The Judicialization of Politics in Latin America

STUDIES OF THE AMERICAS

Edited by James Dunkerley
Institute for the Study of the Americas
University of London
School of Advanced Study

Titles in this series published by Palgrave Macmillan:

Cuba's Military 1990–2005: Revolutionary Soldiers during
Counter-Revolutionary Times
By Hal Klepak

The Judicialization of Politics in Latin America
Edited by Rachel Sieder, Line Schjolden, and Alan Angell

Characterizing Latin America
By Laurence Whitehead

The Judicialization of Politics in Latin America

Edited by
Rachel Sieder,
Line Schjolden,
and
Alan Angell

THE JUDICIALIZATION OF POLITICS IN LATIN AMERICA

First published in 2005 by
PALGRAVE MACMILLAN™
175 Fifth Avenue, New York, N.Y. 10010 and
Houndmills, Basingstoke, Hampshire, England RG21 6XS
Companies and representatives throughout the world.

PALGRAVE MACMILLAN is the global academic imprint of the Palgrave Macmillan division of St. Martin's Press, LLC and of Palgrave Macmillan Ltd. Macmillan® is a registered trademark in the United States, United Kingdom and other countries. Palgrave is a registered trademark in the European Union and other countries.

ISBN 1–4039–7086–6

Library of Congress Cataloging-in-Publication Data is available from the Library of Congress.

A catalogue record for this book is available from the British Library.

Design by Newgen Imaging Systems (P) Ltd., Chennai, India.

First edition: December 2005

10 9 8 7 6 5 4 3 2 1

Printed in the United States of America.

Transferred to digital printing in 2006.

Contents

List of Illustrations

Tables

Figures

Acknowledgments

The editors would like to extend their grateful thanks to the William and Flora Hewlett Foundation for the generous support extended to this project. We also wish to thank our colleagues at the Institute for the Study of the Americas, University of London, and the Latin American Centre at St Antony's, University of Oxford for their support of this joint venture. We particularly wish to thank Olga Jiménez at ISA for her invaluable work on the conference and workshop held in March 2004. Maxine Molyneux and Helga Baitenmann generously gave of their time and expertise to act as commentators in the workshop. We are also extremely grateful to Guillermo O'Donnell for finding time to attend the workshop and for generously agreeing to writing an afterword for the volume. Cath Collins expertly translated the chapter by Rogelio Pérez-Perdomo, our thanks are due to her too.

Notes on Contributors

Rogério B. Arantes holds a doctorate in Political Science from the Universidade de São Paulo and is Professor and Head of the Department of Politics at the Pontifícia Universidade Católica de São Paulo, Brazil. Since 1990 he has been engaged in research and political analysis of justice institutions. He is currently working on a research project on the relationship between the constitution, democracy, and the decision-making process in Brazil in a comparative perspective. He is the author of various articles on judicial issues and two books concerning the political role of judicial institutions: *Ministério Público e Política no Brasil* (São Paulo: Sumaré/Educ, 2002) and *Judiciário e Política no Brasil* (São Paulo: Idesp/Sumaré/Educ, 1997).

Manuel José Cepeda Espinosa is Justice of the Colombian Constitutional Court (2001–2009). He was Dean of the Law School of the Universidad de los Andes where he also taught constitutional law. He was presidential adviser to the Constituent Assembly of President César Gaviria Trujillo and presidential adviser to President Virgilio Barco. He has been the Colombian ambassador to UNESCO and Switzerland. He is the author of several books on constitutional law and holds a law degree (Magna Cum Laude) from the Universidad de los Andes (1986) and an LLM from Harvard Law School (1987).

Javier A. Couso is Associate Professor of Law and Political Science at the Universidad Diego Portales in Santiago, Chile. He is also Director of the Centre for Legal Studies at the Law School of that same institution. Professor Couso has a law degree from the Universidad Católica de Chile and a Ph.D. in Jurisprudence and Social Policy from the University of California, Berkeley. He specializes in comparative public law and judicial politics. His recent publications include "Judicial Independence in Latin America: The Lessons of History in the Search for an Always Elusive Ideal" in Tom Ginsburg and Robert A. Kagan (eds.), *Institutions and Public Law: Comparative Approaches*

(New York: Peter Lang Publishing Inc., 2005) and "The Politics of Judicial Review in Chile in the Era of Democratic Transition, 1999–2002," in *Democratization*, vol. 10, no. 4 (2003).

Pilar Domingo currently works as a researcher at the Instituto de Estudios de Iberoamérica y Portugal at the University of Salamanca. Until recently she was lecturer in the Politics Department at Queen Mary, University of London. Her research interests include the study of rule of law, judicial politics, and human rights in Latin America. Her recent publications include: "Judicialization of Politics or Politicization of the Judiciary? Recent Trends in Latin America," in *Democratization*, vol. 11, no. 1 (2004); *Proclaiming Revolution: Bolivia in Comparative Perspective* coedited with Merilee Grindle (London/Harvard: ILAS/Harvard University Press, 2003), and *Rule of Law in Latin America: The International Promotion of Judicial Reform*, coedited with Rachel Sieder (London: Institute of Latin American Studies, 2001).

Julio Faundez is Professor of Law at the University of Warwick and holds an LCJ from the Catholic University in Chile, and an LLM and SJD from Harvard. His recent books include *Governance, Development and Globalization* (coeditor) (Blackstone Press, 2000); *Good Government and Law* (editor) (Macmillan, 1997), and *Affirmative Action: International Perspectives* (ILO, Geneva, 1994 and Defensoría del Pueblo, Lima [Spanish edition], 2000). He has recently completed two major projects in the area of legal reform: an evaluation of legal and judicial reform projects in Latin America (for the Inter-American Development Bank) and a study on community justice programs in Colombia and Peru (for the UK Department for International Development). In addition to his work on Latin America, he has also served as adviser to the governments of South Africa and Namibia on affirmative action legislation and the Republic of South Korea on free trade agreements.

Fiona Macaulay is Lecturer in Development Studies, Department of Peace Studies, University of Bradford. She was previously Lecturer in Political Sociology at the Institute of Latin American Studies, University of London, and Research Associate at the Centre for Brazilian Studies, University of Oxford. She works in the area of comparative politics, on issues concerning gender, law, human rights, social policy, political institutions, and criminal justice, with a focus on Brazil. Some recent relevant publications include book chapters on gender policy, domestic violence, and reform of the judiciary in Brazil, and on feminist legal literacy initiatives in Latin America. Her latest book is *Gender Politics* *in Brazil and Chile: The Role of Political Parties in Local and National Policy-making* (New York: Palgrave Macmillan, 2005).

Guillermo O'Donnell is Helen Kellogg Professor of Government at the University of Notre Dame, where he was also Academic Director of the Helen Kellogg Institute for International Studies between 1983 and 1998. O'Donnell holds a Ph.D. in Political Science from Yale University and has published widely on issues of the state, democracy, development, and the rule of law in Latin America. His recent books include *The Quality of Democracy: Theory and Applications*, coedited with Osvaldo Iazzetta and Jorge Vargas Cullel (University of Notre Dame Press, 2004) [Spanish edition, 2003]; *Counterpoints: Selected Essays on Authoritarianism and Democratization* (Notre Dame: University of Notre Dame Press, 1999), and *The (Un)Rule of Law and the Underprivileged in Latin America*, coedited with Juan Méndez and Paulo Sérgio Pinheiro (Notre Dame: University of Notre Dame Press, 1999).

Rogelio Pérez Perdomo is Dean of the Law School at the Universidad Metropolitana, Caracas, Venezuela. He recently published a history of Latin American lawyers *Los abogados de América Latina: una Introducción Histórica* (Universidad Externado de Colombia, Bogotá, 2004) and edited, with Lawrence Friedman, *Legal Culture in the Age of Globalization: Latin America and Latin Europe* (Stanford University Press, 2003).

Kathryn Sikkink is the Arleen C. Carlson Professor of Political Science at the University of Minnesota. She has an M.A. and a Ph.D. in political science from Columbia University. Her publications include: *Mixed Signals: U.S. Human Rights Policy and Latin America* (Cornell University Press, 2004); *Restructuring World Politics: Transnational Social Movements, Networks and Norms*, coedited with Sanjeev Khagram and James Riker (University of Minnesota Press, 2002); *The Power of Human Rights: International Norms and Domestic Change*, coedited with Thomas Risse and Stephen Ropp (Cambridge University Press, 1999), and *Activists Beyond Borders: Advocacy Networks in International Politics*, coauthored with Margaret Keck (Cornell University Press, 1998). She is a member of the editorial boards of the journals *International Organization, The American Political Science Review*, and *International Studies Quarterly*, and a fellow of the Council on Foreign Relations and the American Association for Arts and Sciences.

Catalina Smulovitz is Professor at the Universidad Torcuato Di Tella in Buenos Aires, Argentina, and Researcher at the Consejo Nacional de Investigaciones Científicas y Tecnológicas (CONICET). She has edited, together with Enrique Peruzzotti, *Controlando la Política: Ciudadanos y Medios en las Nuevas Democracias Latinoamericanas* (Temas: 2002). Her recent book chapters and articles include: "How Can the Rule of Law Rule?" in José María Maravall and Adam Przeworksi (eds.), *Democracy and the Rule of Law* (Cambridge University Press, 2003); "The Discovery of the Law: Political Consequences in the Argentine Experience" in Yves Dezalay and Bryant Garth (eds.), *Global Prescriptions: The Production, Exportation, and Importation of a New Legal Orthodoxy* (University of Michigan Press, 2002) and "Societal Accountability in Latin America" in *Journal of Democracy* (October 2000) (with E. Peruzzotti).

Bruce M. Wilson holds a Ph.D. from Washington University, St. Louis and is Associate Professor of Political Science at the University of Central Florida, Orlando. He is the editor of *The Latin Americanist*, a multi-disciplinary, international, peer-reviewed journal. He is the author of *Costa Rica: Politics, Economics, and Democracy* (Lynne Rienner Publishers, 1998). His research focuses on politics in Central America and the Caribbean, as well as comparative judicial reform with a focus on Latin America. Wilson's articles have appeared in many journals, including *Comparative Political Studies, the Journal of Latin American Studies,* and *Comparative Politics.* He is currently engaged on a collaborative project examining the impact of judicial reform across all Central American countries.

Glossary of Terms

acción de tutela (or just *tutela*) (Colombia) = writ of protection of fundamental rights.

actio popularis (Colombia) = a legal action that can be initiated by any citizen—without legal counsel and without the need to show that he or she has a concrete interest in the outcome of the case. It covers both laws and decrees in abstract defense of the principles enshrined in the constitution.

amicus curiae = participation or brief filed by a party or an organization interested in a case in which that party or organization is not one of the litigants.

amparo (several countries, among them Costa Rica, Venezuela, Argentina, Mexico) = a judicial injunction to protect a fundamental right. In Mexico there exists a distinction between the *amparo de legalidad* and the *amparo de inconstitucionalidad*.

erga omnes effect = when the effect of a judicial decision applies generally.

habeas corpus = a protection against illegal detention.

inter partes effect = when the effect of a judicial decision applies only to the case in question and to the parties involved in that case.

recurso de protección (Chile) = the equivalent of *amparo*.

Chapter 1

Introduction

Rachel Sieder, Line Schjolden, and
Alan Angell

Since the 1980s, courts—supreme courts, constitutional courts, and lower courts—have been playing an increasingly important political role across Latin America. This is taking place not only in countries which have reestablished democracy after periods of prolonged military rule, but also in countries that escaped the breakdown of their civilian regimes (Colombia and Costa Rica), and in contexts of acute regime crisis (Venezuela). It would be wrong to exaggerate the contrast between a currently activist judiciary and a previously passive one. Courts have been significant political actors in some countries during specific periods in the twentieth century, playing both progressive and conservative roles. For example, in early twentieth century Argentina, selective judicial decisions effectively expanded labor rights prior to the passing of specific labor legislation, while in Chile the supreme court played a significant role in blocking the project of Unidad Popular during the early 1970s.[1]

However, there has undoubtedly been a marked change in the nature and character of judicial involvement in political matters since the 1980s and ever greater recourse to the courts is now a marked feature of the region's contemporary democracies. During the 1990s, constitutional review became increasingly important, and in many countries constitutional courts and supreme courts are now more active in counterbalancing executive and congressional power than at any previous time. In addition, the weakness of effective citizenship rights, the insecurities and hardships produced by economic crisis, and the failure of neoliberal policies to alleviate poverty have prompted ordinary people to resort to the courts or court-like structures to try to press their claims and secure their rights. Nongovernmental agencies and networks of activist lawyers are supporting and advancing such processes of legal mobilization. Legal globalization—the transnational spread of legal norms, institutions, and practices—is undoubtedly playing an important role in these complex and varied developments.[2] Pressure from international agencies such as the World Bank, the IMF and the Inter-American Development Bank for justice reform, has helped to give the courts a new political prominence.

While it is true that the judiciary serves as an instrument for people to assert their rights and as a way to hold governments and politicians accountable, the causes and consequences of this judicialization of politics may not always be positive for democracy. Evidence from Latin America suggests that rights are increasingly being asserted in the courts in many countries because they are not effectively guaranteed by the executive or the legislature. This trend toward "judicializing politics" raises fundamental issues about the appropriate balance of power and responsibilities between representative and elected bodies, and appointed members of the judiciary. Important decisions of constitutional interpretation are increasingly being taken by constitutional courts, with widespread implications for the nature of policy and politics.

In addition, in some cases, the increased resort to the courts by different social and political actors has politicized the judiciary, leading to attempts by executives to weaken its independence. As Pilar Domingo (2004) has pointed out, the judicialization of politics is more likely where regime legitimacy is increasingly linked to the capacity to deliver on rule of law promises of rights, due process, and government accountability. This is increasingly the case in Latin America's post-transitional democracies. Although the rule of law does not depend on the judicial system alone, but on a wide range of institutional and societal factors, if people invest unrealistic hopes in a legal system that is unable to deliver justice, then the level of disenchantment with democracy will undoubtedly rise.

This volume analyzes the diverse manifestations of the judicialization of politics in contemporary Latin America, assessing their positive and negative consequences. It represents an initial attempt to explore a comparative framework for thinking about the nature and effects of the judicialization of politics, particularly in terms of its consequences for the region's existing democracies. Our aim is to reflect on the interplay between institutional change, changing social attitudes, and actions before the courts or court-like instances, and the broader nature of Latin American democracy in the 1990s and 2000s.

Judicialization of Politics: Toward a Definition

A number of different features of judicialization are identified in the individual chapters in this volume. Some relate specifically to the judicialization of politics and others to more general aspects of judicialization, which may or may not be of political significance. With respect to the judicialization of politics, clearly one important dimension is the way in which judges who carry out constitutional judicial review end up making, or substantially contributing to the making of public policy, thus broadening the scope of "judge-made law." As Tate and Vallinder have argued (1995), this kind of judicialization is the process by which courts and judges (typically high courts or constitutional courts) come to make or increasingly dominate the making of public policies that had previously been made by other government agencies, especially legislatures and executives. In tandem with this, as legal arguments are raised in the political process as a consequence of relevant judicial decisions, politicians become more attuned to the actions—or possible actions—of the judiciary.[3] In this respect, as Manuel Cepeda emphasizes in his chapter, a dual process occurs whereby politicians are made more aware of the review power of the judiciary and the judiciary, through judges' actions, increasingly shape substantive policies.

However, the judicialization of politics is not only about judicial review. A broader definition of judicialization encompasses the increased presence of judicial processes and court rulings in political and social life, and the increasing resolution of political, social, or state-society conflicts in the courts. This, in turn, is linked to a process by which a diverse range of political and social actors increasingly perceive advantage in invoking legal strategies and resorting to the courts to advance their interests. In his chapter, Javier Couso makes reference to Charles Epp's notion of "rights-enhancing judicialization," whereby courts create or expand existing individual civil rights and liberties through their evolving jurisprudence.[4] Epp's framework has great appeal for many activists who adopt strategies of legal mobilization in pursuit of their claims.

Not all judicialization in Latin America is rights enhancing, as Couso's own examination of Chile shows. Legal mobilization from below does not necessarily produce an activist judiciary. Conversely, it is also the case that greater activism on the part of the courts does not necessarily or automatically signal the strengthening of individual or group rights: as Epp himself argues, a confluence of factors is necessary to sustain a "rights revolution." Courts can also be active in ways that do not always enhance democracy—the defense of property rights when they are distributed in very unequal ways worsens equity. In some regions of a country, courts may act to defend rights. But in others—the areas that O'Donnell refers to as "brown areas"—the courts may be active in the perpetuation of local elite or even mafia rule. Such tendencies may be particularly marked in federal systems, where subnational actors can use the state courts to reverse or block national decisions.

Epp's analysis of the "rights revolution" focuses on the creation of new rights through judicial reinterpretation of existing constitutions. However, the extent to which processes of judicialization in Latin America today are about the creation of new rights is debatable. In many cases they center on claims for the enforcement of existing rights where those rights have not previously been effectively enforced or upheld in practice. The transitions to democracy in the 1980s focused the attention of organized groups, particularly the left, on the rule of law and the value of legal guarantees of civil and political rights. In a dramatic change in the thinking of the left from the doctrinaire Marxism–Leninism of the 1970s and 1980s, the rule of law, accountable and transparent government, and decentralization of power became the new watchwords. Indeed, the demands of social movements during the authoritarian period were often focused on demands that states uphold their constitutional and statutory obligations to guarantee fundamental rights.

In addition, in contrast to the United States (where the constitution is brief and vague), the civil law constitutional tradition in Latin America is for constitutions to be extensive and detailed—even though constitutional guarantees have been routinely ignored in practice, they have often included extensive citizenship rights, including social and economic rights. Contemporary patterns of constitution-making have favored the enactment of increasingly detailed and extensive charters. The 1988 Brazilian Constitution for example, had over 1,855 original provisions—in turn raising expectations that such rights would be upheld in practice, not least because the constitution itself was based upon a widespread process of popular consultation. Judicialization may encompass the creation of new rights through judicial reinterpretation of the constitution and statutes, or it may simply involve the more effective application of existing, codified rights. In other cases, as Catalina Smulovitz points out, legal mobilization by certain individuals or groups may represent claims for rights that are not yet recognized as such to *become* legal.

Clearly, processes of judicialization of politics can be driven "from above," "from below" or even, at least in part, "from abroad." From above they are driven by elite actors, typically constitutional court or supreme court judges who challenge the constitutionality of certain laws or governmental practices, or by politicians who may resort to judicial review to try to block or change certain policies. Another form of "top down" judicialization of politics is that encouraged by processes of institutional reform, such as the creation of constitutional courts or measures adopted to increase the independence of the judiciary, such as the creation of judicial councils to control the nomination and promotion of judges. Such institutional changes were implemented in many countries in Latin America following their transitions from authoritarian rule in the 1980s, or in others (Costa Rica, Colombia) as part of efforts to deepen and strengthen existing electoral democracies in the 1990s. And the new institutions were given a free rein to be active by the promulgation of new constitutions—in Brazil and Colombia, for example—with very broad commitment to a whole raft of social and economic rights. By contrast, a judicialization of politics "from below" occurs when certain sectors of society gain greater consciousness of their legal rights and entitlements, and when citizens adopt strategies of legal mobilization to press claims through the courts for their existing rights to be upheld, or use legal discourses to develop new rights not yet protected or codified in law.

Evidently, the spread of legal discourses and legalistic rules and procedures into a range of spheres and forums is a general feature of judicialization. Tate and Vallinder (1995) refer to this as the process by which nonjudicial negotiating and decision-making forums come to be dominated by quasi-judicial (legalistic) rules and procedures. Matters that were formerly negotiated in informal—or nonjudicial—ways gradually come to be dominated by legal rules (a process evident, for example, within some of the non-state justice systems discussed by Julio Faundez in his chapter). The triggers for the judicialization of politics rarely derive "from abroad" alone, but as Kathryn Sikkink's chapter shows, domestic processes of judicialization can develop in tandem with extraterritorial developments, such as advances in international human rights jurisprudence, the bringing of cases in third country courts, or transnational activism on the part of NGOs.

It is invariably difficult to distinguish "judicialization of politics from above" from "judicialization of politics from below" (or, for that matter, "from abroad"). As the cases discussed in this volume illustrate, the triggers for legal mobilization are multiple and often interdependent—a more activist, rights-defending judiciary, for example, tends to encourage more groups to take their claims before the courts. Nonetheless, judicialization of politics can also occur in the absence of widespread social mobilization and rights consciousness, as the case of Costa Rica discussed by Bruce Wilson shows.

Increased recourse to the courts may look like a region-wide feature of Latin America's contemporary democracies, but what does greater resort to the courts or activism on the part of judges tell us? As signaled above, judicial activism can lead to a judicialization of politics—when lawmaking and policy implementation is increasingly displaced from the executive and congressional branches toward the judiciary. A range of actors may initiate this kind of judicialization. These can include opposition parties, particularly those in a minority within legislatures, who may use the legal route to try to block certain policies, for example by appealing against the constitutionality of a particular government initiative (a dynamic common in both Brazil and Costa Rica, as demonstrated in this volume by Rogério Arantes and Bruce Wilson, respectively).

Pressure on the courts for political decisions can come from the government as well as from the opposition. Venezuela presents an unusually sharp case of political conflict between the government and the opposition where the government of Hugo Chávez Frías has attempted to dominate the courts and the opposition has resorted to using legal means to oppose the government, as recounted in the chapter by Rogelio Pérez-Perdomo. This is more than a set of demands for the recognition of rights. Rather, it is a fundamental and bitter conflict over the very legitimacy of the government and the political order that stems from the Chávez revolution. Both sides in the conflict seek the legitimacy that comes from the supreme court's recognition of the justice of one or other of the conflicting forces, and from the recognition or non-recognition of the legal validity of the electoral outcomes. The centrality of legal approval in this conflict highlights another dimension of the judicialization of politics, and is one that may well be repeated in other political systems that face systemic crises on the Venezuelan scale. It could also be seen as yet another way in which the representative institutions of government have abdicated their responsibility for solving political conflicts by transferring them to the legal arena.

However, it is not only the national governments who find themselves relying on the courts to solve institutional conflicts but also the subnational levels of government that have become increasingly important in recent years as political decentralization has afforded greater representation to subnational institutions and actors. Within federal structures, state or provincial governments can and often do challenge the federal government through the courts; this has been a notable feature of the redefinition of the federal pact in Mexico during that country's extended democratic transition, as Pilar Domingo signals in her chapter, and has also been important in the case of Brazil, analyzed here by Rogério Arantes.

Either complementary to, or independent of, this judicialization of politics from above by elite actors, is a judicialization of politics from below. Social movements may try to secure commitments from the governments to provide certain kinds of services, such as, for example, subsidized healthcare for AIDS patients, by appealing to the judiciary to uphold the constitutional rights of certain groups or individuals (in this case, the right to life).[5] Catalina Smulovitz's chapter describes the processes whereby thousands of individuals in Argentina tried to secure their rights to a pension or to access their savings by appealing to the judiciary to protect their constitutional rights. Similarly, struggles by indigenous peoples' organizations across Latin America for governments to implement policies to observe their international and constitutional obligations to uphold indigenous rights have often included a legal dimension. A wide range of nongovernmental organizations throughout Latin America have adopted such strategies of legal mobilization and strategic litigation, and there is currently much transnational sharing of knowledge and tactics. Indeed, such cross-national information sharing is supported by international non-governmental agencies such as the Ford Foundation, pointing to the importance of international factors in explaining processes of judicialization.[6]

Whatever be the specific agency triggering the judicialization of politics, it seems that in contrast to the traditional notion that courts in Latin America have historically adhered to the formal interpretation and application of legislator-made law, today courts in Latin America are increasingly *making* law and citizens are increasingly resorting to the courts to resolve issues previously reserved for the political sphere. To the casual observer, it might appear that the judicial is displacing the political as a means of political mediation and lawmaking, though, paradoxically, the courts generally share the low standing in the opinion polls of parties and congresses (though it is difficult to know if this is a specific verdict on the courts or the reflection of a more general rejection of the institutions of the state). But even if the courts enjoy little popularity, the recourse to law on the behalf of many citizens in defense of their rights appears to be increasing.

Other forms of judicialization—such as the increased resort by women to the courts to try to obtain protection and redress in cases of domestic violence (discussed by Fiona Macaulay in her chapter on Brazil), or the increased demands for consumer rights—may represent not so much the judicialization of politics, understood as claims against government made through the courts, as the judicialization of social relations. Some of this is not new; for example, women in Latin America have resorted to the courts to try to contest unequal gender relations within the family and society since the colonial period. Nonetheless, the transnationalization of certain rights discourses in the latter part of the twentieth century has favored an increasingly transnationalized judicialization of social life. Sometimes this may be linked to broader political strategies—as when women's social movements bring pressure to bear on governments for reforms to laws related to domestic violence. This may not always be the case, however; the judicialization of social relations may have little direct impact on politics and specifically on the business of government, even when its impact within society is considerable. Instead of the judicialization of social relations automatically leading to the judicialization of politics, Guillermo O'Donnell suggests in his afterword that we should consider the judicialization of politics as *part* of the broader phenomenon of the judicialization and juridification of social relations overall.

Another illustration of the complex relationship between law and politics is Julio Faundez's discussion of non-state justice systems, where it becomes clear that indigenous peoples and communities have always engaged in forms of regulation and dispute resolution outside the formal court system. He argues that in these communities the distinction between law and politics is in some senses an artificial one; the common aim is the creation of a viable overall system of governance. In many areas of Latin America these quasi-judicial forms continue with little direct relevance for national politics. However, the current tendency to recognize and incorporate such non-state justice systems into the administrative and legal apparatus of the state is increasingly leading to an overlap between non-state justice systems and the courts, in turn changing the nature of governance and politics in Latin America. The extent to which such changes are empowering or disempowering these communities and constituencies remains open to question, as does the question of how far the informal systems contribute or detract from the quality of democracy overall.[7]

In short, the contemporary phenomenon of judicialization examined in this volume is broad and is certainly not limited to the sphere of constitutional review alone. It involves a wide range of institutions and actors and may or may not have consequences for the political system as a whole. Indeed, one of the questions considered by the different contributors is precisely the overall political significance of judicialization. Guillermo O'Donnell has focused our attention on normative questions and outcomes, asking to what extent judicialization is good or bad for democracy, governance, and citizens in Latin America today. This is a highly complex issue: judicialization might be good for certain groups, for example, by securing specific guarantees for government resources for a particular set of claims, but bad for governance overall—for example, if it leads to increasing fiscal pressure on a resource-poor state or to the inability of democratically elected governments to decide budgetary priorities. Decisions to insist on certain health rights, for example, have enormous fiscal implications and can be detrimental to hard-pressed governments trying to reduce fiscal deficits. Such developments may also be bad for democracy if minority interests can block the will of the majority through resort to the courts. One of the standard criticisms of "judge-made law" is that it leads to unelected and unaccountable judges replacing elected officials in the policy-making process. However, counter to this, many would argue that activist judiciaries can be *good* for democracy if they uphold and protect the interests of the weak and the underprivileged—who after all in many countries are the overall majority—against the rich and powerful.

The judicialization of politics may also lead to direct attempts to politicize the judiciary. If judges try to limit the scope of politicians' actions, then those same politicians are likely to try to limit the powers of the courts, for example through court packing or institutional redesign—as happened in Argentina under President Menem—or even bribery and attempts to undermine individual judges. This process of backlash is evident in the case of Colombia, analyzed here by Manuel Cepeda, where the remarkable activism of the constitutional court since its creation in 1991 has led to criticism from political circles and even other branches of the judiciary, as well as efforts by the government of Alvaro Uribe to limit its powers. It is also clearly a factor in the conflict between pro and anti-Chávez forces in Venezuela and the fate of the new supreme court, analyzed by Rogelio Pérez-Perdomo. Such trends can have a negative impact on democracy, by limiting the power of the courts to uphold constitutional, statutory, and human rights and limit the arbitrary actions of government.

The political consequences of judicialization are thus of enormous importance, and we return to the question of outcomes and the impact on democracy later. For the moment, however, we focus less on the normative dimensions of judicialization and look more at functional and "process-led" definitions in order to explore elements of a common framework for comparative analysis.

Explaining the Relationship between Judicialization (or its Absence) and Politics in Latin America

This book aims to highlight the specific features of the judicialization of politics and judicialization in general in Latin America in the 1990s and 2000s, identifying the specificities and commonalities of such processes in a range of countries across the region. This raises the obvious question of the base line for that comparison. Are we comparing Latin America today to the region's past? The courts were hardly absent from political involvement in earlier years, and there are examples of judicial activism in favor of rights at a much earlier time. But the question remains of how far there has been a change, and in what way? Or is our comparison with some normative notion of the "ideal" balance of powers (often implicit in writing on the subject)? Most of the contributors to this volume adopt a longitudinal rather than a normative approach, comparing past and present and asking what—if anything—is new about current patterns of judicialization.

All the countries discussed here are electoral democracies and all are civil law systems. Some experienced transitions from authoritarian regimes in the 1980s and 1990s, albeit of very different natures (Argentina, Brazil, Chile, Peru, Mexico); others maintained traditions of constitutional, elected government in the latter half of the twentieth century, even though in some cases those democracies were highly flawed and were struggling to contain profound social and political conflicts (Colombia, Venezuela). A number of the chapters suggest the importance of a foundational or constitutional moment in explaining subsequent patterns of judicialization. The nature of this "constitutional moment" or critical juncture varies across the cases, but can include the election of a constituent assembly and the subsequent drafting of a new constitution (Colombia, 1991; Venezuela, 1999; Brazil, 1988; Peru, 1993; Argentina, 1994), or the transition from authoritarian government to elected constitutional rule involving the continuation or restitution of a previous constitution (Argentina, 1983–1984; Chile, 1989–1990). Two of the countries discussed here, Mexico and Costa Rica, did not experience a clear "constitutional moment" in the 1980s and 1990s, and are therefore instructive cases to examine in order to consider the relative importance of constitutional innovation or redesign in explaining subsequent patterns of judicialization of politics.[8]

While it is certainly not our desire to develop a multi-variable model for the comparative analysis of judicialization, we endorse the utility of a comparative approach in helping to identify the specific factors which have driven processes of judicialization of politics at particular times in specific countries and in identifying the temporal and thematic commonalities in different national experiences. The essays here, then, analyze who or what is driving both a judicialization of politics and judicialization in general, the different forms that judicialization has taken and the extent to which current patterns of judicialization can be understood as a radical departure from the past.

Focusing attention on the increased resort to the courts, legal mobilization from below and judicial activism may suggest that rights activism is consolidating democracy in Latin America, or at least increasing the protection of individual rights for citizens and of selected collective rights, for example, those of indigenous peoples. This is not necessarily the case—not least because protection of rights also depends upon other institutions, notably the police. Indeed, it may be the very weaknesses of contemporary democracy in Latin America that are driving judicialization. For example, in some countries the extensive use of executive decree by governments to implement controversial economic policy measures has circumvented the legislature and thus encouraged challenges to economic policies in the courts.

Citizenship rights remain poorly protected in many countries, or vary sharply between different areas of the country or between different social sectors, and the acute weakness of rights observance in practice partly explains some aspects of judicialization from below. As Guillermo O'Donnell has emphasized, it is instructive to ask where judicialization is occurring and where it is not. What kinds of rights issues are increasingly coming before the courts? Who is taking the initiative in the legal cases? Is there evidence of broader legal mobilization behind certain issues or not? Are there particular social groups that do not have access to the courts? Or specific issues which are more or less judicialized than others? Latin American countries present a peculiar paradox; the prestige of the judicial branch is generally low and public mistrust of the judiciary often high. According to the Latinobarómetro in 2003, only 20 percent of respondents expressed any degree of confidence in the judiciary—only congress with 17 percent of respondents expressing confidence, and the parties with 11 percent, were less well regarded. This also represents a decline in the figure for the judiciary from a high point of 36 percent in 1997.[9] However, as Catalina Smulovitz points out in her chapter, even in such circumstances the judicialization of rights claims is occurring. This raises the question of the extent to which legal mobilization aims to secure specific *judicial* outcomes. It may be that it is aimed more broadly at producing political outcomes and responses. Or indeed, it may be about legitimating certain rights claims in society, irrespective of the more immediate legal and political results.

Elements for a Comparative Analysis of Judicialization

While we cannot hope to explain all the national variations in patterns of judicialization across Latin America here, we can certainly identify a number of factors that, through their constantly changing and dynamic interaction, can facilitate or limit such processes. Through comparative reflection, we hope to shed light on the relationship between judicialization in general and the judicialization of politics.

First is the question of the *institutional architecture* and *institutional changes.* This includes the nature of the constitutional charters themselves and the range of individual and collective rights—political, civil, social, economic, and cultural—they cover. In this respect some constitutions are restrictive—for example, the 1980 Chilean Constitution, while others, such as the Brazilian Constitution of 1988, are extremely expansive. Other critical institutional factors include the nature and scope of judicial review powers, and linked to this are the powers of the ordinary courts as well as those of constitutional courts or chambers. The introduction of new quasi-judicial institutions can also be a significant factor in judicialization, for example, the institutional reconstruction of the Public Ministry in Brazil, described by Rogério Arantes, which has a broad remit to defend and advance collective and diffuse rights. The introduction of ombudsman's offices in Central America and Peru with a mandate to initiate legal cases to defend collective interests is another instance of institutional innovation favoring judicialization.[10] In countries with federal constitutions, the degree to which resort to subnational courts affect patterns of judicialization is another key comparative element.

Judicial reform programs implemented in most Latin American countries since the 1980s attempted to strengthen the independence of the judiciary, through such measures as the creation of judicial councils or the introduction of new mechanisms for selection of high court judges.[11] They also generally increased the budgetary allocations to the judicial branch and expanded access to justice, for example, through augmenting the coverage of lower courts, justices of the peace or other kinds of small claims courts and nonjudicial dispute resolution forums throughout the national territory. Often important in this process of judicial change were the various international agencies involved—from the nongovernmental organizations to the International Financial Institutions (IFIs). All these factors potentially affect patterns of judicialization. As Fiona Macaulay's chapter shows, the introduction of new courts in Brazil stimulated new demands. The many new layers and arenas of the justice system, formal and informal, are, then, an important factor in our analysis.

A *second* element is that of *legal culture.* This is a notoriously slippery term, but Laurence Friedman and Rogelio Pérez-Perdomo use it to refer to "the cluster of attitudes, ideas, expectations, and values that people hold with regard to their legal system, legal institutions, and legal rules" (2003, p. 2). Friedman's and Pérez-Perdomo's distinction between internal and external legal culture is a useful one for the purposes of disaggregation: internal legal culture refers to the norms, attitudes, and practices of lawyers and jurists, while external legal culture refers to broader perceptions within society. With reference to internal legal culture, the training of lawyers, judges, and public prosecutors is obviously an important element, as is accepted practice within the legal profession. Does legal training remain formalistic and weak, as it has tended to be in Latin America? Or is this changing? Do criminal defense lawyers or civil litigation lawyers see their role as securing constitutional guarantees or protecting human rights? Is there an emerging trend, for example, of lawyers taking class actions? Or does the practice of the law not necessarily imply a vocation for—or practice of—defending rights? Do judges see themselves as active defenders of the constitution with a mandate to develop jurisprudence, or merely as judicial operators who should resolve individual conflicts and apply the law to the letter?[12] Do public prosecutors actively pursue members of government for abuse of their powers? And do extra-national norms and jurisprudence (for example, international human rights) inform the interpretations of senior judges to a greater extent than in the past?

In addition, it is certainly useful to ask how deep the process of judicialization extends: does it affect all judges, including lower court judges, and judicial operators more widely? Or is it restricted to a number of activist judges in the constitutional court?[13] Conversely, if the supreme or constitutional court is subordinate to executive power (for example, Menem's packed court in Argentina during the 1990s) does this mean that the lower courts will be similarly lacking in independence? In other parts of the world, the mindset of some senior judges and their adoption of a more political stance has been an important factor in the judicialization of certain issues:[14] can we identify individual judges or groups of judges who are leading judicial activism in Latin America?

Linked to the idea of the external legal culture is the *third* factor: that of *patterns of legal mobilization*. In particular, this involves a focus on the *actors* driving such processes, whether from below or from above. Legal aid is all but nonexistent in most Latin American countries, so a significant increase in litigation by the poorest sectors of society invariably involves legal advocacy by social movements or nongovernmental organizations. This was particularly notable in the case of human rights organizations, which presented thousands of writs of habeas corpus on behalf of the detained-disappeared and their families during the military dictatorships. Such organizations have continued to campaign for the rights of disadvantaged sectors since the transition to democracy, for example by taking cases against sexual, racial, or ethnic discrimination before the courts.

However, it is not only the poorest sectors and their advocates who can drive legal mobilization. Middle class plaintiffs initiated thousands of civil claims in the *corralito* cases described by Catalina Smulovitz. Individuals may pursue their interests in a range of instances, including labor courts, civil courts, commercial courts, and quasi-judicial or non-state justice forums. The media can also play an important role in processes of legal mobilization; by focusing on certain issues (corruption, violation of due process rights by the police, discrimination, etc.) they can stimulate and support judicial actions by individual citizens or organizations. Lastly, it may not be forces in civil society, but rather politicians and political parties who are the driving forces in certain attempts to secure judicial review, as described by Rogério Arantes for the Brazilian case, Bruce Wilson for Costa Rica and Pilar Domingo for Mexico. Who initiates judicialization, what kinds of legal discourses of probity and entitlement they deploy, and what legal processes they resort to evidently matter a lot.

Fourth, the question of *access to justice* is critical. Who can file what sort of claims and how easily? What are the costs of petitioning? What sorts of rights are covered by the different writs of protection of an individual's constitutional rights, known variously as *recursos de amparo, recursos de tutela*, or *recursos de protección*? Where can such writs be admitted? In some countries, only constitutional courts have powers of judicial review, but in others, such as Brazil, lower courts can exercise powers of concrete review. Colombia, Brazil, and Costa Rica are countries where there is a highly accessible system of judicial review available to all citizens. This is less the case, for example, in Chile, partly because of judicial conservatism but also perhaps because of a greater degree of responsiveness in the political system. In the case of the non-state justice systems, as Julio Faundez observes, they represent the only justice system to which indigenous or isolated communities may have access.

In terms of outcomes, however, the question of access to justice is far from unproblematic: the quality of justice varies enormously across issues and different judicial arenas. In this respect, Fiona Macaulay's chapter on access to justice and domestic violence is a timely reminder, asking what *kind* of justice different legal avenues deliver to plaintiffs in practice. Clearly, judicialization in the form of increased litigation may not necessarily translate into effective enforcement of a positive judgment in many parts of Latin America.

The *fifth* element, of increasing importance, is the *transnational* or *international* dimensions of judicialization. Kathryn Sikkink's chapter rightly focuses on the different "transnational opportunity structures" that encourage or inhibit the judicialization of certain claims. These opportunity structures include international and regional legal norms and frameworks, and transnational alliances or networks. They also vary across time and across issues—for example, as Sikkink's work has shown, transnational human rights networks represent a resource for campaigners in individual countries and a means of bringing pressure to bear on their own governments through boomerang or spiral patterns of influence (Keck and Sikkink, 1998; Risse, Ropp and Sikkink, 1999). As Lutz and Sikkink have noted, Latin America experienced a "norms cascade" with respect to human rights in the 1980s and 1990s, and in contrast to other regions in the developing world has a relatively high density of regional human rights norms and structures (Lutz and Sikkink, 2001).

By contrast, however, emerging global trade rules may effectively "seal off" certain areas from domestic judicial action, for example, encouraging the increased transfer of contract law to London, Geneva, or New York, thus in effect "de-nationalising" certain areas of the law. Indeed, in general terms and despite the introduction of more expansive constitutions in Latin America in the 1980s and 1990s, the range of social and economic rights that it is possible to fight for *and secure* at a national level has become ever more constrained by economic globalization in the last two decades. As well as normative and substantive issues of law, the international dimension also includes the issue of institutional change and judicial reform. Intergovernmental agencies, such as the Inter-American Development Bank and the World Bank, have been instrumental in promoting certain kinds of judicial reform in Latin America. While the impact of such efforts is far from uniform (it is a significant factor in some countries and not in others), in some instances it can be an important element underpinning certain patterns of judicialization or indeed de-judicialization, such as, for example, the World Bank's promotion of commercial dispute resolution, which takes certain kinds of conflicts out of the courts and into quasi-legal forums.

The *sixth* factor to be taken into account when comparing the phenomenon of judicialization is the nature of the political system as a whole. Certain patterns of executive-legislative relations can inhibit recourse to top-down judicialization by political elites, whereas others can encourage them.[15] Overwhelming government majorities, for example, and ineffective mechanisms for legislative consultation may encourage minority parties to pursue their agendas through the courts. Another example of judicialization linked to the political system is a lack of consensus on electoral oversight mechanisms, which may also lead to challenges to electoral outcomes before the courts, as occurred in Mexico during the 1990s. In addition, the nature of the party system and the degree of consensus or conflict—or unity and fragmentation—within it can play a major role in explaining the presence or absence of the judicialization of politics. For example, as Javier Couso argues, the consensus within the Concertación alliance on social and economic rights combined with the restrictive nature of the 1980 Constitution, means that such issues are not a topic for judicial deliberation in Chile.

By contrast, relatively weak party discipline in Costa Rica, as Bruce Wilson shows, means that deputies sometimes ask for constitutional consults against their own party's legislation. This raises the fundamental and broader question of the extent to which judicialization represents politics by other means. If politicians are blocked in the legislature by overwhelming government majorities or ineffective mechanisms for congressional deliberation, they may resort to the courts to try to change or block legislative initiatives. Similarly, if parties are weak and do not adequately represent voters' demands, then individuals and groups may find that action before the courts is the most expeditious or effective way to secure legislation on a particular topic, particularly if governments react preemptively by passing legislation to try to stem a flood of cases before the courts. This raises fundamental issues in democratic theory that go beyond the scope of this book. Nonetheless, the various chapters shed light on these issues for the particular country cases discussed.

Evaluating Judicialization: Results and Outcomes

In analyzing processes of legal mobilization and judicialization, we need to distinguish between *process* and *outcomes*. We also need to distinguish between the *levels* where the impact of judicialization can be observed: executive or legislative behavior, on social movements and civil society actors, or on society more generally. As Catalina Smulovitz has pointed out, it is far from simple to measure the success of judicialization strategies. Does success entail obtaining positive judgments in individual cases about rights that are enshrined in law? Is it judged by the extent to which legal mobilization manages to bring certain cases or issues to the attention of the public or politicians, some of which may be unregulated or "aspirational" rights? Is it less about winning individual cases and more about provoking legislative change or changes in administrative practices?

This raises the broader question of the extent to which we can employ normative criteria when discussing the effects of judicialization. This volume certainly aims to explore the relationship between judicialization and the nature of democratic consolidation—or deconsolidation—occurring across Latin America. How is the relationship between law and politics changing? What are the implications of these shifting dynamics for governance and for democracy in the different countries examined here? To what extent does judicialization lead to improved prospects for the rule of law? Does it lead to greater horizontal or societal accountability (Schedler, Diamond and Platter, 1999; Smulovitz, 2002)? Or to a "rights revolution" and the consolidation of a rights culture within government and society? Or does it reinforce tendencies toward the illiberal (un)rule of law already present in Latin America and increase tendencies toward greater political interference with the judiciary (Méndez, O'Donnell and Pinheiro, 1999)? In short, is the resort to a legal or judicial route a complement to other forms of politics? Or is the sub-optimal nature of democracy in Latin America leading to an ever-greater tendency to channel political and social claims through the courts, with uneven and unpredictable results?

Aside from the normative criteria of whether such developments are good or bad for governance and democracy, there is a common issue about court overload if claims before the courts are exponentially increasing. This depends on institutional factors, such as the freedom with which constitutional courts are able to select from the cases presented to them; it is, however, a growing concern across the region. It may be too early to tell to what extent current trends toward judicialization in Latin America are sustainable. It may be the case that the return to democracy in a number of countries led to an explosion of demands—perhaps fuelled by the creation of Truth and Justice Commissions—and that with the passing of time a more "normal" process may develop. However, Epp refers to a "rights revolution" as a "sustained developmental process" (1998, p. 7). While there may be evidence of this in some of the countries analyzed in this volume, the potential for backlash, regression, and popular frustration is considerable. We hope that this volume will shed light on this evolving process and suggest new avenues for comparative and country-specific research on the topic of judicialization.

Notes

1. See Schjolden, 2002 on Argentina and Novoa, 1978 on Chile.
2. On legal globalization see Dezalay and Garth, 2002a, 2002b; Santos, 1998; Thome, 2000; Trubek et al., 1994; Twining, 2000.

3. The fact that many legislators in Latin America have law degrees may make this recourse to legal argument more palatable.

4. Epp's comparative analysis distinguishes the case of the United States of America, where constitutional rights of property and contract were expanded by judicial interpretation of U.S. constitutional law and statutes in the second half of the twentieth century to include freedom of speech, free exercise of religion, antidiscrimination, rights to privacy, and rights to due process (1998, p. 7).

5. In Argentina, the Centro de Estudios Legales y Sociales (CELS) recently won a case before the Buenos Aires federal court upholding the rights of HIV patients to treatment. See http://www.cels.org.ar.

6. See The Ford Foundation, 2000.

7. For a useful discussion see Van Cott, 2003.

8. Mexico's democratic transition has been gradual and distended and has not involved the drafting of a new constitution, although during the 1990s extensive revision of the 1917 charter occurred; Costa Rica's democracy and constitution date from the outcome of the 1948 civil war.

9. Press Release. Latinobarómetro, October 2003, p. 26.

10. See Uggla, 2004.

11. The appropriate balance between judicial accountability and judicial independence is a complex and much debated question. For an insightful analysis of a case of too much judicial independence see Santiso, 2003.

12. The latitude of judges to develop jurisprudence tends to be lower in civil law systems than in common law systems; in the former, interpreting codes—as opposed to building precedent through case law—has traditionally been the mainstay of judicial activity. However, this distinction is somewhat arbitrary; precedent and case law do play an important role in deciding judicial outcomes within civil law systems (directly or indirectly) and codes and statutes increasingly restrict the abilities of common law judges to develop law through case precedent.

13. For an analysis that considers constitutional court activism alongside the operation of ordinary justice for the case of Colombia, see Rodríguez, García Villegas and Uprimny, 2003.

14. For example, in the United Kingdom in the early to mid-1990s some of the most senior judges were clearly identified with the welfare state and openly opposed to Conservative attempts to dismantle it. They were also concerned about the domination of the executive and sought to limit its power and pushed for a bill of rights as a protection for the citizen. The editors are indebted to Professor Diane Woodhouse for this observation.

15. For example, Epp argues that "in the United States, at least, the relatively broad arena of judicial action and the limits on legislative power are plausibly due less to the Bill of Rights alone than to the many veto points in the legislative process . . ." (1998, p. 13).

References

Dezalay, Yves and Bryant G. Garth (eds.) (2002a) *The Internationalization of Palace Wars: Lawyers, Economists, and the Contest to Transform Latin American States* (Chicago and London: The University of Chicago Press).

——— (2002b) *Global Prescriptions: The Production, Exportation and Importation of a New Legal Orthodoxy* (Ann Arbor: University of Michigan Press).

Domingo, Pilar, "Judicialization of Politics or Politicization of the Judiciary? Recent Trends in Latin America," *Democratization*, vol. 11, no. 1 (2004), pp. 104–26.

Epp, Charles (1998) *The Rights Revolution: Lawyers, Activists and Supreme Courts in Comparative Perspective* (Chicago: University of Chicago Press).

Ford Foundation (2000) *Many Roads to Justice: The Law Related Work of the Ford Foundation Grantees Around the World* (New York: The Ford Foundation).

Friedman, Lawrence M. and Rogelio Pérez-Perdomo (eds.) (2003) *Legal Culture in the Age of Globalization: Latin America and Latin Europe* (Stanford: Stanford University Press).

Keck, Margaret and Kathryn Sikkink (1998) *Activists Beyond Borders: Advocacy Networks in International Politics* (Ithaca: Cornell University Press).

Lutz, Ellen and Kathryn Sikkink, "The Justice Cascade: The Evolution and Impact of Human Rights Trials in Latin America," *Chicago Journal of International Law*, vol. 2, no. 1 (2001), pp. 1–33.

Méndez, Juan, Guillermo O'Donnell and Paulo Sérgio Pinheiro (eds.) (1999) *The (Un)Rule of Law and the Underprivileged in Latin America* (South Bend, Indiana: University of Notre Dame Press).

Novoa, Eduardo (1978) *Vía legal hacia el socialismo?* (Caracas, Venezuela: Editorial Jurídica Venezolana).

Risse, Thomas, Stephen C. Ropp and Kathryn Sikkink (1999) *The Power of Principles: International Human Rights Norms and Domestic Change* (Cambridge: Cambridge University Press).

Rodríguez, César A., Mauricio García-Villegas, and Rodrigo Uprimny (2003), "Justice and Society in Colombia: A Sociolegal Analysis of Colombian Courts," in Friedman and Pérez-Perdomo (eds.), *Legal Culture in the Age of Globalization*, pp. 134–83.

Santiso, Carlos, "Economic Reform and Judicial Governance in Brazil: Balancing Independence with Accountability," *Democratization*, vol. 10, no. 4 (2003) (Special issue on Democratization and the Judiciary), pp. 161–80.

Santos, Boaventura de Sousa (1998) *La globalización del derecho: Los nuevos caminos de la regulación y la emancipación* (Bogotá: ILSA/Universidad Nacional de Colombia, Bogotá).

Schedler, Andreas, Larry Diamond, and Marc F. Plattner (eds.) (1999) *The Self-Restraining State: Power and Accountability in New Democracies* (Boulder, CO: Lynne Reiner).

Schjolden, Line (2002) "Suing for Justice: Labor and the Courts in Argentina, 1900–1943" (Ph.D. dissertation, University of California, Berkeley).

Smulovitz, Catalina (2002) "The Discovery of Law: Political Consequences in the Argentine Case," in Yves Dezalay and Bryant G. Garth (eds.), *Global Prescriptions* (Ann Arbor: University of Michigan Press), pp. 249–75.

Tate, C. Neal and Torbjörn Vallinder (eds.) (1995) *The Global Expansion of Judicial Power* (New York: New York University Press).

Thome, Joseph R., "Heading South but Looking North: Globalization and Law Reform in Latin America," *Wisconsin Law Review*, no. 3 (2000), pp. 691–712.

Trubek, David M., Yves Dezalay, Ruth Buchanan and John R. Davis, "Global Restructuring and the Law: Studies of the Internationalization of Legal Fields and the Creation of Transnational Arenas," *Case Western Reserve Law Review*, vol. 44, no. 2 (1994), pp. 407–98.

Twining, William (2000) *Globalisation and Legal Theory* (London, Edinburgh and Dublin: Butterworths).

Uggla, Fredrik, "The Ombudsman in Latin America," *Journal of Latin American Studies*, vol. 36, no. 3 (2004), pp. 423–50.

Van Cott, Donna Lee (2003) "Legal Pluralism and Informal Community Justice Administration in Latin America" (Paper prepared for the conference "Informal Institutions and Politics in Latin America," Notre Dame, Indiana, April 24–25).

Chapter 2

Judicialization of Politics: The Changing Political Role of the Judiciary in Mexico

Pilar Domingo

Introduction

This chapter seeks to explore the impact of judicialization of politics on the prospects of rule of law construction in democratizing societies. Mexico presents an interesting case study as, since the mid-1990s, the judiciary has engaged in unprecedented levels of judicial activism with important political and economic consequences. The chapter aims to shed some light on our understanding of what we mean by the judicialization of politics, and its connection to the prospects of rule of law construction in young democracies. The first section develops a conceptual characterization of the phenomenon of the judicialization of politics. The judicialization of politics is in general terms a feature of the modern democratic state. In systems which have less than adequate rule of law and where the state is weakly embedded in society it is likely to take a different form in contrast to its impact in more established and developed democracies. In this regard, the chapter asks whether the judicialization of politics improves the prospects of rule of law construction, or alternatively whether its emergence in contexts of delegative democracy and weak state–society relations can in fact reenforce illiberal habits of "un-rule of law." The second section reviews the Mexican case, with an emphasis on the politics of the supreme court in recent years.

Defining the Judicialization of Politics

The judicialization of politics has increasingly come to be recognized as a feature of modern political development.[1] In Latin America, studying the role of judicial institutions became a feature of political analysis in the 1990s, motivated by the concern with rule of law construction as part of the aspiration to democratic consolidation. The judicialization of politics first suggests a greater presence of judicial processes and court rulings in political and social life. Second, it is a manifestation that political, social, or state-society conflict is increasingly resolved in the courts. Third, it is the consequence of the process by which political and/or social actors increasingly see advantage in invoking legal strategies and the arbitration of judges to advance certain interests. The mobilization of legal strategies to some extent empowers judges in political decision-making processes. Finally, the judicialization of politics to some degree reflects the tendency by which regime legitimacy is increasingly perceived to be linked to the state's capacity to deliver on rule of law promises of rights, due process, and legally accountable government.

The judicialization of politics, thus, indicates a greater involvement by judges in lawmaking and social control. Its occurrence suggests that rulers are allowing this to happen, and in some cases may even be facilitating processes of institutional reform that increase the powers of judges either as arbiters of conflict or in their lawmaking faculties. For this to occur, rulers must see some benefit in delegating powers to judges, especially as this is not a risk-free process. It is possible, however, that the empowerment of courts also can lead to a reassessment of changing institutional relationships, which can in turn increase the temptation of power-holders to reestablish either a weaker judicial function (more difficult to achieve), or to seek to control the courts (either through court packing, or outright corruption).

The judicialization of politics may also be discursively linked to regime legitimization around rule of law and rights-based democracy. In appearing to bow before court rulings, power-holders can stake a more credible claim to be observing the principles of rule of law and limited government. In times of regime or political crisis this may emerge as a useful strategy in terms of bolstering legitimacy. Where other branches of power are perceived as deficient or lacking in credibility, facilitating the judicialization of politics can give credence to a public discourse of attachment to rule of law, acceptance of limited government, and commitment to strengthening rights protection mechanisms.

It is important to stress that the definition of judicialization of politics adopted here refers to more than a repositioning of the courts in relation to the executive. Not only does it include a redefinition of the balance of power between the judiciary and other branches of state, but it also refers to the repositioning of the courts in social and state–society relations. The judicialization of politics thus also concerns changing legal and political cultures regarding rule of law and rights entitlements, and also the recourse to courts as a channel for social redress and rights claims. Legal mobilization from below is thus also an important part of the phenomenon of the judicialization of politics, as the editors of this volume point out in their introduction.[2]

The Judicialization of Politics and the Rule of Law

The judicialization of politics is a phenomenon of modern democratic rule. How does it affect the nature and prospects of rule of law? Moreover, is there a useful distinction to be made about its consequences in terms of the degree of prior embeddedness and consolidation of the practice and culture of rule of law? Where rule of law is weak, will judicialization contribute to its advancement? Where rule of law exists in a minimally credible manner, does it create new ways of thinking about law and legal strategies? What is the impact of the judicialization of politics on improving mechanisms of restraint and legal accountability on rulers? And does it contribute in meaningful ways to advancing a rights culture and democratic citizenship? Finally, what are its implications for the prospects of deepening democracy?

The connection between rule of law construction and the judicialization of politics is far from straightforward. The form that the judicialization of politics takes and its specific characteristics in particular political, institutional, and social contexts is more likely to determine the impact of the phenomenon on rule of law and democratization than the fact itself of judges acquiring greater public prominence. Nonetheless, there is a connection between the judicialization of politics and the development of mechanisms of legal accountability of rulers and rights protection in any given polity and society. In as far as the judicialization of politics involves rulers relinquishing law-making power to judges, it suggests that mechanisms of "horizontal accountability" are being activated. The discussion about the different forms of political accountability is useful for understanding the consequences of judicialization of politics. Here I refer particularly to the concepts of "horizontal accountability" and "societal accountability" (O'Donnell, 2003; Smulovitz and Peruzzotti, 2003). Horizontal accountability, according to O'Donnell, refers to "a legally grounded and legally activated interaction between state agencies in view of presumed unlawful actions or omissions (encroachment or corruption)."[3] To the extent that this involves judges acquiring a more active role in their oversight functions, the effective activation of horizontal accountability is conditional upon at least the following features. First, that judges operate with sufficient political autonomy and that they do not collude with attempts by rulers or powerful groups in society to favor certain outcomes (political, social, or economic). Where collusion is evident, then the mechanisms of horizontal accountability are discredited to the detriment of rule of law construction (O'Donnell, 2003). Second, judges must act in good faith in their role of adjudication and constitutional guardianship (Ferejohn, 1998). Finally, their rulings must have the effect of enforcement. Their judgments must matter for horizontal accountability to be effective and to become respected.

The judicialization of politics would suggest that judicial rulings acquire greater presence at the horizontal accountability level, but they may not necessarily be inspired by a commitment to rule of law on behalf of the judges. Judges can be motivated to pass more emboldened and confrontational rulings with respect to the executive, for reasons other than a commitment to protecting constitutional principles (for instance on behalf of other powerful groups, thus marring the principle of legal equality). Equally, the decision to invoke judges' oversight functions (or to abide by their rulings) by political actors may not be motivated by a genuine commitment to limited government, but may instead be the outcome of short-term strategies responding to electoral pressures, to a legitimacy crisis or to the attempt to delegate unpopular decision making on political and social matters to courts. Over time, though, greater political presence of the courts may activate a "proper" functioning of horizontal accountability mechanisms which may become self-enforcing through repetition and routinization of oversight mechanisms.

The judicialization of politics can also be activated from within society. Here the concept of "societal accountability" developed by Peruzotti and Smulovitz is particularly useful and broadens the definition of forms of political accountability (Smulovitz and Peruzzotti, 2003). It is a vertical and non-electoral form of control, which includes legal mobilization strategies, and can contribute to raising the public and political profile of judges—for better or for worse. Societal accountability, claim the authors, can activate the judicial functions of oversight and rights protection. Moreover, its "watchdog" characteristics, however diffuse or even unstructured, can lead to public forms of oversight of the judicial control functions themselves. Judges who do not meet with public expectations that have been unleashed either on matters of rights protection or rendering government accountability through particular cases, risk being discredited. Thus, "societal accountability" processes can create costs in terms of reputation which both judges and rulers may care not to dismiss too easily and which can over time perhaps create incentives for a more careful fulfillment of the judicial function on the part of judges. It is important to stress that legal mobilization from below is not sufficient in itself to assure greater judicial activism, either on rights protection or with regard to judicial oversight functions, in the sense of counteracting government decisions. In the end judges need also to be sensitive to societal demands, and willing to take potentially controversial decisions on political, social, or economic matters (Gloppen, 2003). To the extent that they do, then courts can provide an institutional voice for social groups which may otherwise have limited access to the political process.

Thus, the judicialization of politics is likely to have an impact on redefining intra-institutional relations, and *may* under certain conditions (including the existence of independent, receptive judges endowed with certain forms of oversight and adjudication powers, who in addition are willing to exercise judicial activism) contribute to enhancing rule of law and certain forms of rights-based development. However, it is important to stress that these by no means are inevitable, or even necessarily likely outcomes of greater judicial presence in politics and society. In this regard it is important to establish what the judicialization of politics is *not*.

The judicialization of politics does not necessarily increase the prospects of predictability in legal rulings, or equality before the law associated with rule of law. The greater public profile or political presence of judges does not assure that they are not acting in the name of private or politically motivated interests. Moreover, greater judicial activism does not necessarily improve the prospects of equality before the law. Active judges may also be prey to powerful social groups who seek special treatment before the law. Thus the judicialization of politics can take place under the aegis of illiberal judges. In the event that judges are committed to advancing rule of law through greater judicial activism, this may activate illiberal strategies by rulers. Even when rulers, say for electoral reasons, have contributed to enhancing the political role of judges, the risks that this involves may prompt them to seek to control the judges through such means as court packing or outright bribery. If controlling the judges becomes unfeasible, then two other strategies can unfold. Rulers may seek to undermine the prestige (deserved or not) of disobedient judges. An additional or parallel strategy might involve appealing to majoritarian sources of legitimacy as a way of counteracting the judicial branch.

Conditions may be such that rulers are pushed toward accepting more effective judicial oversight of their actions, for instance during moments of legitimacy crisis. When this coincides with independent judicial rulings undertaken in good faith to uphold constitutional principles (as opposed to acting in collusion with political or private interests), then some advancement toward rule of law takes place— notwithstanding the corresponding caveats regarding the inevitable tension between the majoritarian component of democracy and judicial review.[4] In this sense, the judicialization of politics is one means by which limited government and effective mechanisms of accountability of power-holders may come into effect. And this is linked to the prospects of rule of law construction, which crucially requires that power-holders accept subordination to a higher constitutional order which expresses a consensual view of the rules of political and state–society interaction. This in itself raises important questions about the conditions under which this acceptance of limits on power becomes a possibility. Moreover, as Holmes usefully reminds us, historically rule of law is the exception rather than the norm, and is by no means the inevitable consequence of modernization (Holmes, 2003).

Rational choice perspectives provide useful insights in this regard. Rule of law emerges when powerful groups (and rulers) reach the strategic decision that it is in their best interests to support it, and that non-abidance to the law is in fact a more costly option.[5] Opting for rule of law may be the outcome of several calculations. Predictability in the application of the general rules that comes with rule of law can be an asset for governing parties in as far as it reduces instability and uncertainty in relations between state and society, and between political contenders. Promoting equality before the law that comes with rule of law, and reducing immunity of the powerful from legal scrutiny generates legitimacy. Legitimacy brings with it benefits in terms of reputation, and increases the prospects of governing by consent. Consent of the governed is more likely if the rulers are willing to abide by their own rules, and if the rules apply more equally across society.[6] Moreover, the consent and cooperation from the governed that might result from rule of law also reduces the costly risk of subversion. In addition, delegating political power to judges by enhancing their lawmaking and adjudication powers has the advantage of being able to defer to the courtroom (and thus draw distance from) unpopular policy decisions.[7]

Rational choice approaches establish a useful starting point for mapping the conditions under which processes of judicialization of politics can contribute to rule of law construction. But we need to look beyond to more structural and institutional processes in state formation that combine to facilitate a greater protagonism of the courts in the solution of political conflict. In the end, rule of law emerges as the result of a combination of long-term structural factors and short-term political calculations. The position of courts in the political system, and the nature of social and political attitudes toward legal institutions and the law, gives us further information about how legally bounded limitations on political power operate and are determined. Looking specifically at the judicial function, the development of the modern state, argues Cappelletti, generates multiple levels of oversight functions—including judicial oversight—as an inevitable outgrowth of greater levels of complexity of government and public administration. In line with a Weberian tradition of social theory, the expansion of the modern state and the increased complexity of government mean that the state intervenes in larger spheres of social and economic activities generating greater areas of potential conflict in which the state is called upon to intervene or resolve (Cappelletti, 1989). The effect of this on the judicial function would suggest both a greater political profile of the courts as well as a more complex and diversified operation of judicial oversight mechanisms.

An additional factor which contributes to enhancing judicial political control mechanisms is the "self-restraining" discourse that comes with the gradual acceptance in more than discursive ways of human rights commitments. This is a feature of the post-1948 global discourse on rights, and both at a national and international level has led to the growing presence of a rights-based political culture of democratic rule. The institutional consequences of this are evident at both the national and international level. At the national level, it has led to the "discovery" of the legal mechanisms as a way of advancing citizen rights. Courts, in fact, can act as an important "equalising" mechanism for rights redress precisely for social groups and individuals who otherwise have no access to political power or representation other than as voters (Cappelletti, 1989). In more established democracies this has taken the form of increasing levels of rights based legal mobilization (Epp, 1998). In more recent processes of democratization, the efforts of human rights movements to prosecute violations of rights committed under authoritarian rule has contributed to promoting legal mobilization strategies from below (Smulovitz, 2002).

Institutional and discursive developments at the international level have an impact on the changes in legal cultures and attitudes toward the law and rights-based development. The consolidation of a widely accepted framework of universal rights is slowly generating in its wake, albeit in very incipient forms, a range of international and regional mechanisms of rights protection, treaties, and symbolic commitments, which over time appear to be adding up to more than purely tokenistic gestures. States which aspire to be accepted by the international community may be willing to pay more than lip service to their international commitments on rights. Judicial activism is slowly making its presence felt at the regional level—certainly in Europe, but also in the Inter-American system of rights protection. Human rights groups have capitalized on the opportunities afforded by rights commitments at both the domestic, regional, and international level (Keck and Sikkink, 1998).

The judicialization of politics and state–society relations may be a feature of modern states, and its particular form will be the result of the interaction between short-term political strategies and calculations, and long-term structural processes of institutional and state-building, the specific constellation and development of social forces, and international and global dynamics. The impact of the judicialization of politics on rule of law is equally varied. Under certain conditions it *may* improve horizontal accountability and limits on power. It may also contribute to effective legal empowerment of society vis-à-vis the power-holders. On the other hand, especially in young democracies where rule of law is weak, the judicialization of politics can very rapidly spiral into a process of politicization of the judiciary with detrimental effects for the credibility of rule of law.

The Judicialization of Politics in Mexico

The Mexican case presents an interesting example of a democratizing context in which the judicial branch, at least at the level of the supreme court, has become a prominent political actor. At the level of horizontal accountability mechanisms of institutional limits on political power, there is little doubt that the supreme court has come to represent an increasingly more effective branch in terms of judicial review and constitutional control within the political system. This marks a historical break in a political tradition in which the supreme court rarely challenged the executive, and was perceived as an ineffective and corrupt branch within the political system. Not only has there been in recent years a judicialization of politics at the level of the relationship between the political branches, but moreover, there is general consensus in the literature that this amounts to a meaningful delegation of power by the executive to the supreme court.

The activation of effective mechanisms of judicial checks and balances on political power has gone hand in hand with a relatively high level of abidance with court rulings, even when these seemed politically inconvenient for the ruling party (Staton, 2002). These changes at the level of the supreme court might well indicate important progress in the direction of rule of law construction. However, this has not been paralleled by similar developments within the administration of justice more broadly at lower levels of the federal system of justice.[8] The following section examines reasons which explain the advances made in terms of better "horizontal accountability" as a result of the judicialization of politics, with important consequences for some aspects of rule of law. These are by no means inconsequential. However, rule of law construction is a complex multilayered process, which, moreover, is not irreversible. It is possible for illiberal enclaves, which may constitute a large proportion of state–society relations, and of political behavior immune to legal scrutiny, to coexist with new legal spaces in which both judges and politicians may be beginning to accept the constraints of constitutional probity. The advances that have been made are signaled here, notably at the level of the supreme court and "horizontal accountability" relations. I also draw attention to some of those areas where rule of law is far from achieved.

The Traditional Role of the Mexican Judiciary

The 1990s saw a qualitative shift in the relationship between the supreme court and the executive. A traditionally passive and politically subservient role of the judicial branch in relation to the executive was rooted in the constitutional process of nineteenth century state-building in Mexico. Two features of the political role of the judicial branch were consolidated by the end of the nineteenth century. First, the principle of nonintervention by the judicial branch in electoral and political conflict was firmly established after some debate on the dangers of the dictatorship of the judges (Moctezuma Barragán, 1994). Second, the *amparo* suit had become the principal form of judicial review, and remains to date the main mechanism for individual rights protection against illegal acts of authority (*amparo de legalidad*) or unconstitutional laws and decisions by government (*amparo de inconstitucionalidad*).

Throughout the revolutionary period, despite a brief interlude of relative independence between 1917 and 1928,[9] the judicial branch maintained a subordinate and compliant role vis-à-vis the executive. In the context of dominant party rule from the 1930s onward, the supreme court played an important role in providing the political system with a far from negligible degree of juridical and constitutional legitimization. Overall, in matters that were politically sensitive the court strove either to keep a low profile, or to support the general policy directives that came from the executive. In this regard, the judicial branch contributed to the effect of political stability structured around a nominal constitutional discourse and practice of regular elections and presidential turnover that constituted the *pax priista* of dominant party rule. The judiciary was an important part of the structures that gave credence to a state of legality of sorts—and this was by no means unimportant for regime legitimization.

Until the 1980s, regime legitimacy rested in large measure on the system's capacity to draw on a political discourse of inclusive and redistributive state corporatism. The redefinition of the Mexican state following a succession of economic crises and the beginnings of economic and political liberalization in the 1980s led to a gradual reconfiguration of the language of regime legitimacy around a more explicit discourse of liberal rule of law and rights. These developments were hardly linear or unequivocal—nor did they represent sincere commitments to improving rule of law on behalf of the political elite. The drawn out nature of the transition process toward a more credible polyarchy was precisely characterized by contradictory processes of political liberalization (acceptance of opposition electoral victories, gradual reform of the electoral system, reform of the judiciary) alongside the persistence of old practices of fraud, politically instigated violence and rights violations, and enclaves of authoritarian practices, in which impunity and being above the law remained the norm. The transition process, however, and the incorporation of a language of liberal democracy would pave the way for a regime discourse which would be more consonant with notions of limited government and effective separation of powers.

The 1994 constitutional reforms at the start of the Zedillo presidency, which altered the standing of the judiciary in relation to the executive, were in line with these changes. Prior to the 1990s, however, it is important to point out that the judicial system had undergone important reforms.[10] The reforms on the whole were dictated by administrative and efficiency-related imperatives. After 1917, there was a progressive increase in the number of supreme court members as a way of dealing with a rapidly increasing backlog in the high tribunal. Collegiate tribunals were set up in 1951 to help deal with *amparos de legalidad* (dealing with the legality of acts and resolutions). Importantly in 1958 a law was passed by which the supreme court had the exclusive competence to rule on *amparos de inconstitucionalidad*, cases in which the constitutionality of laws are challenged. The constitutional review faculties of the supreme court were further centralized in a reform of 1987 by which the high tribunal would no longer see *amparos de legalidad*, now dealt with solely by the collegiate tribunals, and would deal essentially with matters of *amparos de inconstitucionalidad*. Thus the high tribunal's character as predominantly a constitutional court was already beginning to be outlined in the 1980s (Fix-Fierro, 2004). Its review powers were still limited due to the "concrete" nature of the *amparo* suit. Court rulings in this regard only apply to the case at hand and do not have *erga omnes* or general effect. Significantly, this has remained unchanged with the reforms of the 1990s.

While reforms prior to 1994 were significant, especially in terms of alleviating caseload problems and delays in the high court, it is also important to point out that no fundamental attitudinal change was discernible in the relationship between the judiciary and the executive. This would not come about until the reforms of the 1990s, and in the particular context of regime transition.

Judicial Reform and Changing Legal Structures in the 1990s

The constitutional reforms of 1994 and 1996 have proven to be crucial turning points in the political history of the judicial branch. Much has been written on their merits and shortcomings.[11] Here I merely outline their main components in as far as they have contributed to a systemic alteration in the workings of horizontal accountability mechanisms.

The 1994 reform increased judicial independence from the executive through a new appointments system of the supreme court, which now requires a two-thirds majority support vote of the senate from a list of candidates presented by the president. This replaces a system of presidential appointment subject to a majority vote of ratification by the senate. The supreme court's review powers were substantially altered first through the reenforcement of its "constitutional controversies" faculty, by which it rules on conflicts which arise between different levels of the public administration and government. The second important addition was the creation of the "constitutionality action," by which, at the behest of a third of the vote in any legislature, either at federal or state level, the court can rule on the constitutionality of a law. The latter is particularly novel due to the general effect of the court ruling in terms of annulling the law in this type of constitutional challenge.[12] Only the legislative branch can resort to this form of review. For individual citizens, the *amparo* suit continues to be the principal form of rights protection and judicial review, and has remained unaltered. Greater budgetary autonomy was granted. A judicial council was created which would be in charge of the administration of the judiciary, including court management, appointments, promotion, and internal disciplinary action. A later reform in 1999 redefined the relationship between the judicial council and the supreme court after some early signs of conflict between the two bodies. The 1999 reform reasserted the supreme court's dominant position vis-à-vis the judicial council.

The 1996 constitutional reform extended the review powers of the judiciary to electoral matters. It fully incorporated the electoral tribunal into the judicial branch, and extended the supreme court's review powers on some electoral disputes.[13] The number of electoral disputes brought before the Federal Electoral Tribunal attests to the marked level of judicial activism that has taken off in this area. Between 1996 and 2000, 11,906 disputes were brought before the electoral tribunal (Berruecos, 2003, p. 808). Moreover, the supreme court has increasingly dealt with cases concerning the constitutionality of electoral laws (Finkel, 2003). Breaking with a long-standing tradition of nonintervention of the courts in electoral disputes, this is an area in which the judicialization of politics has become most evident. The earlier cases were marked by great controversy, in part due to the novelty of resolving electoral disputes in the courts, but also in part due to the still prevalent suspicion that the supreme court would rule according to political criteria. Several issues are worth noting. First, there was a displacement of the practice of "negotiating" electoral results with the ruling Partido Revolutionario Institutional (PRI) toward a system in which disputes could credibly be resolved by legal means. This marked the beginning not only of better conditions for electoral competition, but of a culture of rule of law as part of the electoral process in a way that was dramatically lacking prior to the 1996 reform. A second development was the growing acceptance by political opponents that there was much to be gained by resorting to the courts. In view of the number of success stories in electoral disputes in favor of political opposition to the PRI, not only did this grant credibility to the legal process as a "fair" mechanism, but moreover, this in turn made it more difficult for the ruling party (now the Partido de Acción Nacional, PAN) to disregard judicial rulings on electoral matters. In no small way, this has contributed to enhancing the image of the supreme court and the electoral tribunal as acting with political autonomy from the executive (at federal and state levels). Given the history of fraudulent practices that characterized Mexican electoral processes in the past, the judicialization of politics in this respect has signified an important step toward rule of law construction.[14]

Judicial activism of the supreme court during the 1990s was not limited to electoral disputes. The 1994 reforms unleashed a process of redefinition of the workings of judicial review more broadly through-out the political system. Through the mechanism of constitutional controversies, in which the supreme court has undertaken to rule in polemical disputes between different levels of municipal, state, and federal government, the judiciary has increasingly contributed to defining the legal boundaries of Mexico's federalism. Berruecos (2002) lucid study reveals first, that opposition parties, somewhat under the initiative of the PAN, were quick to catch on to the potential benefits of resorting to this legal instrument to challenge PRI governments at the state and federal level on perceived encroachments of jurisdictional boundaries between the different levels of government. In this sense, legal mobilization was discovered as a useful means of asserting jurisdictional boundaries that in the past had been more nebulous and subject to political negotiation. Second, judicial rulings indicated a willingness by the supreme court to act independently of the executive branch. As the possibility of successful legal challenges became evident to political opponents, this in turn reinforced the perceived usefulness of this legal space and increased the likelihood that it will continue to be resorted to. It is indeed the case that political parties at various levels of government and in the opposition have found a supreme court which has shown itself to be receptive and active. Third, the dramatic increase in the numbers of constitutional controversies that were taken up in the 1990s led to the supreme court becoming a key actor in the complex redefinition of federalism that is part of Mexico's political transition toward democratic rule.[15] There is no clear direction in this redefinition of the "federal pact" in the rulings, other than through what does seem to be a clearer setting of legal boundaries on the relations and competences of different levels of government. This in itself is a marked change from the old federal arrangement which consisted of "unwritten" rules of the game in the negotiation between central and state levels of government. Another important development was the process of assertion of municipal authorities vis-à-vis state and federal government. The court played an important part in this process.[16]

Judicial activism at the level of the supreme court has extended to areas in which in the past it preferred to keep a low profile. In addition to dealing with constitutional controversies, and its new powers of constitutional control though the "constitutional action" suit, the court is ruling audaciously on a wide range of matters, and in its use of the traditional *amparo* suit. It is this change of behavior in *amparo* rulings which is particularly interesting. Overall, judicial rulings have included controversial decisions on tax laws, the constitutional definition of trade union membership, the constitutionality of the interest rates that banks sought to charge after the 1994 economic crisis, the constitutional jurisdiction of which level of government can decide on implementing summer time, controversial extradition rulings, the constitutionality of the indigenous law, and the FOBAPROA (Fondo Bancario de Protección al Ahorro) case, to name but a few.[17] The rulings have not been free of controversy. However, what seems to have also emerged is a growing public acknowledgement that the court is genuinely seeking to distance itself from its politically dependent reputation, and to take its role of constitutional guardian seriously. It is also important to note that there is no clear ideological or political bias to the rulings, which has added to the sense that the judicialization of politics is on the whole not skewed in favor of any single set of political or economic interests.[18] This has contributed to the novel image of judicial independence that is developing at the level of the supreme court.

From the perspective of political parties in Mexico, the supreme court has become an institutional actor that needs to be reckoned with. As the supreme court acquires greater legitimacy and credibility, as well as a more prominent public presence, the costs of not complying with its rulings become higher for governing groups.[19] In this sense, horizontal accountability mechanisms appear to be kicking in an unprecedented manner in terms of judicial review. The growing credibility of the court makes it harder for reluctant political actors to undermine it, to co-opt it as in the past, or to ignore it. Moreover, to the degree that its public and independent presence has been assimilated into the political imagination, then resorting to legal strategies has also become a useful—and *normal*—tool to be used by diverse political actors for advancing certain political interests.

It is evident that the judicialization of politics has gone hand in hand also with the transformation of the supreme court's own self-perception. Since 1994 the supreme court has engaged in a self-conscious effort to carve out for itself a new role in a rapidly changing political environment and to distance itself from its politically subservient past.[20] The change has taken place at various levels. First, the court has sought to reaffirm its new political independence with regard to the executive. Second, it has chosen to promote judicial activism in areas where in the past it sought obscurity from the public limelight. Third, the court has undergone more than a cosmetic change in seeking to revamp its image. It has engaged in an enterprising public relations campaign which has included among other things, developing a new public face through advertisements, publishing an array of books and pamphlets on its democratic function and its rulings, and improving considerably the information made publicly available on its internal workings.[21]

Thus, institutional change has, in the Mexican case, in an important way contributed to a process of judicialization of politics at the level of the relationship between the supreme court and the executive branch. The court has become an effective and credible forum for the resolution of a range of political and social conflicts. In terms of rule of law construction, it has added considerably to the mechanisms of judicial oversight and constitutional checks and balances within the political system. Nonetheless it is important to stress that these changes are most prominent at the level of the supreme court. At lower levels of the judicial system and especially in state judiciaries, these changes are not visible in any significant manner—with some notable exceptions. In this respect, the societal mechanisms of exercising legal accountability have not been strengthened in the same degree. This may respond in part to the nature of the transition process—discussed further—which in Mexico has been far more gradual and top-down. But also the nature of the judicialization phenomenon in part derives from the fact that judicial reforms have especially been instituted at the level of the supreme court and far less so at the lower levels of the judicial hierarchy.

It is important to note that while judicialization of politics in the case of Mexico seems to have gone hand in hand with the self-assertion of—to all appearances—a politically independent court, this should not be mistaken for a reason to unduly increase the political powers of the court in the future. During recent political debates on judicial reform in Mexico, the supreme court has lobbied for greater review powers, but it is possible that an over-empowerment of the courts could in the long run prove to be problematic for the institutionalization of democracy.

Judicialization of Politics and Regime Transition

This undisputable process of judicialization of politics, and the manner in which it has developed—with the historically unprecedented, and somewhat surprising establishment of a relatively politically independent judicial branch—has clearly signified in the Mexican case that the ruling parties (first the PRI and now the PAN) have ultimately accepted delegating a greater degree of political decision-making power to the judicial branch, and the consequences of judicial oversight and limited government in ways which are far removed from the old PRI political system. How has effectively limited government come into being amid a political tradition of impunity and judicial improbity? To what extent can this judicialization of politics be understood as a consequence of the type of regime transition that Mexico has undergone?

The 1994 reforms with which Zedillo inaugurated his presidency unleashed a process of institutional re-accommodation that was reinforced by changing political circumstances and a new constellation of political forces around more competitive and pluralist party competition. The reforms might not have been prompted by a genuine commitment to strengthening rule of law, but nonetheless signaled a policy response to a number of factors in 1994 that were pressing on the regime. First, it typified a practice of beginning presidential terms with the promise of combating corruption and the weakness of rule of law. In previous presidential administrations similar gestures had been made, such as the spectacular arrest of corrupt public officials. Second, the political violence and image of corruption that had characterized the final months of the Salinas administration provided a distinct pressure on the new government to make amends in the form of some kind of political or legislative gesture to combat impunity. Third, the international context was not irrelevant. Salinas had already made some concessions to international pressures regarding human rights issues through the creation of the Comisión Nacional de Derechos Humanos (CNDH) in 1992. The signing of NAFTA was not irrelevant in pushing for rule of law reform, although clearly the treaty's success was not contingent on judicial reforms—it had already been signed.[22] Finally, while politically attractive in the short run, the far-reaching consequences of the 1994 reform were probably not foreseen at the time of their passage. At some level, however, they may also have reflected Zedillo's personal penchant for pushing toward more substantive political reform than the PRI was used to—as would become evident with later reforms—as well as the need to respond to the crisis of political legitimacy that had gripped the country since the Zapatista rebellion, and the political assassinations of 1994.[23] Nonetheless, there was probably little expectation at the time, given the history of political compliance of the judiciary, and the habit of executive dominance, that the supreme court would either undergo a profound transformation of its role in the political system, or that it would really choose to activate its new powers as it did.

The transition process in Mexico was characterized by a sort of democratization *by stealth*. There was no sudden rupture, nor has there been a clear foundational or constitutional moment. The 2000 electoral defeat of the PRI, if anything was the culmination of a long process which had started at least in the 1980s, and could be traced perhaps as far back as the electoral reform of 1977. The PRI had already incurred important electoral losses at the state level well before 2000, and in the 1997 midterm elections where it lost its congressional majority. Many of the institutional forms of democratic rule (competitive elections, a more effective separation of powers and so forth) were already in place before Fox's victory. At the same time, many elements of democratic rule are still deficient in many ways, with ineffective rule of law and rights protection at other levels of the justice system, for instance.[24] If we examine the judicialisation of politics within this complex process of stop-and-go regime change, the attitudinal transformation within the supreme court toward greater judicial activism following the 1994 and 1996 constitutional reforms was both a consequence of and a contributing factor toward the transition process.

The Zedillo administration was particularly characterized by this deepening of the political trends toward greater political party competition and pluralism, which of course was not without ambivalence and contradictions. The PRI lost its congressional majority in 1997 and then, in 2000, the presidency. The changing political landscape against which the 1994 reforms were carried out contributed to changing the incentive structures for both the behavior of supreme court members on the one hand, and political actors with regard to the newly empowered judicial branch on the other. Attitudinal changes within the supreme court were in some ways prompted not only by the reforms, but also by the growing awareness of a changed political climate in which the judiciary's political role was open, along with other institutions, to redefinition as the PRI was losing its hegemonic position.

For contending political parties, the opportunities generated by new judicial review powers in the context of greater political competition increased the incentives to invoke the judiciary as arbiter of political conflicts which in the past had typically been resolved through other forms of political negotiation with central government. To some extent, this was spearheaded by the PAN at the level of municipal and state government, as constitutional controversies were registered with increasing enthusiasm.[25] Clearly it is the case that sustained recourse to legal strategies requires that they yield positive results. The judicialization of politics in the 1990s combined not only a greater willingness by emerging political parties to confide in the resolution capabilities of the court in their favor, but significantly also an increasing degree of receptiveness and, over time, proven autonomy in supreme court rulings as well as an empowered judicial branch by the 1994 and later 1996 reforms. That the supreme court now regularly rules on a wide range of political, social, and economic issues is no longer the exception, but rather the rule.

The Mexican case, therefore, is clearly an example of power-holders being pressed to make concessions in the rules of the political game in a bid to resolve an accumulating crisis of legitimacy. As these concessions were activated they contributed in turn to systemic changes in patterns of accountability—at least with respect to the "horizontal" level. Mexico is also therefore an example of how the acceptance of self-restraining rules, for short-term political gain, has had unforeseen long-term political consequences. To the extent that this is leading to a *normalization* of better checks and balances and mechanisms of horizontal accountability than in the past, then the judicialisation of politics at this "high" level will have some impact on the complex construction of rule of law.

Several caveats need to be pointed out. First, although the particular conditions of greater judicial activism in Mexico at the supreme court level have apparently led to an improvement in horizontal accountability, this is not an inevitable consequence of the judicialization of politics. Nor can we rule out that the court may yet undergo a process of *politicization* by which the autonomy which has begun to characterize its rulings could begin to weaken. Second, a better functioning and more active supreme court has not wiped out many "brown areas" in Mexico's justice system, where rule of law is weak. Corruption in political office, while perhaps somewhat more checked now than in the past, continues to be a critical problem in Mexico's political system. The criminal justice system is fraught with human rights abuses, impunity, and inefficiency. In this sense it is important to distinguish several points. First, that judicialization may or may not contribute to rule of law construction and modernization of the justice system—this will depend on the particular configuration of the judicialization process in each country context. Second, that rule of law construction in any case is a complex and multilayered process in which different levels and qualities of legal accountability or effectiveness in adjudication can coexist. At best there may be a contagion effect between improved areas and those that lag behind, but this is not an inevitable process. To the extent that the Mexican transition process has been led from "above," and especially so in the case of judicial reform, this has led to a judicialization of "high" politics, and an improvement in the high tribunal's levels of public credibility.

Changes in the social context have not been irrelevant, although the judicialization of politics in the Mexican case has been as yet less dramatically susceptible to bottom-up processes of legal mobilization.[26] While the judicialization of politics has led to an important reconfiguration of relations between the powers of state, and the beginnings of more effective means of horizontal accountability, there has been less of a sense of societal appropriation of legal strategies as a way of advancing rights claims or a broader sense of "societal accountability" based on legal mobilization—with a few notable examples. However, this is slowly changing. Mexican society, in part in reflection of patterns of urbanization and modernization, has become more demanding of rule of law and rights protection (Domingo, 1999). This is all the more so with the collapse of old structures of state corporatism and a weakened discourse of re-distributive inclusion in the revolutionary project. Political liberalization has gone hand in hand with a discourse of rights which has become incorporated into the public aspiration toward democratic citizenship. It is, albeit, important to emphasize that the manner in which citizenship and its related rights are defined in Mexican society is far from homogenous, all the more so in view of indigenous demands for recognition of community forms of justice. Generally, "societal accountability" through legal mobilization from below has been slow in Mexico, say in comparison to Argentina. It has not, however, been entirely absent and its presence, albeit in a fragmented and uneven form, is contributing to the political and societal developments that shape the complex patchwork of regime transition and, hopefully, rule of law construction. The societal discovery of a rights language has in part been prompted to some extent by a growing mobilization of NGOs around issues of human rights violations, past and present, with as yet unclear judicial effect (although the recent call to indict ex-President Echeverria for his role in repressive actions against demonstrators in 1971 marks an interesting development in this regard).[27] The establishment of the CNDH, with all the caveats regarding its workings, especially in the early days, has further advanced a discourse of rights and rule of law. The mobilization of the Barzon social movement in defense of small scale borrowers unable to pay back interest on loans following the 1994 financial crisis was an interesting case of collective recourse to the courts in demand of social and economic redress.[28] These slow changes are important in signaling a gradual "discovery" of the law by societal actors as a means of advancing rights claims, even though rulings are not necessarily always in favor of the mobilized interests (there is no clear pattern in this regard). Overall, however, the judicialization of politics in Mexico has been less the result of legal mobilization from below, than from political parties making use of the new judicial review powers. Moreover, high levels of public distrust in the court system also persist as a consequence of the poor image of the criminal justice system, both in terms of its reputation for human rights abuses, and its image of corruption and ineffectiveness in improving public security and combating crime.[29]

An important consequence of the transition process has been the gradual opening of the system to international legal structures and norms. Mexico's increased commitments to international and regional treaties have rendered the state more liable to international norms and standards on due process and rights. Human rights activism has incorporated to good effect recourse to the Inter-American system of rights protection with some impact on government actions.[30] The political elite, in contrast to the past, is now more careful not to disregard its international and regional rights commitments. While Mexico's social context has changed considerably, as have societal expectations about democratic rule, public opinion continues to hold the general justice system in low esteem. Judicialization of politics in the upper echelons of the judicial branch has not directly translated into better lower level justice administration (although reform processes are taking place at the state level; Fix-Fierro, 2004). This mixed baggage of how rule of law operates is highly problematic precisely because of the obstacles it creates to rule of law construction and the possibility of rights-based citizenship. The failure of a more socially embedded and trustworthy justice system over time creates structural problems for democratic advancement. The "brown areas" of misrule of law and impunity can persist indefinitely, and are not necessarily affected by top-down judicialization processes. At best a "contagion" effect can develop; at worst, parallel qualities of justice administration can coexist indefinitely.

Conclusions

Fundamental changes at some levels of the judicial function of rights protection and limited government coexist in Mexico with deeply embedded illiberal structures of justice administration. Unsurprisingly a complex overlapping of processes of change with continuities from the past that project into the future is what we find in the Mexican justice system. Parallel progress in all spheres of the justice system is difficult to achieve, but the sum of changing institutions, perceptions, and opportunities for legal mobilization in the direction of rights protection should not be underestimated. In some respects, Mexico has been experiencing an important break with the old system of dominant party rule in which there was rule *by* law, but where rule of law was far more the exception than it is today.

To what extent is this the result of a process of judicialization of politics? At the level of horizontal accountability mechanisms, the judicialization of politics appears to be resulting in improved forms of limited government, which is no mean achievement in the context of Mexico's drawn out transition process and given its history of "meta-constitutional" presidentialism. But this is very much a feature of top-down reform processes and high-level politics. Reform has led to effective delegation of power from the executive to the judicial branch, which has translated, probably beyond original expectations, into the rapid development of fairly autonomous supreme court judicial activism. This delegation of power to the judicial branch was a concession to a rule of law discourse at a time when regime legitimacy needed boosting. As the Mexican political system has inched its way toward liberal democracy of sorts, the language of rights and rule of law has become both a more explicit political promise, and a more pressing public demand. The international context has not been irrelevant, but generally has played an indirect role in encouraging a redefinition of the workings of the legal system.

What are the lessons to be learned from the judicialization of politics in the Mexican case? Clearly the link to rule of law construction exists but is tenuous and complex. Judicialization processes can activate habits of better legal accountability—as in the case of Mexico's supreme court—but this is not inevitable. Greater judicial activism can also be promoted by powerful political and social interests, with the danger that courts act not autonomously but in collusion with these groups. It is also possible to envisage judicialization processes in which judges enjoy far less credibility. Thus while the Mexican case for now seems to have led to improved mechanisms of horizontal accountability between the executive and judicial branch, this cannot be applied as a rule elsewhere. Finally, it is important to warn against the perils of over-empowering judges for the long-term prospect of democratic rule.

Notes

1. See Guarnieri and Pederzoli, 1999; Waltman and Holland, 1988; Tate and Vallinder, 1995; Cappelletti, 1989; Domingo, 2004.
2. See Epp, 1998; Smulovitz, 2003; and Smulovitz and Peruzzotti, 2003.
3. For discussions of the concept of accountability see the works in Schedler et al., 1999 and in Mainwaring and Welna, 2003.
4. It is important to stress that while judges may play an important role in advancing the cause of limited government, we must not lose sight of the potentially "undemocratic" characteristics of "rule by the judiciary." Gargarella (2003) in particular develops a critical view of the assumptions behind mechanisms of checks and balances based on counter-majoritarian and basically "undemocratic" forms of rule of law construction around un-elected judicial powers.
5. See chapters in Maravall and Przeworski, 2003 for suggestive discussions by the different authors on rule of law construction.

6. Equality before the law can at best only be an approximation. Power asymmetries in society will always have a distorting effect in terms of how rules apply and how rights are weighted.
7. See Holmes, 2003 for an insightful discussion of rule of law construction.
8. At the state level there have been similar "high" level reforms in the judiciary regarding state supreme courts, and the establishment of judicial councils that have been taking place throughout the country since 1995. See Fix-Fierro, 2004. With regard to other aspects of the justice system, recently, sweeping reforms have been announced in a political bid by President Fox to show that the government views the problem of public security seriously.
9. During this period, the court was endowed with more independent characteristics, such as its appointment mechanisms, but also had the reputation of ruling in a conservative way (Cardenas Gracia, 1996; Leon González, 1990).
10. See Fix-Fierro, 2000, 2004 for a detailed discussion of the reforms and their impact.
11. Berruecos, 2002, 2003; Fix-Fierro, 2004; López Ayllón and Fix-Fierro, 2000; Fix-Fierro, 2000; Domingo, 2000; Arteaga Nava, 1995; Vargas, 1996; Melgar Adalid, 1995, among others.
12. The impact of this new review power was somewhat diminished by several qualifications: first, the requirement that rulings require an eight out of eleven vote; and seconds, by the time limit that was established for members of congress to mobilize and present a constitutional challenge before the court.
13. See Berruecos, 2003 and Finkel, 2003 for in-depth analyses of the political impact of the 1996 reform.
14. It is clear that an important aspect of the judicialization of politics in Mexico has revolved around electoral disputes. This is understood especially in the context of a long-standing tradition of political control of electoral competition and its outcome. As political alternation becomes "normal," it is likely that legal challenges to electoral processes are likely to diminish, although the watchdog function of the courts in this respect will continue to be important.
15. Between 1917 and 1994 only 55 constitutional controversies were brought before the court. Between 1994 and 1998, 144 controversies were submitted. Between 1998 and 2000, 140 cases were presented. In 2001 alone, 300 cases were submitted, in connection with the controversial indigenous law. See Berruecos, 2002 for a detailed study of this aspect of judicialization of politics.
16. For instance, in Nuevo León, the municipality of San Nicolás de los Garza went against the state government on fiscal matters and in 1997 received a partially favourable ruling by the supreme court. Río Bravo, a PAN-governed municipality was also an early example of a favourable supreme court ruling in a constitutional controversy case against the state government on matters of public security and transit. Recently, the supreme court has also became the battleground for

conflicts between the local government of the Federal Capital, under Andrés López Obrador (PRD), and the national government of Vicente Fox (PAN). See Berruecos, 2002.

17. See Fix-Fierro and López Ayllón, 2001; Staton, 2002, 2003; Berruecos, 2002, 2003, among others.

18. Clearly, "losing" parties may claim political manipulation when a ruling goes against their interests. Overall, though, there is a growing acceptance that the court is not necessarily favoring a clear set of political or economic interests over others. It has shown itself to be progressive in some areas (for instance human rights cases) and conservative in others, but a clear pattern is not discernible.

19. Staton (2002) develops an interesting study on the differences in law abidance by the different ruling parties in the federal government, who are more vulnerable to the costs of non-abidance in terms of not accepting court rulings than either local or state governments, where the tradition of impunity is harder to overturn and the costs of disobedience are perceived as less damaging. Ultimately, though, even at this level it is becoming harder to resist implementing supreme court rulings.

20. As a result of the 1994 constitutional reforms, the supreme court was completely re-created when all its previous members were dismissed and replaced. It was suggested at the time that Zedillo had taken the opportunity to pack the court with judges loyal to the PRI. In fact, the subsequent behavior of the court does not support this claim. Already from the 1980s there appears to have been a gradual depoliticization of the members of the supreme court in terms of their background and political affiliation. See Domingo, 1999.

21. See Staton, 2003 for an in-depth analysis and assessment of the supreme court's public relations exercise, and the degree to which it has improved both its public standing, and its political leverage in being able to influence future judicial reform initiatives. Staton makes the important point that despite this invigorated effort by the court to become a political actor not only in judicial matters but also in legislative processes, it has not really resulted in significantly better prospects of determining the legislative agenda with regard to judicial reform.

22. Erfani (1995) argues that the United States had already secured for itself sufficient legal guarantees in the terms of NAFTA to play too important a role in pushing for further reforms.

23. It is worth noting that the questionable way in which the members of the new supreme court were appointed signaled a last minute attempt to regain control of a judicial reform which risked altering relations between the judicial and executive branch. Ultimately, though, the executive was unable to effectively co-opt the new high tribunal.

24. The impact of the supreme court on lower-level courts is slow to filter through the system, although, as the supreme court has asserted its control over the judicial council, it may be that (for better or for worse) this enhances its control over lower-level courts. The supreme

court also has far less direct control over the state judiciaries than over the lower courts in the federal justice system.

25. Berruecos, 2002.
26. Indigenous groups did mobilize through the courts against the constitutionality of legislation on indigenous rights, passed under Fox, which fell short of the San Andrés agreement with the Zapatista rebels. Nevertheless, the law was upheld by a supreme court ruling. This proved to be a disheartening experience for indigenous groups, but the legal mobilization from below was in itself quite novel. Authoritarian structures in Mexican society and the recent nature of democratic procedures go a long way toward explaining why legal mobilization from below has been slow.
27. See Welna, 1997.
28. See Fix-Fierro and López Ayllón, 2002 and http://www.elbarzon.org
29. Human Rights Watch, 1999; UN Economic and Social Council, 2002, among others.
30. The release of General Gallardo in 2002, following the recommendations of the IACHR, was a small victory in this sense. General Gallardo had been arrested in 1993 after criticizing human rights violations by the Mexican armed forces. He was initially adopted as a prisoner of conscience by Amnesty International, and his case subsequently went through the Inter-American system.

References

Arteaga Nava (1995) "Las nuevas facultades de la Suprema Corte de la Nación," in Mario Melgar Adalid (ed.), *Reformas al Poder Judicial* (UNAM: Mexico).

Berruecos, Susana (2002) "The Mexican Supreme Court under New Federalism: An Analysis of Constitutional Controversies (1995–2000)" (Paper delivered at Centro de Investigación y Docencia Económica [CIDE]).

———, "Electoral Justice in Mexico: The Role of the Electoral Tribunal under new Federalism," *Journal of Latin American Studies*, vol. 35 (2003), pp. 801–25.

Cappelletti, Mauro (1989) *The Judicial Process in Comparative Perspective* (Oxford: Clarendon Press).

Cárdenas Gracia, Jaime (1996) *Una Constitución para la democracia: Propuestas para un nuevo orden constitucional* (UNAM: México).

Domingo, Pilar, "Rule of Law, Citizenship and Access to Justice in Mexico," *Mexican Studies*, vol. 15, no.1 (1999), pp. 151–91.

———, "Judicial Independence: The Politics of the Supreme Court in Mexico," *Journal of Latin American Studies*, vol. 32, no.3 (2000), pp. 705–35.

———, "Judicialization of Politics or Politicization of the Judiciary? Recent Trends in Latin America," *Democratization*, vol. 11, no. 1 (2004), pp. 104–26.

Epp, Charles (1998) *The Rights Revolution: Lawyers, Activists and Supreme Courts in Comparative Perspective* (Chicago: University of Chicago Press).

Erfani, Julie A. (1995) *The Paradox of the Mexican State: Rereading Sovereignty from Independence to NAFTA* (Boulder: Lynne Rienner Publisher).

Ferejohn (1998) "Dynamics of Judicial Independence: Independent Judge, Dependent Judicary" (Unpublished manuscript).

Finkel, Jodie, "Supreme Court Decisions on Electoral Rules after Mexico's 1994 Judicial Reform: An Empowered Court," *Journal of Latin American Studies*, vol. 35, no. 4 (2003), pp. 777–99.

Fix Fierro, Héctor (2000) "Poder Judicial," in María del Refugio González and Sergio López Ayllón (eds.), *Transiciones y diseños institucionales* (UNAM: México), pp. 162–217.

—— (2004) "La Reforma en México: Entre la eficacia autoritaria y la incertidumbre democrática," in Luis Pásara (ed.), *En busca de una justicia distinta: Experiencias de reforma en América Latina* (Lima: Consorcio Justicia Viva), pp. 249–88.

Fix Fierro, Héctor and Sergio López Ayllón "Legitimidad contra Legalidad: Los dilemas de la transición jurídica y el Estado de Derecho en México," *Política y Gobierno*, vol. 8 (2001), pp. 347–93.

—— (2002) "Cambio jurídico y autonomía del derecho: Un modelo de la transición juridical en México," in José María Serna de la Garza and José Antonio Caballero Juárez (eds.), *Estado de derecho y transición jurídica* (México: Universidad Nacional Autónoma de México (UNAM)), pp. 95–137.

Gargarella, Roberto (2003) "The Majoritarian Reading of the Rule of Law," in José Maria Maravall and Adam Przeworski (eds.), *Democracy and the Rule of Law* (Cambridge: Cambridge University Press), pp. 147–67.

Gloppen, Siri (2003) "Analyzing the Role of Courts in Social Transformation: Social Rights Litigation, Court Responsiveness and Capability" (Presented at the workshop "Human Rights, Democracy and Social Transformation: When do Rights Work?" at the University of Witwatersrand).

Guarnieri, Carlo and Patrizia Pederzoli (1999) *Los jueces y la política: Poder judicial y democracia* (Madrid: Taurus).

Holmes, Stephen (2003) "Lineages of the Rule of Law," in José Maria Maravall and Adam Przeworski (eds.), *Democracy and the Rule of Law*, (Cambridge: Cambridge University Press) pp. 19–61.

Human Rights Watch (1999) *Torture, Disappearance and Extrajudicial Execution* (New York: Human Rights Watch).

Keck, Margaret and Kathryn Sikkink (1998) *Activists Beyond Borders: Advocacy Networks in International Politics* (Ithaca: Cornell University Press).

León González, S.G. (1990), "Decisiones Constituyentes 1921–1938" (Unpublished degree thesis, Mexico UNAM).

López Ayllón, Sergio and Héctor Fix-Fierro (2000) *Tan cerca, tan lejos! Estado de derecho y cambio jurídico en México (1979–1999)* (Mexico UNAM) (http://info.juridicias.unam.mx).

Mainwaring, Scott and Christopher Welna (2003) *Democratic Accountability in Latin America* (Oxford: Oxford University Press).

Maravall, José María and Adam Przeworski (eds.) (2003) *Democracy and the Rule of Law* (Cambridge: Cambridge University Press).

Melgar Adalid, Mario (ed.) (1995) *Reformas al Poder Judicial* (Mexico UNAM).

Moctezuma Barragán, Javier (1994) *Jose María Iglesias y la Justicia Electoral* (Mexico UNAM).

O'Donnell, Guillermo (2003) "Horizontal Accountability: The Legal Institutionalisation of Mistrust," in Scott Mainwaring and Christopher Welna (eds.), *Democratic Accountability in Latin America* (Oxford: Oxford University Press), pp. 34–54.

Schedler, Andreas Larry Diamond and Marc Plattner (eds.) (1999) *The Self-Restraining State: Power and Accountability in New Democracies* (Boulder: Lynne Rienner Publisher).

Smulovitz, Catalina, (2002) "The Discovery of Law: Political Consequences in the Argentine Case," in Yves Dezalay and Bryant Garth (eds.), *Global Prescriptions* (Ann Arbor: Michigan University Press), pp. 249–75.

——— (2003) "How can the Rule of Law Rule? Cost Imposition Through Decentralized Mechanisms," in José Maria Maravall and Adam Przeworski (eds.), *Democracy and the Rule of Law* (Cambridge: Cambridge University Press) pp. 168–87.

Smulovitz, Catalina and Enrique Peruzzotti (2003) "Societal and Horizontal Control: Two Cases of a Fruitful Relationship," in Scott Mainwaring and Christopher Welna (eds.), *Democratic Accountability in Latin America* (Oxford: Oxford University Press), pp. 309–32.

——— (2002) "Public Support and Spin: Judicial Policy Implementation in Mexico City and Mérida" (Paper presented at Washington University).

Staton, Jeffrey (2003) "Lobbying for Reform: The role of the Mexican Supreme Court in Institutional Selection" (USMEX 2003-03 Working Paper Series).

Tate, Neal and Torbjorn Vallinder (eds.) (1995) *The Global Expansion of Judicial Power* (New York: New York University Press).

UN Economic and Social Council (ECOSOC) (2002) "Civil and Political Rights, Including Question of: Independence of the Judiciary, Administration of Justice, Impunity" (Report of the Special Rapporteur on the Independence of Judges and Lawyers, by Dato' Param Cumaraswamy).

Vargas, Jorge A. "Mexico's Legal Revolution: An Appraisal of Its Recent Constitutional Changes, 1988–1994," *Georgia Journal of International and Comparative Law*, vol. 25, no. 3 (1996), pp. 497–559.

Waltman, Jerold L. and Kenneth M. Holland (eds.) (1988) *The Political Role of Law in Modern Democracies* (London: Macmillan Press).

Welna, Christopher (1997) *Explaining Non-Governmental Organizations: Human Rights NGOs and Institutions of Justice in Mexico* (Duke University).

Chapter 3

Changing Dynamics: The Political Impact of Costa Rica's Constitutional Court

Bruce M. Wilson

Introduction

Immediately after its creation in 1989, the new constitutional court (Sala Constitucional, or Sala IV) became a major actor in Costa Rican politics and one of the most influential and activist courts in Latin America. The constitutional amendment that created the court sparked a judicial revolution that shook the country's judicial system out of a 200-year slumber and has touched virtually every aspect of the country's social, economic, and political life. This chapter assesses this new constitutional chamber's impact on the political system and society at large during its first 14 years of existence. I argue that the consequences can be found on three levels that all have direct consequences for the policy-making process in particular and politics in general. First, the court limits the policy-making autonomy of the government by requiring all new and existing legislation to pass a strict test of constitutionality. Second, policy makers within the legislative assembly can and must anticipate the reaction of the court, and thus impose limits on legislation before it becomes law to pre-empt the court's intervention. This dynamic has granted minority parties considerably more power than they had prior to the introduction of the new court, thus shifting the relative power of political parties within the congress. Third, social groups or individuals that were marginalized from the political process and whose agendas were rarely addressed by the major parties—such as gays, people infected by the AIDS virus, indigenous people, or trade unions—have used the court as an effective alternative avenue to participate in the political process and safeguard their constitutional rights. Together, these factors amount to a redistribution of power within the state that is not always obvious, yet profound. In fact, power has been decentralized from the elected bodies of the government to the court and to groups that were historically weak and passive participants in the political process.

The next section briefly describes the creation and function of the Sala IV to provide the background against which the consequent ongoing changes in Costa Rican politics can be understood. I then develop the three main points about the way in which the creation of the new court has affected the policy-making process in Costa Rica. I conclude by looking at the broader implications of these processes for politics in Costa Rica and at some of the challenges to the court.

Awakening the Judicial Branch

The Court Prior to the Reform

As noted in the introduction to this book, many of the increasingly activist judiciaries in Latin America were products of a "constitutional moment," such as the writing of new constitutions or a transition to democracy. In the case of Costa Rica, though, there was no judicial response to the country's "constitutional moment": a short, bloody civil war and the promulgation of a new constitution in 1949. Yet, in the late 1980s, without a "constitutional moment" or a critical juncture of any sort, a new constitutional court was created, which rapidly became one of the most active in Latin America.

Multiple factors, largely domestic, motivated the creation of the constitutional court. The idea of a constitutional court had been discussed for many years, but it took a series of events to catapult the debate into the assembly in the 1980s. Several corruption scandals erupted in the early 1980s in which some supreme court magistrates were implicated. Simultaneously, Costa Rica entered its worst economic crisis since the Great Depression, a crisis that continued unabated during the Rodrigo Carazo Odio administration (Unidad, 1978–1982). There was a pervasive fear that the economic crisis would become a crisis of political legitimacy and ultimately result in a democratic regime collapse as happened in Uruguay in 1973. In August 1989, the legislative assembly passed Law 7.128, which created a constitutional chamber of the supreme court. Unlike many other countries in Latin America, this was not part of a constitutional moment. Indeed, in the case of Costa Rica, the only institutional change to take place at this time was the creation of the constitutional court. All other parts of the constitution remained unchanged.

The 1949 constitution requires the supreme court to check the powers of the popular branches. It contains more than 50 articles detailing individual and social rights and guarantees, as well as numerous other articles that outline both limits to and expectations from the state, such as the freedom of religion (Article 74), voting rights (Articles 93–98), and education rights (Articles 77–89). The Constitution also guaranteed significant financial and political autonomy to the judicial branch (Articles 152–167 and Article 177).[1] Yet, prior to the 1989 judicial reforms, the role of Costa Rica's supreme court, like those in other Latin American countries, was "minor, if not irrelevant" (Correa Sutil, 1999). As one prominent scholar of Costa Rican courts recently noted, "Previous to the creation of the Sala IV, the Constitution was on the top shelf of our [lawyers] bookcases, just like an old book. Now it must be in hand next to the Labour Code, Family Code, Civil Code, or Criminal Code."[2]

The supreme court ruled against the popular branches very rarely and only if their actions were clearly unconstitutional. A number of factors have been identified for the court's judicial inaction: poor legal training of magistrates, political socialization, and the civil law tradition in which supreme courts were expected to be deferential to the elected branches of government (Merryman, 1985; Wilson and Handberg, 1999, pp. 147–48). These factors were compounded by a series of institutional rules that hindered judicial activity, including a required super majority of two-thirds of the entire supreme court to declare a law or decree unconstitutional (Murillo, 1994, pp. 19–20). The original court was also very conscious of proper legal procedure, which encouraged it to reject many cases on technical rather than legal grounds. Thus, the court removed itself from having to address legal issues (Wilson and Handberg, 1999, p. 533). Political actors recognized this lack of legal opportunity structure and seldom attempted a legal strategy to block or overturn unfavorable government decisions. This is reflected in the low caseload of the pre-reform supreme court.

Operation of the Sala IV

In order to understand the behavior of the new constitutional chamber of the supreme court, it is necessary to examine some of the new rules under which the new court operated. The 1989 amendment to the constitution embedded the new court as a chamber of the existing supreme court rather than a separate, autonomous court. Supreme court membership was expanded from 17 to 22 magistrates, 5 in each of the 3 existing chambers and 7 on the new constitutional chamber.[3] The political autonomy of Sala IV magistrates is guaranteed through the requirement of a two-thirds vote of the legislative assembly for magistrates,[4] which requires candidates for the court to be acceptable to deputies of different political parties in the congress. Reelection of magistrates to subsequent terms is automatic, barring a two-thirds negative vote of the assembly (Article 158 of the Constitution).[5] Supreme court magistrates effectively enjoy life tenure.

As well as significant political autonomy, the new court enjoys much broader powers than the pre-reformed court. With a simple majority vote, the Sala IV can declare any and all laws unconstitutional.[6] These rulings cannot be appealed; they are binding on lower courts and set the precedent for all similar cases. Other branches of the supreme court, all lower courts, and other branches of the state can also request a constitutional clarification from the Sala IV.

The Sala IV also has the power of habeas corpus and a more general right of appeal, the *recurso de amparo* (Article 48 of the Constitution).[7] In effect, all actions, rules, decrees, orders or laws contrary to the constitution can be appealed directly before the Sala IV. Congress is required to seek a constitutional consult from the Sala IV while discussing any constitutional amendments. Furthermore, ten deputies together can request that any bill being discussed in congress be sent to the Sala IV for a consult. As discussed further, these broad powers and responsibilities granted to the new court have been used by political parties, interest groups, individuals and weak, marginalized groups to promote their agendas. The result has been to move the balance of power away from the popular branches of government toward the judiciary.

Changes in Caseload

The Sala IV's actions have had a more profound impact on the country's political, economic, and social life than its architects or critics anticipated. According to Maruja Chacón, a former Costa Rican minister of justice, most deputies in the legislative assembly did not understand the policy-making implications of their decision to create the new court. Instead, much of the debate in the assembly revolved around technical and legal details. Former PLN deputy Ottón Solís Fallas supports Chacón's view. Solís argues that deputies were preoccupied with a desire for Costa Rica to be considered an even more democratic country, an image that implied the necessity of a strong constitutional court.[8] Indeed, one of the major arguments against the creation of a constitutional court came from the sitting supreme court magistrates who argued that the caseload of the existing court was not sufficient to warrant the creation of a constitutional court. The judicial branch opposed the reform of Article 152 of the constitution principally on the grounds of a lack of need for such a court. In 1980, only one case of unconstitutionality and 11 *recursos de amparo* were filed with the supreme court secretariat (Rodríguez Cordero, 2002a, p. 43, footnote 67). The lack of recognition of the potential significance of the new court was reflected in the lack of newspaper coverage of the congressional debates.[9] Yet, since its inception, there have been very few political or social issues that have not been addressed by the court.[10] The rapid growth in the number of cases filed with the Sala IV demonstrates the growing importance of the institution. In 1990 (its first full year of operation), the court received almost 2,300 cases, and it currently receives more than 13,400 cases per year (2002).

Table 3.1 shows the average number of cases filed by type for the first and second five-year period of the court's operation and includes cases filed for 2002, the last year in which full data are available.[11] The number of habeas corpus cases jumped from the first to the second period, but now appears to have stabilized at approximately 1,300 cases per year. Unconstitutionality cases stabilized early and remain at about 300 per year. In the case of legislative and judicial consults, the second five-year period is considerably higher than the first. The drop in number is perhaps a reflection of the lack of legislative activity due to the election in 2002 rather than an abandonment of the legal strategy. This may be corroborated by the growing number of cases of *amparo* filed, which almost doubled in each period. These cases are generally filed by individuals and interest groups concerning issues that are not necessarily affected by the election cycle. The court has thus taken on a vast role and the caseload lends evidence to the claim that its function has become fundamental in Costa Rican politics. The next section assesses the impact of the Sala IV's role on politics in Costa Rica in more detail.

Table 3.1 Average number of cases presented to the Sala IV (by case type) 1990–1995, 1996–2001, and 2002

Case Type	1990–1995	1996–2001	2002
Habeas Corpus	829	1,330	1,355
Recurso de amparo	3,553	6,229	11,665
Unconstitutionality	358	355	289
Legislative Consults	27	41	37
Judicial Consults	68	186	83
Others	3	2	2
Total	*4,838*	*8,143*	*13,431*

Source: Based on a table created by J. C. Rodríguez, statistics from the Poder Judicial (Sección de Estadísticas del Departamento de Planificación) y *Noveno Informe sobre el Estado de la Nación en Desarrollo Humano Sostenible* (Proyecto Estado de la Nación en Desarrollo Humano Sostenible-CONARE).

Re-equilibrating Political Power across Institutions and Society

The new court's willingness to challenge existing laws and constitutional amendments served notice to the popular branches that the court no longer recognized their presumed policy-making sovereignty. Historically, deputies believed their "power to legislate was absolute" (Urcuyo Fournier, 1995, p. 44), but the Sala IV has severely curtailed that sovereignty through mandatory constitutional consultations. In effect, the elected branches, and especially the dominant actors within these branches, witnessed a decrease in their power and policy-making autonomy. In turn, the power of formerly less central actors was expanded. These power shifts can be observed at three levels. First, and maybe most obviously, some of the power was moved from the legislature to the judicial branch. What might be less obvious here, though, is the extent to which the legislature's policy-making autonomy has been constrained. The court has shown its clear willingness to hear and rule on all issues of constitutionality, many of which have shifted political power among state institutions. The second level of power shifts concerns the dominance of political parties within the legislature itself, affecting the dynamics of the legislative process. While traditionally, the largest parties clearly dominated the policy-making process, the new role of the court has allowed minor parties to take on a more active and pivotal role in policy making. The third broad area of impact is the protection and promotion of constitutionally mandated civil rights and liberties. Although these rights and liberties have been constitutionally protected since the promulgation of the current 1949 Constitution, the supreme court's inactivity meant they were little more than rights on paper. The new court's openness has allowed weak, marginalized, and poorly organized groups, largely ignored or excluded from policy-making avenues, to seek legal redress from the Sala IV. This has, in turn, diminished the role of the legislative assembly and empowered new political actors. I discuss these three points in turn.

Reigning in Legislative Power

The historical presumption of constitutionality of laws written by the legislative assembly existed only until the creation of the Sala IV (Gutiérrez Gutiérrez, 1993, pp. 200–03). The new court quickly dispelled this belief with a series of rulings that sent a clear signal to the legislative assembly and other branches of government that all laws and decrees would have to pass a constitutionality test. The role of the court in limiting the policy-making autonomy of the legislature is powerfully illustrated by two examples of Sala IV rulings that challenge the popular branch's political supremacy: presidential reelection and privatization of state-owned industries.

Presidential Reelection

Costa Rica's constitution provides for one of the weakest executives in Latin America (Mainwaring and Shugart, 1997, p. 432; Wilson, 1998, pp. 51–54). This deliberate diminution of presidential power was motivated, in part, by a desire to prevent a return to the pre-civil war era's *caudillo* politics. The 1949 Constitution devolves policymaking power across numerous state agencies with the legislative assembly being the more powerful body. All issues and laws involving elections were historically handled by the Supreme Elections Tribunal (Tribunal Supremo de Elecciones, TSE); the supreme court is the highest court in the country and there are various autonomous institutions, which are given constitutionally mandated tasks such as the provision of electricity, telephones, insurance, and so forth.

In 1969, a constitutional amendment to Article 132 (Law 4.339) prohibited presidential reelection, which further weakened the presidency; upon their inauguration, presidents are lame ducks with little influence over deputies' voting behavior. Politicians seeking to extend their political careers beyond a single four-year term in the assembly necessarily have to form alliances with the party's next presidential candidate, not the sitting president. Presidential power was very limited and became more so with the prohibition on reelection (Carey, 1996; Taylor, 1992; Wilson, 1998).

This prohibition on presidential reelection was accepted as legitimate and remained unchallenged until the late 1990s, when former president Oscar Arias Sánchez (PLN, 1986–1990) encouraged ten PLN deputies to introduce a bill to congress to repeal the amendment. Arias argued that the correct path to remove the reelection prohibition was through a "constitutional amendment in the legislative assembly." He stated that to request the Sala IV to declare the prohibition unconstitutional would be "an undemocratic action."[12]

In spite of public opinion polls that showed overwhelming support for presidential reelection in the abstract, and of Oscar Arias specifically,[13] the bill made little headway in the assembly. In response to the legislative delay, Arias reversed his position and filed a case of unconstitutionality with the Sala IV even before congress had voted on the issue. In a five to four split decision, the court rejected the case (Expediente no. 7428–7990). A week after the Sala IV's decision, the legislative assembly debated the presidential reelection issue and voted overwhelmingly (32 votes to 13) not to discuss it further and sent it to the archive, which effectively killed any possible legislative resolution that would have allowed an Arias candidacy in the 2002 presidential election.

In early 2003, a second case of unconstitutionality was filed by two lawyers who argued that the prohibition on reelection was discriminatory and questioned the right of the legislative assembly to pass such a constitutional amendment. The legal argument was different from the 2000 case, but more significantly, in the intervening three years the composition of the court had changed. The Sala IV's presidency had moved from Luis Paulino Mora Mora (who voted against reelection) to Luis Fernando Solano Carrera (who voted in favor). More importantly, two magistrates who voted against lifting the ban on reelection had retired from the court and were replaced by magistrates who favored presidential reelection. On April 4, 2003, in a five to seven split decision, the Sala IV annulled the prohibition on presidential reelection. The court majority argued that the prohibition limited the constitutional right of individuals to seek election and of voters to vote for candidates of their choosing.[14]

This ruling has two related momentous impacts on the political life of the country. First, the ruling is likely to re-equilibrate the balance of power between the legislative assembly and the executive. The historical dominance of the assembly might easily be eclipsed once former presidents are able to seek reelection; even after eight years on the sidelines, former presidents will regain an influence over sitting deputies that has not existed since the 1969 constitutional amendment. Currently, deputies are not closely tied to the sitting president from their party, but generally take their voting directions from the various party pre-candidates seeking the presidential nomination. With presidential reelection now a possibility, the political calculations of sitting deputies will necessarily change, which in turn may influence their voting behavior in Congress.

On another more immediate level, the Sala IV's ruling dealt a severe blow to the assembly's policy-making sovereignty. The assembly had, with overwhelming majorities, twice rejected the reintroduction of presidential reelection in 2000. On the most obvious level, the court's ruling was a public statement limiting the legislative assembly's presumed powers. However, an even more profound attack on the assembly was contained in the court's explanation for rejecting the amendment that prohibited presidential reelection. The Sala IV ruled constitutional amendment 132 (the prohibition on presidential reelection) unconstitutional because it impinged on citizens' fundamental rights to be elected and to elect people. The court declared the assembly had and has no power to amend the constitution to restrict citizens' fundamental rights (as defined by the court). The congress, it was noted, "cannot reduce, amputate, or limit rights and fundamental guarantees, or political rights of the citizens, or the essential aspects of the country's political organisation."[15] According to the court, deputies exceeded their powers by passing the 1969 constitutional amendment in the first place and were now explicitly informed of their limited capacity to amend the Constitution in the future.[16]

Economic Policy-Making

The second illustrative case addresses the government's autonomy in regulating the economy. The 1980s and the 1990s marked a transitional period in Costa Rica's economic development model. The 1980s economic crisis also marked the final stage of the gradual increase in the role of the state in the economy. In the post–civil war period, successive governments pursued an expanded role for the state in the provision of social and economic goods. By the 1980s, the state was one of the largest employers in the country and had become a major competitor for private companies whose growth it had previously fostered. It has been argued that this expansion of the role of the state encouraged lawmakers to disrespect "the Constitution and fundamental rights" and to pass routinely "unjust discriminatory laws" (Murillo, 1994, pp. 34–37). During the last two decades, then, the long push to increase the role of the state in the economy and in the provision of social services was being modified and, in places, replaced by an increasing role for the market in determining economic policy. While there were clear political forces limiting this transition (Wilson, 1994), the assembly and the executive were controlled by the same party, PLN, and were able to pass some laws that decreased the role of the state in the economy. One goal during these two PLN administrations was to increase private sector involvement in industries traditionally controlled by the state, for example, banking and telecommunications. Early in the post-war period, the government had nationalized the production and supply of most of the country's utilities and many other services.

In the case of electricity and telephones, a state corporation, Instituto Costarricense de Electricidad (Costa Rican Electricity Institute, ICE), was granted a monopoly on the supply of both telephones and electricity.[17] In 1987, the Arias administration passed a law to allow a U.S. company, Millicom, to provide a cellular telephone service in Costa Rica. The contract with Millicom produced little legislative resistance and, once passed into law, was not challenged in the courts.

The ICE labor unions, however, were against the contract and believed that the opening of the telecommunications market to private companies, even if it was just cellular phones, was the start of a more extensive privatization program, which would probably result in job losses for their members. Over the next six years, Millicom invested millions of dollars in the provision of cellular telephone service while the administrations of Arias (PLN, 1986–1990) and Rafael Angel Calderon (PUSC, 1990–1994) weathered protests and political pressure to rescind the contract.

In October 1993, the ICE unions switched their strategy and supplemented their lobbying activities by filing a case of unconstitutionality with the Sala IV. The court agreed to hear the case and accepted the unions' argument. The Sala IV ruled that cellular phone service was a form of telephone service and thus a constitutionally protected state monopoly. As a result of this ruling, subsequent governments could not sign contracts to grant private companies access to the telephone market (*La Nación*, May 15–30, 1995; Wilson, 1998). The unions' success, at the expense of the legislative assembly, demonstrated the importance of the new court in the policy-making process, and underscored a new reality that the Sala IV no longer presumed all acts of congress to be constitutional. Similar rulings that constrained the autonomy of governments to regulate the economy occurred in areas of price fixing for utilities—especially gas,—the national budget— especially concerning monies constitutionally allocated to ensure the autonomy of the judiciary—and the requirement to abide by international conventions to which Costa Rica was a signatory. This last requirement was used to prevent the administration of Abel Pacheco (PUSC, 2002–) from reducing educational expenditures by cutting the number of days in the school year.[18]

The Effect of the Sala IV on Party Dynamics in the Legislature

The Sala IV was granted a central role in adjudicating laws passed and/or under consideration by the legislative assembly. Since 1989, all constitutional reform bills must be sent to the Sala IV for its recommendation through a mandatory consult (*consulta preceptiva*).[19] If the Sala IV makes procedural corrections, those become legally binding on the legislative assembly and must be resolved before the reform can become law. Deputies, then, must pay close attention to the Sala IV's recommendations.[20] It has been argued that "the *consultas previa* of legislative bills has demolished parliamentary sovereignty in legislative material" (Jiménez Zeledón and Rojas Saborío, 1995, p. 110).

This function of the Sala IV is enhanced by another provision that allows deputies to send any bill to the court for a constitutional consult. With just ten deputies' signatures, any parliamentary project can be sent to the Sala IV for a consult. This can and has become a favorite tool for smaller parties in the legislature hoping that the court will veto the measure, or at the very least require changes to the bill that might delay its implementation.

The extent to which this tactic has been used is reflected in the parliamentary behavior of deputy Otto Guevara Guth of the minor third party Movimiento Libertario during the 1998–2002 legislative period. Deputy Guevara Guth collected nine other deputies' signatures (frequently from other parties) to send 21 bills to the Sala IV for constitutional consults. A study by Echeverría Martín (2000, p. 216) of deputy Guevara Guth's constitutional consults finds that the Sala IV discovered constitutional defects in 43 percent of those bills, which required additional effort and time in the assembly to rectify the bills' problems. This legal avenue to affect the content of government legislation was not possible before the creation of the court.

After the February 2002 general election, three political parties had more than the required ten deputies to send bills to the Sala IV (Wilson, 2003). It is expected that there will be an increase in the use (or abuse) of this type of legal action as a form of political control (Echeverría Martín, 2000).

The Sala IV thus profoundly affects the legislative process itself and severely limits the policy-making autonomy of the government in three main ways: (1) by deputies anticipating a potential court ruling and thus modifying bills before they are sent to the court, effectively preempting legal ruling; (2) through constitutional consult, primarily initiated by deputies from minority parties; (3) through mandatory consults for any modifications to the constitution and international treaties. Parallel to curtailing the power of the ruling party and president, minority parties have, in turn, experienced an increase in their power to affect legislation, a process that has on one level implicitly empowered the legislature as an institution. This may sound paradoxical since I argued earlier that the legislature lost power to the judicial branch. At the same time, however, the function of the legislature has increased as it can no longer be considered a rubber-stamp body where majority parties automatically and unilaterally make policy decisions. Furthermore, by increasing the influence of minor parties on pending legislation, third parties have witnessed an exponential increase in their power, which may well be linked to concomitant changes in the party system in the late 1990s where third parties have experienced unprecedented electoral success. As Seitzer (1999, p. 45) observes, this behavior can make "the threat of a court challenge an effective legislative tactic, for parliamentary minorities can gain concessions from majorities concerned to avoid a possible adverse court judgment."

Redistribution of Power within Society

As discussed earlier, the 1949 Constitution grants numerous social and economic rights, more so than many other constitutions in the region, but in the first forty years of its existence, many of these resembled paper rights rather than real ones. Indeed, during this period infringements of constitutional rights were rarely challenged and the constitution was reduced "to a second place, turning it into an inapplicable programmatic text [that gave] secondary laws (codes and statutes) an excessively privileged position."[21] However, since the creation of the Sala IV, individuals and groups who were previously marginalized from political processes and who exercised little influence over the policy-making process have found that the Sala IV can afford new opportunities to safeguard their constitutionally guaranteed rights. This has to do with the rules that guide the functioning of the Sala IV. For one, access is broad and inexpensive as there are no minimal requirements as to who can file or which procedures have to be followed: cases can be brought before the court by any individual, without legal counsel, and without filing any formal paperwork.[22] Individuals can file a claim with the court at any time of the day or night, any day of the year. The claim can be written on anything, by anyone, including minors and noncitizens, without filing fees or the need for legal council. These new procedural rules have broadened access to the court to individuals and groups with few resources. Second, due to the low costs associated with filing a case with the court, it becomes strategically possible for individuals and groups to lose a case and then refile a similar case shortly afterward. As the following examples show, this has not just resulted in the court's limiting the policy autonomy of the legislature, but has also effectively redistributed some power in society from traditionally privileged actors to those previously politically marginalized.

Marginalized Groups

The traditional (pre-Sala IV) policy-making process in Costa Rica generally excluded marginalized groups. The two major parties, PLN and PUSC, dominated the executive branch and consistently captured more than 90 percent of congressional seats. Interest groups have generally taken advantage of the dispersal of political power and used various tactics to influence policy discussions and decisions.[23] However, poorly organized, socially marginalized groups were generally not courted by the two major political parties and were unable to summon the necessary resources to lobby the government and its agencies. Finally, the pre-reformed Supreme court's strict procedures, expensive filing fees, and slow pace of resolving cases meant few cases were ever successfully filed with the court. It was difficult even for established, well-funded interest groups to use the court and virtually impossible for marginalized groups and individuals.[24]

A recent study documents the use of the Sala IV by marginalized groups. Among some of the most prominent cases where specific groups of people have been able to use the court to their advantage are homosexuals, people living with the AIDS virus, and trade unions. These groups have widely different agendas, but they had all previously been unsuccessful in convincing legislators to support their agenda. When they resorted to use the new court, however, they were considerably more successful in protecting their rights.[25] People living with AIDS, for instance, had engaged in previous attempts to get the state health agencies (1992) to fund the costs for drugs to minimize the impact of the virus on their health, but lost the case (Resolution no. 280–292). The state had refused to pay for the drugs arguing that they were prohibitively expensive at approximately US$800 per person per year (Soriano, 1997). The case was probably harmed by the social stigma attached to people testing positive for HIV (Stern, 1998). In 1997, a second case concerning AIDS medications was filed, but this time the Sala IV sided with the AIDS patients and against the government. The Sala IV argued: "What good are the rest of the rights and guarantees . . . the advantages and benefits of our system of liberties, if a person cannot count on the right to life and health assured?" (Resolution no. 5934–5997). The right to state-funded medical care, the court argued, was a constitutional right. As a result, state coverage for drugs for people living with AIDS is now generally and readily available (Wilson and Rodríguez Cordero, 2006).

Homosexuals, another poorly organized and socially marginalized group, had a somewhat different agenda and generally sought protection from police violence, an end to discrimination, and the enforcement of their civil rights. Their court victories are perhaps less spectacular; yet police brutality against gays has substantially been reduced and gay organizations now receive the same legal recognition and protections as heterosexual groups. Again, gays had previously occupied a marginalized position in Costa Rican politics. Social stigma had made it difficult to find political allies to champion their cause and had also made it difficult to organize since many individuals feared the potential economic and social repercussions that could result from openly championing gay rights. The Sala IV effectively lifted these requirements for collective action, as neither political nor economic resources are required to seek the protection of rights through the court (Wilson and Rodríguez Cordero, 2006).

Trade unions, for their part, had previously been unsuccessful in their attempt to guard the constitutional right to strike. This right had been severely limited by the parallel existence of a Labour Code that restricted the right of public workers to strike and defined them in such a way that a large percentage of Costa Rican workers fell under this rubric. Political parties had shown little interest in supporting the union agenda of modifying the Labour Code. When the unions filed with the Sala IV, though, the court decided that the Labour Code was in parts unconstitutional and restored the right to strike for a large share of Costa Rican workers (Resolution no. 1317–1398). Beyond having obvious implications for economic policies with strikes now being a real threat in previously exempted sectors, the ruling also real-located political power between different social groups and gave new powers to unions and workers.

While it is possible for groups to join together or to form alliances with political parties to challenge government policies in the courts, or to have their rights upheld, it is not necessary. Indeed, there is lit-tle evidence to suggest a concerted effort by interest groups to link with politicians in pursuing a judicial strategy. The open access and low cost of taking cases to the Sala IV removes any need to muster large numbers of people or resources. The case of marginalized groups, such as AIDS patients, is most striking. This was a very small group with no political allies and considerable social animosity toward them that challenged government decisions concerning the funding of anti-retroviral medications. In spite of all these drawbacks and weak-nesses, the group was able to successfully reverse government policy and force the state to expend considerable sums to fund the medications. These cases of weak, socially and politically marginalized groups and individuals successfully pursuing a judicial strategy illustrates a significant strengthening of civil society, allowing independent actions by diverse social groups and individuals.

Conclusions: The Impact of the Sala IV on Politics and Popular Reactions

What might have appeared as the creation of another passive oversight agency when the Sala IV was created in 1989 has resulted in a major overhaul of Costa Rican politics with far-reaching implications for the legislative process, the distribution of power between state institutions and social groups. The function of the elected bodies has been reduced, although it could be argued that the newly found importance of third parties in the legislative assembly has actually added to the weight of this body in the policy-making process. Similarly, the autonomy of the government has suffered, as the Sala IV is unwilling to accept the supremacy of the legislature. At the same time, groups and individuals that had previously been marginalized in Costa Rican politics have found a new avenue to safeguard their rights. Unsurprisingly, these processes, which have effectively decentralized governmental power, have been linked to questions concerning the quality of democracy and have not been universally embraced.

For instance, the expansion of powers assumed by the Sala IV has not gone without comment. Since its inception, many deputies have complained about their own loss of powers. In a very unusual move, the Attorney General Román Solís discussed in the national press his frustration and fear that Sala IV effectively leaves the executive and legislative assembly with little power.[26] He also filed a brief in the presidential reelection case, arguing that the Sala IV had no constitutional right to hear the case (*La Nación*, September 1, 2000).

More recently, criticisms of the court have grown louder. With the court's annulment of constitutional amendment 132, which prohibited presidential reelection, the Sala IV also explicitly limited the powers of the legislative assembly to modify the constitution. This ruling produced a vitriolic backlash from deputies in both major parties in the congress. Ex-deputy Alberto Cañas, for example, classified the Sala IV's reelection ruling as a "*golpe de estado*," or coup d'état. Another PLN militant claimed the court's ruling was a "judicial barbarity." Jorge Eduardo Sánchez, the secretary general of the PUSC, claimed that the Sala IV had usurped powers and had become a "co-administrator and co-legislator."[27]

These debates clearly indicate that the effects of the new court on Costa Rica's democracy are contentious, at least at the level of political elites. Yet, the court's caseload also seems to indicate that its role has been popularly accepted as a guarantor of constitutional rights and that a considerable number of people have welcomed the opportunity to enforce rights outside the structures of elected politics. The court has produced new winners and new losers, which has added a new dynamic to Costa Rican politics. The effects on the quality of democracy are yet to be seen. It seems that on the one hand, elective bodies have lost power. Yet, this is not necessarily a negative thing for democracy since the new constraints on the actions of popularly elected representatives link policies more clearly to fundamental rights and provisions contained in the constitution, which is the basic document of the country's democratic order. On the other hand, it could be argued that Costa Rica's democracy has become more inclusive of minor parties as well as marginalized individuals and groups that were previously discriminated against and demand that the state respect their constitutionally mandated rights. While these developments can easily be interpreted as adding to the quality of Costa Rica's democracy, the consequences for policy stability and democratic governance are less clear.

Notes

1. Since 1957, Article 177 of the constitution guarantees the judicial branch at least 6% of the state's ordinary budget (all citations are from the 1949 Constitution, 2001 edition).
2. Personal correspondence with Costa Rican constitutional scholar and lawyer, Juan Carlos Rodríguez Cordero, July 6, 2004.
3. There are also approximately 40 supplemental magistrates (12 assigned to the Sala IV) who can hear cases and make rulings in place of any magistrate who is unable to attend (Ley de la Jurisdicción 1989; Armando Mayorga, "Inminente fracaso de la Sala Cuarta," *La Nación*, May 23, 1989 and Armando Mayorga, "Asamblea aprobó Sala Cuarta," *La Nación*, June 13, 1989. (*La Nación*: http://www.nacion.com).
4. Until 2003, a simple majority was used to select the rest of the supreme court. The current law is that all magistrates are selected by the legislative assembly by a two-thirds majority vote of the deputies.
5. This has never happened to date.
6. Previously, this required a two-thirds vote of the plenary court.
7. *Amparo*, which is contained in Article 48 of the constitution, guarantees everyone, without limitation, the right to appeal to the Sala IV to maintain or reestablish all other rights guaranteed in the constitution (individual and social guarantees, sections IV and V) and not already included under the habeas corpus provision.
8. Interviews by the author, San José, Costa Rica, August 1997.
9. During the congressional debate over constitutional reforms to create the Sala IV, newspapers gave it scant attention. A content analysis of the country's leading daily newspaper, *La Nación*, between February and November 1989, revealed very little coverage until the congressional debate over the selection of magistrates for the new court.
10. Gudmundson (1996, pp. 84–85) argues that "virtually every major economic interest group faced with the loss of its former protection or subsidy . . . has appealed to the Sala IV."
11. Data from 2002 are atypical for some case types as it was an election year. The elections take place in February and then the new administration is not inaugurated until May of that year. Thus, the level of congressional activity is generally lower than in nonelection years.

12. Alejandro Urbina, "Reelección contra el impasse," *La Nación*, December 6, 1999.

13. Various percentages were noted for popular support of the constitutional amendment to allow presidential reelection, ranging from 60% (Alejandro Urbina "Reelección contra el impasse," *La Nación*, December 6, 1999) to 88% (Berlioth Herrera y Hazel Feigenblat, "Arias: 88% dijo sí a reelección," *La Nación*, March 13, 2000).

14. *Expediente* N° 02–005494–007–CO; Resolution N° 2003–02771.

15. Mauricio Herrera U., "Congreso no puede cercenar derechos," *La Nación*, July 17, 2003.

16. *La Nación*, April 5, 2003.

17. The monopoly included the production and supply of electricity, although it was possible for private companies to produce a small part of the country's electricity if they sold it to ICE.

18. In this case the Sala IV ruled that a previous government had signed the Convenio Centroamericano sobre la unificación Básica de la Educación, which promised a 200-day minimum school year (Wilson, Rodríguez Cordero and Handberg, 2004).

19. However, other political actors, such as the *Defensoría de los Habitantes, the Tribunal Supremo de Elecciones and the Contraloría General de la República* can consult aspects of certain legislative bills (Article 96, *Ley de la Jurisdicción Constitucional*).

20. A recent criticism of the Sala IV's tendency to give opinions concerning issues of substance in these bills considers this practice to be imposing conditions on the constitutional power (Arias Ramírez, 2000, p. 209).

21. Calzada, 2001.

22. Cases of unconstitutionality do have some minimum legal requirements including the need for legal council.

23. The historical role of interest groups is discussed in Arias, 1987; interest group behavior from the civil war through the 1990s is discussed in Wilson, 1998, pp. 66–74.

24. A recent examination of cases filed by marginalized groups revealed that from the end of the 1948 civil war to the creation of the Sala IV there were only a handful of cases filed with the supreme court to address minority interests (Wilson and Rodríguez Cordero, 2006).

25. This is not to suggest that they were always successful in pursuing their claims, but that they were often able to employ a legal opportunity to pursue their respective agendas.

26. William Méndez Garita, "Procuradores Solis y Beirute Sala IV decide aquí," *La Nación*, November 13, 2000.

27. Dóriam Díaz, "Lluvia de críticas a la Sala IV," *La Nación*, April 6, 2003.

References

Arias Ramírez, Bernal, "Incompetencia de la Sala Constitucional para enjuiciar por el fondo proyectos de ley de reforma constitucional," *Revista Parlamentaria*, vol. 8, no. 3 (2000), pp. 173–211.

Arias Sánchez, Oscar (1987) *Grupos de presión en Costa Rica* (San José: Editorial Costa Rica).

Calzada, Ana Virginia (2001) "Prologue" in *Constitución Política de la República de Costa Rica* [1949] (San José, Costa Rica: Editorial Juricentro).

Carey, John M. (1996) *Term Limits and Legislative Representation* (Cambridge: Cambridge University Press).

Correa Sutil, Jorge (1999) "Judicial Reform in Latin America: Good News for the Underprivileged?" in Juan E. Méndez, Guillermo O'Donnell, and Paulo Sérgio Pinheiro (eds.), *The (Un)Rule of Law and the Underprivileged in Latin America* (Notre Dame: University of Notre Dame Press), pp. 255–77.

Echeverría Martín, Gloriana, "La consulta facultativa de constitucionalidad como instrumento de control politico," *Revista Parlamentaria*, vol. 8, no. 3 (2000), pp. 213–23.

Gudmundson, Lowell (1996) "Costa Rica: New Issues and Alignments," in Jorge I. Domínguez and Abraham F. Lowenthal (eds.), *Constructing Democratic Governance: Latin America and the Caribbean in the 1990s* (Baltimore: The Johns Hopkins University Press).

Gutiérrez Gutiérrez, Carlos José (1993) "Evolución de la justicia constitucional en Costa Rica," in *La Jurisdicción Constitucional: III Aniversario de la creación de la Sala Constitucional*, vol. 1 (San José, Costa Rica: Editorial Juricentro).

Jiménez Zeledón, Mariano and Ingrid Rojas Saborío, "El poder de la Sala Constitucional de Costa Rica," *Revista Parlamentaria*, vol. 3, no. 3 (1995), pp. 93–116.

Mainwaring, Scott and Matthew Soberg Shugart (eds.) (1997) *Presidentialism and Democracy in Latin America* (New York: Cambridge University Press).

Merryman, John Henry (1985) *The Civil Law Tradition: An Introduction to the Legal Systems of Western Europe and Latin America* (2nd Ed.) (Stanford, CA: Stanford University Press).

Murillo Víquez, Jaime (1994) *La Sala Constitucional: Una revolución político–jurídica en Costa Rica* (San José, Costa Rica: Editorial Guayacán).

Rodríguez Cordero, Juan Carlos (2002a) *Entre curules & estrados: La consulta preceptiva de las reformas constitucionales en Costa Rica* (San José, Costa Rica: Investigaciones Jurídicas).

Rodríguez Cordero, Juan Carlos (2002b) "(Re)equilibrios políticos en Costa Rica: El poder constituyente y el control de constitucionalidad," *South Eastern Latin Americanist*, vol. 45, nos. 3–4 (2002), pp. 15–28.

Seitzer, Jeffrey (1999) "Experimental Constitutionalism: A Comparative Analysis of the Institutional Bases of Rights Enforcement in Post-Communist Hungary," in Kenney, et al. (eds.), *Constitutional Dialogues in Comparative Perspective* (London: St. Martin's Press).

Soriano, George, "AIDS Victim Wins Right to Drugs," *Tico Times*, vol. 3, no. 38 (1997), p. 38.

Stern, Richard (1998) "Lobbying Vital for AIDS Treatment—The Lesson from Central America," from *Panos*, http://www.oneworld.org/panos/news/34sept98.htm

Taylor, Michelle M., "Formal Versus Informal Incentive Structures and Legislative Behavior: Evidence from Costa Rica," *Journal of Politics*, vol. 54, no. 4 (1992), pp. 1055–73.

Urcuyo Fournier, Constantino, "La Sala Constitucional: Necesarios límites al poder," *Revista Parlamentaria*, vol. 3, no. 3 (1995), pp. 37–48.

Wilson, Bruce M., "When Social Democrats Choose Neoliberal Economic Policies: The Case of Costa Rica," *Comparative Politics*, vol. 26, no. 2 (1994), pp. 149–68.

Wilson, Bruce M. (1998) *Costa Rica: Politics, Economics, and Democracy* (Boulder, Colorado: Lynne Rienner).

Wilson, Bruce M., "The Elections in Costa Rica, February and April 2002," *Electoral Studies*, vol. 22, no. 3 (2003), pp. 509–16.

Wilson, Bruce M. and Roger Handberg, "From Judicial Passivity to Judicial Activism: Explaining the Change within Costa Rica's Supreme Court," *NAFTA: Law and Business Review of the Americas*, vol. 5, no. 4 (1999), pp. 522–43.

Wilson, Bruce M. and Juan Carlos Rodríguez Cordero, "Legal Opportunity Structures and Social Movements: The Effects of Institutional Change on Costa Rican Politics," *Comparative Political Studies*, vol. 39, no. 3 (2006).

Wilson, Bruce M., Juan Carlos Rodríguez Cordero, and Roger Handberg, "The Best Laid Schemes . . . Gang aft a-gley: Judicial Reform in Latin America—Evidence from Costa Rica," *Journal of Latin American Studies*, vol. 36, no. 3 (2004), pp. 507–31.

Chapter 4

The Judicialization of Politics in Colombia: The Old and the New

Manuel José Cepeda Espinosa

The scope and intensity of judicialization of politics described in this chapter may sound surprising and even incredible for those unfamiliar with Colombia. In a country associated with political violence and the drug trade, a strong tradition of judicial review may appear strange. It is as if there were two countries: one where force reigns, another based on the rule of law. In this chapter, I do not attempt to describe nor explain this paradox. I shall only recall a few basic facts. Colombia has approximately 44 million inhabitants, while guerrilla and paramilitary organizations gather 50,000 armed individuals at the most. These organizations operate mainly in the rural areas of a very large country where 75 percent of the population is urban. The impact of the guerrilla organizations on the country's institutional processes was dramatically and tragically made evident in 1985 with the violent seizure of the Palace of Justice in Bogotá, which resulted in the destruction of the premises and the death of half of the sitting magistrates of the supreme court. However, this did not prevent the supreme court from reassuming its functions two months later, nor did it prevent the strengthening of the administration of justice in general, and of constitutional justice in particular by the creation of a constitutional court, with the adoption of the 1991 constitution. Although several presidential candidates have become victims of violence, Colombia has held regular elections for congress and territorial authorities for over a century, as well as for the direct election of the president of the republic since 1910. Even during the two brief dictatorships of the twentieth century (1900–1904 and 1953–1957), judicial review continued to operate, and moreover, during these periods some decisions were adopted which invalidated particular laws and decrees.

Constitutional judicial review and the judicialization of politics have been constant features of the Colombian political system. Active judicial review of legislation has operated continuously, with more or less intensity, since the middle of the nineteenth century—more specifically since the enactment of the 1863 federal constitution, which empowered the Supreme Court of Justice to temporarily suspend the application of laws approved by the federated states and accused of unconstitutionality by citizens, deferring the final decision on the matter to the senate. Later in the century, as the custodian of the 1886 constitution, the supreme court was empowered to strike down bills adopted by congress whenever they were unsuccessfully vetoed by the president of the republic for reasons of unconstitutionality. The supreme court first invalidated a bill on July 6, 1887;[1] since then, only three years have passed in which no legal provision at all has been invalidated.[2]

The judicialization of politics is a twofold process by which, first, legal arguments are raised in the course of the political process, as a consequence of relevant judicial decisions—in other words, the language of the law is absorbed by the political discourse, thereby affecting the normal course of political processes, especially legislative ones. Second, constitutional judges end up substantially contributing to the orientation of public policy. On the grounds of this double definition, three factors are evident:

(a) In Colombia, the judicialization of politics has been constant since the early twentieth century.
(b) The judicialization of politics in Colombia responds to the coexistence of a violent conflict. On the one hand, constitutional amendments play the part of peace agreements between warring enemies; on the other, the judicialization of politics is linked to flaws in the political system, which does not respond adequately to ordinary social conflicts.
(c) Since 1991, the process of judicialization of politics has been substantially enhanced so as to cover most of the areas of everyday Colombian life, turning the constitutional court into a critical actor within the democratic process, with an unprecedented and permanent presence and impact in the political system.

The Judicialization of Politics is an Old Phenomenon in Colombia

Colombian politics has *always* been subject to *some* degree of judicialization, at least since the beginning of the twentieth century.

Between the 1886 and the 1991 constitutions, key stages in the historical development of the Colombian political system have been marked by constitutional amendments (1910, 1936, 1957, and 1968) that play the part of peace agreements between conflicting political groups, usually as a means to put an end to violent conflicts. Central components of these amendments have focused on the adaptation of the system of constitutional judicial review, so as to adjust it to the requirements of each historical period. Once put into practice, this system of judicial review in turn affected different aspects of the political system.

At the initiative of a Constituent Assembly comprised of members of the traditional Liberal and Conservative parties, the 1910 constitutional reform broadened the system of judicial review introduced by the 1886 constitution. Most significantly, it did this, first, by introducing a public unconstitutionality *actio popularis*, which could be brought by any citizen before the supreme court of justice in order to strike down national laws that violated the constitution. Second, the reform secured a balance of powers by which supreme court justices were elected by congress from among lists of candidates submitted by the president. Both of these reforms were introduced, among several others, as a reaction to the authoritarian five-year presidency of Rafael Reyes. They represented a means to safeguard the rights of the opposition within a clearly presidentialist regime, and to reinstate democratic means of participation, as well as an equilibrium between the branches of government. Important social and political guarantees, such as freedom of religion, trade union rights, and agrarian reform provisions were subsequently incorporated into the text of the constitution in 1936. This responded to the most salient social concerns and the growing political pressures of the time in Colombia, marked by a change in patterns of land use and occupation and the emergence of a vocal working class. The supreme court was entrusted with the power of interpreting these open clauses and adopted a number of controversial decisions in these fields.

In 1957 a new system for designating supreme court judges was introduced. Since the end of the 1940s, the country had been ravaged by systematic violence between the liberal and conservative parties. After a brief period of military dictatorship, an agreement between the leaders of the two political parties (the so-called National Front) was enshrined in the constitution. According to the terms of this, beginning in 1958 and for a period of 16 years, the presidential office was to be occupied successively by members of the Liberal and the Conservative parties, so as to secure political alternation between them. All posts in ministries, municipal councils, and departmental assemblies were to be evenly distributed between the political parties, and—most importantly—the same was to happen with the members of the supreme court of justice, who were now to be elected from Conservative and Liberal benches by the magistrates themselves. This was the so-called system of "*co-option*" (*co-optación*) and political parity, introduced with the aim of sealing the judicial branch off from political confrontations. In 1968, the supreme court was constitutionally mandated to carry out ex officio review of legislative decrees issued by the president of the republic during so-called "states of siege" or "states of economic emergency." This reform was introduced to set limits to presidentialism in a context of incorporation of dissident political forces that challenged the exclusive parity arrangements of the National Front and government by state of siege decrees as contrary to pluralism and the rule of law.

These historical examples indicate that, in Colombia, different stages in the evolution of the political system have been accompanied by constitutional reforms, which in turn have reformed the prevailing system of constitutional judicial review. These revisions have usually created new ways to access the court and expanded its judicial review powers so as to protect the basic political agreements enshrined in each constitutional reform, aimed at building democratic institutions and peace. A very close historical and structural link therefore exists between politics, peace, and constitutional judicial review. Since its inception, constitutional judicial review has been designed to serve, inter alia, purposes of a political nature. This does not mean that the independence of the individual judges or courts who carry out judicial review has been curtailed, but rather that the system *as a whole* serves a given function within the country's political system. In the context of the violent political conflicts that have shaken Colombia since the nineteenth century, constitutional reforms, devised as means to attain peace, have paid considerable attention to constitutional judicial review as a tool to ensure respect for the basic agreements reflected in the constitutional text. They have also introduced new constitutional provisions and enforcement mechanisms that, once put into practice, have influenced the functioning of political processes and institutions, thus establishing a close relationship between sociopolitical realities and judicial enforcement of the constitution.

For reasons of space, it is impossible to examine in any detail the cases that illustrate the judicialization of politics before 1991. However, to provide an indication, table 4.1 enumerates just some of the salient judgments adopted by the supreme court of justice. The examples were selected on the grounds of four criteria: (1) judgments that reflect a prominent phase of constitutional judicial review, as occurred with the decisions of the so-called "admirable" supreme court of the 1930s; (2) judgments that deal with landmark stages of constitutional evolution, such as those that controlled constitutional amendment processes; (3) decisions that show how timid the supreme court was in carrying out judicial review over presidential powers, in particular during states of exception; and (4) some decisions on electoral matters.

The creation of the constitutional court in 1991 represented a profound institutional change, which was nevertheless compatible with the historical trend outlined earlier. The new constitution was brought to life by a constituent assembly elected in 1990. This assembly, which was composed of 72 individual members from all political backgrounds—including four guerrilla groups and several previously excluded

Table 4.1   Some controversial decisions by the supreme court of justice before 1991

Date	Holding	Voting
June 23, 1913	The constitution allows congress to temporarily delegate its legislative powers to the president of the republic during times of peace.	7–3
September 16, 1932	The constitution allows the restriction of voting rights for members of the army, the national police, and permanent armed forces while they are in service.	12–1
March 13, 1937	Masonic societies may be granted legal personality in accordance with the constitution.	13–5
November 12, 1937	Employment cessation benefits should extend to current workers who were hired before the law that established such benefits.	8–6
March 10, 1938	Expropriation may be constitutionally carried out before the full value of compensation has been paid, in the context of the agrarian reform. Payments with long-term bonds allowed.	Un.
September 4, 1939	State intervention in the banana industry is constitutional insofar as it is carried out by congressional statute–it is unconstitutional to authorize the president to restrict freedom of contract and carry out expropriations in such industry.	8–5
September 14, 1955	It is contrary to the constitution to transfer the votes received during elections by different lists, even if they belong to the same party.	12–5
November 28, 1957	The summoning of a plebiscite by a military *junta* in order to reinstate democracy is a political matter not subject to judicial review.	14–7
December 14, 1973	Presidential intervention in the economy by means of a monetary commission (*junta monetaria*) may not be restricted by congress.	13–12

Continued

Table 4.1   Continued

Date	Holding	Voting
March 9, 1978	Upholds the constitutionality of a state of siege decree by which any criminal act committed by members of the armed forces—including homicide—would be justified, if it took place during previously planned operations launched to prevent and repress kidnapping and activities related to drug trafficking.	19–6
May 5, 1978	The supreme court of justice is empowered to review constitutional amendments passed by congress. The constitution forbids the delegation by congress to a constituent Assembly of the power to amend the constitution.	15–10
October 30, 1978	It is constitutional to repress a trade union protest and to restrict freedom of information (with mechanisms that are tantamount to censorship), by means of state of siege decrees.	19–6
April 12, 1983	It is unconstitutional to adopt a tax reform by means of presidential decrees issued under a state of economic emergency.	13–11
July 24, 1986	The constitution allows the law to impose limits upon contributions to, and expenses of, electoral campaigns.	Un.
October 2, 1986	It is constitutional for the law to grant a more favorable tax treatment to those who contribute to the financing of electoral campaigns.	Un.
December 12, 1986	The law that approves the 1979 Colombia–US Extradition Treaty is declared unconstitutional on formal grounds—i.e., sanction by a minister (who is delegated authority by the president) while on an official trip.	16–10
March 5, 1987	It is unconstitutional for military tribunals to investigate and try civilians.	18–7
March 3, 1988	It is unconstitutional for the armed forces and the police to enter physical premises and carry out searches without previous judicial authorization, even during states of siege and in the fight against terrorism.	Un.
May 24, 1990	It is constitutional for the president to authorize, through the exercise of state of siege powers, the electoral organization to count the votes that may result in favor of, or against, the summoning of a Constituent Assembly by the people.	Un.
October 9, 1990	The constitution may be reformed by a Constituent Assembly directly elected by the people, insofar as no material limits are imposed upon its powers. Thus, the specific themes for the amendment for which the assembly was summoned were struck down.	13–12

social, sectors, such as indigenous peoples and religious minorities—promulgated a constitution characterized by democratic inclusiveness, a very strong bill of rights with a solid judicial enforcement mechanism, and a constitutional court, all of which placed Colombia in line with prevailing global tendencies of constitutionalism. In contrast with the earlier period, the members of the body in charge of judicial review were not to be elected by co-option, or on the basis of political parity, but by a very different system. Candidates, who do not have to be public law experts (although they should have different legal specializations), are now elected by the senate of the republic (the second chamber of Congress, popularly elected by national constituency), among lists of three candidates presented by the supreme court, the council of state and the president of the republic, each of these submitting three lists. Constitutional court judges serve a fixed, nonrenewable eight-year period, which secures their independence from members of congress and the executive, who serve four-year terms. Such a system was designed to harmonize the independence of constitutional court judges with indirect political legitimacy. This was a necessary counterbalance to the strong powers invested in the court as guardian of the 1991 constitution, a constitution that effectively represented a peaceful, institutional rebellion against exclusion and, moreover, was supported by a peace agreement among some of the actors of the violent conflict, notably the M-19 guerrilla.

Principal Features of the 1991 System of Constitutional Judicial Review

The Constitutional court has the mandate to preserve the integrity of the 1991 constitution, principally to enforce a very generous Bill of Rights and the new constitutional principles of participatory democracy, the "social state" (*estado social*) and human dignity. The court is the head of a mixed system of judicial review. It has some features of the diffuse system (any judge can defend the constitution in a concrete case), but the constitutional jurisdiction (as opposed to the civil, criminal, and employment/labor jurisdictions headed by the supreme court of justice and the administrative jurisdiction headed by the council of state) is headed by the constitutional court, the body in charge of carrying out the abstract review of legislation and the final review of all *tutela* judgments rendered by any judge in the country (see further). In abstract judicial review, the court may hold that a norm (statute, decree, treaty, constitutional amendment, referendum, and so forth) is invalid and therefore strike it from the legal system. Such decisions have *erga omnes* effects. In concrete review of *tutela* cases, the court decides a conflict between parties concerning a threat or violation of a fundamental right. In such cases its decisions have *inter partes* effects.

With these reforms the supreme court lost constitutional judicial review powers altogether.[3] In order to adjust the judicial review system to the innovative and protective spirit of the 1991 constitution, the Constituent Assembly not only created the constitutional court, but in addition approved several reforms that made it even easier for citizens to access the court and expanded its jurisdiction, in both abstract and concrete judicial review.[4] Here only the most important one, known as *tutela*, is signaled. The scope of application of constitutional judicial review in individual specific cases—that is to say, concrete review—was introduced with the creation of a writ of protection of fundamental rights, the *acción de tutela*. This may be brought forward by any person before any judge with territorial jurisdiction in order to prevent or stop the violation of her/his constitutionally protected rights.[5] It should be emphasized that the generous catalogue of rights protected by the 1991 constitution has led *tutela* judges to issue rulings on a very diverse range of subjects. *Tutela* lawsuits must be decided through relatively simple and fast judicial procedures (a maximum term of 10 days is granted by law for deciding in first instance), which enable judges to adopt any measure deemed necessary to protect threatened human rights in accordance with the specific requirements of the case. In addition, every single *tutela* judgment adopted in the country may be appealed before a higher judge and, in any case, reviewed by the constitutional court, which will, at its total discretion, (1) select those that it regards as incorrectly decided, or pertinent for the development of its own case-law, and later (2) issue the corresponding judgment.

Evidently the constitutional court has been granted a considerable degree of power to fulfill its mandate as guardian of the integrity of the constitution. An additional feature, which is crucial for the judicialization of politics, is that access to the court is very easy. Colombia has, perhaps, the most open system of judicial review. There are four mechanisms of access to the Court: (1) the unconstitutionality *actio popularis*;[6] (2) ex-officio abstract review of referendum bills, laws that approve treaties, statutory legislation, and states of emergency decrees; (3) the review of bills unsuccessfully vetoed by the president of the republic; and (4) the discretionary review of *tutela* judgments. Thus virtually every single law passed by congress may be immediately subjected to judicial review, as well as every constitutional amendment (on formal grounds), certain special types of presidential decrees, and *tutela* decisions issued by all judges in the country. In effect, all administrative decisions that violate or threaten fundamental rights, together with all judicial decisions that openly disregard the mandates of the constitution and several types of "private powers" are subject to the court's scrutiny. No wonder, then, that the constitutional court has issued judgments on nearly every aspect of Colombian life.

The Judicialization of Politics After 1991

The significant expansion of the issues and topics regulated by the constitution in 1991 has been accompanied by a corresponding broadening of the scope of judicial review, which has contributed to the emergence, merely a decade later, of a striking social, political, and legal process. The constitution—and constitutional law along with it—has begun to permeate most aspects of the complex Colombian reality, all the way from the highest spheres of government to ordinary neighborhood conflicts, infusing them with a wholly new *constitutional* and, moreover, *rights-oriented* type of discourse of yet unknown effects. Through the production of an extraordinary amount of case law in regards to practically every phase of Colombian affairs, the "constitutional" jurisdiction, headed by the constitutional court, has become a vital actor. With its decisions it has started to modify the markedly unequal distribution of power among social and political forces, giving increasingly legitimate—albeit in no few cases controversial—responses to the most sensitive and difficult problems facing the country. Moreover, the submission of conflicts to the constitutional judge for their resolution has become one of the prominent forms of participation by ordinary Colombians in the conduct of public and private affairs. Politics, of course, could not be the exception— the field of politics was one of the first to be affected, and indeed transformed, by the 1991 Constituent Assembly's stated aim of making the constitution a superior law to be taken seriously at all levels (see further).

Constitutional litigation has also seen a sharp increase since 1992, in relation to both abstract and concrete review. Citizens, individually or collectively organized for such purposes, have made active recourse to judicial procedures in order to enforce relevant constitutional provisions in all sorts of settings, many of which deal with wholly new topics, issues, and areas which had not been previously regulated by the constitution. On the one hand, the *acción de tutela* has been used with increasing frequency by citizens, for a number of reasons of a political and social nature. First, after 1991, Colombians soon realized that the protection given by the constitution to their fundamental rights could have a direct bearing upon their ordinary lives. Second, due to economic recession and social disruption, very high numbers of persons seek the enforcement of their social rights through this procedural channel, most prominently those related to health, retirement pensions, and salaries. Third, in no few cases what is at stake is the resolution, on a case-by-case basis, of pressing socioeconomic problems that the political system has been unable to solve at a more collective level. On the other hand, citizens are also making ever-increasing use of unconstitutionality *actio popularis*, which was initially designed to trigger abstract review of legislation, but is increasingly being filed to challenge the constitutionality of certain legal provisions on the grounds of their effects upon the enjoyment of fundamental rights. This is, perhaps, a side effect of two factors: the existence of the *acción de tutela* and its impact upon citizens' grasp of the constitution's potential and relevance for their ordinary lives, coupled with the inability of normal political channels to deal with the pressing problems that affect Colombians on a daily basis, which are thus deferred to judicial resolution.

The Impact of the Court on the Legal and Social Realms

The contribution of the constitutional court to the realization and development of the 1991 constitution has had deep implications for most aspects of Colombian life. This can be appreciated both in quantitative and qualitative terms. Between 1992 and 2002, the constitutional court adopted a total of 9,442 decisions—an approximate annual average of 840 judgments, in both abstract and concrete review (see table 4.2). This figure is not just an indication of the court's efficiency; it also reveals its workload, which has now become almost eight times higher than that of the Supreme Court of Justice in the pre-1991 period. As of 2002, the percentage of abstract review decisions declaring the unconstitutionality of legal provisions was 27 percent, while 58 percent of concrete review decisions granted protection to fundamental rights in specific cases. It is therefore hardly surprising that politics, along with every other aspect of life in Colombia, has been affected by an independent and activist process of judicial enforcement of the constitution.

Four factors serve to indicate the magnitude of the process of judicialization of politics in Colombia: (1) when newspapers speak of "the Court," it is almost immediately assumed that they refer to the constitutional court, although there are several different high courts in Colombia; (2) at least once a week, the media broadcast news about decisions of the court, and around every two months, the most broadly circulated newspapers devote their editorial pages to one or several of the court's decisions; (3) the court's power and role is a prominent issue within the national political agenda; and (4) since 1991, every single president of the republic has proposed a constitutional amendment in response to a judgement by the court (see table 4.3). An ongoing government-sponsored proposal to thoroughly

Table 4.2   The work of the court, 1999–2002

Year	Total number of decisions	Number of *tutela* decisions	% of total	Number of abstract review decisions	% of the total
1992	235	182	77.44	53	22.55
1993	598	394	65.88	204	34.11
1994	582	360	61.85	222	38.14
1995	630	403	63.96	227	36.03
1996	718	370	51.53	348	48.46
1997	680	376	55.29	304	44.7
1998	805	565	70.18	240	29.81
1999	993	705	70.99	288	29.01
2000	1734	1340	77.27	394	22.72
2001	1344	976	72.62	368	27.38
2002	1123	784	69.81	339	30.19
Total	9442	6455	68.36	2987	31.64

amend the functioning of the administration of justice sums up the attempts of the executive to undermine the powers of the court.

It is more difficult to describe the qualitative dimension of judicialization of politics; another chapter would be needed simply to summarize the court's most salient decisions.[7] Moreover, given that judicialization of politics permeates several fields, it would clearly be insufficient to select a couple of cases in order to show the general impact of the constitutional court. Nevertheless, the enunciation of these fields indicates the scope of judicialization of politics. Although no area of Colombian life has been immune to this phenomenon, the main areas affected are:

(a) The economy—in areas such as the national budget, public salaries, taxes, social public expenditure, fiscal restraint reforms, or financial autonomy of territorial entities.
(b) Social issues—such as women's rights, the rights of homosexuals, euthanasia, abortion, or the personal use of narcotic drugs.
(c) Public order—in matters such as amnesties, states of emergency, restriction of rights to reinstate public order, the distinction between combatants and non-combatants, or presidential authority to temporarily withdraw the military, police, and judicial authorities from areas of the country in order to foster peace talks with the guerrilla.
(d) International affairs—including, inter alia, the review of all sorts of treaties and of the laws that approve them, such as the

Table 4.3 Constitutional amendments overruling the court

Constitutional amendments approved by congress through legislative acts

Legislative Act 01 of 1995	Regulates in detail the participation of territorial entities in the national budget funds classified as "ordinary national income," as well as the destination that they should be given. Approved in response to decision C–520 of 1994, which gave strict application to the previous constitutional mandate, by which these funds should be applied exclusively to "social investment," not personnel costs.
Legislative Act 02 of 1995	States that military courts or tribunals can be composed of both active and retired military personnel. Approved in response to decision C–141 of 1995, which stated that only retired military personnel or civilians could be part of such bodies.
Legislative Act 01 of 1999	Abolishes the possibility, open since 1936, of carrying out expropriation for reasons of equity without previous compensation. Approved in response to several decisions by the court, which struck down Bilateral Investment Treaty clauses that protected foreign investment by assuring payment of just compensation in cases of expropriation.

Failed legislative act proposals

Proposal launched by a group of congressional representatives to prohibit the adoption of "modulative judgements" by the court (several initiatives since 1995).

Proposal launched by a group of congressional representatives to forbid the admissibility of *tutela* claims against judicial decisions (several initiatives since 1992).

Proposal launched by a group of congressional representatives to impose the requirement of qualified majority voting to declare the unconstitutionality of a law (several initiatives since 1995).

Failed constitutional referendum initiatives

Referendum initiative launched by the Catholic Church in 1993 to introduce a constitutional article authorizing a Concordat with the Holy See, against decision C–027 of 1993, which struck down the central provisions of such treaty.

Two referendum initiatives launched with governmental support (in 1994 and 2003), to authorize the criminalization of the possession and use of personal doses of drugs, against decision C–221 of 1994, which struck down the relevant provision in the Criminal Code.

Partially failed referendum (October, 2003)

Referendum bill, introduced by President Alvaro Uribe Vélez to amend several parts of the constitution. Approved by congress through Law 796 of 2003, summoning the referendum. The text of the referendum had three reforms, among a total of eight, which were directed to overrule previous decisions of the constitutional court: (a) the abolition of special pension rights for high officials, interpreted broadly by the court in several *tutela* decisions; (b) the authorization to completely freeze public salaries which were above two minimum wages (for a period of two years for middle-rank salaries, and four years for high-rank salaries), partially and temporarily disregarding decision C–1064 of 2001; and (c) an authorization to criminalize the consumption of personal doses of drugs, directed against decision C–221 of 1994. The third one was struck from the text of the referendum by the constitutional court on procedural grounds. The remaining questions did not obtain the minimum voting threshold once the referendum was carried out.

Concordat with the Holy See, environmental and human rights conventions and international instruments to repress crime.

(e) The fight against the drug trade—on topics such as the termination of property rights over illegally acquired assets, extradition, the constitutive elements of the crimes related to the drug trade, and the aerial fumigation of illegal crops, or procedural guarantees for criminal defendants.

As to the specific areas of impact of the court upon the political field, one should mention:

(f) The admissibility of referenda.

(g) The basic rules of representative democracy—including issues such as campaign and party financing, access by candidates to the mass media, the distortion of political processes through the deviation of public expenditure, or the protection of the rights of political parties, movements, and candidates.

(h) Political scandals that have ended up in criminal procedures or in the removal of offenders from congressional seats, in which the corresponding judicial decisions have been challenged through *tutela*.

The intensity of judicialization can be appreciated in the list of some of the most controversial decisions of the court. Table 4.4 concerns concrete fundamental rights cases, and table 4.5 concerns abstract review decisions. In addition, table 4.6 refers to the concrete review cases in which the court has resorted to the figure of "unconstitutional state of affairs," given the structural causes of the fundamental rights violations at stake. The last decision, for example, protected over two million internally displaced persons.

It is not possible to identify a common pattern in the political processes preceding these judgments, or to identify those civil society organizations or actors that have been active in advancing the judicialization of politics in Colombia. Nonetheless, at the risk of simplification, it is possible to point to the following common elements. First, the plaintiff is rarely a social organization, but is usually rather a citizen acting on his or her own behalf, who may or may not be discretely backed by a social group. Nevertheless, in cases concerning public order issues, human rights NGOs file amicus curiae, and in cases that relate to social affairs, trade unions usually intervene. Private sector organizations tend to resort less to the court, although they have done so to defend specific interests. Second, during parliamentary debates congressional representatives who feel they are in a

Table 4.4 Some of the most controversial decisions of the court—concrete review

Subject	Year, ref.	Rule/decision	Voting		
			Affirm	Dissent	Concur
Right to health	T–534/1992, among hundreds ("Necessary treatment" cases)	The right to health, although not fundamental in itself, may be protected through *tutela* whenever such protection is necessary to preserve threatened fundamental rights, such as the right to life and personal integrity (concerning diagnostic services, medicines, treatment, surgeries, etc.), or the right to human dignity.	3	0	0
	SU–043/1995 ("Children's fundamental right to health" cases)	Children's right to health is fundamental in itself.The right to health includes the right to receive treatment, even in the case of incurable diseases that can be controlled.	9	0	0
	SU–480/1997 ("AIDS patients" cases)	AIDS patients who cannot finance their own treatment are entitled to receive it from the social security system, even if the medications or interventions they require have not been officially foreseen in the catalogue of available treatments.	9	0	0
	SU–819/1999 ("Overseas treatment" cases)	The right to health, under certain conditions, can entitle social security affiliates to receive treatment abroad, when no national treatments are available.	9	0	0
Indigenous Peoples' Rights	T–428/1992 ("Road in indigenous territory" case)	National authorities may not disregard the rights of indigenous communities when building infrastructure, such as roads. These constructions must always be preceded by an adequate consultation process with the affected aboriginal groups.	3	0	1

	SU–039/1997 ("U'wa case")	Indigenous communities have fundamental collective rights to preserve their cultural identity and all that is necessary for that purpose. This includes the right to previous consultation whenever natural resources are to be exploited in their territory. On these grounds, an important oil exploration project in U'wa territory was barred (SU–039/97).	5	4	0
	T–523/1997 ("Whip case")	Indigenous individuals have a right to be judged by traditional indigenous authorities, even if that entails the imposition of penalties that would be deemed unacceptable in a nonindigenous context.	3	0	0
	SU–510/1998 ("Protestant church case")	Indigenous authorities have the right to exclude nonindigenous religious groups or churches from preaching and encouraging conversions in their territory, in order to preserve their cultural integrity	6	3	0
Right to minimum subsistence income	T–426/1992 among hundreds ("Vital minimum cases")	Whenever the minimum subsistence conditions are not satisfied, and there exists an emergency or severe circumstances, people are entitled to demand positive actions by the state to fulfill their unresolved basic needs, even if that entails public expenditure.	3	0	0
Right to rectification	T–066/1998 and	Individuals affected in their reputation by	3	0	0

Continued

Table 4.4 Continued

Subject	Year, ref.	Rule/decision	Voting		
			Affirm	Dissent	Concur
	dozens of others ("Fair rectification cases")	untruthful information disseminated through the mass media, have the right to rectification of such information, in conditions of fairness.	9	0	0
Displaced population	SU–1150/2000 ("Forcible displacement" case)	Individuals who have been forcibly displaced from their land due to the violent conflict suffer from massive, multiple, and continuous violations of their fundamental rights. These must be attended to and resolved by the state, in particular the executive, through adequate programs that fulfill their basic unsatisfied needs.			
Admissibility of *tutela* against judicial decisions	T–006/1992, T–231/1994 and dozens of others ("*Tutela* against judgements" cases)	Judicial decisions may be attacked through the *acción de tutela* whenever they incur in gross legal irregularities (*vías de hecho*), regardless of their *res iudicata* effects.	3 3	0 0	1 0
Labor union rights	SU–342/1995 ("Trade union persecution" cases)	Employers may not discriminate against workers who belong to trade unions, inter alia by granting better working conditions or benefits to workers who are not associated therewith or by firing unionized workers.	5	4	0
Right to education	SU–624/1999 and dozens of others	Academic institutions may not exclude students who have not been able to pay their	8	1	0

	("Poor Students" cases)	tution fees, at least during the academic year. They may not retain grades certificates either, even if there has been an unjustified lack of payment by students' guardians.		
Right to free development of one's own personality	SU–642/98 ("Personal appearance" cases)	The state and private organizations may not interfere with an individual's life options, insofar as they do not unreasonably restrict or violate third parties' rights or the legal order. This includes, inter alia, the right to determine one's own appearance, especially within academic institutions.	8	1	0
Right to determine one's own gender identity	SU–337/99 ("Hermaphrodite" case)	Given specific circumstances, parents or legal guardians may not in principle grant substitute consent for the performance of sexual re-adequation procedures, without the affected minor's acceptance of the intervention.	9	0	0
Sexual orientation— homosexual couples	SU–623/2001 ("Homosexual couples" case)	Homosexual individuals may not be discriminated because of their sexual orientation, but they may not be equated to heterosexual couples for purposes of constituting "family" or receiving social security benefits.	5	4	0
Parliamentary inviolability	SU–047/1999 ("Impeachment of the President" case)	Congressional representatives may not be prosecuted for the opinions they express in the exercise of their functions, or for the way they vote, even when they are reviewing the actions of high public officials in the exercise of congressional judicial powers.	7	2	0

Continued

84

Table 4.4 Continued

| Subject | Year, ref. | Rule/decision | Voting | | |
			Affirm	Dissent	Concur
Arbitral Awards *ex aequo et bono*	SU–837/2002 ("Awards in equity" case)	Arbitral awards in equity (*ex aequo et bono*), produced to solve labor conflicts in which collective bargaining has failed, may not be arbitrary, and they must be adequately motivated in order to respect the constitution.	9	0	1
Protection of informal salespersons	T–772/2003 ("informal salesmen" case)	Persons who occupy public space carrying out informal sales activities cannot be the object of police arbitrariness or mistreatment, and whenever they are working in good faith, they must be offered reasonable reallocation alternatives by the authorities before being removed from public space.	3	0	0
Fumigation of illicit drug crops	SU–383/03 ("fumigations in indigenous land" case)	The court upheld the constitutionality of the aerial fumigations of illicit coca and poppy crops, but subject to strict conditions when carried out in the ancestral land of indigenous peoples.	6	3	0

Table 4.5 The most controversial decisions of the court—abstract review

Year	Subject	Reference	Rule/decision	Affirm	Dissent	Concur
					Voting	
1993	Equality of religions	C–027	Unconstitutionality of the main articles of the 1974 Concordat between Colombia and the Holy See, which privileged the Catholic Church.	8	1	0
1994	Abortion	C–133	Constitutionality of the criminal provision penalizing abortion, given the prevalence of the right to life.	6	3	0
2001		C–647	Modified in 2001, upholding a legal exemption to punishment, whenever abortion is performed in "extraordinary circumstances," such as after sexual assault.	5	2	4
1994	Access by political candidates to the media	C–089	Constitutionality of the legal provision that preserves the opposition parties and political minorities to have access to state media in direct proportion to their number of Congressional representatives, since the "right to a radio and TV antenna" is necessary for allowing the opposition to fulfill its critical function within the political system.	5	4	2
1994	Personal dose of drugs	C–221	Unconstitutionality of the criminal provision imposing penalties for possession and consumption of personal doses of narcotic drugs.	5	4	0
1997	Euthanasia	C–239	Impossibility to criminalize doctors who apply euthanasia to terminally ill patients in cases of extreme suffering and informed consent.	6	3	3

Continued

Table 4.5 Continued

Year	Subject	Rule/decision	Reference	Voting		
				Affirm	Dissent	Concur
1997	Security services by armed civilians	Constitutionality of provision allowing organized communities to provide private security services by armed civilians, insofar as the weapons they use have not been restricted to exclusive use by the armed forces.	C–572	5	4	1
1998	Journalism Law	Unconstitutionality of licensing system for the exercise of journalism.	C–087	9	0	1
1998	Television Law	Rejected unconstitutionality *actio popularis* against the law that prohibited the renewal of concession contracts with television providers, with the consequent exclusion of the news channels that criticized public figures during the "8,000 Criminal Process," on the grounds that the discriminatory purpose or impact of the law had not been proven.	C–456	6	3	0
1999	UPAC decisions	Unconstitutionality of the basic features of the system for financing the construction and acquisition of housing	C–383 C–700 C–747	7 6 6	2 3 3	0 2 2
2000	Female quotas	Constitutionality of the law establishing mandatory participation of women in at least 30 percent of decision-making positions in the executive branch.	C–371	5	4	1
2000	National Development plan	Unconstitutionality of the law that approved the National Development Plan for 1999–2002, due to procedural defects.	C–557	8	1	0

Year	Topic	Description	Case			
2000	Increase in public salaries	Unconstitutionality of part of the national budget, for not having appropriated enough funds to increase all public wages at least in a percentage equivalent to the previous year's inflation rate(2000).	C–1433/2000	7	2	0
2001		Later modified in 2001 and 2003, when the court established that, in times of fiscal deficit, public salaries above two minimum wages need not be increased in the same proportion as the previous year's inflation rate.	C–1064/2001	5	4	0
			C–1017/2003	6	3	
2001	Intervention in the financial autonomy of territorial entities	Congress may regulate matters that are initially within the financial autonomy of territorial entities, in order to preserve the macroeconomic stability of the nation.	C–579/2001	5	4	2
2001	Prohibition of pork barrel (*auxilios parlamentarios*)	All authorities who intervene in the process of elaborating the budget must give clear and explicit justifications for the reasons why a given project is financed with public funds. Congressional representatives may not be granted "disguised" discretionary allocation funds in the national budget, nor given the opportunity to bear individual commanding influence upon the expenditure of such funds, by virtue of the constitutional prohibition of *auxilios parlamentarios* and the principle of legality of public expenditure.	C–1168/2001	6	3	1
2002	National Security Law	Unconstitutionality of a national security law that relied on the notion of "national power," which implied incorporating civilians into the armed conflict and the fusion of separated powers.	C–251	7	2	0

Continued

Table 4.5 Continued

Year	Subject	Rule/decision	Reference	Voting		
				Affirm	Dissent	Concur
More than one, 1994–2003	States of exception	Unconstitutionality of decrees declaring or maintaining states of internal commotion or economic emergency, because constitutional requirements had not been met. In one case, the unconstitutionality was partial (1997).	C-300/1994 C-466/1995 C-122/1997 C-327/2003	6 7 6 5	3 2 3 4	1 2 4 0
2003	Value-added tax for first-necessity goods and service.	Unconstitutionality of the legal provision that extends the value-added tax to first necessity goods and services, because (1) it was indiscriminate and had been adopted without a minimum level of public debate in Congress, (2) it was adopted in the context of serious flaws in the tax system, countering the principle of progressiveness, and (3) it covered goods and services which provide, in the context of a seriously insufficient system of social welfare, the grounds for the effective enjoyment of the most basic living conditions by the majority of the population.	C-776	9	0	0
2003	Referendum	The court must verify whether congress had the competence to convoke a referendum to amend the constitution. Although there are not intangible constitutional articles, a referendum must refrain from repealing, subverting, or substituting the constitution. The court upheld most of the referendum, but struck down parts of it in order to protect freedom of choice by the voters and avoid the risk of transforming the referendum into a plebiscite.	C-551	6	2	0

minority are ever more likely to invoke the judgements of the court in order to support their political position with legal arguments. If they fail to gain a sympathetic hearing, then they increasingly promote the presentation of an unconstitutionality *actio popularis* before the court. Third, the government always intervenes in abstract review procedures in defense of the legal provision concerned whereas, on the contrary, congressional representatives within the majority that adopted such provisions hardly ever intervene in their favor. Fourth, national mass media do not give coverage to the political or judicial processes before the judgment, but they do report on the rulings and the reactions of those affected by them. Fifth, the link to international actors is exceptional. Judicialization of politics in Colombia tends to follow endogenous dynamics.[8] Sixth, the court's decisions tend to be complied with. When a given judgment has a negative economic impact or limits presidential powers in matters of public order, the corresponding minister publicly expresses his or her disagreement, but always points out that the government will obey the court's decision, and in practice it does. The Supreme Court of Justice is the only exception, being the only public entity that has publicly opposed the possibility of having its own judgments in civil, criminal, or labor/employment matters invalidated by the constitutional court by means of *tutela* rulings. In five cases, the supreme court has refused to comply with the orders of the constitutional court, which has then adopted special decisions (*autos*) obtaining the enforcement of the *tutela* judgment regardless of the supreme court's opposition and without its co-operation.[9]

Except for the five cases of *tutela* decisions against judgments by the Supreme Court of Justice, the doctrine of the constitutional court is usually followed by lower court judges. Until the mid-1990s, these doctrines encountered some resistance, given that constitutional case law seemed very innovative and because lower court judges did not depend on the constitutional court for their evaluation, permanence, or promotion. Nevertheless, the court has consistently decided to select and review those *tutela* judgments by lower court judges that depart from its doctrine, given that every single *tutela* decision adopted by the country's judges is sent to the constitutional court in order for the latter to verify whether its doctrine has been respected. This has led most judges to follow the court's rulings as if they were precedents within a common law system. From an approximate total of 180,000 *tutela* judgments per year rendered by lower court judges, the court only has to select around 600 in order to ensure respect for its precedents.

In *tutela* cases, the court imparts specific orders to administrative authorities or private individuals, in the sense of carrying out an action or an abstention. These orders are usually obeyed. The court is rarely asked to modify an order so that it may be fulfilled within the corresponding term. If an order by the court, or by any *tutela* judge, is disregarded, noncompliance may be punished with successive penalties, such as arrest and fines. This does not occur very often, but it has happened even at the highest levels. Ministers, directors of national public entities, mayors, governors and deans of universities—to quote the most notorious cases—have been arrested for not complying with *tutela* rulings, and they have subsequently carried out the mandate. Only the supreme court of justice has not been punished. This is because only congress may impose disciplinary measures on supreme court judges.

In addition, when an abstract judicial review decision invalidates a legal provision, its implementation is automatic because the judgment invalidates the norm within the legal system with *erga omnes* effects. No authority can subsequently invoke the norm, nor apply it. If they do so by mistake, *tutela* can be used to undo the arbitrariness, as well as to invoke disciplinary or criminal measures.

The Effects of the Judicialization of Politics in Colombia

The judicialization of politics has generated several effects within the Colombian political system. First, constitutional case law has prompted the inclusion of previously marginal topics within the national political agenda, as well as a reordering of priorities. The rights of homosexuals, euthanasia, abortion, and the use of drugs are just some of the most notorious examples of topics which, having first been the subject-matter of decisions by the court, have later become the centre of public debate, inter alia in the legislative sphere and the press. Second, decisions by the constitutional court have become weighty factors in the process of formation and definition of collective actors and identities which, in turn, have become visible and active in the political field. One good example is that of indigenous peoples, for whom constitutional case law has become a key tool in the preservation and development of their cultural identity and in the promotion of their collective fundamental rights.[10]

Third, discrete balances of power within Colombian society have been substantially altered by the strict judicial enforcement of the constitution, which introduced several mechanisms to control the arbitrary exercise of power by private parties over individuals and groups.[11] Through the far-reaching application of the *acción de tutela* to private relations, the court's case law has contributed to an important process of individual empowerment, especially of those who would be deemed, before 1991, as relatively weak. These have included retired workers vis-à-vis their former employers,[12] residents of buildings and residential compounds in relation to the respective co-owners' assemblies and administration bodies,[13] users or clients of financial entities who unduly disseminate their personal data,[14] inhabitants of residential areas affected by the smells and noises emanating from their neighbors' animal-raising activities or other irregularly operated industries,[15] and housewives who were the constant victims of domestic violence.[16] These are only a few examples of the many categories of private individuals who were empowered by the constitution to have their rights respected at all levels. In short, through *tutela*, the weak often win. This is why this legal instrument has been referred to as "the power of the powerless."

Fourth, the dynamics of the political process, as well as its outcomes, have also been affected by constitutional judicial review. It is now commonplace for congressional representatives to speculate, during legislative debates, whether a given provision will withstand a constitutionality test once it gets to the court. Constitutional mandates, as well as the interpretative guidelines established by constitutional case law, have thus been incorporated as significant deciding criteria at the moment of drafting and approving any given law, thereby affecting the results of the process. This is the so-called "anticipation effect," by which the design of legal provisions, their content, the language used for their justification and the debates around their enactment both within the government and in congress are infused by judicial decisions adopted by the court. To cite one eloquent example: in a recent judgement cited above,[17] the court struck down a legal provision that imposed a value-added tax on essential goods and services which had previously been excluded or exempted from such taxes. Once adopted, this decision by the court gave rise to fierce debates in congress, during which the reasons of unconstitutionality invoked by the court were explicitly incorporated as guiding criteria for the adoption of a tax reform to attack the flaws in the system (mainly the evasion of progressive taxes), and for the creation of taxes that affect the wealthier strata of the population.

Fifth, social actors have in many cases begun to adjust their ordinary preferences and choices to the dictates of constitutional case law. One clear example is that of personal appearance in schools, now viewed as part of the right to personal autonomy. While it was very common, before 1991, for schools to impose extensive restrictions upon students' personal appearance, for example by determining a maximum hair length, prohibiting the use of make-up, or making certain types of attire mandatory in school, constant use by students of the *acción de tutela* against these rules has led, if not to their total abandonment, to a visible process of "liberalisation" of the aesthetic requirements imposed on them by schools. Lastly, the dynamics and channels of public deliberation have also been modified in response to the application of constitutional mandates to matters previously excluded from judicial review. The most salient example is that of personal drug consumption. The court declared the unconstitutionality of the legal provision that criminalized the possession and use of personal doses of drugs. This decision, obviously controversial in a country devastated by drug trafficking, gave rise to two different government-sponsored referenda initiatives in which the people were to be asked directly whether they approved the criminalization of this conduct. The first of these referenda initiatives failed, since it did not gather the number of signatures required as a threshold for presenting the proposal. The second was part of a recently conducted referendum in which a number of different constitutional amendments were to be submitted to popular approval, but the court, on procedural grounds, struck down the question pertaining to this particular issue when it reviewed its constitutionality. Such a strong reaction in the democratic field to one decision by the constitutional court is quite remarkable.

Factors Underpinning the Judicialization of Politics

A number of Colombia's unique social, political, and institutional characteristics are especially relevant to explaining the current judicialization of politics in the country. As a consequence of its Hispanic colonial heritage and republican tradition, Colombia has a highly "legalistic" culture, which has led political confrontations to be transformed into constitutional amendments that play the part of peace treaties between belligerent factions. It has also meant that political and social issues have often been converted into legal, and moreover, constitutional controversies. Given that Colombia has traditionally been a country of laws, and that laws are constantly being issued with the illusion that new norms will solve the country's pressing national problems, almost every social, political, or economic problem has a corresponding law that governs it. It is therefore quite easy to formulate such problems as matters of regulation, and to question the rules before the court. In addition to this, fundamental constitutional rights are applicable in every phase and aspect of life, which allows every concrete situation to be formulated as a constitutional case. Colombia could easily have been the subject of Alexis de Tocqueville's famous affirmation about the United States: every social or political issue sooner or later becomes a legal one. A very high number of lawyers and law schools complement this cultural panorama.

Second, the Colombian political system is affected by flaws that lead people to resort to alternative or judicial means to solve problems that the political forum is not capable of dealing with. These flaws are of a very diverse nature and here I signal only those that have a direct bearing upon the process of judicialization of politics:

(a) Due to the central position traditionally granted in Colombia to the president of the republic, the executive branch exerts permanent influence over congress, which in turn contributes to diminish—and in many cases distort—the system of checks and balances between the political branches of power. Although the 1991 constitution sought to strengthen congress, in practice it still has a rather precarious institutional capacity to exercise its powers, for both technical reasons (such as poorly qualified and insufficient staff, and limited access to autonomous information), as well as political causes (poor party discipline, clientelistic local electoral bases, and so forth). Additionally, following presidential elections, congressional representatives tend to divide between supporters and opponents of the president. The president usually manages to build a majority in congress which would help support his policies. Therefore, in many cases congress adopts its decisions with the aim of backing the executive. Given that congress often fails to check the power of the executive because of political compromise, the "losers" of the process go to the court. Citizens and social organizations usually look to the court in order to seek the enforcement of limits to the government's policies or laws. For this they rely on constitutional grounds and arguments, rather than political means. Resort to judicial review also demands less effort in terms of political organization, which renders it a much more attractive alternative than the traditional confrontations in the political field.

(b) In spite of the important reforms of 1991, there is still a prevailing feeling of disappointment within public opinion about political practices, which are perceived as clientelistic and as benefiting politicians rather than ordinary people. This has prompted a situation in which laws are seldom seen by citizens to represent the consent of society or of a solid political majority. The court's decisions to strike them down are usually met either with indifference or with popular approval.

(c) Although Colombia is a country with one of the most stable constitutional and electoral traditions in Latin America, there are still very clear manifestations of social exclusion—indeed, recent figures show that Colombian society is markedly unequal, in particular with respect to the distribution of wealth—and political under-representation. In short, people do not feel represented by political parties or movements, to such a degree that over one half of the electorate define themselves as "independent."

(d) Judicial fora tend to be more sensitive to human rights issues—which are relatively prominent in the media—than congress or other popularly elected bodies at the local level. This is because courts are less directly affected by considerations of political expediency. It is also due to the strong protections of fundamental rights granted by the constitution.

(e) As opposed to what happens in most countries, in Colombia violence is a real, everyday and—of course—illegal mechanism for the resolution of conflicts. It is a widespread and devastating phenomenon, which has been occurring on a national scale and with different levels of intensity, actors, and driving forces for decades. Given that politics often seems unable to function efficiently as a channel for the peaceful expression and resolution of social conflicts, the highest degree of institutional legitimacy and credibility is thus placed upon the judiciary. The judiciary is called upon by social actors to resolve issues that are not adequately addressed by the political process, and that are—or could be—aggravated by so-called violent solutions. That is why the *acción de tutela* has been praised in the Colombian context as an instrument of peace, because the intervention of a judge has helped solve conflicts that could have been addressed by arbitrary means, often as serious as personal intimidation or murder.

Third, the quality of Colombian public policies and public administration is not the best. Policies are frequently improvised, mechanisms to respond to the changing needs of the population are not implemented, key policies often fail during the stage of implementation, and follow-up or evaluation of the results obtained is rarely carried out. Such poor performance encourages citizens to resort to the judiciary, generally by means of *tutela*, in order to control the flaws that threaten or violate constitutional fundamental rights. A brief synthesis of the main decisions in which the court—through the doctrine of "unconstitutional state of affairs," introduced in 1997 by constitutional case law—has dealt with the major flaws of public policies and the regulatory system is presented in table 4.6.

Fourth, it should be pointed out that some social groups, together with a handful of activist citizens, quickly understood the implications of having such an open and easily accessible system of constitutional judicial review, and made rapid use of the constitutional channels to file their petitions before the court. This is not a massive mobilization, because constitutional procedure rules do not require a significant number of citizens to come together around an issue. Since rights protect each individual, it is enough for one active citizen to take the time to write a short lawsuit before the court, or a brief request of review for a *tutela*, in order for the court to have to adopt a decision

Table 4.6 Unconstitutional state of affairs: Grave regulatory and policy failures identified by the court

Decision	Holding
SU–559/1997	The court ordered local and national authorities to pay the social security benefits of public teachers in order to protect their fundamental right to social security.
T–068/1998	The Court ordered the National Retirement Fund (*Caja Nacional de Previsión*) to adopt, within six months, efficient administrative procedures to respond to petitions duly filed, in order to protect the right to social security of the elderly population.
T–153/1998	The court ordered national authorities to design (within three months) and implement (within four years) a prison plan, in order to reduce overcrowding and dignify prison inmates' living conditions and thereby protect their fundamental rights.
SU–250/1999; T–1635/2000	The court ordered the competent authorities to summon a public competition within six months in order to appoint public notaries in the entire national territory. It later ordered the same authorities to correct the mistakes that occurred in the original competition.
T–590/1998	The court ordered national and local authorities to stop all practices endangering the lives of human rights activists, and to adopt measures to protect them.
T–606/1998 and T–607/1998	The court ordered the competent authorities to protect the right to health of prison inmates, and—to achieve this—instructed them to engage public health service providers. It was to be in full operation within six months of the court's decision.
T–525/1999	The court ordered the treasury and local authorities to adopt, within the second semester of 1999, all budgetary measures necessary to pay the outstanding salaries and pensions of the retired workers of the Department of Bolívar, to protect their right to social security.
SU–090/2000	The court ordered the treasury and local authorities to disburse, within three months, the funds legally allocated to pay the outstanding pensions of the retired workers of the Department of Chocó, to protect their right to social security.
T–847/2000	The court ordered the competent authorities to separate, within ten days, persons under preventive detention in police stations from convicted offenders and persons being criminally prosecuted.
T–025/2004	To protect the rights of internally displaced persons, the court ordered the government authorities to allocate, within a timetable designed by the court, the resources necessary to enforce the existing attention and protection plan—as designed by the corresponding law—or, otherwise, to redefine state priorities for the protection of the internally displaced, but always securing the minimum standard of protection established by the constitution and relevant international instruments.

on the matter, even if it does not always delve into the merits of every claim. Indeed, after 1991, many social actors—as opposed to political parties or groups and high-ranking public officials—have begun to make use of constitutional law in order to advance their own interests. Some common denominators of social actors' uses of constitutional law to attain political objectives can be identified.

The social actors who make the most frequent use of constitutional law are those that have the least power within the decision-making processes that affect them. This is the case, for example, of indigenous peoples in relation to the protection of their collective fundamental rights, informal salespersons who need to protect their right to work on the streets,[18] or people in extreme conditions of poverty who lack access to social security benefits.[19] Constitutional controversies are generally formulated in terms of violations or threats to fundamental rights, and absolute protection of the latter is claimed in abstract or concrete review. For example, debtors of the social housing financing system phrase their claims in terms of the right to dignified housing; retired workers who are not granted their pension in due course file *tutela* claims for their rights to social security and to the minimum material conditions to lead a dignified life;[20] or students who have been expelled from school due to their parents' tardiness in paying tuition fees formulate the conflict in terms of their right to education.[21] *Tutela* suits are usually filed by the affected individuals, but with the support of social organizations that later disseminate the content of the court's decision so that its benefits will be known to other people in similar situations.

Given the magnitude and innovative character of the legal problems that were brought to their attention, judges were quite reticent at the beginning of the 1990s to act in relation to the protection of fundamental rights. However, once the constitutional court started issuing its decisions and determining the scope and limits of such rights, their judicial protection and enforcement became increasingly common. Finally, since congress has so far issued very few statutory laws that harmonize conflicting fundamental rights or define their scope and their limits, it has been the court that has been called upon to draw the line. It has done this in a generally balanced manner, modulating the orders to be imparted in accordance with the problem under review.

Conclusions: A Controversial Institutional Actor

Bearing in mind the weaknesses in the political resolution of conflicts, combined with the traditional ineffectiveness of public administration, it is hardly surprising that not only politics, but most of the spheres of Colombian life have become more or less judicialized. However, judicialization has prompted increasing controversy about the role and power of the court. Some say that the court is invading every aspect of Colombian life, and formulating public policies on every conceivable topic. Others argue that the court should have gone further in most of its decisions, because substantial sectors of the population remain excluded from, or underrepresented in, Colombian politics. In this sense, I would emphasize that it is not that the court is meddling with every issue that it can imagine; it is more that ordinary citizens and political actors bring their everyday problems and interests to the court, which is then mandated to adjudicate on a notoriously diverse range of subjects. Given that it has to decide on such a broad array of issues, the court has had to adapt constitutional law to new and ever-expanding challenges. Having behaved as an independent and activist constitutional arbiter, the court has also consistently sought to design and apply a number of self-restraint mechanisms.[22] In addition to these self-restraint mechanisms, when brought to decide upon complex or controversial matters, the court has usually sought to strike a balance between conflicting interests, refraining from "all-or-nothing" judgments that benefit one of the actors or parties in conflict and trying to establish an equilibrium between their respective concerns. These self-restraint mechanisms and balanced decisions are critical for the sustainability of the system of judicial review as a whole. Indeed, the first condition for the survival of the system is the preservation of the court's neutrality, while enforcing the constitution in sensitive areas. Insofar as the highest constitutional arbiter is perceived as an impartial body, which decides according to the law and following fair and clear procedural rules (a distinctive trait of the judicial, not the political, process) to which citizens and groups can have recourse in order to safeguard their constitutional rights, the system as a whole will be more likely to prove sustainable and preserve its legitimacy.

The public perception that the court decides in accordance with the law is facilitated by the degree of detail of constitutional provisions in Colombia. It is clear that the more detailed a constitution is, the broader the spectrum of political decisions that may be adopted on the grounds of a specific, relevant, public, and accepted rule. This has the dual effect of stimulating the judicialization of politics and granting judges enough objective and clear legal grounds to adopt decisions on issues that have previously been perceived as exclusively political, but which have been judicialized by way of these specific provisions. At the same time, the opposite effect may occur: general and indeterminate constitutional principles open a broader margin of interpretation to constitutional judges, which may prompt their deciding on almost any type of problem, as happens in the United States. The Colombian constitution contains both types of clauses: it is detailed in relation to social and economic rights and economic institutions, although to a far lesser degree than the constitutions of Brazil and other countries. It also contains general fundamental principles that define the state and enumerate civil and political rights with a degree of generality even higher than that of several European constitutions.

Some observers argue that the constitutional court lacks sufficient democratic legitimacy to assume the role described above. Given that this argument had also been invoked in the past against the supreme court, it was expressly addressed in the 1991 constitution. In order to increase the representative character of the court, the constituent Assembly abolished the preexisting "co-option" system for the designation of judges, replacing it with an indirect popular election system. The senate, popularly elected by national constituency, elects in turn all the judges of the constitutional court. The composition of the court reflects the relationship between political forces in congress, and even the different factions within each party. In addition, the court's decision-making process is highly participatory. Essentially, any citizen may draft a document stating his or her position in favor or against a legal provision that is being reviewed by the court. The court also invites experts, social organizations, and authorities to formally express their opinions. The court's work schedule is public, as are the minutes of its sessions. For symbolic purposes, the court's judgments must be headed as follows: "by mandate of the Constitution and in the name of the People." Finally, since judges serve a non-renewable eight-year term, political forces can periodically evaluate the work of the court and elect judges with different points of view from those of their predecessors. This does not affect their future independence, because they may not be removed and their salary is constitutionally linked to that of congressional representatives.

The very same court has been very careful in defining its mission, expressly stating that in a democracy it is up to congress to adopt the most important political decisions. That is why it has crafted self-restraint doctrines in order to limit the cases in which it intervenes, the degree of strictness with which it will decide upon a given matter, and how it will modulate the effect of its rulings in order to allow congress to amend its mistakes. Moreover, as opposed to the United States and most countries with strong judicial review systems, the Colombian constitution establishes two mechanisms through which the congress may "guard the guardian." The first is that of special-hierarchy legislation, by which Congress may limit judicial discretion in the interpretation of rights. These statutes—called "statutory laws"—may only be reviewed by the court before they enter into force, and they may not be invalidated thereafter. The second is that of constitutional amendments. The Colombian constitution is easy to amend. It takes less than a year to do so. Congress has approved an average of two constitutional amendments per year. Several of these bound the court to modify its doctrine in order to comply with the change in the constitutional text. In turn, several constitutional amendment initiatives directed against specific decisions by the court have failed. This proves that congressional majorities have eventually come to share the decisions of the constitutional court, which reinforces the latter's democratic legitimacy and the acceptance of its rulings.

This is especially evident in decisions with macroeconomic implications, since none of the constitutional amendment initiatives on this subject have been successful. The constitutional court, like any other court, is not mandated to consider the source of fiscal resources that will finance compliance with a given decision. However, this does not make the court fiscally irresponsible. With few exceptions, the court has incorporated existing fiscal restrictions as a constitutionally relevant factor in its judgments with economic implications. It has even designed kinds of argument and evidence rules that allow it to assess the goals of macroeconomic policy at the moment of adopting judgments with fiscal effects. It has also deferred the effectiveness of its decisions toward the future in order to reduce or avoid negative macroeconomic impact. For example, in 2001 the court deferred for one year the effect of the declaration of unconstitutionality of a statute regulating foreign investment in oil fields. Nevertheless, one of the constitutional amendments proposed in 2004 concerns the judgments of the court with fiscal implications. Some of the proposals aim to restrict the court's powers, while others broaden it.

The court's work in the aforementioned spheres, among others, has generated pressure for the reform of other state institutions in order for their structure and functioning to adequately respond to the 1991 constitution. This is due to the fact that such institutions and social actors must adapt to the constitution in order to comply with a decision by the court or to prevent disfavorable rulings. Nevertheless, easy access to the court has generated the negative effect of discouraging the adoption of reforms through political fora.

In the end, the court has been very careful to maintain an equilibrium that preserves its position as an impartial arbiter in delicate issues. This has contributed, so far, to the overall sustainability of the system. Opinion polls and surveys would seem to back this claim: the *acción de tutela* is the legal institution with the highest level of favorable public opinion in Colombia (nearly 80 percent), and the constitutional court has solid citizen support (55 percent positive image)[23]—figures which may be compared to the significantly lower level of popularity of Congress (39 percent positive image),[24] or to the high percentage of the population which has expressed its mistrust with regard to other institutions (71 percent have expressed their distrust toward public administration, 79 percent toward Congress and 89 percent toward political parties, whereas in the same survey, only 58 percent said they distrusted the administration of justice in general) Cuellar, 2000, p. 63).

The difficult question is whether or not the system designed in 1991 is ultimately sustainable. The "losers" are often powerful interests that may combine forces to push forward constitutional amendments to reduce the power of the court. Since in 2004 and 2005 the court will have to decide on very sensitive issues concerning economic reform and fiscal restraints, measures against terrorism, profound electoral changes and, perhaps, amendments to the powers of the court itself, the coming years will pose the toughest challenges to the sustainability of the constitutional judicial review system designed in 1991, and to its independent and active enforcement by the constitutional court.

Notes

I am grateful to Federico Guzmán for his invaluable support in the elaboration of this paper.

1. See *Gaceta Judicial*, vol. 1, p. 235. The decision involved a pension problem.
2. These years were 1956, 1957, and 1968. For the first decisions of the supreme court of justice and a general balance of one hundred years of constitutional judicial review, see Cepeda, 2004a.
3. The pre-1991 scheme progressively lost support due to internal disadvantages, among which were: (1) the nondemocratic system of "co-option" (*cooptación*) by which supreme court justices were elected; (2) the imprecise definition of the supreme court's functions and its frequent conflicts of jurisdiction with other authorities; (3) the court's excessively formal approach to the interpretation and application of constitutional mandates. This was in addition to external factors, including; (4) the marked distance between the constitution and citizens' ordinary lives; (5) certain controversial decisions adopted by the supreme court (such as striking down two constitutional reforms and several "emergency powers" decrees); and (6) the weak protection granted by the overall system to human rights. Together, these factors contributed to creating a broad gap that separated the constitution and its system of judicial review from everyday social and political life, and eventually undermined the legitimacy of the system as a whole.

4. (a) Ex officio review was expanded to new types of norms, so as to include not only (i) decrees issued under any of the so-called "states of exception," but also (ii) all laws that approve international treaties, as well as the treaties themselves, which need to be adopted by congress and reviewed by the court before the executive can ratify them; (iii) statutory laws (laws that regulate specific matters enumerated in the constitution, such as fundamental rights, participation mechanisms, states of exception, the administration of justice, and other important topics deemed to be best protected through a statutory law's special adoption procedure), which must also be reviewed by the court before the president signs them; (iv) acts that summon a constituent assembly or a referendum to modify the constitution, which can only be reviewed with respect to their procedural validity; and (v) referendums carried out in relation to the approval or derogation of laws, as well as other democratic participation mechanisms such as national popular consultations and national plebiscites (the latter only with respect to their procedural validity). (b) The scope of application of the unconstitutional *actio popularis* was broadened, since it may now be filed, without formalities, by any citizen or by the public ombudsman (*Defensor del Pueblo*) against laws, constitutional amendments (with regard to their procedural validity), decrees issued by the government in exercise of delegated legislative powers, and pre-1991 laws that approve international treaties (post-1991 laws in the same sense are subject to automatic review by the court before their promulgation). Abstract review procedures allow for the participation of any citizen who wishes to support or oppose the claim, the *Procurador General de la Nación*, whose intervention is mandatory as part of her/his function as promoter of society's interests, and authorities who took part in the adoption of the norm subject to review—if they wish to do so. (c) In order to contextualize abstract judicial review of norms and bring it down to reality, the constitution enabled the court to seek and obtain any type of specialized information that may aid in the delivery of its judgments, including the possibilities of (i) requiring specialized technical or professional opinions; (ii) taking into account the opinion of the relevant ministries; and (iii) summoning public hearings to better assess the implications and the context of the decision at hand.

5. All judges can hear *tutela* cases. In other words, there is a constitutional jurisdiction that consists of judges and magistrates of all the different legal disciplines (criminal law, civil law, labor law, administrative law, etc.), at the head of which is the constitutional court.

6. *Actio popularis* is a legal action that can be initiated by any Colombian citizen—without legal counsel and without the necessity to show that he or she has a concrete interest in the outcome of the case. It covers both laws and decrees in abstract defense of the principles enshrined in the constitution. The possibility to initiate an *actio popularis* is considered a fundamental political right.

7. See, for example, Cepeda, 2004b.

8. Nevertheless, international schools and trends do bear an influence upon the Colombian system in three ways: they provide legal arguments, given that the court must interpret rights in accordance with international treaties on human rights; they increase the tension between economic liberalization measures—in response to economic globalization—and claims for the protection of employment/labor and environmental rights, in accordance with ILO covenants and international agreements on the protection of the environment; and they introduce a delicate dimension whenever cases under review are related to the drug trade and its repression, given the interest of the U.S. government in the matter. It is not clear quite what the weight of the international dimension will be with regard to cases pertaining to terrorism. In August 2004 the court declared the Anti-Terrorist Statute, approved at the end of 2003, null and void. The Statute, which would have allowed the military to arrest individuals, raid homes and offices, and intercept communications without judicial warrant, was widely criticised by international and domestic human rights organizations.

9. In two such cases, the beneficiaries of the constitutional court's judgment resorted to the Inter-American Court of Human Rights in 2003 with the goal of either obtaining enforcement of the judgment, or a declaration of Colombia's responsibility for disregarding the right to effective judicial remedies, as enshrined in the American Convention of Human Rights.

10. See, for example, Sánchez Botero, 1998, 2002.

11. The most notorious of these is the possibility of filing a *tutela* suit against private parties when they threaten or violate fundamental rights. According to the court's well-established doctrine, the *acción de tutela* may be used against private parties whenever (1) the plaintiff is in a position of subordination or defenselessness in relation to the private party against whom the claim is directed; (2) whenever such private parties seriously harm collective interests; or (3) whenever they are in charge of providing public services or utilities

12. Decision T–524 of 2000.

13. Decisions T–418 of 1999, T–333 of 1995 and T–233 of 1994.

14. Decision T–261 of 1995.

15. Decisions T–115 of 1997 and T–099 of 1998.

16. Decisions T–436 of 1995 and T–458 of 1995.

17. Decision C–776 of 2003.

18. See, inter alia, decision T–772 of 2003.

19. Decisions T–533 of 1992, T–401 of 1992, T–046 of 1997 and T–1330 of 2001, inter alia.

20. Decision T–426 of 1992.

21. See, among others, decisions SU–624 of 1999 and T–208 of 1996.

22. The court has, for example, placed limitations on the mandatory effect of its opinions for other judges. While the decision and its *ratio decidendi* are binding, the arguments that support the decision are not. It has also affirmed that, in principle, its *tutela* decisions have *inter partes*

effects, except when the Court explicitly ascribes *inter pares* or *inter communis* effects to its judgments. The court has also limited its own possibility of reviewing other judges' work in ordinary criminal, labor, civil, and administrative matters by striking down the provision by which *acción de tutela* could be filed against judicial decisions (Decision C–543 of 1992). The only exception to this rule is when these judicial decisions are opposed to the law in such a gross manner that they can only be considered "factual arbitrariness" and not "legal" pronouncements. In cases where unconstitutional *actio popularis* is filed against a law on the claim that it breaches the principle of equality, the court applies particularly strict requirements on the plaintiff's arguments— something that can be understood as a self-restricting mechanism. In addition, the court proceeds on a case-by-case basis, it does not adopt general solutions; it restricts the scope of its analysis to the specific laws or articles accused of unconstitutionality, without examining other parts of the same provision, and it only strikes down legal provisions when they cannot in any way be reconciled with the constitution.

23. Opinion poll published by the newspaper *El Tiempo* on July 23, 2003.
24. Ibid.

References

Cepeda, Manuel José (2004a) "La defensa judicial de la Constitución: Una tradición centenaria e ininterrumpida," in Fernando Cepeda Ulloa (ed.), *Fortalezas Institucionales de Colombia* (Bogotá: Ariel-BID), pp. 145–211.

———— (2004b) "Judicial Activism in a Violent Context: The Origin, Role, and Impact of the Colombian Constitutional Court," *Washington University Global Studies Law Review* (special issue), vol. 3 (2004), pp. 537–700.

Cuellar, María Mercedes (2000) *Colombia: Un proyecto inconcluso*, vol. 1 (Bogotá: Universidad Externado de Colombia).

Sánchez Botero, Esther (1998) *Justicia y pueblos indígenas de Colombia: La tutela como medio para la construcción del entendimiento intercultural* (Santafe de Bogotá: Universidad Nacional de Colombia).

———— (2002) *Diez años de ejercicio de la jurisdicción especial* (Bogotá: Procuraduría General de la Nación).

Chapter 5

The Judicialization of Chilean Politics: The Rights Revolution That Never Was

Javier A. Couso

Introduction

Ever since the arrest of General Augusto Pinochet by British authorities in October 1998—and the trial that followed it over the next two years—the judicialization of Chilean politics has been associated with this landmark case. Indeed, given the spectacular nature of the trial of one of the world's most notorious dictators in a procedure that seemed to inaugurate the era of universal jurisdiction in cases involving gross human rights violations, it is only natural that journalistic and academic attention has focused on the role of the Chilean courts in this case, as well as in others dealing with human rights violations perpetrated during the 17-year-long regime initiated with the military coup of 1973. As a result of this interest, there has been a considerable amount of research over the past few years that have addressed the origins, trajectory, and potential consequences of the Pinochet and related trials for the future of Chile's democratic system.[1]

In spite of its importance, however, the overwhelming interest in the judicial treatment of past human rights violations has overshadowed the study of the extent to which the Chilean courts have defended fundamental rights *during* the era of democratic transition. This is regrettable, because in the 14 years since the return to democratic rule, the courts have been increasingly asked to defend civil and political rights as well as social and economic ones—as in many other Latin American countries. In this chapter, I make an assessment of the response by the judiciary to such demands. First, I discuss the notion of the "judicialisation of politics," then I proceed to give a brief historical background to the political and legal context of post-authoritarian Chile. The chapter ends with a survey of the record of both the constitutional court and the regular judiciary in the area of free speech and nondiscrimination law under democratic rule.

Conceptualizing Judicialization

Before analyzing the role played by the Chilean courts in furthering human rights since the return of democracy, a basic conceptual issue that is commonly overlooked should be addressed: the meaning of the term "judicialisation of politics," the very subject of our inquiry. Because it is a rather equivocal concept, it needs to be defined. Efforts at conceptualizing this notion started during the early 1990s, with the now well-known rendering provided by Tate and Vallinder, for whom the concept of "judicialisation of politics" has two core meanings:

(a) The process by which courts and judges come to make or increasingly dominate the making of public policies that had previously been made (or, it is widely believed, ought to be made) by other governmental agencies, especially legislatures and executives; and

(b) The process by which nonjudicial negotiating and decision-making forums come to be dominated by quasi-judicial (legalistic) rules and procedures (Tate and Vallinder, 1995).

As can be seen from this classification, the conceptualization offered by Tate and Vallinder comprises two very different aspects that are worth distinguishing for analytical purposes. Thus, while the first alludes to court-led social change—typically exercised by high courts or specially created constitutional courts—the second refers to the process by which matters formerly negotiated in informal ways gradually begin to be governed by legal rules.

In this chapter, I use the first of Tate and Vallinder's definitions of this concept. This does not mean, of course, that in Chile there are not instances of the second form of judicialization, as identified by these authors. The reason for constraining the analysis to the former is simply because it is the one most likely to have an impact on the fundamental rights of individuals, and because it has more relevance for democratic consolidation. Moreover, this variant fits the paradigmatic example of the Supreme Court of the United States during the so-called Warren Court era, in which for the first time it engaged in judicial activism on behalf of the disadvantaged, in areas such as racial discrimination, the rights of criminal defendants, and freedom of speech, among others.[2]

From the point of view of the legal techniques involved in this variant of judicialization of politics, it is perhaps useful to recall that judicial policy-making and rights-creation is typically associated with the institution of judicial review of the constitutionality of laws, a concept that also requires careful definition.[3]

According to a classical definition introduced by Henry Abraham, judicial review consists in "the power of any court to hold unconstitutional and hence unenforceable any law, any official action based upon a law, and any other action by a public official that it deems . . . to be in conflict with the Basic Law" (Abraham, 1968, p. 283). Abrahams' definition can be complemented by adding that in some jurisdictions—such as France, Germany, and many Latin American countries—the power of constitutional judicial review lies not with "any courts," but with specially created constitutional courts. The significance of this mechanism is that it reallocates power from the elected branches of government to the judiciary, by giving the latter the privilege of authoritatively defining the meaning of the constitution (no matter what the other branches of government think). Through this veto power courts can block policy initiatives and, depending on the degree of leadership and activism of the courts, they can contribute to the development of policy initiatives that have been ignored by the political process.[4]

It is relevant to stress that for judicial review of the constitution to operate as a process of rights-creation or judicially led policy-making, it is necessary that the courts endowed with powers of constitutional review actually used them in an active way. This may sound self-evident, but the fact is that even though by the end of the twentieth century most nations had formally given judicial review powers to specially created constitutional courts or to the ordinary judiciary, the actual number of countries with an effective system of constitutional judicial review is significantly smaller than the number that have formally introduced it. As Holland puts it: "Judicial activism is a phenomenon distinct from judicial review. Judicial review is expressly provided for in Swedish and Japanese law, but the Supreme court of Sweden has never found a law of the *Riksdag* to be repugnant to the constitution" (Holland, 1991, p. 2). Indeed, in the same way that the number of states who actually enforce the individual rights recognized in their bills of rights is smaller than the number which formally recognize them, only a small portion of the courts with judicial review powers actually exercise them in an active way.

The complicating factor is that the very notion of "judicial activism" is itself elusive. For a start, most comparative courts scholars seem to agree that an "activist" constitutional court can be identified by the degree to which it goes further than a mere application of the constitution, venturing into policy-making. Thus, Holland argues that we can recognize judicial activism "when courts do not confine themselves to adjudicate legal conflicts but venture to make social policy ..." (Holland, 1991, p. 1). This creative jurisprudence would confer political power to the courts.[5] As a result, "the activism of a court ... can be measured by the degree of power that it exercises over citizens, the legislature, and the administration" (Holland, 1991, p. 1).

Another interesting approach for identifying judicial activism was introduced by Charles Epp, who in a comparative study of factors contributing to what he calls "rights revolutions," defines judicial activism as the process by which a constitutional court "creates or expands a host of new constitutional rights" (Epp, 1998, p. 2). This is a more demanding standard than Holland's, because it is conceivable that a court could make social policy without actually expanding the set of constitutional rights available to the people.

As this brief discussion suggests, there are a number of paths that can be followed when attempting to judge the degree of judicialization in a given country. In this chapter, I follow Charles Epp's understanding of this process in my examination of the degree to which the Chilean courts have actively engaged in the creation or expansion of rights through their powers of constitutional review.

The Political and Legal Background of the Transition to Democracy in Chile

In order to assess the degree to which Chilean politics has been judicialized since the return to democratic rule, it is useful first to provide a brief background to Chile's recent political and constitutional history, particularly with regard to changes in the legal system and the courts.

The Military Regime and the Constitution of 1980

Just days after the 1973 coup that interrupted decades of republican rule, the new military authorities organized a small commission entrusted with drafting a new constitution.[6] Some years later, in 1980, General Pinochet, who had by then consolidated his leadership, announced a plebiscite aimed at providing popular support for the new constitutional charter. Even though the latter was probably fraudulent, the new constitution was promulgated on March 11, 1981.

The Constitution of 1980 established a "new institutional order" (*nueva institucionalidad*) that was meant to be the formal expression of the foundational project in which the military regime had been engaged since 1973. The new charter aimed at ensuring that Chile would not return in the future to what Pinochet dismissively called a "*partidocracia*," by which he meant the demagogic capture of the state by the elites of political parties. As one observer put it: "The Constitution of 1980 thus embodied the ideals of a-politicism, technocratic efficiency, anti-communism and laissez-faire economics that the military regime of Pinochet had already been implementing" (Bauer, 1995, p. 9). The idea was to ensure the continuity of this project, while giving the regime a certain degree of legitimacy.

In order to make the constitution of 1980 enforceable in the future, subsequent to any return to democratic rule, the drafters introduced a variety of mechanisms of constitutional review. The resulting scheme is rather peculiar, since it contemplates a mixed or "disseminated" (Gómez, 1999, p. 93) system of control of the constitutionality of laws and administrative acts, characterized by a division of labor between a constitutional court (Tribunal Constitucional), in charge of the preventive control of the constitutionality of laws and executive decrees, and the high courts of the regular judiciary, which also have powers of review of the constitutionality of law through the so-called *recurso de inaplicabilidad* and the *recurso de protección*. Thus, while the constitutional court performs an "abstract" review of the constitutionality of legislation—that is, the review of bills approved by Congress but not yet promulgated—the regular judiciary performs a "concrete" review of already existing laws and executive decrees through the writs of *inaplicabilidad* and *protección*. In spite the intentions of the drafters, however, this system of constitutional review has some evident shortcomings. The first concerns the constitutional court's lack of jurisdiction with respect to the validity of already existing legislation, which is therefore immune to constitutional challenges. True, an individual affected by such preexisting legislation can always file an *inaplicabilidad* suit before the supreme court, but this is a bad remedy, given both the limited scope of this writ and the reluctance of the court to actually use it. Another problem with the constitutional court is that few actors are allowed to trigger its action. Indeed, the system does not permit the general public to object to the constitutionality of either a law or a presidential decree. The lack of what comparative legal doctrine labels "popular action" is a central feature of Chile's constitutional court, which, as we shall see further, has had important consequences.

The Courts During the Era of Democratic Transition

On March 11, 1990, Chile returned to democratic rule. After long years of authoritarianism, the country was returning to its republican past and to the civil and political freedoms that it had enjoyed in the previous half century. With regard to human rights policy, the issue was mostly framed as a question of how to handle "past human rights violations" (or what the literature now calls "transitional justice" issues), not so much how to deepen the reach of human rights in the future. Accordingly, most of the new coalition's human rights program dealt with the consequences of the violations perpetrated during the military regime. Having said this, a few concrete steps were taken by the new government regarding the future enforcement of human rights, such as the ratification of a number of international treaties furthering human rights protections;[7] the inclusion of human rights courses in the curricula of schools and law enforcement agencies; and the creation of a special unit within the Ministry of Foreign Relations (Lira and Loveman, 1999, p. 345).

The new president, former senator Patricio Aylwin, was an experienced politician who demonstrated great political skill in helping to consolidate a government coalition.[8] In his four-year term (1990–1994), Aylwin had to carefully navigate the tensest moments of Chile's transition to democracy, in particular those involving General Pinochet's quasi-subversive showdowns, which he repeatedly carried out in response to events he deemed hostile to himself or the military.[9] The first of such incidents took place in December 1990, in response to the government sponsored Truth and Reconciliation Commission, which was about to issue a report establishing the fate of the victims of the most serious human rights violations during the authoritarian era.[10] In addition to sponsoring the Truth and Reconciliation Commission, President Aylwin publicly requested the supreme court to end its refusal to investigate human rights cases that had been amnestied by the military in 1978.[11]

During those first years of the democratic transition, the judicial branch came under intense public criticism, both from the government and the opposition—for different reasons. In the case of the government, the core criticism was the passivity exhibited by the courts vis-à-vis the widespread human rights violations during the Pinochet years. In the case of the pro-military opposition, criticism of the judiciary spun from what they regarded as an inefficient and corrupt judiciary, which was thus utterly unsuited to the needs of a modern economy.[12] Confronted with such strong criticism of its performance during the military regime, the supreme court reacted by issuing a complete condemnation of the report of the Truth and Reconciliation Commission,[13] stating that it was "passionate, reckless, and biased,"[14] and arguing that the Commission had violated the separation of powers by its intromission in judicial matters (Correa, 1999, p. 302). President Aylwin rebuffed the court's response by going on national television and declaring that the Chilean courts "had shown a lack of moral courage in face of the vast human rights violations perpetrated by the military regime" (Correa, 1999, p. 303). The supreme court in turn reacted by accusing the government of undermining the judiciary's independence and endangering the rule of law. It defended its trajectory during the military regime by declaring that the mission of the courts was just to obey the existing law, not judge the justice or injustice of it, which, in the case of its action under the authoritarian regime meant that they limited themselves to applying laws that made it impossible for the courts to defend human rights (Matus, 1999, p. 61). In the case of the criticism mounted by the right-wing opposition, this was an expression of a technocratic concern, rather than a humanist one, which viewed the Chilean courts as an obstacle to the development of a modern economy. From this viewpoint, the courts were slow, corrupted, and unable to adjudicate properly the complex legal conflicts arising from a sophisticated economic model. Thus, a complete overhaul of the judiciary was required.[15]

The combined criticism of the courts by the entire political party spectrum led to a sense of political fragility within the judiciary. In Jorge Correa's words:

> The decade of the 1990s thus started with a Judicial Branch that was in the worst of worlds. It did not have the democratic legitimacy that the new government authorities wanted for all state institutions, nor the (technocratic) aura of modernity of other state institutions. The right wing, although it considered the Supreme Court one of the core enclaves for the defense of the new institutionality, regarded it as an organ incapable of modernising itself. Particularly within entrepreneurial circles, the judicial branch was perceived as inadequate for for the resolution of their disputes. The "Concertación" (government coalition), for its part, regarded the judicial branch as an entity whose behavior before human rights violations had demonstrated its lack of adherence to the democratic system. (Correa, 1999, p. 292, my translation)

The national consensus on the need to reform the judiciary eventually persuaded the government to send to congress a set of reforms which included, among other things, the creation of a National Judicial Council in charge of the administration of the judiciary; a bill increasing the number of justices of the supreme court from 17 to 21; and the creation of a National School of Magistrates, in charge of the training of judges. The supreme court's reaction to the reform package was, predictably, negative. Although it recognized that there were some problems of delay in the courts, it took issue with the accusation of widespread corruption among judicial personnel, and strongly opposed the introduction of a National Council for the Judiciary, declaring that it posed the risk of politicizing the courts.[16] The general sense that the Chilean courts had become more corrupt during the authoritarian years eventually led to a series of constitutional impeachment procedures filed by congress against justices of the supreme court throughout the decade. The first such incident was in fact promoted by a coalition of senators from both the government and the opposition—in December 1992—and resulted in the removal of one justice.[17]

A final aspect of the government-judiciary relationship during this period which is worth mentioning was the gradual change in the membership at the top of the judicial hierarchy. The three consecutive presidents of the Christian Democratic-Socialist coalition have appointed more than half of the current members of Chile's high courts.

The "Pinochet Case" and Its Aftermath

No account of the judicialization of politics in Chile during the post-authoritarian period can be rendered without at least a mention of the prosecution of Augusto Pinochet. Given the vast literature available on this topic, and because the focus of this work is the judicial treatment of fundamental rights since the return to democracy, this section addresses only the most salient features of the Pinochet case.

The case began in the most unexpected way, when the British authorities arrested the former dictator in October of 1998. Before that, Pinochet had remained almost untouched by lawsuits.[18] Thanks to his arrest—and the year and a half of house arrest and legal proceedings which followed—the social and political dynamic in Chile concerning the former ruler changed dramatically. The critical moment came when the British government—on grounds of the general's incapacity to face trial due to his frail health—released him. Upon his arrival in Santiago (in March 2000), the government was immediately reminded of its constant statements during the previous eighteen months, calling for Chile's sovereign courts to try Pinochet. In the meantime, human rights groups and relatives of the victims had filed over a hundred criminal cases against him. This led to the loss of his senatorial immunity and his subsequent indictment, which in turn forced the defense team to resort to the humiliating excuse that Pinochet was "insane," since that is the only way to suspend a criminal procedure in Chilean penal law.

The new political context opened up by the prosecution of General Pinochet contributed to a number of important developments concerning past human rights violations. First, there was the introduction of a special instance of dialogue between the government, human rights lawyers, and representatives of the armed forces (in what was known as the Mesa de Diálogo) which led to a number of initiatives, such as the introduction of judges with the exclusive task of finding the bodies of the disappeared, the recognition by the Chilean armed forces of the legitimacy of the Truth and Reconciliation Commission Report, and the formal recognition by the Commander in Chief of the Army of the unacceptable nature of the human rights violations perpetrated during the military regime.

Of all the events just described, the most important was the introduction of the "exclusive judges," whose dedicated work eventually led to the discovery of the remains of many people listed as disappeared, and the prosecution of scores of members of the armed forces. At the time of writing, there were hundreds of cases dealing with the human rights violations of the authoritarian regime of General Pinochet pending, with dozens of military men under arrest. In these cases, the courts have interpreted the Amnesty Law of 1978 in agreement with the changing interpretation suggested years before by President Aylwin, but the Chilean Supreme Court is yet to rule on the issue.

Constitutional Review of Fundamental Rights in Post-Authoritarian Chile

Coming back to Charles Epp's notion of judicial activism, we now turn to evaluate whether or not the Chilean courts have actually "expanded or created a host of constitutional rights," in the years since the return to democracy. At this point, it is important to bear in mind that although the country has a reasonably good human rights record in this period, there are a number of areas in which both the government and the legislature have failed to live up to the constitution and the international human rights treaties that are now part of Chile's domestic law. Another element worth considering is that, over the last decade, the country has consolidated the kind of support structures that Epp considers necessary for a "rights revolution" to emerge; that is, a network of nongovernmental groups able to mobilize social groups and provide them with lawyers to advise them in court. Indeed, on top of the traditional human rights groups that had originated during the military regime, a variety of new groups emerged, including nongovernmental organizations committed to the advancement of the rights of women, children, sexual minorities, AIDS patients, and indigenous peoples. Furthermore, by the mid-1990s, a critical mass of lawyers familiar with human rights law and the techniques of public interest litigation had also emerged.[19] Finally, thanks to changes in the regional human rights scene (the Inter-American Human Rights Commission and the Court started to make itself more accessible to requests from the different countries of the continent), Chilean public interest lawyers and activists joined a Latin American network of human rights groups that started to meet regularly to exchange experiences in their litigation strategies.[20]

Given the above, and taking into consideration that Chile is among those Latin American nations where the rule of law is most consolidated, one would have expected the courts to be assertive in the defense and expansion of individual rights. This, however, has not been the case. To the contrary, the Chilean courts have by and large refused to actively use their constitutional powers of review to enhance individual rights. In the following section, we see examples of the rather disappointing record exhibited both by the Chilean Constitutional Court and the regular judiciary with respect to a crucial subset of the domain of civil and political human rights law: free speech and equal protection.

The Constitutional Court's Record

As explained in the section describing the different mechanisms of control of the constitutionality of law existing in Chile, the constitutional court is in charge of the abstract and a priori review of legislation. While review of the so-called "organic laws"—regulating fundamental rights, the organization of the state bureaucracy, and others—is mandatory, in the case of regular legislation the court can only act if the president or at least a portion of the senate or the Chamber of Deputies formally asks for its intervention.

Due to the fact that during the last stage of the dictatorship the constitutional court rendered a couple of decisions that were critical for the end to the military regime,[21] many expected that it would play a major role in the transition to democracy. During the more than 14 years working under democratic rule, however, the court has been largely passive, usually deferring to the legislature's judgment concerning the constitutionality of the laws it passes. Indeed, there is widespread agreement among constitutional scholars that this body has not been a significant source of rights-enhancing jurisprudence, limiting itself to a rather formalistic, mechanical analysis of the constitutionality of the law projects it has reviewed (Gómez, 1999). This conclusion is supported by the experience of those who have the most to fear from an activist constitutional court, that is, those holding executive power.[22] Indeed, as I have reported elsewhere, the first two presidents of the democratic era—Aylwin and Frei, whose administrations covered the first ten years of transition to democracy—candidly recognize that the constitutional court did not represent an obstacle to their respective legislative agendas.[23]

This perception is confirmed by the disappointing record exhibited by the court during the last 14 years. Indeed, instead of developing a jurisprudence that enhances fundamental human rights, it has restricted itself to the rather insubstantial role of objecting to minor technical deficiencies of the legislation it reviews. For this reason—as opposed to the case of say, the Costa Rican Sala IV—the Chilean Tribunal Constitucional remains largely unknown by most of the population. Another indicator of its political insignificance is the peculiar way in which the members of the constitutional courts perform their duty; that is, as a part-time position, which they complement with the practice of other types of law before the regular judiciary.

From a structural point of view, no doubt the fact that the court cannot accept constitutional lawsuits brought by ordinary citizens, combined with the impossibility of reviewing existing legislation, accounts at least in part for the relative obscurity of the Tribunal in the eyes of the public. Having said this, it is important to point out that the very jurisprudence of the constitutional court has contributed to its diminished status. Indeed, as a long-time observer and supporter of the Court, Patricio Zapata, has put it:

> In the majority of the decisions [of the Tribunal], can be recognised a very healthy disposition to respect the domain of the democratically elected bodies. This moderation—or "deference"—constitutes another valuable aspect of the jurisprudence of the Chilean constitutional court. With the adoption of this policy of deference, the court has distanced itself from approaches that confuse constitutional [adjudication] with a form of government . . . , and from those who would like to substitute enlightened judicial despotism for democratic deliberation. (Zapata, 2002, p. 159, my translation)

In this passage, this supporter of the constitutional court's performance reiterates a traditional discourse hostile to judicial activism in constitutional adjudication which—although common among many Chilean lawyers—is incompatible with even a modest degree of "rights revolution." After this laudatory comment, Zapata then explains that the courts' deference to the democratically elected branches of government was developed over a series of decisions passed during the democratic transition. In one of these, *Convenio Sobre Pueblos Indígenas*,[24] the constitutional court specifically stated that: "Laws approved by the elected branches of the state are to be presumed valid and legitimate. Therefore, it is only possible to declare their unconstitutionality when the reviewers arrive at the intimate conviction that the incompatibility between law and the Constitution is patent, so that it is impossible to harmonise the two of them. . ." (Zapata, 2002, p. 82, my translation).

The judicial restraint that the "principle of deference" entails is supplemented with another jurisprudential creation of the court that further restricts the scope of its role; namely, the "principle of legislative autonomy," which states that the latter cannot rule on the policy implicit in the proposed legislation that comes under its review (Zapata, 2002, pp. 72–73). This principle, first established toward the end of the authoritarian period in the *Partidos Políticos* decision,[25] have been confirmed by the court over the 14 years of democratic transition, particularly in the cases *Municipalidades III* (1992),[26] and *DFL 192 Sobre Riesgos del Trabajo y Enfermedades Profesionales* (1996).[27]

Another illustration of the deferential stance exhibited by the constitutional court in the post-authoritarian era is Decision No. 332, issued on July 17, 2001. This case involved the review of a bill passed to allow one of Chile's main political parties, the Christian Democrats (of the ruling coalition), to register its candidates for a congressional election due later that year. As it turned out, the party had made a gross bureaucratic mistake in the registration of its candidates, leaving it with less than 10 percent of the intended number of candidates. The next day, one of the opposition parties, the Democratic Union Party (UDI), agreed with the government to approve special legislation extending the deadline retroactively, thus allowing the Christian Democrats to register again, arguing that it would be bad for the political system to have an election without the participation of one of the main political parties (the Christian Democrats usually take between 18 and 27 percent of the vote in national elections). Although constitutional experts and members of the other opposition party, National Renovation (RN), had strong constitutional objections to this ad hoc legislation, the bill was approved by congress that afternoon and sent to the constitutional court that same night. Then, within hours of receiving the bill for review, the court unanimously approved the bill,[28] with almost no discussion of the constitutional objections raised by scholars and one of its own members.[29] This case is significant, because it shows the extent to which the Court is willing to please the political branches in dealing with the review of politically sensitive legislation.

The Regular Judiciary's Record

Chile's peculiar institutional design includes a two-tier system in which the Tribunal Constitucional shares its role as guardian of the constitution with the superior courts of the regular judiciary, which are in charge of protecting fundamental rights when they are violated by existing legislation. This subset of constitutional jurisprudence is critical, because the country still has substantial areas of law that are in conflict with the charter of rights included in the constitution of 1980 and the international human rights treaties ratified by Chile.

This background, and the fact that the regular judiciary is endowed with powerful mechanisms for review of the constitution—in particular the so-called *recurso de protección*—created great expectations among human rights activists and academic observers of the possibility of a judicially triggered "rights revolution."[30] As in the case of the constitutional court, however, the record of the regular judiciary over the last 14 years of democratic rule is also extremely unsatisfactory.

The first domain in which the courts failed to perform an assertive defense of individual rights against government and legislative encroachment, is freedom of speech. Indeed, although strictly political speech is rarely suppressed (i.e., political campaigns), artistic and journalistic discourse are often censored or penalized on grounds of obscenity or defamation. Accordingly, scores of both artistic and journalistic works have been censored over the last decade, which led Human Rights Watch to declare that "although Chile lives under a democratic regime and under a rule of law system . . . the right to free speech is under severe restrictions not found in any other Western democracy" (Human Rights Watch, 1998, p. 4).

The list of cases involving a violation of freedom of speech over the last 14 years is large. The most prominent are:[31]

Luksic v. Martorell/Editorial Planeta *(1993)*

This case involved the censorship of a journalistic book reporting on sexual scandals of Argentinean diplomats and Chilean politicians and entrepreneurs. One of the most prominent businessmen mentioned in the book, Andrónico Luksic, member of the wealthiest family in the country, filed a *protección* suit asking the Santiago Court of Appeals to prevent the publication of the book because it was libelous. The court granted relief for Luksic, issuing a judicial order that prevented the publication of the book in what amounts to nothing short of judicial censorship of journalistic speech.

Chamber of Deputies v. Francisco Javier Cuadra *(1995)*

This case involved another libel suit, filed by the Chamber of Deputies against a politician who denounced in an interview to a newspaper, the existence of drug consumption among some congressmen whom he did not mention by name. The legislative body, incensed by the accusation, requested Mr. Cuadra to provide the names or face legal consequences. Because the Chilean criminal code requires the naming of a person in a libel case, the Chamber of Deputies accused Cuadra of having violated a statute inherited from the dictatorship, the Internal State Security Law, which criminalizes offences against "the public order," which presumably had been the case with his accusations.[32] Eventually the case ended up in the supreme court, which confirmed Cuadra's conviction. This led Cuadra to take his case to the Inter-American Human Rights Court, which condemned the Chilean state.

The Last Temptation of Christ *(1996–1997)*

This was a case in which a Chilean Catholic fundamentalist group asked the Santiago Court of Appeals to ban the showing of this film by Martin Scorsese—which had already been approved by a government agency—on the grounds that it offended the mostly Catholic population of the country. The decision was to grant relief to the plaintiffs, and was later confirmed by the supreme court. Again, this clear violation of free speech led to a condemnation of the Chilean state by the Inter-American Human Rights Court.

Libro Negro de la Justicia Chilena *(1999)*

In what amounts to a confirmation of its previous record of privileging the protection of honor over free speech, in this case the supreme court banned the publication of a journalistic book dealing with corruption in the judiciary. The action was in response to a request by a member of the supreme court who was mentioned in the book as a corrupt judge. The author of the book, Alejandra Matus, took asylum in the United States, fearing prison. She appealed the decision before the Inter-American Human Rights Court.

Cecilia: La vida en llamas *(2002–2003)*

This case[33] involved a non-authorized biography of a singer who had been famous in the 1960s. The book documented her struggle against alcohol and drug addiction, and her lesbian inclination. The singer filed a suit asking a lower court to prevent the publication of the book, which it did. This was later confirmed by the Santiago Court of Appeals. This time, however, the book was eventually allowed to be published, once the court was informed that the case was going to be heard by the Inter-American Human Rights system.

The most shocking aspect of all these episodes of censorship, is that they were not ordered by the government, but by the courts themselves. Thus, instead of protecting the right to free speech against governmental or legislative encroachment, the courts have been the perpetrators of its violation. Confronted with criticism by jurists and human rights activists, the judiciary has insisted on the argument that they are merely applying laws that give preeminence to the protection of honor over speech, and that if the law is bad, the political branches ought to change it. Of course, this is a completely disingenuous answer, since constitutional "law" allows the courts to protect fundamental rights against laws that violate them.

Whereas the Chilean courts' jurisprudence in the domain of freedom of speech is nothing short of scandalous, the situation in the area of nondiscrimination—although somewhat better—is still poor. The following cases illustrate the reaction of the regular judiciary to violations of the constitutional clause guaranteeing equal protection:

Discrimination of Disabled Passengers in Airline *(1999)*
This case involved a blind passenger who was denied access to an international flight because she was flying alone, in violation of airline policy that requested blind passengers to travel accompanied by another person or a trained dog. The court of appeals dismissed the *protección* suit on the grounds that there was no violation of the nondiscrimination clause of the constitution, because the conflict involved a relation between two private parties. It also decided that international antidiscrimination law was not applicable to the situation in question. The supreme court confirmed the decision without much commentary.[34]

HIV Patients I *(2000)*
This case involved a *protección* suit against the Ministry of Health, for failing to provide medical treatment to a group of HIV patients. The plaintiffs asked the court of appeals of Santiago to order the ministry to provide them with the same therapy that was been given to other HIV patients (the ministry had denied the plaintiffs the best available therapy, arguing that it lacked enough economic resources for providing it to all Chilean HIV patients).[35] According to the lawsuit, denying the treatment to the petitioners constituted a violation of the right to life and equal protection. The court of appeals ruled against the plaintiffs,

arguing that the law governing the public provision of health care (Law No. 2763 of 1979), prescribed that "the Ministry of Health would provide health care in accordance with the resources it has at its disposition," and that the lack of economic resources cited by the ministry as the explanation for failing to provide the best available treatment to the petitioners was reasonable, therefore it did not violate their right to life and equal protection. This decision was later confirmed by the supreme court, which did not provide any justification for its ruling.

HIV Patients II *(2001)*

The following year, three patients in a more critical condition than the ones who had filed the suit the previous year, sued the Ministry of Health for the same reason. This time, the court of appeals of Santiago ruled in favor of the petitioners, ordering the ministry to provide them immediately with the best available treatment. Later, the supreme court reversed the ruling, arguing that the ministry had acted in accordance with the law. At any rate, the patients were ultimately successful, because the Ministry decided on its own to provide treatment to the plaintiffs after all.

Equal Access for the Disabled Case *(2003)*

This case involved a suit on behalf of people living with physical disabilities against the Ministry of Public Works and Transportation, for failing to enforce legislation providing for the construction of disabled-friendly access to public buildings. The court of appeals dismissed the case, declaring that "the government has future plans for helping the disabled . . . and it is not clear that there is here a violation of the right to non-discrimination against the disabled, since there is no intention by the authorities to discriminate against them . . . ." The supreme court confirmed the ruling.

Singh v. Almacenes París *(2003)*

This case started when a big retail store in Santiago published an advertisement in a local newspaper offering a position to a "twenty-six year old male." Maria Teresa Singh, a woman of 46, felt that the advertisement discriminated against her on the grounds of her gender and age. After filing a *recurso de protection* against the store, the court of appeals dismissed the case without much explanation. When the case was appealed to the supreme court, the decision was confirmed, rejecting the petitioner's claim on the ground that "the fact that the store returned the application material to the petitioner, does not in itself show a discriminatory intent against Ms. Singh." The case is now before the Inter-American Court of Justice.

Judge Atala Case *(2003–2004)*

This case, which eventually became the centre of national controversy, involved a lesbian judge who lost custody of her two daughters on the ground that she was unfit to take care of them, because of her sexual condition. The case began when Judge Atala's former husband filed a custody suit when he heard that Atala's partner had moved in to live with her. Arguing that it would set a bad example for the girls, he eventually obtained the support of the supreme court, which ruled that it was in the best interest of the children that they live with their father and not with their lesbian mother.

Venusterio Case *(2001)*

This case involved the denial of conjugal visits to women serving preventive detention in a national correctional facility. Given that this represented a discriminatory treatment vis-à-vis other inmates at the same prison—women already sentenced were allowed to meet their husbands—a group of inmates under preventive detention filed a *protección* suit against the correctional authorities. The court of appeals dismissed the case on a technicality, and the supreme court did not accept the appeal.

As it can be appreciated from these decisions, the response of the regular judiciary in the domain of free speech and nondiscrimination is highly unsatisfactory, to say the least. Even after the end of authoritarian rule, the Chilean judiciary has been remarkably passive about—if not actively contributing to—violations of those fundamental rights. Such denial of judicial redress is also apparent in what the courts have not done against statutes in blatant violation of the constitution. Indeed, to this day the Mapuche movement—made up of members of the country's most important indigenous population—is repressed by the government with the help of antiterrorist legislation that should have been declared unconstitutional a long time ago, both because it is applied to social protest which does not amount to terrorism,[36] and because it allows the government to violate due process guarantees.[37] The judiciary has so far been silent on this issue. Another example of judicial deference to statutory law and the political branches was the decades long inaction on behalf of the Chilean courts with regard to the legal discrimination against children born out of wedlock, who for decades had far less rights than "legitimate" children. This situation lasted until a new law was passed (Atria, 2000, p. 372).

All the cases of deference to statutory law described in this chapter represent instances of a clear pattern of behavior exhibited by the judiciary over the last 14 years: courts have never expanded—let alone created new—constitutional rights. In Chile, constitutional rights have so far been implemented or expanded only when both the legislative and executive branches agree to do so, not as a result of the constitutional jurisprudence of either the constitutional court or the regular judiciary.[38]

This pattern of judicial behavior is also apparent when examining the single most important human rights advancement of Chile's post-authoritarian period: the modernization of its criminal procedures code. This reform, which replaced an archaic system which did not protect even the most basic due process guarantees, was brought about by the executive's will to modernize the nation's criminal procedures code, not by anything done by the courts, which never once questioned the constitutionality of the old code.

The passivity of the courts can also be linked to the existing "legal culture" in Chile. The Chilean judicial system represents an extreme version of the continental European model of a judicial bureaucracy organized in a highly hierarchical and bureaucratic fashion. It is composed of judges whose careers start when they are just out of law school, and who then slowly become socialized as professionals over the many years it takes for them to gain promotion to the top ranks of the court system. Their socialization as judges is heavily shaped by the emulation of their superiors, since career advancement within the judiciary crucially depends on the annual evaluations of the lower courts by the superior courts. Furthermore, because judges can spend several decades in the judiciary before reaching the superior echelons of the judicial bureaucracy, by the time they "arrive," most of them have become accustomed to the traditional understanding of the role of the judiciary, which is averse to politically controversial cases.

There are other elements that contribute to the disciplined behavior showed by the lower courts in following the deferential attitude of the superior courts. One is a legal education which stresses a formalist interpretation of the law. Another is the strong corporate identity of the Chilean judiciary, which partly comes from the socialization process described above, but also from the judges' isolation from other social forces. Thus, most judges share the traditional notion that the judiciary should not be involved in "political" matters, and that it should remain as far removed as possible from political debates.

All this suggests that the Chilean regular courts still operate as if constitutional law is not "real" law. They do their work of enforcing the legality of administrative action—often better than most other Latin American countries—but are almost always deferential when a law violates the constitution.

Conclusions

Interest in the judicialization of politics in Latin America is often linked to the expectation that courts will contribute to the consolidation of the rule of law and deepen the processes of democratization in the countries of the region. Thus, many hope that the courts will bring about the respect for fundamental rights and the political accountability that the "regular" political system has been unable to provide. The case of Chile represents a peculiar case from such a perspective, because, although it is often held up as one of the most successful cases of democratic consolidation in Latin America, it has shown a very low degree of judicialization of politics.

Although the Chilean judiciary performs relatively well in protecting the legal rights of the population vis-à-vis executive action—checking the *legality* of executive action—it has shown almost no willingness to check the *constitutionality* of law, let alone to expand or create new constitutional rights, as Charles Epp's definition of judicial activism would have it. In fact, the reluctance of the Chilean courts to actively engage in rights protection is paradoxical, given that other Latin American judiciaries with far less support structures and judicial independence have been far more activist (although this has effectively put many of them out of business).

Confronted with the rather anomalous case of Chile, some scholars have blamed judicial deference to the political branches on the illiberal nature of its judges (Hilbink, 1999, Chapter 8). Others have blamed this passivity on the corporatist and self-centered nature of the Chilean courts, which avoid entering into politically charged domains from fear of intervention by other the branches of government if they actively use their powers of constitutional review (Couso, 2003; Peña, 1996). Finally, there are those who blame judicial deference to statutory law on the private law mind-set of Chile's constitutional judges, hoping that when a sufficient number of young judges make it to the highest positions in the judicial hierarchy, the situation will change (González, 2004). From this point of view, only then would the judicialization of Chilean politics become a reality.

The correct answer is probably a combination of all of the above, plus elements that still elude us. What is clear, however, is that the jurisprudential record exhibited over the last decade and a half by the Chilean courts in the domain of constitutional adjudication, can only be characterized as a "rights revolution" that never happened.

Notes

1. See Burbach, 2004; Davis, 2003; Brody and Ratner, 2000; and Woodhouse, 2000.
2. It represents what Lucas Powe calls the "history's Warren Court," that is, the U.S. Supreme Court during the period from 1962 to 1968. This was when the myth of a court at the service of the marginalized groups arose, due to its defense of the rights of the poor, the politically disenfranchised, and the criminally accused. See Lucas Powe's excellent history of the subject (Powe, 2000).
3. In attempting a definition of this concept, I hope to avoid a common vice noted by Theodore Becker: "Definitions of judicial review float about like so much flotsam. As is par for any course in academe, each definition is fitted to the eccentric purposes of the individual definer. So it is here" (Becker, 1987, p. 204).
4. See McCann, 1994.
5. Note the role that interpretive creativity plays in Holland's approach to judicial activism. In his view, for a constitutional court to be "activist," it has to make use of a non-positivistic approach to constitutional adjudication. He also makes the point that there are countries—for example Germanay—where judges object to judicial activism, considering it a pejorative referring to a judge who engages in social engineering (Holland, 1991, p. 1).
6. The drafting body, called Comisión de Estudios de la Nueva Constitución Política del Estado, was set up through Decree no. 1064, of September 24, 1973. It stated: "There is a need for a new Constitution in order to reconstruct, renew, and improve the fundamental institutional order of the Republic" (Huneeus, 2000, p. 231).
7. Chile ratified the American Convention on Human Rights (or Pacto de San José), the United Nations Protocol on the Pact on Civil and Political Rights, and the Additional Protocols I and II to the Geneva Convention (Lira and Loveman, 1999, p. 346).
8. For a good analysis of the process of creation of the Christian Democratic and Socialist coalition, see Huneeus, 2000.
9. For an account of these incidents, see Cavallo, 1998, pp. 76–85 and Lira and Loveman, 2000, pp. 531–39.
10. See Comisión Nacional de Verdad y Reconciliación, 1991.
11. In August of 1990, the supreme court, sitting en bloc, had confirmed the constitutionality of the 1978 Amnesty Law by an 11–4 vote (Lira and Loveman, 2000, p. 498).
12. This account follows closely Jorge Correa's argument (Correa, 1999, p. 302). Within the opposition, the most vocal critic of the judiciary's performance and outdated practices was the Centro de Estudios Públicos, a moderate right-wing think tank that in 1991 published a book calling for the modernization of the Chilean judiciary. See Centro de Estudios Públicos, 1991.
13. Corte Suprema, "Respuesta de la Corte Suprema al Informe de la Comisión de Verdad y Reconciliación."

14. From the text of the Supreme Court's response to the Rettig Commission Report, issued on May 17, 1991, quoted in Matus, 1999, p. 59.

15. This was a criticism shared by the Centro de Estudios Públicos, close to one of Chile's most important entrepreneurial groups.

16. The proposed council would have taken away from the supreme court the annual evaluation of judicial personnel and the preparation of the list from which the president nominates new judges (Cavallo, 1998, p. 41).

17. The impeached justices were Hernán Cereceda, Lionel Beraud, Germán Valenzuela, and Fernando Torres Silva. Of these, only Cereceda was eventually expelled from the Supreme Court by the Senate (Lira and Loveman, 1999, p. 359).

18. Although Lira and Loveman report that before the detention there had been a handful of cases filed against Pinochet—including one by the head of the communist party and widow of a disappeared man, Gladys Marín—the fact is that those cases were inactive at the time of his arrest in London (Lira and Loveman, 1999, p. 368).

19. The Human Rights Clinic of the Faculty of Law at the Universidad Diego Portales and FORJA (Formación Jurídica para la Acción) are the most prominent ones.

20. This network, which started in 1995, gathers law schools and NGOs from all Latin America. These are, in Argentina: the University of Buenos Aires/CELS (Centro de Estudios Legales y Sociales); the University of Palermo; the National University of Comahue; CEDA (Center of Studies of Environmental Law) in Córdoba; and the National University of Tucumán. In Chile: Diego Portales University and the Catholic University of Temuco. In Peru: the Catholic University of Lima; the National University of San Agustín in Arequipa; and the National University San Antonio Abad in Cusco. In Colombia: the University of Rosario; the University of Los Andes; and the University of Medellín. In Ecuador: the University of San Francisco in Quito. Lastly, in México: the Instituto Tecnológico Autónomo of México (ITAM); CIDE; and the Iberoamericana University.

21. Particularly a decision ruling that the plebiscite of 1988 was to be held under the oversight of an Electoral Court.

22. This is because in Chile's highly presidential regime, the executive has enormous legislative powers.

23. In the case of former President Aylwin, asked whether the constitutional tribunal had been an obstacle to the policies of his administration, he said: "I was at first concerned about the role that the 'Tribunal Constitucional' could play, because most of the justices were from the opposition to our government and therefore I expected that this would mean that we would lose in cases of constitutional conflict. This, however, did not turn out to be the case. Indeed, to be frank with you, although the membership of the 'Tribunal' did not satisfy us, I, as the President of the Republic, never experienced it as a significant

obstacle to the central tenets of our political program." Aylwin's experience was echoed by his successor, President Eduardo Frei (1994–2000), who also expressed his satisfaction with the relatively easy way in which his government was able to handle the constitutional complaints presented by the opposition. He reported: "In general terms, our experience with the Constitutional Tribunal was very positive. We did serious work in our responses to the complaints presented to the Tribunal, and I am happy to say that of the 10 or 12 really important cases it decided during my administration, we prevailed in almost all of them. This great rate of success was possible, first because we were constitutionally right, and second, because we presented thorough, well-thought defenses" (Couso, 2003, p. 77).

24. Decision No. 309, issued August 4, 2000.
25. Decision No. 43, issued February 24, 1987.
26. Decision No. 141, issued February 12, 1992.
27. Decision No. 231, issued March 18, 1996.
28. The haste of the constitutional court was astonishing. This is apparent just by reading the ruling, which is dated July 17, 2001, and which starts with the following sentence: "The Chamber of Deputies has sent this Court the note number 3.428, of July 17th 2001, informing the approval of an amendment of the law of popular elections for its review . . ." See Decision No. 332 of the Chilean constitutional court.
29. The justice, Luz Bulnes, in the end joined the rest of the court in a unanimous decision.
30. The *recurso de protección* is an injunction-type writ of a constitutional character, which allows any person whose constitutional rights have been violated to go directly to a court of appeals and sue the government or any other perpetrator of a human rights violation. It was first introduced in the 1980 constitution, and Chilean jurists and practicing lawyers at first thought the courts would use it in a highly activist way to police constitutional rights. This has not been the case, however, as the rest of this paper indicates.
31. I follow Lisa Hilbink's account here. See Hilbink, 1999, p. 528.
32. The State Security Law, No. 12.927, grants special protection to state authorities' honor, sanctioning with higher penalties libelous or defamatory acts against them.
33. The case is numbered 63.135–2002.
34. For a detailed account of this case, see Cisternas, 2001, p. 36.
35. The ministry had given the best available treatment to only 2000 patients, leaving behind 1,500.
36. This group of rather desperate and marginalized indigenous people have expressed their frustration with chronic destitution and discrimination in public demonstrations that occasionally end in street disorders and destruction of public signs and the like. In the most serious cases there has also been destruction of private property. However, although reprehensible, this behavior does not come even close to terrorism.

37. For a good account of the government's response to the protest of the Mapuche movement, see Facultad de Derecho de la Universidad Diego Portales, 2003.
38. This deference to the legislative and executive branches of government and lack of judicial activism in the Chilean courts is evident also in the field of past human rights violations. In fact, the courts were remarkably "inactive" in dealing with the human rights abuses of the military dictatorship until the executive explicitly asked the courts to change this policy (in a famous letter to the supreme court written by President Aylwin). Also, it was only after the arrest of General Pinochet in London and the Chilean government's declaration that he should be allowed to come back "to be tried by the Chilean courts" that the courts felt free to become "active" in this area. In conclusion, to regard the jurisprudence of the Chilean courts in matters of past human rights violations as an example of judicial "activism," is not an accurate description. In fact the opposite is true, since the eventual shift of the Chilean courts to start prosecuting human rights violators is most accurately seen as a result of deference to the government, rather than of judicial activism.

References

Abraham, Henry (1968) *The Judicial Process: An Introductory Analysis of the Courts of the United States, England, and France* (New York: Oxford University Press).

Atria, Fernando, "Revisión judicial: El síndrome de la víctima insatisfecha," *Estudios Públicos*, no. 79 (2000), pp. 347–402.

Bauer, Carl, "The Contradictory Role of the Judiciary in Chile's Neoliberal Economic Model" (Paper presented at the First Congress of the Latin American and Caribbean Association of Law and Economics, Mexico City, February 2–3, 1995).

Becker, Theodore (1987) *Comparative Judicial Politics: The Political Functioning of Courts* (Washington, DC: University Press of America).

Brody, Reed and Michael Ratner (eds.) (2000) *The Pinochet Papers: The Case of Augusto Pinochet in Spain and Britain* (Leiden, Holland: Martinus Nijhoff).

Burbach, Roger (2004) *The Pinochet Affair: State Terrorism and Global Justice* (London: Zed Books).

Cavallo, Ascanio (1998) *La historia oculta de la transición: Memoria de una época, 1990–1998* (Santiago, Chile: Editorial Grijalbo).

Centro de Estudios Públicos (1991) *Proposiciones para la reforma judicial* (Santiago, Chile: Centro de Estudios Públicos).

Cisternas, María Soledad (2001) "La discapacidad en Chile: Un tema de proyección urgente," in Felipe González (ed.), *Discriminación e Interés Público* (Santiago, Chile: Cuadernos de Análisis Jurídico de la Facultad de Derecho, Universidad Diego Portales), pp. 9–63.

Comisión Nacional de Verdad y Reconciliación (1991) *Informe*. In translation by Phillip E. Berryman (1993) (Notre Dame: University of Notre Dame Press).

Correa, Jorge (1999) "La Cenicienta se queda en la fiesta: El poder judicial chileno en la década de los 90," in Paul Drake and Iván Jaksic (eds.), *El modelo chileno: Democracia y desarrollo en los noventa* (Santiago, Chile: LOM Ediciones), pp. 281–315.

Corte Suprema, "Respuesta de la Corte Suprema al Informe de la Comisión de Verdad y Reconciliación," *Estudios Públicos*, no. 42 (1991), pp. 237–50.

Couso, Javier, "The Politics of Judicial Review in Chile in the Era of Democratic Transition, 1990–2002," *Democratization*, vol. 10, no. 4 (2003), pp. 70–91.

Davis, Madeleine (ed.) (2003) *The Pinochet Case: Origins, Progress, and Implications* (London: Institute of Latin American Studies).

Epp, Charles (1998) *The Rights Revolution: Lawyers, Activists, and Supreme Courts in Comparative Perspective* (Chicago: University of Chicago Press).

Facultad de Derecho de la Universidad Diego Portales (2003) *Informe anual de derechos humanos: Hechos del 2002* (Facultad de Derecho, Universidad Diego Portales).

Gómez, Gastón (1999) "Algunas ideas críticas sobre la jurisdicción constitucional en Chile," in Gastón Gómez (ed.), *La jurisdicción constitucional chilena ante la reforma* (Santiago, Chile: Cuadernos de Análisis Jurídicos de la Universidad Diego Portales, vol. 41), pp. 89–107.

González, Felipe (2004) "Cultura judicial y enseñanza del derecho en Chile: Una aproximación," in *Informe de Investigación* (Santiago, Chile: Facultad de Derecho, Universidad Diego Portales), pp. 293–319.

Hilbink, Lisa (1999) "Legalism against Democracy: The Political Role of the Judiciary in Chile, 1964–1994" (Ph.D. dissertation, University of California, San Diego).

Holland, Kenneth (ed.) (1991) *Judicial Activism in Comparative Perspective* (London: Macmillan).

Human Rights Watch (1998) *The Limits to Tolerance: Freedom of Expression and Public Debate in Chile* (New York: Human Rights Watch).

Huneeus, Carlos (2000) *El régimen de Pinochet* (Santiago, Chile: Editorial Sudamericana).

Lira, Elizabeth and Brian Loveman (1999) "Derechos humanos en la 'Transición Modelo,' " in Paul Drake and Iván Jaksic (eds.), *El modelo chileno: Democracia y desarrollo en los noventa* (Santiago, Chile: LOM Ediciones), pp. 339–74.

Loveman, Brian and Elizabeth Lira (2000) *Las ardientes cenizas del olvido: Vía chilena de reconciliación política, 1932–1994* (Santiago, Chile: LOM Ediciones).

Matus, Alejandra (1999) *El libro negro de la justicia chilena* (Buenos Aires: Editorial Planeta).

McCann, Michael (1994) *Rights at Work: Pay Equity and the Politics of Legal Mobilization* (Chicago: University of Chicago Press).

Peña, Carlos (1996) *Práctica constitucional y derechos fundamentales* (Santiago, Chile: Colección Estudios no 5, Corporación Nacional de Reparación y Reconciliación).

Powe, Lucas (2000) *The Warren Court and American Politics* (Cambridge, MA: Harvard University Press).

Tate, C. Neal and Torbjörn Vallinder (eds.) (1995) *The Global Expansion of Judicial Power* (New York: New York University Press).

Woodhouse, Diana (ed.) (2000) *The Pinochet Case: A Legal and Constitutional Analysis* (Oxford, UK: Hart Publishing).

Zapata, Patricio (2002) *La jurisprudencia del Tribunal Constitucional* (Santiago, Chile: Biblioteca Americana, Universidad Andrés Bello).

Chapter 6

Judicialization and Regime Transformation: The Venezuelan Supreme Court

Rogelio Pérez Perdomo

Introduction

During the 1990s, Venezuela experienced an accelerated process of judicialization of politics. The profound political changes that the country has experienced since 1992 have deeply affected the nature and behavior of the supreme court, the focus of analysis of this chapter. This period of judicialization of Venezuelan politics can be divided into two distinct phases: 1992–1999, when the supreme court became increasingly active, yet continued to adhere to a formalist practice, and 1999 to the present, when both government and opposition attempted to use the courts to advance their agendas or block their opponents during a period of acute political crisis and threatened regime collapse. This second phase followed the election of Hugo Chávez Frías to the presidency, the election of a constituent assembly and the approval of the new Bolivarian constitution, which dissolved the former supreme court and replaced it with a Supreme Tribunal. The judicialization of politics in Venezuela stands in sharp contrast to that experienced elsewhere in the region. This is not a case of judicialization in a "post-transitional" regime, nor was judicialization conceived of as a means to deepen the existing democratic system. Rather, at a time of threatened regime breakdown, political elites increasingly resorted to the courts. In this sense then, Venezuela represents a case of "top-down" judicialization, as it is driven by political elites rather than by social movements and marginalized groups seeking redress through the courts.

In February 1992 a young, middle-ranking military officer by the name of Lieutenant-Colonel Hugo Chávez led an unsuccessful coup attempt. The existing regime of party democracy was subject to severe criticism. The parties were dominated by oligarchic elites, and democratic oversight consisted of little more than a choice between discredited parties. The general view was that political parties had colonized the state, and that the corruption and inefficiency of politicians and civil servants was preventing the public sector from functioning on behalf of the majority of Venezuelans. The coup attempt was a complete military failure, and in a matter of a few hours Chávez and his companions were imprisoned.

However, subsequent events demonstrated the level of popular disenchantment with the political situation. The two main parties, AD (Acción Democrática) and COPEI (Comité de Organización Política Electoral Independiente), did extremely poorly in the 1993 elections, which were won by Rafael Caldera, a longtime politician and former president who had taken the gamble of forming his own movement and accepting the support of the left, particularly of the Movimiento al Socialismo (MAS). Caldera pardoned Chávez, who promptly emerged as a popular contender, expressing himself in the language of the traditional left. This earned him the support of left-wing parties including the MAS. He also gained the support of the (very small) Communist Party, Patria Para Todos and Bandera Roja.[1] With the aid of politically unaffiliated individuals and others prepared to switch their political allegiances, Chávez founded the Movimiento V República (MVR) as his political vehicle, although it was presided over by well-known left-wing leader Luis Miquilena. In December 1998, Chávez was elected to the presidency. His political platform was extremely radical: the convocation of a constitutional assembly to change the constitution and refound the republic. He also proposed to end malfeasance and do away with corrupt political parties.

The Venezuelan political system has undergone radical change since 1999. The National Constituent Assembly was elected, containing a huge majority of Chávez supporters. It convened in July 1999, and produced a new constitution in December in the same year. Amongst the many changes instituted was that of the country's name, which became the "Bolivarian Republic of Venezuela."[2] President Chávez has presented himself as the champion of the poor and marginalized, and as a leader of the anti-globalization movement. He has clashed repeatedly with the United States, business leaders, and the Catholic Church. More than a few rural and urban properties have been taken over by his supporters. His governing style is also inimical to the traditions of party democracy that previously existed in Venezuela. He has armed his supporters, and at times has not hesitated to use violence against the opposition, which he has denounced as illegitimate.[3]

In 2000, Chávez was authorized by the National Assembly to legislate by presidential decree, and in November of the same year he approved a package of 39 decree laws which transformed Venezuela's legal framework, moving it strongly toward the left (although economic policy is neither orthodox socialist nor capitalist). The new legislation affected the interests of virtually all sectors, and the complete lack of consultation over its implementation offended many of Chávez's own supporters. The National Assembly designated a commission, chaired by an eminent leader of the MVR, to hear complaints and attempt to reconcile divergent interests. Chávez opposed any revision of the package of decrees whatsoever, and consequently the MAS and other parties of the left withdrew their support from the government. The MVR also split, with Luis Miquilena and other leaders leaving to found Solidaridad, a new political grouping. Chávez, however, preserved his control of the National Assembly. He also retained as allies the comptroller general, the ombudsman and the attorney general of the republic, who had formerly been his vice president. However, his popularity rapidly declined and the opposition began to organize massive protest rallies on the streets of Caracas. In April 2001, military commanders deposed Chávez and held him prisoner, following an armed attack on an opposition demonstration in which around 20 people died and approximately 100 were injured. However, attempts to install the country's main business leader in the presidency met with widespread rejection and Chávez was returned to power within 48 hours.

Controversy over the nature of Chávez's regime and the projects of its opponents are commonplace in Venezuela. However, the government has become increasingly repressive, and the Venezuelan government has been condemned for human rights violations by international organizations such as Amnesty International and Human Rights Watch.[4] The Inter-American Human Rights Commission and the Inter-American Court of Human Rights have emitted resolutions on behalf of journalists, editors, and opposition political leaders, as several journalists have been assassinated or injured by Chávez supporters and frequent attacks have been carried out against newspaper offices and TV stations.[5] Most left-wing intellectuals, and various political parties with socialist leanings (particularly the MAS, Causa R, and Bandera Roja) reject any assertion that Chávez is left-wing or revolutionary. They insist that his policies can only lead to unemployment, corruption, and a worsening of poverty, and the term "*rob-olución*" has been coined to refer to the regime. The majority of trade unions also oppose the regime.

In 2001, opposition parties and various NGOs formed the Coordinadora Democrática, an ideologically diverse political alliance whose main purpose was to combat Chávez by democratic means. Its first challenge was to differentiate itself from those who have attempted to unseat Chávez via military intervention, a costly error committed by business leaders who entered into a pact with the military high command.[6] By the second half of 2002, the political situation had grown so tense that the Organization of American States (OAS) stepped in with a proposal for mediation. OAS Secretary-General César Gaviria practically took up residence in Caracas for an extended period, and former U.S. president Jimmy Carter visited the capital on numerous occasions. A "group of friends" was formed—comprising Brazil, the United States, Chile, Spain, and Portugal—to help mediate the conflict. By May 2003, an agreement had been reached that a referendum to revoke the president's mandate, as set out in Article 72 of the 1999 constitution, was the most peaceful, constitutional, and democratic way to resolve the political crisis. The referendum was held in August 2004, resulting in a comfortable victory for Chávez (58 percent). The opposition denounced fraud and its defeat has since thrown it into disarray.[7]

The aim of the present chapter is to describe and analyze the role of judges, in particular that of the magistrates of the Supreme Court of Justice (later Supreme Tribunal of Justice), in the complex political situation unfolding in Venezuela. The goal is to analyze how the Supreme Tribunal has been transformed, a transformation partly driven by broader political changes; and at the same time to analyze the extent to which the court has fulfilled the role assigned to it by the constitution and has influenced the institutional architecture of government. The first section describes changes in the way the judicial hierarchy interacts with politics and sets out some criteria for analyzing the actions of the supreme tribunal. The second section examines cases that have proved particularly controversial. The concluding section reflects on the relationship between the judicialization of politics in Venezuela and the transformation of the country's legal culture.

Political Change and Judicialization

From Supreme Court to Supreme Tribunal

The constitution of 1961 established the supreme court as Venezuela's highest tribunal and placed it at the apex of the judicial branch (Article 204). The constitution also envisaged the creation of a Judicial Council, to "ensure the independence, effectiveness, discipline and decorum of the courts and . . . guarantee the benefits of the judicial career to judges" (Article 217). The council was duly constituted in 1969, and came to be responsible for the administration of the judicial branch and the appointment, evaluation, and disciplining of judges. It was comprised of magistrates designated by the supreme court, but also by other branches of state. Most of the Judicial Council's powers had previously been exercised by the Ministry of Justice, with some oversight from the supreme court. The creation of the Judicial Council instituted a judiciary that was formally less dependent on the executive, but completely bicephalous: headed by the supreme court in jurisdictional matters and in all other matters by the Judicial Council (Pérez Perdomo, 2003b).

Yet in practice the judicial branch was not politically independent. Supreme court judges were appointed by congress for a nine-year period, subdivided into renewable three-year terms. However, it was common knowledge that appointments were made by political parties, without reference to qualifications and with a complete lack of transparency. The main factors taken into account were political and personal loyalties. The magistrates of the Judicial Council, although appointed by the supreme court, the president of the republic and congress, were also appointed by political parties as part of an overt bargaining process. Judges were effectively appointed according to the quota of political power wielded by each of the parties involved in the nomination (Brito González, 1978; Quintero, 1988; Pérez Perdomo, 2003b).

Given this clientelist approach to the assigning of judicial posts, the judiciary understandably lacked prestige. When the party system was working well, party leaders negotiated between themselves, settling most conflicts through channels of internal negotiation. Where economic interests were at stake, especially in cases where private citizens were pitted against the state, political leaders could also act as mediators. The importance of the judicial system, and in particular of the supreme court, was limited.[8] However, once the parties lost internal cohesion and became—effectively—federations of warring groups, the political system lost its capacity to regulate social, political, and economic conflicts. Judicial intervention was required, but judges were not prepared for this new role. They were consequently upbraided for being excessively subservient to political forces, for making no effort to hold politicians accountable for the improper or unsatisfactory exercise of their functions, and, in particular, for not sanctioning politicians involved in notorious corruption cases. In December 1991, an open letter published by well-known intellectuals and journalists, known as the "Letter of the Notables," drew attention to the disgraceful impunity associated with crimes of corruption and demanded the resignation of the supreme court justices. Politicians finally became worried when, in February 1992, the coup attempt carried out by a group of young officers, led by Lieutenant Colonel Chávez, exposed the minimal levels of political support enjoyed by the democratic party system. In May that year, when judicial appointments fell due, the most compromised judges were removed. After a public consultation, more politically independent figures were brought into the court.

During the remainder of the 1990s the supreme court was forced to become an arbiter in a period of increasing political and economic conflict. There was practically no major political or economic issue that was not taken before the court. This led to a huge case backlog, and the court adopted a practice of careful attention to procedural issues. A badly or incorrectly presented case was usually dismissed before the court entered into the substance of the matter. The backlog also led to considerable delays in the resolution of cases. A good number of crimes or infractions lapsed before magistrates had made decisions, as occurred in the well-known "jeeps case," a corruption case involving former President Lusinchi. Persistent criticism of the supreme court led it to propose its own reform, and in 1997 the republic signed an agreement with the World Bank for a US$7.3 million modernization project (Pérez Perdomo, 2004).[9] The court did not always act slowly, however; the 1993 trial of President Carlos Andrés Pérez for misappropriation of funds saw him suspended and sentenced within a matter of months.

Following the election of Hugo Chávez as president of the republic in 1998, the supreme court was faced with the problem of his proposal to have the constitution redrafted by means of a Constituent Assembly. This was not a method recognized in the existing charter. However, the court decided that, even though there were no written provisions for such a body, democratic principles could be satisfied if the population, consulted in a referendum, were to vote in favor of the convoking of such an assembly.[10] Shortly afterward, the court obliged Chávez to define the terms of the convocation.

In summary, between 1993 and 1999 the Supreme Court of Justice displayed ever greater political prominence during a period of increasing judicialization of politics. The supreme court played a clear and decisive role, although its formalism tended to limit its actions. Cecilia Sosa, the first woman to preside over the Supreme Court of Justice, became a figure familiar to all Venezuelans through her appearances at press conferences, providing straightforward, informative explanations of the court's major decisions. In 1999 the National Constituent Assembly was elected, with President Chávez' supporters winning a sweeping majority. One of its first acts, before starting work on the draft constitution, was to declare the judicial branch in crisis on August 18, 1999. The assembly designated a Judicial Emergency Commission, whose task was to evaluate the functioning and performance of the supreme court and the National Judicial Council. The commission would also undertake the purging of judicial personnel and the introduction of new procedures for the appointment of judges. The assembly's decision rocked the supreme court. On August 23, 1999, in a divided ruling, the court recognized the legitimacy of the commission and authorized one of its own magistrates to participate. The dissenting opinion of magistrate Cecilia Sosa, president of the court, was particularly dramatic. She pointed out that the Emergency Commission was taking upon itself the administration of the judicial branch, thereby displacing the supreme court and placing the court itself under the commission's supervision. In a public statement she declared that the supreme court had effectively committed suicide to preempt its own assassination, and resigned.

The constitution of the Bolivarian Republic of Venezuela, approved in 1999, significantly transformed the judicial branch. It abolished the Judicial Council, handing over its functions to a new Supreme Tribunal of Justice, which replaced both the supreme court and the Judicial Council. The number of judges was increased to 20, distributed across six "salas" or benches.[11] Each was to have three magistrates, except the Sala Constitucional (the bench charged with interpreting and guaranteeing the constitution), which had five. Provision was made for a "Sala Plena" (a full sitting of all the court's judges), but this was given fewer attributions than the now-defunct supreme court. The powers attributed to the supreme tribunal by the 1999 constitution are very broad. They include the power of judicial review, the interpretation of laws, the resolution of jurisdictional disputes between organs of state, and a very important role in the impeachment or trial of the president and other high-ranking state officials (Articles 266, 335, and 336). In the case of omissions by national, state-level, or municipal legislatures, the tribunal is even authorized to dictate necessary measures to ensure the constitution is adhered to (Article 336, paragraph 7). In this respect, the supreme tribunal is a much more powerful organism than the previous Supreme Court of Justice.

Once the constitution had been approved, the constituent assembly provisionally appointed the 20 judges of the Supreme Tribunal of Justice, on December 22, 1999. A year later, on December 20,

2000, the National Assembly made definitive appointments. These sequential rounds of appointments were used to politically purge the judicial corps, and few of the original court magistrates survived. Iván Rincón Urdaneta, one of those who did, was elected president of the tribunal and continued the task of modernization. Supreme tribunal magistrates were chosen from among those law professors and lawyers of prestige who had shown a certain inclination toward the left-wing parties. Only three magistrates had clear links with opposition political parties. As a result of new organizational and administrative systems that were put into place, the supreme tribunal is no longer burdened by an enormous caseload. It frequently announces itself "up-to-date"; that is, with no backlog of old cases and able, therefore, to decide cases with relative celerity. The processing of cases and decisions has been computerized, and it is now possible to access bench calendars, case status, and decisions via the Internet.

This modernized supreme tribunal has been called upon to act in an extremely difficult situation. On the one hand, it has the elevated status of interpreter of a new constitution, one which changed substantial aspects of Venezuelan law and which, due to the haste with which it was drafted, is often ambiguous or inconsistent. It is the supreme tribunal that has to decide which parts of the old Venezuelan legal edifice remain valid and which have been swept away. On the other hand, it has had to act in a period of enormous political conflict, accentuated since 2002. The next section examines to what extent the new supreme tribunal has met the expectations of diverse and opposing sectors of the national community.

Judicialization and Activism in the New Supreme Tribunal

The judicialization of politics occurs because courts, in particular supreme courts, take on a more active role, or because political actors invite judges to intervene in the resolution of political conflicts. In some senses these are two sides of the same coin; it is difficult to conceive of politicians taking their conflicts to the justice system unless they have some expectations of it. During the 1990s in Venezuela, social and political actors put increasing pressure on judges to intervene in political problems and, in response, judges progressively began to adopt a more proactive role.

Table 6.1 shows the output of the supreme court and supreme tribunal between 1997 and 2003. The measure used is volume, rather

Table 6.1   Output of the supreme court and supreme tribunal, 1997–2003

Cases	1997*	1998*	1999*	2000	2001	2002	2003
Received	5,659	5,659	4,516**	6,488	6,851	7,018	8,039
Resolved	3,999	5,180	7,202	7,681	8,844	7,207	8,974

Notes: * The Supreme Court of Justice was in operation until 1999. From 2000 it was replaced by the Supreme Tribunal of Justice.

** The source does not supply data for the number of cases brought before the Sala de Casación Penal. To avoid major distortion, an estimate of 1,800 cases received has been adopted. This figure represents the average of cases received in 1998 and 2000.

Sources: For 1997: Supreme Court of Justice, *1998 Report*, p. 30. For all other years: Supreme Tribunal of Justice at www.tsj.gov.ve, consulted March 25, 2004.

than relative importance of cases. However, it can be seen that in 1997, the supreme court was seriously congested, with the rate of resolution well below the number of cases received.

The table shows a sustained increase in cases received and a marked growth in output since the administrative reform of 1997. In fact the tribunal has doubled the number of decisions made, in the face of a significantly increased caseload.

A qualitative analysis, taking into consideration the relative importance of cases presented and decisions made, is a much more complex undertaking. Our current research project specifies a procedure for identifying those decisions of the supreme tribunal that may be considered of most political significance, particularly those that may have contributed most to shaping the new political system and the Venezuelan state in general. The procedure adopted involves consultation of magistrates and qualified academic experts, and remains in its early stages. This chapter will simply deal with those cases that have attracted most media attention, either because they took place at particularly key moments in the political process or because they dealt directly with matters central to the Chávez government. The aim is to consider the constraints or dilemmas confronting magistrates as interpreters of the law and frontline political actors.

The term "professional" or "internal" constraint refers to the dilemma between acting in accordance with traditional canons of legal interpretation (known in Latin America as "legal formalism"), or in accordance with a more contextually informed, "case-led" stance. "Anti-formalism" is clearly more conducive to judicial activism, as it leaves judges less tied to legal texts and juridical formalities. The second constraint on judges—"external" in nature—derives from their political role. They are selected and designated by the principal political actors, and play an important political role, being called on to adjudicate in many cases in which the government may have a direct or indirect interest. By virtue of their position in the politico-legal system, judges have to maintain discretion about their own political views, but it is inevitable that their decisions will be read as either favorable or unfavorable to—or in deference to or independent of—the government.

In accordance with the 1999 constitution, supreme tribunal magistrates are appointed by the National Assembly. Dismissal of a magistrate requires the intervention of the so-called Moral Council of the Republic (made up of the attorney general, the comptroller general and the ombudsman). The members of this council are themselves appointed by a qualified majority vote in the National Assembly. When the definitive appointment of the new magistrates took place in December 2000, the president had a solid majority in the National Assembly and popular approval ratings of around 80 percent. As noted above, the majority of the magistrates were university law professors or prestigious left-wing lawyers who had not been part of the judicial hierarchy when it was controlled by the political parties. It is generally believed that the selection of magistrates in 2000 was mainly carried out by Luis Miquilena, veteran left-wing leader, president of the MVR and considered at the time to be Chávez' chief advisor.[12]

By January 2002, the authoritarian radicalization of the government had become evident. The MAS and other left-wing parties withdrew their support. Miquilena, president of the MVR, together with other political leaders, formed a new party, which became part of the opposition. Venezuelan politics became increasingly polarized. Yet, given the restrictions on political expression placed on judges, it was not immediately apparent whether individual magistrates of the new supreme tribunal favored the government or the opposition.

The degree of external pressure brought to bear on judges and supreme court justices is hard to estimate, but it is fairly commonplace in Latin America. It certainly occurred in Venezuela during the era of party democracy, even though the pressures were rarely made public or explicit. However, Chávez is well known for his outspokenness in this regard. He does not hesitate to use radio and television to indicate to magistrates what decisions they ought to reach, and later to comment on their decisions without the slightest restraint. This does not, of course, mean that more discreet pressures, threats, or unspoken ways of letting magistrates know what is expected of them are not also employed. The opposition is also far from reticent in expressing its condemnation of particular decisions or magistrates. Various magistrates have been "caceroleados," that is, subjected to noisy protests,[13] and in one unfortunate incident tribunal president Iván Rincón was physically attacked.[14]

Molina (2002) carried out an early evaluation of the decisions of the supreme tribunal, especially those of its Sala Constitucional, in its first year of operations. His well-documented research pointed to an activist tribunal, unwavering in confronting the most serious challenges of legal interpretation and capable of making bold decisions. This was particularly true of the Sala Constitucional. On encountering legislation contrary to the principles enshrined in the new constitution, the Sala Constitucional frequently declared the legislation unconstitutional and went on to decide the new rules that should be applicable. This led to the creation of new rules, and even new procedures. When the tribunal found that a lawyer had framed a problem incorrectly, they had no compunction in pointing this out and rejecting the petition. However, if they found an underlying principle worthy of attention, they would proceed to rule on it. This activist stance on the part of the supreme tribunal is a striking new departure for Venezuela and differs substantially from the legal formalism so prevalent in Latin America. The supreme court of justice was characteristically both extremely slow to make decisions and exceedingly sensitive to procedural detail. A small procedural flaw would lead to the rejection of a case without any reference to the matters of substance involved. In other words, the formalist and timid attitude predominant in the former supreme court[15] has been replaced by an interpretive boldness and a clear desire to renew the legal order under the new supreme tribunal, in particular its Sala Constitucional. If we accept Molina's analysis, the renewal of the supreme tribunal has not only been organizational and technical, but has also extended to an overhaul of legal thinking and practice.

The personalist authoritarian or revolutionary project of Chávez has placed the supreme tribunal under enormous strain. The biographies of the magistrates concerned show that at the time they were nominated, they were politically close to the ambiguous project of renewal that predominated during the first year of the Chávez presidency. By late 2001 and early 2002, however, when Chávez began to show his more authoritarian side and total lack of vocation for compromise, his supporters split, and magistrates appeared to do likewise. Nevertheless, as one might expect given strong professional constraints, magistrates did not automatically align themselves with either government or opposition.

Case Analysis

The Case of the Coup and Its Consequences

Perhaps the most dramatic case, and the one which put the Supreme Tribunal of Justice in the headlines for weeks, was the initial *antejuicio de mérito*, or pretrial hearing, of the high-ranking military officers who had deposed President Chávez on April 11, 2002 in an attempted coup. The officers involved held the rank of general. In accordance with the 1999 constitution, a trial of military officers of such rank required a pretrial hearing before the supreme tribunal. The officers could only be accused and processed if the tribunal was in agreement.[16] The attorney general had demanded a pretrial hearing before the full sitting of the supreme tribunal, on the grounds that the officers had committed the crime of military rebellion (Military Justice Code, Article 476). The attorney general's petition held no political surprises, except in that it did not include the most senior of the officers, who had moreover been the one to announce to the country in the early hours of April 12, 2002 that the officers had requested, and received, the president's resignation. Indeed Commander-in-Chief Lucas Rincón not only escaped trial but was subsequently named Minister of Defense.

A brief explanation of the background to the case is in order here. On April 9, 2002 a general strike began, called by the central workers' association, CTV, and the business leaders' association, Fedecámaras. On April 11, the strike culminated in a huge demonstration that marched on the Miraflores Palace, the seat of government, demanding the president's resignation. President Chávez decided to activate the so-called Ávila Plan, a military plan for the defense of the capital, and to protect the presidential palace with tanks and heavy armaments. Since the military chiefs of staff refused to respond to his calls, it was armed civilians of the government party who fired on the crowds, provoking around 20 deaths and 100 injuries. Meanwhile, the president imposed a virtual blockade[17] on television and radio stations, obliging them to transmit official information instead of reports of what was happening on the streets. Private television stations opted to transmit on a split screen, with half showing the official programming and the other half live coverage of the events. The government's response was to attempt to block television transmissions although, due to new information technology, this was only partially successful. At that point, the military high command announced publicly that they would not obey the president. The president went voluntarily to the main army headquarters in Caracas, where the generals demanded his resignation. He was taken prisoner and transported to the naval base of La Orchila, a small island in the Caribbean. At dawn, General Rincón announced the president's resignation, and shortly afterwards Pedro Carmona, a business leader and the president of Fedecámaras, announced that he was provisionally assuming the presidency. He subsequently dissolved the national assembly and the Supreme Tribunal of Justice, and appointed a cabinet. None of these actions had any basis in the constitution, which provides for a completely different procedure in the case of the resignation of the president. Groups of Chávez's supporters went out onto the streets in violent mode, and shops were looted in street riots. The commanders of several important military groups were in disagreement with the generals, who in turn withdrew support from Carmona. Chávez was restored to the presidency on April 13, 2002. In a dramatic televised speech he asked his enemies' pardon, promised a change of attitude, and called for national harmony. Shortly afterward he replaced the most controversial of his ministers and named Commander in Chief Lucas Rincón as the new defense minister.

When the magistrates began their deliberations, it became clear that the majority were reluctant to accept the attorney general's arguments. In a televised speech, Chávez indicated that the tribunal ought to authorize the trial because the officers had carried out a coup and had illegally held him captive. He suggested that the people would not accept any other decision and might react violently. The sentence of August 14, 2002 is long and contains complex arguments. Its main legal reasoning could be considered formalist, as it emphasizes that the high military officials did not "rise up in arms"; rather, they had refused to order a mobilization of troops in accordance with the president's instructions.[18] The supreme tribunal also found that, by omission of the legislature, no penalty had been specified for this crime. It is noteworthy that the attorney general should have chosen the crime of military rebellion, rather than that of "disobedience" (as spelt out in Article 519 of the Military Justice Code). The decision is understandable in that the attorney general almost certainly did not want to provoke discussion of what Chávez's orders had actually been. This would have led to disputes over the legitimacy of the orders, and in this respect the military's position could have been more clearly justifiable, since the constitution forbids the use of arms or "noxious substances" to disperse peaceful protests (Article 68). The dissenting magistrates' votes emphasized that there had been an attempted coup, that the pretrial hearing was merely a procedural requisite, and that it would be for state prosecutors and judges to investigate further and determine what crime the high officials had actually committed. The bottom line was whether the conduct of the president and the military had been correct, although this was not directly stated.

The sentence exposed a profound schism within the group of magistrates. The vote of the full sitting was divided 11–8, with one magistrate absent. However, this majority was made possible because two magistrates who had condemned the coup in the press were duly excluded from the deliberations for having expressed an opinion. Their replacements voted one on each side. Had it not been for these exclusions, plus the absence of one magistrate, the court would have been split 10–10 and its president would have had to emit the deciding vote. The sentence was dictated while violent and ardent groups of Chávez supporters surrounded the supreme tribunal building, which was being guarded by a large military and police contingent. Chávez kept silent, making no attempt to pacify his supporters. He later described the decision as "*plasta*," or complete rubbish.[19] Within the next few days, shots were fired at the building of the tribunal. This series of events demonstrated that the president had no respect whatsoever for the magistrates and was not inclined to respect their independence.

For its part, the National Assembly decided on August 15, 2002 to designate a special commission to investigate the "crisis of the judicial branch." One outcome of its investigations was a check on the credentials of magistrate Franklin Arriechi, who had played a key role in the *antejuicio* case. The commission found that his qualifications had not been satisfactorily proven and proceeded to annul his appointment on the grounds that, since the claims made on his resumé were not substantiated, he could be presumed to have deceived both the Constituent Assembly (which had appointed him in December 1999) and the National Assembly, which had ratified the appointment in December 2000. With that argument, the assembly decided on December 3, 2002 to annul Magistrate Arriechi's appointment. This amounted in practice to a dismissal, albeit via a procedure very different to the one set out in the constitution. Magistrate Arriechi asked for a constitutional *amparo* against the National Assembly's decision, requesting the temporary suspension of its effects and its eventual overturning.[20] On December 10, 2002, the Sala Constitucional accepted the *amparo* writ and the protective measures that had been solicited (the provisional suspension of the effects of the assembly's decision). Surprisingly, given the importance of the case and the fact that the supreme tribunal is generally said to be up to date with its caseload, a definitive resolution of the case was not forthcoming. On June 15, 2004, in an action of questionable legal basis, the National Assembly once again annulled Magistrate Arriechi's appointment. On June 22, 2004, the pro-Chávez majority of the Sala Constitucional denied the admissibility of the *amparo* and Arriechi was finally dismissed.

In summary, this case demonstrated that President Chávez did not have control of the supreme tribunal and that the tribunal itself was deeply divided. The schism continued, and the tribunal has failed to designate its new directorate. It was clear, however, that Chávez supporters were prepared to undertake almost any measure in order to get rid of problematic magistrates.

The Case of the Corte Primera de lo Contencioso Administrativo

The Corte Primera de lo Contencioso Administrativo is a tribunal of particular importance in the Venezuelan judicial system. It was created by the organic law of the Supreme Court of Justice of 1976, as a way of decentralizing and increasing the efficiency of the Sala Político Administrativa.[21] The appreciation of its significance requires a brief excursion into Venezuelan judicial history.

The 1961 constitution maintained the separation of ordinary jurisdiction from administrative jurisdiction or jurisdiction of public law, following the French tradition. However, that constitution did not create an administrative Council of State. Instead, it gave jurisdiction of major administrative controversies to the Sala Político Administrativa, the body that inherited the mantle of the Federal Court or Sala Federal of previous arrangements. The increase in state size and functions that occurred in the 1960s and 1970s led to a significant increase in the number of cases which came before the Sala Político Administrativa. The organic law establishing the Supreme Court of Justice in 1976 established contentious administrative jurisdiction, and created this new tribunal to tackle the existing case overload. The 1976 law gave higher civil courts competence over charges of illegality regarding administrative acts carried out by municipal and federal authorities, as well as over claims involving relatively minor charges made against the republic, autonomous institutions, or state businesses (Article 181). The Corte Primera de lo Contencioso Administrativo was created as a second-tier instance to oversee the decisions of those courts. Its decisions were final—that is, they could not be appealed before the Supreme Court of Justice. In other matters, the Corte Primera de lo Contencioso Administrativo acted as a first instance court whose decisions could be appealed before the Sala Político Administrativa (Article 185).

The law establishing the Supreme Court of Justice placed the Corte Primera de lo Contencioso Administrativo under the charge of five magistrates (similar to the individual benches of the supreme court), and special qualifications were required of its magistrates.[22] Nor was the normal procedure for the naming of magistrates by the Judicial Council followed. Instead, magistrates were chosen directly by the Sala Político Administrativa of the supreme court. In practice, magistrates of the Corte Primera were highly qualified, and the court enjoyed considerable prestige in academic circles. It is a relatively large entity; each magistrate is advised by some seven lawyers who assist in the analysis of cases and the preparation of decisions.

In 2000, the magistrates of the Corte Primera de lo Contencioso Administrativo were appointed by the Sala Político Administrativa of the new Supreme Tribunal of Justice. Months later, as a consequence of the renewal of the supreme tribunal, the Corte Primera was also overhauled. On this occasion, the magistrates were appointed by a full sitting of the supreme tribunal. It was quite evident that those who were named as magistrates in the Corte Primera were, likewise, people of left-wing tendencies or with links to left-wing groups. The Corte Primera always heard cases of considerable political and economic significance, since it was responsible for overseeing the legality of administrative acts. For instance, during the 1990s, government interventions in the banking sector gave rise to various disputes which were taken before the Corte Primera. In any era of radical transformation and political conflict, the Corte Primera will naturally have to preside over cases of great importance. For example, when the National Treasury failed to hand over funds to state governors, the governors resorted to the Corte Primera in an attempt to resolve what was, in effect, a conflict between the president of the republic and governors of states controlled by the opposition.[23] In any event, the case also demonstrated that the Corte Primera intervenes not only to annul administrative acts but also to rectify administrative omissions.

In short, this tribunal has a vast field of competence and can be decisive at certain moments. One particularly important case, which the Corte Primera decided by majority vote, was the so-called Plan Barrio Adentro. Under the terms of this plan, over a thousand Cuban doctors were invited to practice in "*barrios*," the poorest districts of Venezuelan cities. It was a controversial initiative, with the opposition regarding the medics as political activists dedicated to the implantation of a Cuban-style regime.[24] The legal point at issue was the validity of an agreement made between the main professional medical association, the Colegio Metropolitano de Médicos, and the Mayoralty of Caracas, both organisms controlled by the government. The agreement contained divergent norms for the appointment of Venezuelan, as distinct from foreign, doctors (no express reference was made to Cubans). While Venezuelan doctors had to go through normal procedures, including open competition on the basis of their qualifications, foreign medics required only a placet or dispensation from the Colegio Metropolitano in order to practice. The agreement sidestepped existing regulation of the medical profession, in the form of a law which requires that all doctors either graduate in Venezuela or have their foreign qualifications validated by a Venezuelan university. The Corte Primera's first decision was to accept the request for nullification and emit a preventive *amparo*, establishing that all doctors had to obey the existing statutes referring to qualifications for exercising the profession. On August 26, 2003 the president of the republic and other functionaries called for the court's preventive measures to be ignored, the president railing against the magistrates in offensive language.[25] That same day, the Sala Constitucional of the supreme tribunal took over the case and suspended the measures. The case has not been finally resolved.

The Corte Primera made various other decisions that irritated the government. For example, it ordered the restoration to active service of General Vázquez Velazco, one of the leaders of the April 11, 2002 coup attempt. The supreme tribunal had not authorized his trial, although he was later subjected to the administrative sanction of demotion.[26]

Another important case was that of "Unapetrol." In the aftermath of a strike that lasted from December 2002 until January 2004, the directors of state oil company PDVSA dismissed 18,000 workers who had taken part in the strike. These included most of the middle and high-level management of the oil industry. Some of those workers, amongst them the leaders of the strike, had solicited the formation of a union and were thereby protected against dismissal. They therefore solicited an *amparo*, seeking to overturn the decision of a labor inspector who had declared that they could be dismissed.

The situation in the Corte Primera was extremely tense. Cases in which the government had a direct interest were usually decided by a majority 3–2 vote, with the magistrates in the minority group generally withholding their votes or registering a dissenting opinion. Confrontations ensued between the magistrates of both factions. On one occasion, one of the magistrates of the minority faction complained to one of the majority about the ease with which certain litigating lawyers, despite holding no official position in the court, were able to enter and leave that particular magistrate's office and access the records of ongoing cases.[27]

On September 18, 2003, the chauffeur of Magistrate Perkins Rocha was intercepted by the DISIP (Dirección de Servicios de

Inteligencia Policial), or political police, while delivering case documents to an external advisory lawyer of the Corte Primera. The chauffeur was accused of the crime of concealment and retention of a public document (Article 78, Anti-Corruption Statute), and was detained without bail. President Chávez immediately made comments about the incident to the press, insisting that a web of corruption in the Corte Primera was about to be exposed. In the days that followed, the DISIP and a prosecutor of the Ministerio Público visited the head-quarters of the Corte Primera, accompanied by a great show of arms, and occupied the offices for about six hours. They were apparently searching for documents related to the case for which the chauffeur was being held. On October 23, 2003, the Sala Penal of the supreme tribunal found the chauffeur's detention to be completely unjustified, since he had been issued with written instructions to transfer the file, and since such transfers were in any case routine judicial practice.

A week later, on October 30, 2003, the Commission for the Functioning and Restructuring of the Judicial System decided to dis-miss four of the Corte Primera's magistrates, and ordered the activa-tion of the previously agreed retirement of the fifth, Evelyn Marrero.[28] The dismissals were motivated by a decision that the Corte Primera had taken in a case relating to the registration of a document, a deci-sion which the Sala Contecioso Administrativa had considered to be a serious error in law. The matter appeared to have no direct relation to either the chauffeur's detention or the events being investigated by the prosecutor and the DISIP. Notwithstanding, the supreme tribunal did not question the commission's competence, nor did it see fit to revise the commission's decision in such an important case. Nor did the supreme tribunal protest over the searching of the premises of the Corte Primera. All of these actions appeared to seriously impair judicial independence, and the supreme tribunal, probably owing to its own internal political divisions, proved itself incapable of acting in its defense. The deans of law schools and the Venezuelan Association for Administrative Law publicly exhorted the supreme tribunal to defend the integrity of contentious administrative judges, to no avail.

The measures taken against magistrates extended as far as the occu-pation of the Corte Primera by DISIP personnel.[29] In the event, the designated replacement magistrates were not called upon, and the court simply ceased to function. Lawyers who had pending cases or who had planned to present demands to the court were left without recourse. The supreme tribunal initially redistributed matters to other tribunals and then, on December 10, 2003, created the Corte Segunda de lo Contencioso Administrativo. As of June 2004, however, neither of the two courts had begun to function.

The final outcome of these events raises more questions than answers. In the end, the public was never told what acts of corruption the Ministerio Público and the DISIP were investigating, nor why those investigations ultimately proved fruitless. If, on the other hand, the objective was to dismiss the magistrates, a full sitting of the supreme tribunal could simply have appointed new magistrates without the need for such a traumatic procedure. The internal divisions within the supreme tribunal were probably what prevented the dismissals being brought before the full sitting of the tribunal and likewise prevented it from acting to reverse them once they had been carried out. It is inexplicable that substitute magistrates were not called upon in order to keep the court functioning. In any event, the Supreme Tribunal failed to defend judicial independence as might be expected.

The Case of the Ley Orgánica of the Supreme Tribunal

The constitution of 1999 established the Supreme Tribunal of Justice as the head of the judicial branch. It replaced the Supreme Court of Justice in this role, but this was no mere change of name. The supreme tribunal retained the powers of the old court, but acquired additional attributes which the old one did not have. It is not a central concern of the present chapter to analyze these differences, but they are mentioned here to explain why the supreme tribunal and the National Assembly have taken an interest in the preparation and approval of the organic law regulating the Supreme Tribunal of Justice, as set down in the constitution (Article 262).

In 2003 various deputies of the MVR, the principal governing party, introduced a legislative proposal, which was rapidly approved at its first reading. The proposal aimed to increase the number of magistrates to the supreme tribunal from 20 to 32 and allow them to be appointed by simple majority. This would effectively allow Chávez's supporters to appoint magistrates and so assure themselves of control of the tribunal. The opposition, conscious of what was at stake, employed all the delaying tactics at its disposal. On August 12, 2003, a group of opposition deputies asked the Sala Constitucional to define the procedure for approval of the statute governing the supreme tribunal. The constitution states that all legislative proposals for organic laws, "with the exception of those stipulated in this Constitution," shall be admitted by the National Assembly by a vote of two-thirds of its members (Article 203). It also says that "this [qualified majority vote] will also apply to the modification of organic laws." Based on the fact that the legislative proposal for the organic law of the Supreme Tribunal of Justice modified the organic law of the

Supreme Court of Justice, the claimants proposed that it should be declared that a two-thirds vote from the National Assembly would be required to initiate discussion of the respective legislative project. On January 28, 2004, in a divided, 3–2 vote, the Sala Constitucional found against the opposition deputies' proposal. The logic of the majority opinion is difficult to understand and the ruling itself displays serious inconsistencies. It is a decision which virtually abolishes the distinction between ordinary and organic laws, without ever expressly saying so. It runs completely counter to the decisive manner in which the Sala Constitucional has confronted other problems of interpretation and suggests that, rather than obeying any internal, legal logic, the outcome was dictated by the need for a decision favorable to the government. The political consequence is to put the modification of the law of the supreme tribunal in the hands of any majority in the National Assembly, however slender. These changes in legislation can increase or reduce the number of magistrates, alter the age of retirement, and make other changes which might facilitate political control of supreme tribunal magistrates.

In April 2004, the National Assembly reinitiated discussion of the organic law, and the opposition adopted the strategy of delaying the debate as much as possible. To counter the obstructionism of the opposition, government deputies consolidated various articles into a single one and opted to take advantage of every possible procedural recourse. After the law had been approved in the chamber, the committee charged with overseeing stylistic aspects opted to make important modifications while denying a fresh debate. The new organic law of the Supreme Tribunal of Justice was published on May 20, 2004. The number of magistrates was increased to 32 (Article 2), and magistrates were henceforth to be elected by a simple majority in the National Assembly (Article 8). The new law encompasses a procedure for dismissal which allows magistrates who have been accused by the Moral Council of the Republic (discussed earlier) to be suspended while the National Assembly rules on their dismissal. Since the aforementioned council is in government hands, the new law not only permits political control in the naming of new magistrates, it also facilitates any purges that might be considered necessary. Government supporters were in such haste to approve the law that they derogated the norms for contentious administrative procedure without providing new ones. Opposition deputies announced that they would ask for the nullification of the law on the grounds of unconstitutionality, and would push for a referendum to abrogate it. Various deans of law schools and law professors, as well as individual lawyers in their own right, have also attempted to bring actions against the law on the grounds of unconstitutionality. However, these may all prove futile gestures given that the National Electoral Council and the Sala Constitucional are currently in the hands of government supporters.

In summary, although the supreme tribunal has produced a few decisions which have not been to the liking of President Chávez, it has clearly failed to place limits on the president's overweening power, or to defend its own judicial independence and that of other courts. In June 2004, the Moral Council of the Republic (controlled by supporters of Chávez) declared that Sala Electoral magistrates Martini Urdaneta, Hernández, and Gravina (the latter a supplementary magistrate) had committed a grave error in their decision in a case that pitted the Sala Electoral against the government. On July 8, the full sitting of the Supreme Tribunal of Justice ordered the retirement of magistrates Martini Urdaneta, Hernández, and Rafael Pérez Perdomo (the latter from the Sala Penal), an action which left the supreme tribunal under government control.

The National Electoral Council and the Issue of the Referendum to Revoke the Presidential Mandate

Venezuela has been subject to enormous political tensions since 2002. Dramatic events have occurred and, in an effort to avoid violence and breakdown, the OAS, a group of friendly countries who have made efforts to influence the government and the opposition—and the Carter Center have jointly attempted to promote negotiations between the different political sectors. In May 2003 the government and the opposition agreed to seek a constitutional, peaceful, and democratic solution in the form of a referendum which could revoke the president's mandate. This is contemplated in Article 72 of the constitution. Nevertheless, the president's supporters initially did everything possible to block this outcome.

In a decision on January 22, 2003, the Sala Electoral of the supreme tribunal declared that the National Electoral Council designated by the National Constituent Assembly no longer had the competence to organize any electoral activity. This decision was controversial both for its content and for the manner in which one of the magistrates manipulated the composition of the bench. In the event, the vice president of the bench accepted the self-disqualification of the president and the third magistrate. He then called together supplementary magistrates, whom he had hand-picked without reference to the established order of selection. The decision of this ad hoc Sala Electoral left the country without a functioning National Electoral Council, obliging the National Assembly to appoint new members to the Council (Brewer Carías, 2004, p. 31). However, this appointment process was beset with political difficulties. The constitution requires that the five members of the National Electoral Council be persons without links to organizations with political objectives (Article 296). Three of them must be proposed by civil society organizations, one by Poder Ciudadano[30] and one by the law faculties of the national universities. They must also be elected by a two-thirds majority in the National Assembly. Negotiations were complicated by the fact that the government did not have such a majority.

When the allotted time span expired without the nomination of the National Electoral Council having taken place, various sectors resorted to the Sala Constitucional, asking it to nominate the council. The constitution stipulates that, if any constitutional provision should fail to be met due to omission by national, municipal, or federal legislatures, the Sala Constitucional can declare the omission to be unconstitutional and set a time limit for it to be rectified. If the omission is not corrected, the Sala Constitucional is authorized to take necessary measures (Article 336, 7°). The Sala declared an omission on the part of the National Assembly on August 4, 2003 and, after the ten-day period it set down had expired, went on to appoint the members of the National Electoral Council (Brewer Carías, 2004, p. 37). Government supporters protested that the Sala Constitucional had exceeded its remit, although their protests were also interpreted in another light: the decision had effectively paved the way for the referendum. The appointments did not correspond exactly to the spirit of the constitution. Four of the members chosen were clearly identified with the government or the opposition (in a two–two split), while the fifth was a political unknown. When this fifth member, who had been named president of the National Electoral Council, began to act, he showed a clear commitment to the government line (Kornblith, 2003).

The National Electoral Council began its mandate by declaring invalid the signatures that had been collected petitioning for a referendum to revoke the president's mandate. The signatures had been collected in February 2003 by the opposition, in an act known as the "*firmazo.*" The council established very strict regulations: in order to petition for a referendum to revoke the presidential mandate, signatures had to be collected on pre-determined days, on special security-marked papers, in an act which could be witnessed by the interested parties. Both the government and the opposition subsequently collected signatures, a week apart, between November and December of 2003.[31] These were major public events, broadcast by many television channels, supervised by the army and by international observers. The convocation sponsored by the government attracted few participants, whereas the opposition's generated huge queues. Around December 20, 2003, both the opposition and the government declared the number of signatures they had collected. The opposition claimed 3,450,000 signatures, a million more than the total required in order to call the referendum.

On March 2, 2004, the three Electoral Council members identified with the government published the provisional results of the official count. They acknowledged 1,800,000 valid signatures, declared around 400,000 invalid and considered that a further 900,000 (a figure which later grew to around 1,200,000) needed to be confirmed. This would require that those people who had signed, but who had not additionally printed their name in their own handwriting, be asked to confirm whether they had in fact signed or not. The two members identified with the opposition alleged that there was no valid basis for requiring confirmation of signatures, and that there were enough signatures to call a referendum.

In the days that followed, government and opposition supporters resorted to the Sala Electoral. Opposition supporters wanted the petitioners' cause to be upheld and called for the referendum. Government supporters pressed for the disqualification of the magistrates supposedly sympathetic to the opposition, to no avail. On March 15, 2004, the Sala Electoral decided that the requirement to check signatures only applied to those people whose signatures could have been obtained by subterfuge. It also ordered the checking of 39,000 signatures that had been rendered void by errors attributable to the electoral administration. This decision made it more than probable that the referendum would go ahead, and in effect guaranteed the electoral and constitutional solution to which government and opposition had both committed themselves. Each decision of the Sala Electoral was met by a contrary decision from the Sala Constitucional, and so a kind of "turf war" grew up between them, exposing the depth of magistrates' political commitments. Each bench contained a majority "line" together with an unswerving minority who delivered dissident votes (Brewer-Carías, 2004).

In Venezuela, the National Electoral Council is the electoral arbiter par excellence. The constitution defines it as one of the five branches of state. The Sala Electoral was conceived of as the mechanism for overseeing the legality of decisions taken by the council. In naming the members of the National Electoral Council by government majority, and subsequently impeding the Sala Electoral from exercising jurisdictional oversight of the council's actions, the Sala Constitucional placed control of all electoral and referendum-related matters squarely in the hands of government supporters. As noted earlier, on the basis of the

Sala Constitucional's decisions, the Moral Council of the Republic declared that the magistrates of the Sala Electoral who had made rulings favorable to the opposition had committed serious errors warranting the initiation of dismissal proceedings.[32]

In the event, the National Electoral Council finally won the day. It was able to maintain the exclusion of the invalid signatures, and over a million more were rendered subject to confirmation. Despite the prevailing atmosphere of coercion, opponents managed to collect enough signatures to call the referendum. The presence of international observers, plus the interventions of former U.S. President Jimmy Carter and of OAS Secretary César Gaviria, were decisive in having the result recognized (Carter, 2004). The referendum was eventually held on August 15, 2004 and the opposition was defeated.

Conclusions: Judicial Culture and Judicialization

An overview of the history of the supreme court over the last few years shows that the magistrates of the supreme court allowed political change to take a constitutional course at the end of the 1990s; whereas in the decade that followed, supreme tribunal magistrates tended to block political opposition. This is particularly true of the Sala Constitucional and its behavior regarding the referendum for the revoking of the presidential mandate.[33] The lack of impartiality evidenced by magistrates raises an important issue: why, if they were aware of the bias displayed by judges, have lawyers nonetheless attempted to make use of judicial recourse? It seems that despite government opposition—or perhaps because of it—lawyers and citizens are prepared to bring controversial cases before the courts and, especially, before the supreme tribunal. What motivates lawyers to take action through the courts even when there is little prospect of success? When interviewed, various lawyers who have represented opposition figures, or who have brought actions that favor opposition interests, expressed the hope of being able to subject individual supreme court judges to persuasion. In other instances, there may be more direct interests at stake. Requests to have laws nullified, or for criminal proceedings against the president of the republic or high regime officials generate considerable publicity[34] and can win lawyers a certain status amongst the opposition. Whatever the motives might be, the fact is that lawyers, like citizens in general, are increasingly using the judicial system as an instrument of political opposition in Venezuela. The attitude that citizens and lawyers take toward the judicial system and its use imply changes in legal culture. The recent history of Venezuela, as well as outside events, has changed patterns of resort to lawyers, law, and the courts. This, perhaps, is the genuine revolution that has occurred. Perhaps once the present difficulties are over, this tendency may lead to the consolidation of the rule of law, a longstanding aspiration in a divided nation.

Notes

This chapter is the first attempt to define a research project which I have undertaken jointly with René Molina. We have had many discussions, and I have benefited greatly from his vast knowledge of supreme tribunal decisions, as well as from the interviews he has carried out with supreme tribunal President Iván Rincón Urdaneta and with Magistrate Antonio García García. I am indebted to Magistrate Rafael Pérez Perdomo for much of my understanding of the workings of the supreme tribunal and how its decisions are made. I am, likewise, grateful to Ana María Ruggieri and Evelyn Marrero, magistrates of the now-defunct Corte Primera de lo Contencioso Administrativo, for agreeing to be interviewed. Humberto Njaim, Rafael Chavero, and Víctor Hugo Guerra have helped me to acquire a better understanding of particular rulings. René Molina and Francisco Plaza helped revise this chapter. Responsibility for the interpretations given here and for any errors remains, of course, entirely my own.

1. Patria Para Todos is a left-wing party of recent origin. Bandera Roja is a small party of the extreme left, usually associated with Trotskyism.
2. The name change is far from incidental. Although Bolívar is a national hero, the political movement founded by Chávez also originally called itself "Bolivarian." The implied message, which Chávez has often made explicit through words and actions, is that anyone who is not "Bolivarian" is not a true Venezuelan or a real citizen. Opposition is unacceptable (Pérez Perdomo, 2003a).
3. For an analysis of Chávez' political project, see Blanco (2002).
4. Amnesty International, "Venezuela: Human Rights under Threat," May 12, 2004, http://web.amnesty.org/library/Index/ENGAMR530082004; Human Rights Watch, "Questions and Answers about Venezuela's Court-Packing Law," July 14, 2004, http://hrw.org/backgrounder/americas/venezuela/2004/
5. This has been reported in newspapers and news programmes. For a general reading, see Comisión Interamericana de Derechos Humanos, 2003.
6. A minority opposition group formed the "Bloque Democrático," who argued that the only way to oppose Chávez was by open, violent resistance.
7. The opposition complained that the electoral registry had been inflated and the new electoral machines manipulated. International observers initially endorsed Chávez's victory, but OAS Secretary César Gaviria later pointed out serious flaws in the election.
8. Dr. Sánchez Risso, secretary of the supreme court between approximately 1958 and 1998, considers that the volume and significance of matters taken before the supreme court was incomparably greater in the 1990s than in the 1960s (personal communication).

9. Agreement 4270-VE. The World Bank provided a US$4.7 million loan, with the republic providing the remainder.

10. Supreme court of Justice, Sala Político Administrativa, decision of January 19, 1999.

11. These were the Sala Constitucional, the Sala Político Administrativa, the Sala Penal, the Sala Civil, and the Sala Electoral.

12. Luis Miquilena was an important left-wing political leader during the 1960s. Following his retirement from active politics he developed a close friendship with businessman Tobías Carrero, whose business interests include the "Multinacional de Seguros," a major insurance firm. Several of the new magistrates of the supreme tribunal, including Cabrera, Rondón Haaz, and Arriechi, were lawyers for that firm.

13. This form of protest involves the banging of pots and pans in front of the victim's house, usually in the early hours of the morning. It can also take place in public places such as restaurants, especially if these are located near places frequented by opposition groups.

14. Presiding Magistrate Iván Rincón Urdaneta happened across a group who had gathered at a funeral home for the wake of a young investigative journalist with links to the opposition. The death was believed to be the result of a political assassination. On catching sight of Rincón the group remonstrated with him, and one person threw coffee at him.

15. I am not aware of any existing analysis of the style of the defunct supreme court, and this assertion is based on the many individual commentaries on sentences, particularly those of law professors at the Central University of Venezuela. It is my impression that, after 1992, the Supreme Court of Justice did pay more attention to the material aspects of the cases before it, moderating its formalism to some degree.

16. Article 266, paragraph 3 of the constitution. This is clearly a procedural privilege established by the constitution of 1961 in order to protect the highest state functionaries from being interrupted in the execution of their duties by frequent accusations. The 1999 constitution extended this same protection to high-ranking officers of the armed forces.

17. In Venezuela the executive can order private radio and television stations to abandon their usual transmissions and re-broadcast programmes mandated by the government. Presidents prior to Chávez had used this faculty to transmit certain important announcements. President Chávez, by contrast, has used it frequently and for various purposes. On April 11, 2001 no significant announcement was made: the objective was to prevent the transmission of information about what was happening on the streets.

18. Article 476 of the Military Justice Code states that military rebellion consists of "[acts] . . . to promote, assist or sustain any armed movement to disturb the internal peace of the Republic; or to impede or obstruct the exercise of government in any of its branches."

19. The complete expression is *"plasta de mierda"* (literally, "a pile of shit"), although the last part is usually omitted. It is considered an insulting and disrespectful phrase in common Venezuelan usage.

20. Amparo is a judicial injunction to protect a fundamental right. It is a quick procedure.

21. Organic laws are the fundamental laws that set up the administration of government. Ordinary laws are the statutes passed by the regular legislature.

22. The preferred requisites were a specialization in public law, as demonstrated by the holding of a professorship or by having practiced as a lawyer in the field for more than ten years. These were more exacting requirements than those set down in the constitution for prospective magistrates of the supreme court.

23. The national treasurer is a civil servant with the rank of director in the treasury department. Various state governors (who are elected representatives) are from the opposition. It was (or is) government policy not to deliver, or to delay, the funds to which they are constitutionally entitled. The person who appears as having failed to fulfill their responsibilities is the national treasurer, hence recourse is to the Corte Primera.

24. There are no exact figures available for the number of Cuban doctors or other Cuban personnel invited to Venezuela. There are also sports coaches, agricultural technicians, and security personnel. One section of Chávez's numerous personal guard is made up of Cubans. Various journalists have alleged that many Cubans enter the country on Venezuelan passports.

25. *El Universal*, August 26, 2003.

26. Ibid., January 22, 2003.

27. Author's interview with Magistrate Evelyn Marrero, February 4, 2004.

28. The Commission for the Functioning and Restructuring of the Judicial System is a remnant of the Judicial Emergency Commission appointed by the constituent assembly in 1999. It originally had seven members, subsequently reduced to three.

29. On February 4, 2004, I was able to confirm in person that the Corte Primera de lo Contencioso Administrativo continued to be inactive and was closed to the public. Access was extremely restricted, and DISIP personnel were requesting identification from those authorized to enter.

30. The Poder Ciudadano is a state power that embodies the idea of a "moral power" that operates in the defense of the public interest. It consists of the Defensor del Pueblo (Ombudsman's Office), the Fiscal General de la República (Attorney General's Office), and the Contralador General de la República (the Treasury Inspector's Office).

31. This regulation can be read as a considerable obstacle to or limitation on citizens' political participation. In this sense, the actions of

the National Electoral Council do not correspond to the definition of participative democracy established by the constitution, nor to the Council's proper function of facilitating electoral participation. The opposition did not protest; instead it converted the requirement to repeat the collection of signatures into a major public act of protest and reaffirmation of faith in democracy (the so-called "*reafirmazo*"). There were probably also practical reasons for their acceptance: the public nature of the act, and the control mechanisms which were put in place, rendered groundless the accusations of fraud which were to be expected from the government—and which Chávez did, in effect, make as soon as the collection of signatures was over. It is particularly noteworthy that the government, which itself controls the electoral body, made the accusations of fraud. International observers declared that they did not witness any fraudulent behavior whatsoever.

32. *El Nacional*, June 19, 2004, pp. A1, A2, and A14.
33. For a more detailed analysis see Brewer-Carías, 2004.
34. There have also been various complaints against Chávez and other high-ranking officials for corruption and crimes against humanity. Some of these complaints have been presented in the Spanish courts (Audiencia Nacional Española) and in the International Criminal Court. Naturally, these cases have generated instant publicity. The public and journalists cannot, for the most part, form an impression of how grounded the claims may be, but the lawyer concerned attracts a significant amount of media attention.

References

Blanco, Carlos (2002) *Revolución y desilusión: La Venezuela de Hugo Chávez* (Madrid: Catarata).

Brewer-Carías, Allan R. (2004) *La Sala Constitucional versus el Estado Democrático de Derecho* (Caracas: Los Libros de El Nacional).

Brito González, José, "Consideraciones acerca de la idea y concreción del Consejo de la Judicatura en el marco del Estado contemporáneo," *Politeia*, vol. 7 (1978), pp. 215–33.

Carter, Jimmy (2004) "President Carter's Trip Report on Venezuela, May 29–June 1, 2004," at http://www.cartercenter.org/viewdoc.asp?docID=1700&submenu=news

Comisión Interamericana de Derechos Humanos (2003) *Informe sobre la situación de los derechos humanos en Venezuela* (24 de octubre) at http://www.cidh.oas.org/countryrep/Venezuela2003sp/indice.htm

Kornblith, Miriam (2003) "Elecciones y representación en tiempos turbulentos," in Patricia Márquez and Ramón Piñango (eds), *En esta Venezuela: Realidades y nuevos caminos* (Caracas: Ediciones IESA).

Márquez, Patricia and Ramón Piñango (eds.) (2003) *En esta Venezuela. Realidades y nuevos caminos* (Caracas: Ediciones IESA).

Molina, René (2002) *Reflexiones sobre una visión constitucional del proceso y su tendencia jurisprudencial ¿Hacia un gobierno judicial?* (Caracas: Ediciones Paredes).

Pérez Perdomo, Rogelio (2003a) "La dimensión constitucional de la crisis política," in Márquez and Piñango, *En esta Venezuela* (Caracas: Ediciones IESA).

——— (2003b) "Venezuela 1958–1999: The Legal System in an Impaired Democracy," in Lawrence Friedman and Rogelio Pérez-Perdomo (eds.), *Legal Culture in the Age of Globalization: Latin America and Latin Europe* (Stanford: Stanford University Press), pp. 414–78.

——— (2004) "Reforma judicial, estado de derecho y revolución en Venezuela," in Luis Pásara (ed.), *En búsqueda de una justicia distinta: Experiencias de reforma en América Latina* (Lima: Consorcio de Justicia Viva), pp. 335–74.

Quintero, Mariolga (1988) *Justicia y realidad* (Caracas: Universidad Central de Venezuela).

Chapter 7

Petitioning and Creating Rights: Judicialization in Argentina

Catalina Smulovitz

Courts and the law are playing an increasingly important political role. Courts are redefining public policies decided by representative authorities, and citizens are using the law and rights-framed discourses as political tools to address private and social demands, as well as to govern everyday social interactions previously regulated by cooperation, trust, or kinship. This increased use of legal procedures and rights-framed discourses is taking place in various forms and in different regions and has given birth to a growing literature on the judicialization of politics.[1] Analysts agree that the process involves the expansion of the domains and roles of the courts, judges, and litigants. While some studies highlight the non-democratic political impact that courts as political agencies, and judges as political actors, have on sovereign decisions; others center on the democratic implications of citizens' increased use of the law as a petitioning tool. Still others emphasize the deleterious consequences of the judicialization of interpersonal and everyday relationships on social life (Glendon, 1991). These outcomes are not mutually exclusive. Indeed, they can take place simultaneously, leading to mixed and ambiguous assessments regarding the consequences of the process of judicialization.

What types of judicialization are taking place in Argentina? And what are their political and social consequences? In this chapter I analyze the specific way in which two particular forms of judicialization— judicialization as a petitioning tool and judicialization as a discourse of rights—are developing in Argentina, as well as the political consequences of their appearance.

Judicialization as Legal Mobilization:
Social Demands and Legal Protest

Judicialization can take different forms. It can involve the growing participation of bodies able to make constitutional reviews of political decisions (see also table 7.8A in Appendix),[2] it can imply the use of a discourse of rights to develop new rights, or it can involve the increased use of ordinary judicial procedures to address conflicts between settled rights and practices violating those rights. In this section I analyze this latter form of judicialization.

Increased ordinary litigation can signal the institutionalization of social relationships. If that is the case, increased litigation rates imply not only that actors choose to use institutionalized procedures to adjust their disagreements, but that they expect the judicial system to efficiently (impartially and promptly) "resolve" their disputes. Over the past few years Argentina has witnessed an increase in the number of proceedings filed at different levels of the judiciary (see table 7.1 and corresponding graph). However, it should also be noted that these increases have taken place in a context characterized by the consistent decrease of the prestige and trust in the efficiency and impartiality of the judiciary (see table 7.8B in Appendix). In a context where the utility of making legal claims is uncertain and where the impartiality of the judiciary is in doubt, we must wonder about the reasons citizens have to make use of this instrument. If litigation does not lead to practical or remedial results, other reasons must be considered to explain the phenomenon.

Why have judicial claims and individual complaints increased despite the discredit of the judiciary? The literature on legal mobilization provides an answer to this apparent paradox. It shows that litigation can increase, even though there are no guarantees about the outcomes of the judicial claims, because rather than as a practical strategy to achieve specific results, legal disputing can also be used to achieve symbolic legitimization, institutional acknowledgment of the claims, and political and social leverage for the petitions (McCann, 1991). If that is the case, an increase in litigation rates can be an indication of a process of legal mobilization rather than an indication of trust in the abilities of the judiciary to solve disputes. According to Frances Zemans "law is . . . mobilised when a desire or want is translated into a demand as an assertion of one's rights" (Zemans, 1983, p. 700). When judicialization appears as legal mobilization, the "majesty of the law" is used to call attention to private or social claims. Although claimants know that partial victories are not warranted, they also know that they are not precluded either. Legal mobilization is a

Table 7.1 Case files submitted to the Supreme Court of Justice, federal courts, and state jurisdictions, 1991–2002 (number of files)

Year	Total national judiciary	Supreme court	Federal courts	State jurisdictions
1991	621,383	5,332	473,710	142,341
1992	694,911	6,546	516,101	172,264
1993	796,749	24,507	589,968	182,274
1994	1,046,813	36,657	690,884	319,272
1995	1,102,671	16,880	736,502	349,289
1996	912,913	23,519	660,690	228,704
1997	1,101,546	9,639	753,023	338,884
1998	1,002,134	7,888	719,451	274,795
1999	1,087,298	13,595	760,398	313,305
2000	1,000,296	17,290	766,084	216,922
2001	944,637	14,262	705,871	224,504
2002	1,330,287	41,860	884,922	403,505

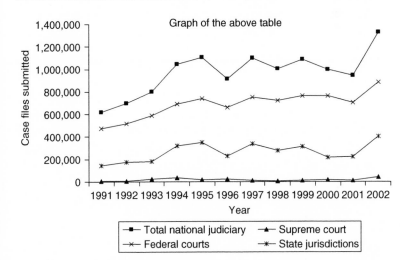

Source: Poder Judicial de la Nación, Corte Suprema de Justicia, *Estadísticas 2000, 2001, and 2002*.

valuable tool for individuals and social movements because when legal disputes are initiated, the legal system is forced to provide some kind of answer.[3] In the process, legal complaints become a mechanism that can turn legal mobilization by citizens into a potential law-enforcing activity. On the other hand, when practical results do not follow, the political and symbolic effects of legal mobilization cannot be avoided. For these reasons, some consider legal mobilization as the paradigmatic form of political involvement in a democracy: it gives actors a voice, it allows them to expand the visibility and scope of their conflicts, and it allows them—at times—to readdress the orientation of certain policies (McCann, 1991; Zemans, 1983).

The use of legal procedures as a tool for social resistance and demand is not new in Argentina. During the last dictatorship, the *habeas data* was used not only to demand protection but also to give visibility to the clandestine and illegal character of the repression that was taking place.[4] More recently, the judicialization of the pension funds dispute and the conflict over the freeze on savings deposits (the so-called *corralito* case) illustrates how ordinary legal proceedings have been used to pursue social claims and readdress policy, to obstruct unfavorable public policy, to expand social alliances and to oversee governmental actions.

The judicialization of the pension fund conflict began in the early 1960s, when deficits in the pension fund system determined the reduction of the amount paid to beneficiaries.[5] According to a 1958 law, retirement benefits were to fluctuate between 70 percent and 82 percent of a worker's salary. This policy was significantly limited in 1960 by another that reduced that amount for medium and high range salaries. Later on, all benefits were de facto reduced due to inflation. All sources recognize that it was at that time when the judicialization process began. Since then, lawsuits have been motivated by claims related to the adjustment criteria used to calculate benefits, to the unconstitutionality of the ceilings set for the benefits, to the inadequate proportionality between salaries and benefits, to the distortion that escalating inflation rates produced in the benefits, as well as to the delays in updating benefits. In addition, there have been lawsuits demanding the execution of court sentences and others questioning the decision to pay debts with national debt bonds. Throughout the period, the government has taken a series of measures that indicate the fiscal and social magnitude of the phenomenon. It sanctioned (twice) decrees establishing a halt in the legal proceedings, it offered schedules to pay debts over a ten year period, it declared the economic emergency of the system, it suspended the execution of court decisions and it offered beneficiaries willing to give up their right to initiate legal proceedings benefit adjustments. In the early 1990s the government recognized that it had a US$12,365.6 million debt with 4,024,837 beneficiaries.[6] Lawsuits initiated after the change to a mixed regime that took place in 1994 have questioned the violation of the right to a prompt trial (3,000 cases) and the criteria used to update benefit payments (70,000 cases). According to an Interamerican Development Bank report, in 2001 when the system counted 3,200,000 beneficiaries, approximately 20,000 lawsuits were being filed each year, 100,000 lawsuits were in process and nearly 120,000 benefits payments were granted.[7]

While the judicialization of the pension funds conflict has been taking place for over 40 years, the judicialization of the freeze on savings deposits dispute (the *corralito* case) is new, and is likely to have a shorter life. Despite this, its explosive development constitutes a condensed illustration of the process of legal mobilization as a political and resistance tool.[8]

On December 1, 2001, Domingo Cavallo, the then economy minister, announced the establishment of restrictions on cash withdrawals from private and company bank accounts.[9] The decision took place in a context characterized by the continuous drainage of private sector deposits. In the last quarter of 2001, the outflow had built up to US$15,500 million and amounted to US$ 1,500 million on November 30, 2001.[10] Three days after this announcement, a house representative of the Partido Justicialista[11] announced that his party intended to present an *amparo*[12] (injunction) against restrictions on withdrawals from salary accounts,[13] and the National Union of Judicial Employees (UEJN) initiated the first collective injunction claiming the unconstitutionality of the economic measures and their immediate rejection due to their "confiscating" character.[14] A week later there were 220 cases denouncing the unconstitutionality of the measure.[15] On January 1, 2002, after middle class and popular anger won the streets, riots, looting, and police repression took place and two presidents resigned (De la Rúa and Rodríguez Saá). The legislative assembly subsequently elected Peronist Eduardo Duhalde as president. In the following two months Duhalde abandoned the ten-year peg of the peso to the dollar, established the total "pesification" (conversion into pesos) of the economy,[16] and a dual exchange rate system—1.40 pesos per dollar for official transactions and a floating one for all other transactions. Debts in dollars within the financial system were converted to pesos at a 1 to 1 exchange rate, while deposits in dollars were "pesified" at a 1 to 1.40 exchange rate. In addition, new restrictions for withdrawals from personal and corporate deposits were imposed, reprogramming their availability. The new restrictions expanded the previously established ones, imposing time limit restrictions of up to three years for withdrawals from savings deposits. It should be noted that by December 2001, 70 percent of the deposits in the banking system were nominated in U.S. dollars[17] and that by July 2002, the floating exchange rate was over 3.5 pesos per dollar.

Before the end of that chaotic December, newspapers were already reporting a wave of judicial cases against the *corralito*, questioning the constitutionality of the measure and a federal judge sanctioned a preliminary measure against the imposed restrictions (at that time, the number of cases amounted to 220).[18] By April 2002, the office of the

Table 7.2 Injunctions presented in federal administrative courts (federal capital and interior), 2001–2002

	2001–2002	2003
Federal capital	143,580	29,241
Rest of the country	194,372	29,548
Total	337,952	58,789

Source: Poder Judicial de la Nación *Estadística*, 2002 and 2003.

Procuración del Tesoro Nacional, published that 210,188 "*amparos* against the *corralito*" had been presented in the federal justice system.[19] The information explicitly specified that these numbers did not include injunctions presented in the provincial justice system, although several sources have mentioned that the number of injunctions at a provincial level were similar to the ones at a federal level.[20] By the end of 2002, the Statistical Bulletin of the National Judiciary informed that *amparos* against the *corralito* amounted to 337,952 (see table 7.2).

In April 2002, the two banking associations—Asociación de Bancos de la Argentina (ABA) and Asociación de Bancos Públicos y Privados de la República Argentina (ABAPPRA)—in a report to the supreme court warned about the risks that favorable judicial treatment of *corralito* demands would bring about, given that the 200,000 existing claims comprised only a small number of the 9,000,000 savers in the financial system.[21] At that time, newspapers also published stories about the initiation of more than 20,000 additional injunctions and about the presentation of two collective demands advanced by the National and Municipal Ombudsman Offices demanding a halt in the application of the Reference Stabilization Coefficient (CER) that was to be applied to credits that were in dollars and had been converted into pesos,[22] as had been established in the decree 214/02. By June 2004, the weekly report of the BCRA on the status of the *corralito* demands indicated that from April 5, 2002 to June 18, 2004, 264,557 writs of *amparo* had received favorable responses[23] (table 7.3 and figure 7.1).

The history of these two cases can be read as an illustration of the "science of muddling through" by legal means, where actors resist the imposition of a policy and readdress its content through the continuous use of legal tools backed by periodic mobilizations. In both conflicts, the initial dispute exceeded its original boundaries and developed into a network of different and related judicial claims. In the pension funds conflict, for example, there were claims concerning

Table 7.3 Total number of injunctions paid and amounts, 2002–2004

Year	Number of cases	Money paid (in million of pesos)
2002	165,384	13,441
2003	81,975	5,244
2004 (June 18)	17,198	1,022
Total	264,557	19,707

Source: Banco Central de la República Argentina, Informe semanal no. 56, June 25, 2004.

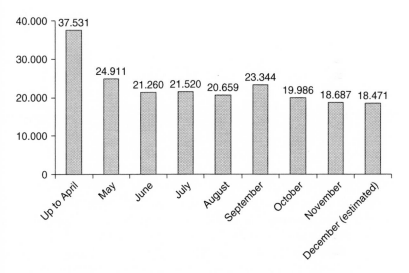

Figure 7.1 Average amount returned per injunction (in dollars) in the year 2002
Source: Banco Central de la República Argentina, Informe semanal No. 8, January 3, 2003.

the amount of the benefits paid, claims contesting the indexes used to update benefits, claims demanding the execution of court sentences, and others questioning the political and legislative changes the government kept introducing. Something similar took place in the *corralito* conflict, where injunctions for violations of property rights were followed by others (more than 20,000) against the retroactive application of the Reference Stabilization Coefficient (CER),[24] by others against measures suspending the right to file demands and still by others claiming the execution of favorable sentences. Indeed, in both cases the strength, effectiveness, and persistence of the legal disputes were highly associated with the continuous remaking and ramification of the original legal claims.

In both cases, throughout the conflict the government tried several responses to deal with the accumulation of claims and the risks of unfavorable court decisions. In the pension funds dispute, the government approved measures suspending the execution of legal sentences on two occasions. At another stage it acknowledged its debts and reprogrammed its payment in exchange of the claimants' resignation of future legal claims, and recently it established additional requirements to the legal procedure in order to increase the costs of litigation. The government used the same tools in the *corralito* case. It sanctioned decrees[25] establishing a six-month suspension in the initiation of claims and in the execution of court decisions, it re-programed its payment with bonds in exchange of claimants' resignation of future legal actions and it passed a law[26] establishing additional procedural requirements for complying with favorable court decisions. In both conflicts governmental reactions led to a succession of nested legal conflicts in which the original legal dispute was followed by "second order" legal conflicts questioning, on different although related grounds, the responses given to the original claim. The net result was that, after some time, the original dispute became an intricate chain of conflicts and the government ended up confronting an increasingly complex array of political, social, and legal contenders.

The analysis of both cases also shows that neither the massive character of the claims nor the successive waves of injunctions and lawsuits were able to totally achieve the litigants' goals. In the pension funds conflict claimants are still unsatisfied with the achieved results, and *corralito* claimants have not been able to achieve a final supreme court decision regarding the unconstitutionality of the freeze or the unconstitutionality of their conversion into pesos.[27] In spite of that, data also show that in both conflicts the achievements have not been irrelevant. A significant number of claims have received favorable judicial decisions and both—pension funds beneficiaries and *corralito* claimants—have achieved important extra-legal results. In the two cases, claimants achieved "piecemeal" successes, such as individual court decisions that eroded, limited, and in some cases reversed governmental policy decisions. In addition, in both cases, the juridical framing of the disputes forced the government to give official and public responses to the claims, restricting, in turn, its ability to impose arbitrary political decisions. Thus, from the claimants' points of view, even though the legal strategy did not achieve all their goals, it has proven to be an effective defensive strategy in so far as it has minimized initial losses.

In addition to the partial satisfaction of the claims, the intervention of the judges provided claimants with legitimacy and public recognition. In transforming their petitions into legal petitions, claimants were able to transform their claims into officially broken promises (Scheingold, 1974) and judges into "guardians of past promises" (Garapon, 1997, p. 20). This transformation created public empathy, brought social allies to their cause and made judges institutional custodians of their demands. Thus, the social and political consequences of judicialization processes do not concentrate only on the punitive potential of judicial decisions. As Galanter (1983), among other authors, has noted, the law is both an operating set of controls and a system of cultural and symbolic meanings. Its use creates threats, promises, blessings, and stigmas (McCann, 1998). These radiating and symbolic effects of law nurture the development of additional agendas and organize political and social movements around the public acknowledgment of their experience as victims of a violation of rights.

These cases show that in Argentina the judicialization of politics understood as legal mobilization has been used to advance demands and to claim rights when conflicts between already settled rights and a practice violating those rights takes place. Legal mobilization has given actors a voice, has expanded the visibility and scope of their conflicts; it has also allowed them to achieve partial goals and to readdress the orientation of certain policies.

Judicialization as the Triumph of a Rights-Based Discourse

In this section I concentrate on the use of legal mobilization as a tool for developing new rights or to extend the judicialization of nonregulated practices. I argue that in recent years in Argentina, the expansion of the domain of law and of a rights-based discourse is reaching new arenas of interpersonal interchanges. The cases analyzed can be read as a manifestation of the perennial expansion of the domain of law into new arenas of social interaction. Some of those interactions are still mainly regulated by trust and cooperation, others were until recently not understood as illegitimate behavior, and still others appear as problems searching for juridification. The cases can also be read as an illustration of the way in which actors use the discourse of rights to call public attention to unheard demands and conflicts even though they are not yet recognized as such by the legislation. In recent times rights claims have increased sharply in areas of consumer rights, professional malpractice, rights of de facto partners and unions, sexual harassment, marital violence and discrimination based on lifestyles. The transformation of these problems into rights-oriented claims implies, on the one hand, the attempt to expand the reach of rights into previously unregulated practices and the attempt to judicialize new arenas of social life. On the other hand, the transformation of these problems into rights-oriented claims highlights that the frontiers of citizenship are becoming contested and that the rules and language that previously governed these relationships are being challenged.

Different empirical evidence confirms the emergence of this type of judicialization in the Argentine case. One relates to the growing number of complaints made at the recently created control agencies, such as consumer defense agencies, ombudsman's offices, and utilities regulatory agencies. It should be remembered that claims submitted to these agencies do not necessarily become judicial disputes. In spite of that, citizen and consumer complaints have been growing. This increase and the fact that these complaints are taking place in public agencies and in private organizations (such as consumer associations), reveal that citizens perceive their injuries as rights, that is, as grievances that deserve the protection of the state and as claims entitled to some sort of reparation. This growing trend can be observed at the municipal ombudsman's office and at regulatory agencies overseeing privatized utilities enterprises (see tables 7.4, 7.5, and 7.6 and corresponding graph). For example, the Defensoría del Pueblo de la Nación, an agency created in 1994, received in its first year, ten complaints per day, while in the following years the average number of daily complaints increased to 100. In 1998, annual complaints at the Dirección de Defensa del Consumidor y Lealtad Comercial (National Consumers' Defence Office), amounted to 25,708, and averaged 2,142 per month, while in November 2003, monthly inquiries amounted to 5,533.[28]

The regulation of professional services is another arena where citizens' interventions shaped and based on a rhetoric of rights is growing. Although no comprehensive statistical data is available, fragmented information reveals an increase in the number of lawsuits filed for civil or professional liability. According to Gerardo Russo, between 1982 and 1993 claims for medical malpractice grew by 1,000 percent and between 1995 and 1996 criminal claims for malpractice increased by 80 percent and civil claims by 26.4 percent.[29] A more recent study about the economic impact of malpractice claims (Tobar et al., 2001) noted that although in Argentina these types of claims are not as common as in the United States, between 1980 and 2000, an estimate of 10,000 medical doctors have been the object of this

Table 7.4 Actions filed at the *Defensoría General de la Nación* (National Consumers' Defence Agency) and at the *Oficina Municipal Del Ombudsman* (Municipal Ombudsman's Office)

	Claims filed at the Defensoría General de la Nación	Claims filed at the Municipal Ombudsman
1988		1,021
1989		934
1990		1,058
1991		1,511
1992 (*)		848
1993		1,478
1994	756	2,851
1995	7,256	2,713
1996	22,697	2,423
1997	25,496	2,280
1998	30,434	1,740
1999	18,000	4,595
2000	14,716	5,501
2001		12,528
2002		26,399

Note: (*) indicates that in this year the continuity of the *Defensor de la Ciudad* (City's Defender) was not certain.

Source: Defensor del Pueblo de la Nación. Informe Anual 1994 y 1995. Controladuría General Municipal. Estadística Informativa del Defensor del Pueblo de la Ciudad de Buenos Aires.

Table 7.5 Number of questions and claims received at the *Dirección de Defensa del Consumidor Y Lealtad Comercial* (Consumer Defence and Commercial Loyalty Authority) (in absolute figures)

Year	Complaints	Inquiries	Complaints and inquiries
1993			8,842
1994			4,248
1995	2,196	23,926	26,122
1996	3,232	26,325	29,857
1997	3,993	37,939	41,932
1998	3,237	25,708	28,945
1999	793*	13,224*	14,017
Total	13,451	127,122	153,963

Note: * indicates data until June 1999.

Source: Defensa al Consumidor: 5 Años de Aplicación de la Ley, Revista de la Dirección de Defensa al Consumidor, 1999.

Table 7.6   Claims filed at utilities' regulatory agencies

	Energas	Etoss	Enre	Total
1993	1,252	1,101	5,567	7,920
1994	2,985	5,037	16,471	24,493
1995	4,441	6,198	12,336	22,975
1996	4,259	7,587	15,307	27,153
1997	4,880	7,485	13,939	26,304
1998	6,243	7,421	11,956	25,620
1999	6,989	9,012	14,081	30,082
2000	7,498	10,924	17,800	36,222
2001	5,578	7,089	25,472	38,139
2002	5,315	4,158	20,385	29,858

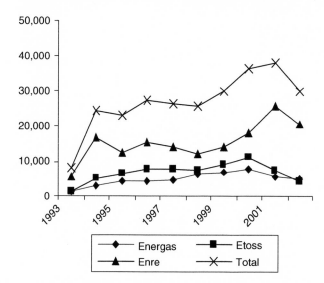

Notes: Energas, Gas Supply Regulatory Agency; Etoss, Water Supply Regulatory Agency; Enre, Electricity Regulatory Agency.

Source: Energas, Etoss, and Enre. Annual Bulletins.

type of demand. The report also asserts that only 20 percent of criminal claims and 25 percent of the civil claims result in sentences. The difference between claims and sentences can be signaling two different and opposite situations. While on the one hand, this distance may be the product of the unfriendly judicial treatment of these claims, on the other, it may also reveal that claimants' perceptions about what constitute their rights may be overestimated. Information provided by insurance companies confirms that citizens' perception about this right is consolidating. According to the Superintendencia de Seguros

Table 7.7 Claims filed in the national courts in the federal capital based on the enforcement of law 24,417 (January 1995–December 2000)

Victim	1995	1996	1997	1998	1999	2000
Minor	199	240	322	400	304	383
Elderly	9	23	24	39	38	32
Handicapped	4	4	2	5	6	7
Women	*749*	*1,240*	*1,447*	*1,651*	*1,696*	*1,859*
Male	32	94	89	120	117	125
Others	3	7	6	8	7	4
Total	1,009	1,601	1,820	2,167	2,160	2,269

Source: Consejo Nacional de la Mujer, *La Mujer y la Violencia en la República Argentina*. Buenos Aires, 2002.

de la Nación, between 1996 and 2000 claims for medical malpractice against insurance corporations have increased 304 percent. According to the Sun Pacific Consulting Agency, between six and ten physicians out of every 100 are sued each year for malpractice in Argentina and lawsuits against Buenos Aires hospitals grew by 26.42 percent between 1995 and 1996.[30] Despite the low probability of being declared guilty, physicians have started contracting some kind of insurance, and in many cases health care professionals are required by prepaid health care organizations to contract insurance in order to be included in their health care provider listings. This data indicates the advancement of a discourse of rights in a relationship that used to be regulated by informal mechanisms such as trust and authority.

Family violence and sexual harassment at the workplace are two other areas where the advancement of a discourse of rights is taking place. In December 1994, after the constitutional reform incorporated the "International Convention Against the Discrimination of Women," a law against family violence was approved (Law 24,417). Both the content of the law and the way in which it has been enforced throughout the 24 provinces have been severely criticized by women and human rights organizations.[31] Despite this, it should be noted that in 1996 and 1997 CELS reported that annual inquiries regarding victims of domestic violence averaged 25,000 and that by March 2001, the national courts at the Federal District had received 11,026 claims denouncing domestic violence (see table 7.7). Again, regardless of the limitations that enacted laws offer, the persistent increase of claims and inquiries shows that a behavior that was previously not legally regulated has become a rights claim and a judicialized dispute.

Sexual harassment in the workplace is another area where the demand for rights and judicialization has been increasing. Although since 1991 different legislative projects[32] have been presented, there is no national legislation punishing sexual harassment in private workplaces. And currently only three districts—the province of Buenos Aires, the city of Buenos Aires, and the province of Santa Fe—have approved legislation punishing sexual harassment in the public sector.[33] Despite this, lawyers involved in those cases have confirmed that sexual harassment claims in private workplaces are being filed "disguised" as claims for emotional damages (*daño moral*) or as compensation claims brought under legislation governing the terms of workers' redundancy. The existence of these claims and the responses they have brought about show, on the one hand, that the accused are responding as if the claims actually had positive legal status.[34] On the other hand, the evolution of the cases confirms, as Martha Minow has noted, that the process of converting aspirations into rights "often occurs outside the courts" (Minow, 1987, p. 1862).

Conclusions

There is no doubt that courts, the law, and the discourses of rights are playing an increasingly important political role in Argentina. The greater number of ordinary litigation cases and the increased use of rights-based discourses ratify their relevance as tools that are shaping the evolution and development of political struggles. The specific form in which the process of judicialization of politics is taking place shows, however, different forms and distinctive results. While the presence of judicialization understood as a mechanism to redefine public policies already determined by elected political officials (i.e. constitutional review) is high; the frequency of constitutional review has not increased. In recent years, two other forms of judicialization have undergone a significant development: judicialization as a tool to address conflicts between settled rights and practice violating those rights, and judicialization as a discourse of rights. While the first type of judicialization involves the use of the judicial procedures to make political and social demands and to resist the enforcement of certain policies, the latter form involves the use of the discourse of rights to transform aspirations into positive rights and to extend the domain of law into social practices that until recently or still are governed by informal mechanisms.

Before considering the consequences of these different forms of judicialization, a few comments are in order. The previous analysis highlights the role that social movements and an active civil society has had in the process of judicialization. Charles Epp (1998) has mentioned that conventional interpretations of the rights revolution identified constitutional guarantees, judicial leadership, and popular rights consciousness as variables that foster the process of judicialization. They are not enough to understand its occurrence but they are not irrelevant either. Although this is not the place to consider the impact of each of them in the Argentine process of judicialization, two short comments regarding the impact of institutions and right consciousness are in order.

Since the late 1960s, when the first cases analyzed in this chapter started to develop, constitutional guarantees have changed on several occasions. Actors initiated claims during periods when rights were widely protected, but also at times when they were not. Pension funds claims, for example, started in the early 1960s when rights were protected, but they continued to be initiated during the 1966–1973 dictatorship. Between 1976 and 1983, when violations of constitutional rights and lack of judicial protection were widespread, certain actors used legal claims, such as *habeas data*, as a tool to defy authority and to reveal the arbitrary and unconstitutional character of the exercise of power. Legal claims largely increased after the 1983 democratic transition and after the 1994 constitutional reform, new rights and guarantees were recognized. The constitutional recognition of the *amparo*, of environmental and consumer rights and the recognition of the right of public interest associations to initiate legal actions (Articles 42 and 43 of the 1994 constitution) are some examples of institutional innovations whose consequences cannot be disregarded. However, although constitutional guarantees and judicial protection are extremely relevant, they are not enough to explain the acceleration of the judicialization phenomenon. The *habeas corpus* cases that took place during the dictatorship show that, in certain circumstances, the use of legal tools can increase precisely in order to denounce the lack of constitutional guarantees. On the other hand, the initially timid use of the *amparos* shows that the introduction of constitutional guarantees does not necessarily result in the immediate increased use of a legal instrument.

What has been the role of rights consciousness in the Argentine case? Elsewhere (Smulovitz, 2002) I have argued that in the early 1980s, Argentine society discovered the benefits of the law. The visibility of the trials against the junta commanders due to human rights violations and other trials that took place in that period transformed the perceptions about the law and the role of the judiciary. Those trials revealed the judiciary as a place where citizens' rights could be realized and the rhetoric of the law as a potentially mobilizing and subversive tool. The central effect of these events was the revelation of an institutional tool and of a space for the resolution of disputes that had hitherto remained hidden. Some of the cases analyzed in this chapter indicate that before this discovery some actors were already using this tool. However, after this revelation occurred, rights claims not only increased and extended to other arenas, but they also experienced new uses. The acceleration of the judicialization process in Argentina rested then, not only on institutional conditions that enable its occurrence, but also on the development of skills, cognitive resources, and organizational capacities that allowed citizens and associations to take advantage of institutional and political opportunities.

Is the expansion of the judicialization process related to the market-oriented economic reforms that took place in the 1990s? Although this variable does not totally explain the explosion of the judicialization process, its consequences were not irrelevant either. On the one hand, it should be recalled that the judicialization process began before the market-oriented reforms started. But, the introduction of these policies affected the judicialization process in so far as they modified the way political and social actors related to the state and the resources they used to advance their political and economic claims. In the past, when exchanges between social actors were framed within a neo-corporatist logic, conflicts between parties were mainly solved through the exercise of political resources and through the intervention of their representatives. In the 1990s, market-oriented economic reforms weakened the ability of collective organizations to protect the interests of their members and the privatization of public utilities reinforced their transformation into individual customers. In this context, individuals, citizens, and customers used the law and quasi-legal claims to demand and deal with those issues and disputes the new social arrangements left unattended. Thus, even though it cannot be asserted that market-oriented economic reforms were the cause of the judicialization process, the transformation they produced created conditions that fostered the use of the law as a mechanism for the resolution of disputes, the protection of rights, and the petition of social demands.

What do the analyzed cases indicate about the consequences of judicialization understood as a protest and resistance mechanism? What have these types of judicialization accomplished? The cases illustrate that legal strategies can yield not only specific material benefits, but that they can also radiate important symbolic and political ones. The historical reconstruction of the cases shows that the legal strategy brought about significant material outcomes for plaintiffs. Although they did not accomplish all their intended goals, a significant percentage[35] of those who used the strategy obtained partially favorable responses. It should also be noted that initially these benefits only reached individuals who resorted to legal strategies.

However, these results do not capture the extra-legal consequences of judicialization as a tool of resistance and demands. The intervention of judges not only resulted in the partial satisfaction of the demands, it also provided the claims with legitimacy and public recognition. Legally framed social and political conflicts produced these results because, in the process, judicial procedures endowed unorganized individuals with a social and collective identity, brought them unexpected social and institutional allies, and created external institutional custodians for the claimants' demands. These results were also possible because social mobilization and media attention were important companions of the legal protest. On the one hand, media visibility illuminated the existence of an uncoordinated social phenomenon (a massive number of pension funds and *corralito* claimants). On the other hand, media visibility and social mobilization disseminated and advertised the availability of specific courses of action and "ready made" solutions for the claimants.

The legal framing of the disputes introduced an additional feature. It situated judges and tribunals as legitimate and authorized parties and as observers of public behavior and it altered, in turn, the resources involved in the "resolution" of the cases. When law becomes the new language of politics and procedures, its grammar, the way conflicts are solved, faces important restrictions (Garapon, 1997, p. 18). Legal precedents, reasonable arguments, and preestablished rules have to be considered in a decision. These requirements imposed constraints on the possible outcomes of the dispute: they enlarged the number of parties involved in the "resolution" of the conflict and they reduced the chances of imposing "solutions" based only on political grounds. The procedural architecture of the legal claim has an additional consequence: it supports the permanence and vitality of the conflicts. Claims have to be answered in certain ways and external time limits set the pace for the protest, presenting plaintiffs with periodical procedural opportunities that recreate the mystic of the protest and provide them with events that force protestors to coordinate actions.

Judicialization also affects the collective organization of actors. The legal strategy allows individual claimants to overcome some of the difficulties they face when attempting to collectively organize their actions. In contrast to other forms of protest, claimants can initiate protest actions without even coordinating with other actors. The cases analyzed show that individual legal protest became a social phenomenon due to the massive character and media visibility it achieved. The cases also show that when these two conditions started to wither away, the procedural architecture of the juridical process started to support the life of the dispute. The rituals and tempos that distinguish legal procedures set the pace of the claimants' actions, preventing the disappearance of the protest and the organization of claimants when external supporters stop paying attention to the demands.

What do the analyzed cases show about the consequences of judicialization understood as the expansion of a discourse of rights? When the discourse of rights does not overlap with positive rights the struggle around rights takes place outside the courts. The process involves, first, the expansion of the notion of entitlement. That is, that rights-based claims are not the product of whims, but that they rather articulate legitimate aspirations intended to remedy behaviors and actions that are now named as "unfair" (Felstiner et al., 1980–1981). Thus, in the struggle for rights, the struggle over their interpretation and meaning is critical. It determines whether rights demands can become a common ground for claimants and a source for the development of a common social identity. If that is the case, rights based discourses will nurture social mobilization and become a rallying point for collective action.

These productive consequences of rights-based discourses take place when rights have not yet become positive rights. At that moment, before the positive dimension of the law constrains and predefines the reach of the claims, rights-based discourses are a political tool that signal group and individual aspirations, while at the same time they attempt to redefine how claimants should be treated (Minow, 1987, p. 1862). The rights discourse can perform this function precisely because it does not yet overlap with formally recognized rights. Its productive and reforming potential lies precisely in its undetermined character. It is a language that articulates demands, and at the same time forces the debate regarding the way in which social burdens should be distributed. Indeed, the transformative dimension of the discourse of rights is not mainly associated with the revelation of new demands and aspirations. This is a task that can also be performed through other political tools. Its subversive potential lies in its ability to force debates and decisions about the conditions in which collective life is or should be organized. Claims formulated as rights-based discourses imply a challenge to the arguments that support the current formalized organization of social relationships. Rights-framed discourses and claims signal the unresolved debate over those justifications creating, in turn, conditions for their change or stability. Whatever the political results of these processes, the rise of rights-based discourses forces the consideration of the way in which social demands conflict and how they should be resolved. In this sense, and regardless of the other dimensions involved in these conflicts, the *corralito* case and the pension funds conflicts opened a debate about the status of individual property rights vis-à-vis welfare community rights, while punishment of marital violence unlocked discussions over the extent of the state's rights to intervene in the private realm. Thus, the main unexpected consequence of rights-based discourses is that they can question and challenge established institutional distributions of societal burdens.

Some authors argue that this expansion of the rights discourse aggravates social conflict and adversarial social relationships. Mary Ann Glendon, for example, considers that the social outcome of the expansion of a rights discourse is social disorder because "right talks, in its absoluteness, . . . inhibits dialogue that might lead toward consensus, accommodation, or at least to the discovery of common ground" (Glendon, 1991, p. 14). In her view, rights discourses reinforce individualism at the expense of community. Others highlight instead that rights arguments strengthen social integration. They note, first, that even though rights discourses give public expression to and translate conflicts, they do not initiate them (Minow, 1987, p. 1871). By contrast they argue that rights discourses reaffirm social integration and social life in so far as they imply an invitation to the larger community and to its authorities to decide on the membership status of the claimants. Those that resort to rights discourses are calling for the intervention and the attention of the larger community. Thus, the use of rights discourses implies claimants' acknowledgment of their social membership. As Martha Minow notes, rights discourse implies stating a claim "in a form devised by those who are powerful in the community (and) expresses a willingness to take part in the community, as well as a tactical decision to play by the rules of the only game recognised by those in charge" (Minow, 1987, p. 1875).

Can these two contending positions be reconciled? The Argentine experience shows that previously tolerated or unquestioned practices are now identified as injurious and that they are being readdressed in the form of rights-oriented claims. It also shows that some old practices have only recently become the object of claims and the rallying point of rights demands. In the process, the use of rights discourses have questioned previously established institutional distributions of burdens and the authority of the representatives that have taken those decisions. Thus, it seems that Glendon's concern about the deleterious effect of right discourses is well taken in so far as rights discourses appears to be eroding citizens' obligations to those decisions, weakening the ability of representatives to exercise their authority and introducing a state of malaise in regard to their authority. However, our assessment about the likely impact of rights discourses changes if we consider the use of rights discourses as a historical and dynamic process. If, as Minow suggests, rights should not be perceived as "trumps" but as the language we use to try to persuade others (Minow, 1987, p. 1875), then rights discourses become a tool within a contingent political process. Rights discourse can, as Glendon notes, have deleterious effects but they can also enlarge social integration. As in any political process, social disorders, maintenance of the status quo or expanded social integration are all possible results. For social analysts, however, it is difficult to evaluate whether the adversarial and disintegrating effects of rights discourses are a transitory stage or a relatively stable resting point. Thus, although the deleterious consequences of rights discourses cannot be ignored, their final impact cannot yet be known.

Appendix

Table 7.8A Constitutionality and unconstitutionality rulings and decisions between 1935 and 1995

Years	Total requests of constitutional review[a]	# and % of decisions that declare the constitutionality of the reviewed laws	# and % of decisions that declare the unconstitutionality of the reviewed laws	Formal error[b]	Annual average of unconstitutional decisions	Annual average of constitutional reviews
1936–1983[c]	1,823	887 48.3%	541 29.4%	409	11.5	38.7
1984–1995	233	148 63.52%	85 36.48%		7.72	21.1

Notes

[a] Only those cases, published in full by the Revista Jurídica La Ley between 1936 and 1995, where a constitutionality or unconstitutionality complaint of a federal or provincial regulation was submitted for review by the court were considered.

[b] Formal error refers to the rejection of a case due to a formal or technical problem.

[c] To calculate the annual average no distinction was made between decisions taken during military and constitutional governments. 47 years were considered.

Source: Data for years 1936–1983 taken from Molinelli (1999), p. 27.
Data for years 1984–1995 taken from Bercholc (2000), p. 11.

Table 7.8B Public opinion survey of institutional prestige

	1984 %	1991 %	1995 %	1999 %	2000 %	2001 %
The church	46	46	47	60	58	50
The education system	54	38	34	33	50	
The press	45	27	34	38	42	36
The military	19	28	23	27	34	28
The police	24	26	23	24	24	17
Congress	72	16	17	11	20	8
Large companies	35	25	29	26	20	19
The justice system	57	26	26	21	18	12
Public officials	49	8	8	7	14	5
Trade unions	30	8	10	12	11	7
Political parties	–	12	9	7	10	7

Source: http://www.justiciaargentina.gov.ar/estadisticas/imag_jus.htm

Notes

1. See McCann, 1994; Tate and Vallinder, 1995; Garapon, 1997; Guarneri and Pederzoli, 1999; Shapiro and Stone Sweet, 2002.
2. Although this paper will not analyze judicialization understood as constitutional review, a short comment regarding its extension in the Argentine case is in order. This form of judicialization results from the growing activity of judicial bodies in carrying out constitutional review of legislation. The judicial bodies carrying out such constitutional review can be either constitutional courts, or—as in the case of Argentina where there is diffuse control of constitutionality—supreme courts. Guillermo Molinelli and Jorge Bercholc evaluated the evolution of constitutional review in Argentina. Their data shows that between 1935 and 1995 the exercise of constitutional control was significant and that its frequency, although higher than in countries such as the United States of America, has decreased in the past few years. The comparison of the two periods they analyze (1935/83 vs. 1984/95) indicates that the annual average of constitutionality reviews and the annual average of norms declared unconstitutional dropped in the last years of the century. Thus, in Argentina, although this particular form of judicialization remains high, their data shows that the country does not follow the upward trend that Tate and Vallinder have described for other areas. See Molinelli, 1999 and Bercholc, 2000.
3. Whether it is positive, negative, or explicitly ignoring the issue, state authorities must provide an official answer to the suit.
4. See Acuña and Smulovitz, 1997.
5. For an extended analysis of the legal mobilization process in the pension funds conflict, see Smulovitz, 2001. The Argentine Retirement and Pension System was created in 1904. It initially comprised a collective capitalization regime and a government-provided regime. Its first members were civil servants. Later on workers from different sectors of the economy began to be included. In 1943, the government promoted the expansion of its coverage. In 1944, the system had 430,000 members (7% of the economically active population), but the number of members rose to 2,300,000 five years later. At the outset each working sector operated its fund under its own regime. Although benefits fluctuated according to contribution levels, they all had a high number of services in exchange for a low salary contribution. By the late 1950s, the loss of capital reserves and the growing deficits led to the abandonment of the capitalization system followed by its replacement of a system based on the mandatory contribution of active workers. According to the Argentine Social Security Research Foundation (FAISS), the adequate relationship between contributions and benefits was lost in the 1970s when the population aged over 65 amounted to 6.9% of the total population. See Fundación Argentina de Investigación de la Seguridad Social (FAISS), "Acerca de los costos de la transición

por la reforma del sistema de previsión social argentino," Documento no. 3, 2000.

6. See *Administración Nacional de la Seguridad Social*, Final Report (2/2), préstamo BID 925 OC-AR, March 2001.

7. Ibid.

8. For an extended analysis of the "*corralito* conflict," see Smulovitz, 2003.

9. See Decree 1570/01. These restrictions are popularly known as the "*corralito*." *Corralito* means enclosure.

10. Ministerio de Economía de la República Argentina, "The Argentine Economy During the Third Quarter 2001 and Recent Evolution," Report 39 (2001).

11. The representative was Jorge Remes Lenicov who was later the first minister of the treasury of the Duhalde administration.

12. An "*amparo*" is a complaint against a violation of constitutional rights when such rights cannot be adequately and promptly protected by other means. See Guillermo Cabanellas de las Cuevas and Eleanor C. Hoague, *Diccionario Jurídico, Law Dictionary* (Editorial Heliasta SRL, 1993).

13. *La Nación*, December 4, 2001.

14. Ibid.

15. Ibid.

16. See Law 25.561; Decree 141/02; Decree 214/02.

17. Fundación de Investigaciones Económicas Latinoamericanas (Buenos Aires), "Indicadores de Coyuntura," no. 419 (January/February 2002).

18. *La Nación*, December 19, 2001.

19. Ibid., March 23, 2002.

20. See Lynch, 2002.

21. *La Nación*, April 23, 2002.

22. Ibid., April 17, 2002.

23. Banco Central de la República Argentina, "Medidas Cautelares," Informe no. 56 (June 25, 2004).

24. CER was the actualization index to be applied to debts that were in dollars before the end of the convertibility plan.

25. D214/02 and D320/02.

26. Law 25.587, popularly known as "Ley Tapón" was supposed to put a lid on the drainage of funds resulting from favorable sentences to *corralito amparos*.

27. On July 13, 2004, the supreme court announced a decision with regard to one of those pending legal conflicts related to the *corralito* dispute. It established that depositors who had voluntarily allowed their frozen bank funds to be returned in pesos could not later obtain the full amount in dollars (*La Nación*, July 14, 2004). The decision gave rise to new demonstrations by bank depositors who on the following day announced they were studying the possibility of taking

their case to international courts. It should be noted, however, that this decision did not define the court position regarding the constitutionality of the "pesification," a claim that is still awaiting a court decision (*La Nación*, July 14, 2004).

28. http://www.mecon.gov.ar/secdef/basehome/0800_sobre_que.htm#. Accessed November 21, 2004.

29. Gerardo Russo, "Mala praxis médica: La nueva industria del juicio," at www.paideianet.com.ar/industria.htm. Accessed November 21, 2004.

30. *La Nación*, September 11, 2001.

31. See CELS, 1998, 2002.

32. According to the Consejo Nacional de la Mujer (2002), there are three legislative projects under study: (1) "Reglamentación del acoso sexual en las relaciones de empleo"; (2) "Incorporación al Codigo Penal del Articulo 127 sobre acoso sexual"; and (3) "Creación de un cuerpo interdisciplinario especializado en discriminación laboral y acoso sexual en el ambito del Ministerio de Trabajo, Empleo y Formación de Recursos Humanos."

33. See CELS, 2002.

34. Lawyers involved in these claims have also mentioned that in order to avoid negative press, extra-judicial arrangements are being used to solve these types of demands because—according to the experience of one of the lawyers interviewed—employers prefer "an unfavourable agreement rather than a good trial."

35. Although no exhaustive information is available regarding claimants in the pension funds conflict, by December 2002, roughly 65% of the individuals who presented legal claims in the *corralito* dispute had received a favorable response.

References

Acuña, Carlos and Catalina Smulovitz (1997) "Guarding the Guardians in Argentina: Some Lessons about the Risks and Benefits of Empowering the Courts," in James McAdams (ed.), *Transitional Justice and the Rule of Law in New Democracies* (Notre Dame: University of Notre Dame Press), pp. 93–122.

Bercholc, Jorge (2000) "Independencia de la Corte Suprema a través del control de constitucionalidad 1935–1983" (MIMEO).

CELS (Centro de Estudios Legales y Sociales) (1998) *Derechos Humanos en Argentina: Informe Anual.*

——— (July 2002) *Argentina: Shadow Report from ONGs to CEDAW Committee* [Committee on the Elimination of Discrimination Against Women].

Consejo Nacional de la Mujer (2002) *La mujer y la violencia en la República Argentina* (Buenos Aires: CNM). See http://www.cnm.gov.ar/areainterv/violencia.htm

Epp, Charles (1998) *The Rights Revolution: Lawyers, Activists, and Supreme Courts in Comparative Perspective* (Chicago: The University of Chicago Press).

Felstiner, William, Richard Abel, and Austin Sarat, "The Emergence and Transformation of Disputes: Naming, Blaming, Claiming . . .," *Law and Society Review*, vol. 15, no. 3–4 (1980–1981), pp. 631–54.

Galanter, Marc (1983) "The Radiating Effects of Courts," in Keith Boyum and Lynn Mather (eds.), *Empirical Theories About Courts* (New York: Longman), pp. 117–42.

Garapon, Antoine (1997) *Juez y democracia* (Madrid: Flor del Viento Ediciones).

Glendon, Mary Ann (1991) *Rights Talk: The Impoverishment of Political Discourse* (New York: The Free Press).

Guarneri, Carlo and Patrizia Pederzoli (1999) *Los jueces y la política: Poder judicial y democracia* (Madrid: Taurus).

Lynch, Horacio, "Emergencia, derecho, justicia y seguridad jurídica (reflexiones sobre la crisis y las libertades económicas)," *La Ley*, vol. 2002-C, pp. 1287–312.

McCann, Michael "Legal Mobilization and Social Reform Movements: Notes on Theory and its Application," *Studies in Law, Politics and Society*, vol. 11 (1991), pp. 225–54.

——— (1994) *Rights at Work: Pay Equity Reform and the Politics of Legal Mobilization* (Chicago: The University of Chicago Press).

——— (1998) "How Does Law Matter for Social Movements?" in Bryant Garth and Austin Sarat (eds.), *How Does Law Matter?* (Evanston, IL: Northwestern University Press), pp. 76–108.

Minow, Martha, "Interpreting Rights: An Essay for Robert Cover," *Yale Law Journal*, vol. 96, no. 8 (July 1987), pp. 1860–1915.

Molinelli, Guillermo (1999) "La Corte Suprema de Justicia de la Nación frente a los poderes políticos a través del control de constitucionalidad, 1983–98" (MIMEO).

Scheingold, Stuart (1974) *The Politics of Rights: Lawyers, Public Policy and Political Change* (New Haven: Yale University Press).

Shapiro, Martin and Alec Stone Sweet (2002) *On Law, Politics and Judicialization* (Oxford: Oxford University Press).

Smulovitz, Catalina (2001) "Judicialización y Accountability Social" (MIMEO).

——— (2002) "The Discovery of Law: Political Consequences in the Argentine Experience," in Bryant Garth and Yves Dezalay (eds.), *Global Prescriptions: The Production, Exportation, and Importation of a New Legal Orthodoxy* (Ann Arbor: The University of Michigan Press), pp. 249–75.

——— (2003) "Protest by Other Means: Legal Mobilization in the Argentinian Crisis" (MIMEO).

Tate, Neal and Torbjorn Vallinder (eds.) (1995) *The Global Expansion of Judicial Power* (New York: New York University Press).

Tobar, Federico, C. Fernández Pardo et al. (2001) "Impacto económico de la mala praxis medica: Costo de las demandas, juicios y seguros en Argentina" (Programa de Investigación Aplicada. Buenos Aires: Instituto Universitario Isalud).

Zemans, Frances, "Legal Mobilization: The Neglected Role of the Law in the Political System," *American Political Science Review*, vol. 77. no. 3 (1983), pp. 690–703.

Chapter 8

Community Justice Institutions and Judicialization: Lessons from Rural Peru

Julio Faundez

As used in this chapter, the term "community justice institutions" refers to institutions that have three main features: first, they administer justice, but are not part of the official judicial system; second, they resolve disputes that, under the prevailing legal system, are within the exclusive jurisdiction of state courts; and third, they do not apply state law, although they often rely on general principles of law that are consistent with those found in the official legal system. In Latin America, this type of community justice is found both in rural and in urban areas. In urban areas they are often found in the shantytowns that encircle most Latin American cities and that stand as symbols of the shortcomings of the process of economic modernization. In rural areas they are often, though not always, associated with indigenous communities.

From a strictly legal perspective, the activities of community justice institutions are illegal as they involve local communities dispensing justice in defiance of the rules of civil and criminal procedure. Accordingly, following a textbook approach on the proper role of courts, the appropriate response to community justice institutions would be to "judicialise" them since they are usurpers of power and, as such, liable to criminal sanctions. This harsh outcome is probably also consistent with the view held by political scientists who characterize areas not reached by the state as "brown" areas (O'Donnell, 1993). This characterization suggests that community justice institutions should not be tolerated and should be brought into the fold of state regulation.

This tough approach to community justice institution could well be justified on human rights grounds. It is undeniable that many community justice institutions are far from embodying the ideal model of liberal legality and they often commit serious violations of human rights. In procedural terms these violations relate to the absence of due process safeguards as their decisions are biased, often inconsistent, and not subject to any form of review. Moreover, the accused often does not have a chance to be heard and/or to be adequately represented. In substantive terms, community justice institutions often adopt measures that are blatantly inconsistent with basic principles of human rights.

An alternative to the harsh approach to judicialization is to recognize community justice institutions as judicial institutions and to incorporate them into the official court system. I call this approach soft judicialization. In Uganda, for example, the Local Council Courts, originally established by the community in areas that the official court system did not reach, are now part of the official court system (Odonga-Mwaka, 2000). In Latin America, the recent recognition of legal pluralism in relation to indigenous peoples is an important first step toward integrating community justice institutions within the national justice systems.[1] In Peru, the 1993 constitution recognizes the ethnic and cultural pluralism of the nation. In terms of the administration of justice, the constitutional provision that has served as a model for countries in the region is Article 246 of the 1991 constitution of Colombia that provides as follows: "The authorities of indigenous peoples may exercise jurisdictional functions within their territories in accordance with their norms and procedures, provided they are not inconsistent with the Constitution and the laws of the Republic. The law shall regulate the way this special jurisdiction will relate to the national judicial system." Similar provisions are found in the constitutions of Bolivia, Ecuador, Nicaragua, Panama, and Paraguay (Van Cott, 1994, 2002). It remains to be seen whether these constitutional provisions will have a significant impact on the political and legal systems.[2]

Judicialization, however, whether in its harsh or soft version, is not the only approach available to engage with community justice institutions. To illustrate this point, this chapter draws from two experiences of community justice in rural Peru: the Rondas Campesinas (hereafter Rondas) and Nucleos Rurales de Administración de Justicia (hereafter NURAJs). As the following discussion shows, a strictly legal approach to community justice institutions can often be counterproductive. In order properly to understand community justice institutions it is necessary to bear in mind that these organizations are not primarily or exclusively judicial. Moreover, the factors that brings about the emergence of these institutions, as well as those that sustain them, are generally related to wider issues of governance: the absence, weakness, or corruption of state institutions at the local level. The wider lens of governance also makes it possible to avoid the common mistake of regarding community justice institutions as exotic cultural artifacts of a bygone age or as marginal political mechanisms. While it is undeniable that some community institutions in Latin America—such as *comunidades campesinas* in Peru—have a long historical lineage, they are not relics of the past. They are dynamic political actors that influence and respond to contemporary political developments, both local and global. The governance perspective should make it possible to understand the contemporary political role of community justice institutions that—for better or worse—often reflect and reproduce the weaknesses and strength of governance in the wider community. Thus, however unsavory some of the activities of these community organizations might be, it is necessary to bear in mind that their very existence is often a consequence of the weakness or corruption of state institutions at national or local levels. Hence, an understanding of why these community organizations come into being and the nature of their activities can offer valuable insights on a variety of issues such as the reach of legal institutions in rural areas, the efficacy of legal regulation and other forms of state intervention, the role of human rights training and the vexed question of decentralization.

This chapter is divided into four sections. The first offers general background information on rural justice in Peru; the second and third sections provide a brief overview of the experience of Rondas and the NURAJs. The final section outlines some of the lessons that policymakers involved in judicial reform can draw from this experience.

Rural Justice in Peru

More than one-third of Peru's population of 20 million lives in rural areas, and the majority of rural inhabitants belong to one of 70 indigenous ethnic groups. In the Andean region, there are seven indigenous ethnic groups, of which the two largest are the Quechuas and Aymaras. In the Amazon, which comprises nearly one-third of Peru's territory, there are some 65 indigenous ethnic groups (CONAPA, n.d). Most of the rural indigenous population lives in small communities: *comunidades campesinas* in the Andean region and *comunidades nativas* in the Amazon region. Members of indigenous communities are among the poorest in the country. A recent government survey found that, from a total of just over six thousand indigenous communities, only 26 were above the poverty line and more than half of the rest were living in extreme poverty or under conditions of misery (Jiménez, 1999; Vega, 1998). Moreover, indigenous people were the main victims of military confrontation against *Sendero Luminoso* (Shining Path), which killed nearly 70,000 people between 1980 and 2000 (Comisión de la Verdad y Reconciliación, 2003).[3]

Though economically impoverished, *comunidades campesinas* and *comunidades nativas* are subject to an elaborate regulatory framework. As already noted, the 1993 Constitution recognizes that *comunidades campesinas* and *comunidades nativas* have the right to administer their own customary law, provided they do so within the limits of the constitution. Several laws regulate other aspects of the rights and duties of the communities, including the requirements for community membership. The law also recognizes that communities have a right to their communal land (Plant and Hvalkof, 2001). Despite this abundant regulation there is a dearth of information about the way *comunidades campesinas* govern their affairs or resolve disputes (for partial exceptions see Drzewieniecki, 1995; Mallon, 1983, 1992; Peña, 1998; Peña et al., 2002; Poole, 1994; Radcliffe, 1990; Vega, 1998). There is also next to no information available about conflicts of jurisdiction between the *comunidades campesinas* and state courts.

The available evidence suggests that the majority of the people in rural areas have a deep distrust of the official justice system. They reject it on the grounds that it is expensive, slow, and that judges and lawyers are more interested in prolonging rather than resolving disputes (Peña, 1998). While these grounds for distrusting the judiciary are shared by urban dwellers in many other countries, rural communities in Peru also distrust state courts because they regard them as unfriendly, even hostile. This view is not surprising given that judges and other court personnel are generally not part of the local community. Moreover, since legal proceedings in state courts are in Spanish and many peasants only speak Quechua or Aymara, it is hardly surprising that rural communities regard state courts as instruments of colonial domination.[4] A survey carried out in Ayacucho confirms that people there distrust the official court system and believe that lawyers and local court personnel discriminate against them (IPAZ, 2000, pp. 17–19). In *comunidades indígenas,* such as Calahuyo, local people regard the official justice system as a threat to their right of self-determination and self-government (Peña, 1998).

The negative views that rural communities hold about the state justice system contrast sharply with the popularity of justices of the peace, *jueces de paz* (hereafter JPs).[5] But JPs did not always enjoy this level of legitimacy. In the first half of the nineteenth century, they were mainly used by landowners to maintain law and order (Lovatón, 2000). As the agrarian reform of the late 1960s disrupted prevailing power structures in the countryside, JPs became closely identified with their local communities. Today, they play an important role in the administration of justice and, in sharp contrast to professional judges, enjoy widespread popular support. JPs act mainly as conciliators (Chunga, 1986; Comisión Andina de Juristas, 1999; La Rosa, 2003). They also have limited jurisdiction to adjudicate in matters such as debts, misdemeanors, alimony, and certain cases of domestic violence. In practice, however, and as a result of demand by local communities, they often exceed their jurisdiction. JPs deal with matters informally and, under the Code of Civil Procedure, are expected to respect local practices and culture (Lovatón, 2000, p. 21). The popularity of JPs within the rural population undoubtedly compensates for the shortcomings of the official court system. Yet, their popularity has not prevented the emergence of grassroots institutions used by local communities to resist or transform state institutions.

Rondas Campesinas—Night Watch Patrols

Rondas Campesinas, or Night Watch Patrols, are the most successful—and controversial—community justice organizations to emerge in rural Peru during the past thirty years. They emerged in the mid-1970s in the Department of Cajamarca in Northern Peru to deal with the problem of cattle rustling and theft generally. Such was their success in controlling crime that communities in several other departments soon replicated their structure. The Rondas also attracted the attention of the state as successive governments attempted to use them in their struggle against rebel movements in the countryside. Yet, while one arm of the state tried to co-opt them, leaders of the Rondas accused of usurping the functions of the police and the judiciary faced criminal charges and, often, imprisonment (Yrigoyen, 2002).

The Department of Cajamarca is comprised of mainly independent commercial farmers who are mestizo and Spanish-speaking. The average size of their individual plots is seven hectares (ASER, 2001). Some plots, however, are too small to provide subsistence. The larger plots extend up to 24 hectares (Gitlitz and Rojas, 1983, pp. 165–67). The Rondas were set up mainly to protect private property (Gitilitz and Rojas, 1983). They came into existence because the community had no confidence that the police or the judiciary were capable of, or willing to protect them from organized gangs involved in the theft of cattle and other violent crimes. In fact, peasants in Cajamarca believed that the police and the local judiciary were involved in supporting these criminal activities. Indeed, according to a report by a local NGO, only 10 percent of criminal cases brought before local courts resulted in convictions (ASER, 2001). While some observers are cautious about whether the police were implicated in cattle theft, they do however believe that they were slow and inefficient in responding to criminal activity. They also believe that more could have been done to control the routes used to move the cattle out of the area and the centers where stolen cattle were traded (Gitilitz and Rojas, 1983, p. 174). Scholars who have studied cattle rustling in other areas of Peru confirm that local elites, the police force, and even schoolteachers are often directly involved in cattle rustling (Paponnet-Cantat, 1994, p. 213).

The first Ronda was established in the hamlet of Cuyumalca, in the Department of Cajamarca (Gitilitz and Rojas, 1983, p. 179). It came about through the efforts of one individual, a relatively prosperous peasant. He secured the backing of the political authorities by means of an agreement in which he undertook that the Rondas would assist the police in crime control and that its members would not carry arms. In practice, however, members of the Rondas carry arms and they are involved in the administration of justice—a matter that was not even contemplated when the first Ronda was established.

The structure of the Ronda follows a common pattern. The General Assembly, made up of peasants who own land in a particular hamlet, elects the members of the Ronda Committee. The committee then divides the area into sectors. Each sector is organized by a delegate appointed by the Rondas. Men between 18 and 60 are required to serve on Ronda patrols. Women generally do not take part in night watch patrols, although they support the work of the Rondas by providing food and other ancillary services.

Rondas generally hand over suspects to the General Assembly, not to the police. The General Assembly is entrusted with the task of deciding whether the suspect has committed a criminal offence, and, if so, what punishment should be administered. The scope of activities of Rondas has expanded. Some Rondas are involved in welfare activities and in the development of public works in the community—such as building medical facilities and improving irrigation schemes. Rondas have also expanded their policing and judicial functions from the protection of property to include more general offences such as slander, damage to crops or animals, drunkenness, assault, and domestic and family disputes.

By 1978, Rondas had largely succeeded in controlling theft in Cajamarca. Their success enhanced their legitimacy and prompted the establishment of Rondas Campesinas in other rural departments.

Thus, Rondas soon emerged in the Departments of Piura, San Martín, Amazonas, Junín, and Ancash. By 1991, Rondas Campesinas had become the most popular grassroots organization in Peru. They covered nearly 3,500 hamlets in Northern Peru, over an area of 150,000 square kilometers (ASER, 2001). In some departments, notably Junín and Ancash, *comunidades campesinas* established them as part of their structure of governance. There thus developed two types of Rondas: the original Rondas, established by independent commercial farmers in Cajamarca, and those established by indigenous peasants as part of their traditional structures of governance.

Administration of Justice

There is an important distinction between Rondas Campesinas established by independent farmers—as is the case in Cajamarca—and those established by indigenous communities. In the former case, Rondas are not allowed by the constitution to become directly involved in the administration of justice. In the latter case, the *comunidad campesina* performs judicial functions and the Rondas assist them.

Despite the intense political controversy that Rondas have attracted, there is little reliable information about the way Rondas administer justice. The two scholars that have studied Rondas in some detail, John Gitlitz (2000) and Orin Starn (1999), confirm that Rondas resort to corporal punishment and that their decisions often lack consistency. Orin Starn points out, however, that, although Rondas make use of corporal punishment, they do so in order to restore harmony in the community (Starn, 1999, p. 135).

Gitlitz offers an interesting account of the way Rondas in two different localities handled cases involving allegations of rape—a matter that under the Peruvian Criminal Code should, in any event, have been referred to state courts. In the first case, punishment was mild, in the second it was brutal.

The first case involved an assault against a female adolescent by a man who, though alcoholic, was well liked by community members. The parents of the victim, however, were not popular, especially the mother. The General Assembly found that attempted rape was a serious offence, but its members were divided as to how to proceed. Some argued that the case had to be referred to the state courts, while others disagreed, maintaining that the community should punish the accused. Ultimately, the latter view prevailed and the accused was required to pay a small sum to the victim's mother as compensation for her daughter's lost reputation. The offender also had to perform six days of community work plus six extra night patrols. At no time did the assembly seek the views of the victim.

The second case involved a man having an affair with the wife of a neighbor. On the day of the incident, he was rejected by the woman, who, aware that her husband was nearby, feared that they would be discovered. As the woman struggled, the husband came to the scene and referred the matter to the local Ronda. The case attracted enormous attention in the vicinity and, after lengthy consultations, the Ronda Assembly decided that the man was guilty and should be subjected to "mass discipline," a punishment that involves two lashes from each person present at the hearings. Since 250 neighbors had attended the hearings, the man stood to receive 500 lashes. After the first 10 lashes, it became clear the man would not survive the remaining 490 lashes, so the president suspended the procedure to consult with the assembly. He proposed that the punishment should be terminated as the man had already been adequately punished. The majority of the assembly, however, disagreed, but conceded that 500 lashes were excessive. In any event, it was agreed that only married women present in the assembly would be allowed to continue administering lashes. Altogether, the man received 70 lashes.

The procedure and different outcome in these cases raise worrying questions about the Rondas as community justice institutions. The cases suggest that the justice of the Rondas is closer to popular justice than to traditional restorative justice of indigenous communities.[6] Recent reports suggest, however, that Rondas tend to rely more on community work as a form of punishment than on corporal punishment (Ardito, 2004b). These reports also indicate that members of the Rondas often decline to deal with serious crimes and refer them instead to local state courts (Aranda, 2003). The available information, however, is insufficient and does not allow any meaningful generalizations. To form a view about this aspect of the activities of the Rondas, more information is required about the way they handle disputes. Most observers point out, however, that local people overwhelmingly prefer to submit their disputes to the Rondas than to the official justice system (Gitlitz and Rojas, 1983; Yrigoyen, 2001a, 2001b, 2002). This view is corroborated by a survey of Rondas Campesinas in the Department of Piura (Starn, 1999, p. 291).

Women and Rondas

The prevailing view among observers is that the Rondas Campesinas are largely male dominated and that their activities are male orientated.

Starn reports, however, that in some localities women have discovered ways of using the Rondas as a device to weaken and split patriarchal hegemony (1999, pp. 174–83). Thus, for example, women often rely on the support of their brothers or fathers to bring matters of domestic violence to the attention of the General Assembly. The outcome of cases of domestic violence in one hamlet in Cajamarca suggests that the Rondas are making progress in tackling the issue of gender equality. According to Starn (1999, p. 181), in 1986, out of eight cases of domestic violence brought to the attention of the General Assembly of Tunnel Six, a locality in Cajamarca, only two were dismissed. In four cases the man was required to agree, in writing, not to abuse his wife. In the remaining two cases, the assembly decided that the men should be punished in accordance with local custom: whipping. It is thus not surprising that local women find that men in their community are a little less bold when dealing with women. This leads Starn to speculate that if women were asked to choose between the official justice system and justice administered by the Rondas, they would choose the Rondas (1999, p. 291). Yet, Starn also reports that in the case of marital disputes 50 percent of women opt for the official court system (see also Aranda, 2003; Ardito, 2004b).

Victims of Their Success

The success of the Rondas in controlling crime and their popularity in Cajamarca inevitably attracted the attention of national politicians. The administration of Alan García (1985–1990) tried, unsuccessfully, to co-opt and politicize the Rondas. These efforts raised their profile and brought about a proliferation of Rondas throughout the countryside (Gitilitz and Rojas, 1983, p. 180). In 1986 the congress enacted legislation that narrowly defined the role of the Rondas, describing them as peaceful, democratic, and autonomous community organizations, but subordinating them entirely to the local police and judicial authorities. They were not given any judicial or enforcement functions. Two years later, the government, through a decree enacted by the Ministry of Interior, attempted to convert them into an arm of the national police. The available evidence suggests that no attempts were made seriously to enforce this decree, which was largely ignored by the Rondas (CEAS, n.d).

During the Fujimori administration (1990–2000), the government once again attempted to intervene. This time the approach was more ruthless as the government attempted to enlist the Rondas in its campaign against Sendero Luminoso. The government promoted the establishment of Self-Defense Committees (Comités de Autodefensa) in some localities, as part of its war against Sendero. These were community organizations organized and armed by the military and aimed mainly at supporting the military campaign against terrorism (Degregori et al., 1996). The Fujimori government and its supporters referred to these organizations as Rondas Campesinas, thus creating considerable confusion and resentment among the members of the genuine, independent Rondas—mainly those from Cajamarca. But the government was determined to bring the Rondas within the framework of their military strategy. Thus, in 1993, it enacted a decree requiring all Rondas to adopt the structure of the Self-Defense Committees. Evidence suggests that most Rondas resisted the implementation of this decree, but were weakened by it (CEAS, n.d).

From a legal perspective, the most serious blow against the Rondas came about with the enactment of the 1993 constitution. Article 149 of the constitution provides that *comunidades campesinas* and *comunidades nativas* can administer justice in accordance with "customary law."[7] It does not give this right to the Rondas. It merely acknowledges that Rondas Campesinas established by *comunidades campesinas* may assist the authorities of the *comunidades* in their judicial functions. As a consequence, Rondas that are not part of a *comunidad campesina*—that is to say, the original Rondas established in Cajamarca—are not allowed to administer justice.

In recent years, the Rondas lobbied vigorously to secure approval by the congress of legislation explicitly acknowledging that they also have the power to administer justice. After a lengthy debate on December 12, 2002, the congress approved a new law for the Rondas. The law acknowledges that Rondas play a role in dispute resolution, but only as mechanisms to facilitate the conciliation of local disputes. While this provision is superfluous, as Rondas did not need a law to perform this function, the new law is nonetheless a positive gesture by the legislature. Indeed, the new law could be seen as a step in the process of negotiating a constitutional amendment that, one day, will give Rondas the right to perform judicial functions.[8]

Given the shortcomings of state regulation, self-regulation has emerged as an alternative. While the legislative debate was taking place in Lima, in June 2001 a federation of Rondas from one of the provinces in Cajamarca (Central Unificada Provincial de Rondas Campesinas de la Provincia de Hualgayoc) adopted its own regulations (CUPROC, 2001), which set out in detail the objectives, function, and structure of the Rondas. It is a long document consisting of some 77 Articles, most of which are divided into several sections and sub-sections.

The section on the administration of justice provides that the Rondas have jurisdiction over public and private disputes. The first category is described as "agricultural matters concerning communal and individual property"; and the second is described as "family matters that may have a bearing on law and order within the community." Under the regulations, there are three organs vested with judicial power: the Executive Committee and the Judicial Committee, both of which deal with cases in the first instance, and the General Assembly, the highest judicial and political organ, which hears appeals from the other two organs.

It is interesting that the regulations say nothing about the law that the Rondas apply. They are therefore ambiguous on the crucial question as to how Ronda justice relates to the formal system. While they acknowledge that serious offences have to be referred to the formal justice system, they also provide that, prior to such referral, the General Assembly has the obligation to investigate the matter (Article 60). Moreover, while the regulations reaffirm that the Rondas will normally not challenge or interfere with the work of the judicial organs of the state, they also provide that the Rondas must remain vigilant and denounce corruption and malpractices by judges, prosecutors, and the police.

The regulations also contain an article explaining why Ronda justice is better than state justice. It claims that this is because members of the Ronda are familiar with the types of disputes that arise from within their communities and are therefore in a better position to resolve them. The state justice system, on the other hand, it is claimed, cannot resolve community disputes since, not only are they unfamiliar with the locality, they also have to rely on testimonies of witnesses who are either bribed or ignorant of the reality of the community.

It is clear that the Peruvian Congress did not take these regulations into account when it adopted the new law. Yet, the regulations are probably a more reliable guide to the practice of the Rondas than the new legislation. It remains to be seen whether in the future the official system adopts a more realistic policy toward the Rondas.

Rural Centers for the Administration of Justice (NURAJs)

The NURAJs or Rural Centres for the Administration of Justice (*Nucleos Rurales para la Administración de Justicia*) were established in the Department of Ayacucho in 1997, in the aftermath of the war against Sendero Luminoso. Their objective is to help peasant communities in the locality reconstitute civil society by providing prompt and efficient access to justice. The experience of the NURAJs is of special interest on two counts. First, because they provide a framework that brings together community leaders and state appointed officials and,

as such, constitute an attempt to refashion and democratize governance structures. And second, because they came into being largely
through the efforts of IPAZ (Instituto de Investigación y Promoción
del Desarrollo y la Paz), a local NGO, thus providing an interesting
perspective on how external agencies can engage with grassroots
organizations (IPAZ, 2000).

The Department of Ayacucho, in the South of Peru, has a population of nearly 500,000; that is 2.3 percent of the country's population. Nearly 80 percent of its inhabitants are classified as poor or
extremely poor. The people of Ayacucho bore the brunt of the atroc-
ities committed by Sendero Luminoso. They were also subjected to
arbitrary and repressive measures by the military during the campaign
against terrorism. As a consequence of the violence, it is estimated
that up to 150,000 people were displaced, of which half had to leave
Ayacucho altogether. Violence disrupted productivity and seriously
dislocated community and family life. Women were the worst affected.
According to a survey of six communities, over 40 percent of women
lost a family member during the war so that most of them became the
sole breadwinners (Laynes, 2004, pp. 12–14). Thus, it is not surprising that rural communities became increasingly isolated and distrust-
ful of any form of public authority. The NURAJs can thus be seen as
an attempt to rebuild trust in state authorities through popular participation in the administration of justice and governance generally.

NURAJs are established within the territorial jurisdiction of a rural
municipality or Consejo Menor. Its members include one delegate
from each of the peasant communities within the municipality, a representative of the local women's association, the mayor, the justice of
the peace (if there is one), and the local police (*teniente gobernador*).
The first NURAJ was set up in the Ayacucho province of Huanta in
1997. By the beginning of 2000, eight more were established, all of
them in the Department of Ayacucho.

Between 1997 and 2000, 84 disputes were brought to the NURAJs.
The disputes fall within the following main categories: domestic
violence (17 cases), assault (15), theft (12), family (10), property (5),
others (25). IPAZ reports that the NURAJs resolved 70 percent of
these cases. The rest were referred to the official court system.

Laura v. Nemesia: A Dispute over Land

There is no detailed information available about the cases decided by
the NURAJs. In March 1999, however, I had the opportunity to visit
Chaca in the province of Huanta, where I observed the NURAJs at
work. The proceedings were conducted in Quechua, but a local

anthropologist offered simultaneous interpretation. What follows is based on notes I made at the time.

Until 1982, Chaca was a privately owned hacienda. Under the agrarian reform some 2600 hectares were transferred to *comunidades campesinas*. Only 18 percent of this land is suitable for cultivation (mainly potatoes and cereals such as wheat and corn), 43 percent is devoted to grazing and 38 percent is inaccessible and economically unviable. Cultivable land is allocated by the community to families and passed on to members of the same family after the death of the head of the family. Grazing land is communal property. Neither the land owned by the community nor family plots are registered.

Family plots were allocated before Sendero Luminoso began its activities in the region. When violence erupted, families were forced to move away from their plots and to form hamlets to protect themselves. As a consequence, some families were unable regularly to work on their plots and there emerged some confusion about the precise demarcation of their properties. Moreover, since many male heads of families were killed or forced to escape from the area, some plots were temporarily abandoned.

The dispute between Laura and Nemesia concerned the precise demarcation of the family plots. It arose as a consequence of the confusion caused by the presence of the Sendero Luminoso in the area. The disputed area was small, about half a hectare in total, but of significant economic value to the parties. Laura claimed that Nemesia was illegally occupying her land. According to Laura, who had lost her husband, the land belonged to her father, who had been forced to leave the area because of Sendero Luminoso's activities. Her father's plot had not been cultivated for a while, but she had recently begun to cultivate it. Nemesia argued that the disputed area belonged to her husband, who had also been forced to flee the area. She had decided to reoccupy the plot because she needed money to support her family. In her speech, she told the members of the NURAJ panel that during her husband's absence she had remained faithful and was working hard to raise her children. She also pointed out that she regularly fulfilled her obligations toward the community.

The members of the panel asked questions to both parties, seeking mainly to establish whether they also cultivated land elsewhere. They also reminded the parties that they could not make claims to grazing areas or firewood that belonged to the community. There then followed a short period of open discussion and deliberation among panel members. Some thought that the decisive factor was the length of time that each woman had occupied the disputed area. Others pointed out that loyalty to the community during the war against terrorism

was a more relevant factor. Most agreed that consistent good citizenship was an important factor. In the end, the panel decided that
Nemesia should be allowed to continue cultivating the plot, but she
was reminded that she was not allowed to take firewood or any other
products from the adjacent plot cultivated by Laura. The panel also
announced that representatives from the NURAJ would inspect
the site and demarcate the land the following day, and when that
procedure was completed, the parties would sign a conciliation
agreement.

The proceedings were brought to a close by the president of the
panel, who congratulated both parties for bringing the dispute to the
attention of the community authorities. In a brief, but moving speech
he stressed the importance of resolving disputes peacefully since—as
he put it—"in this community all of us are poor and should learn to
get along with each other." He also reminded both parties of the
importance of complying with the terms of the conciliation agreement.
Finally, he asked the women to embrace each other.

Conflict Resolved

This case is interesting for several reasons. First, although Nemesia
prevailed, the president of the NURAJ described the outcome as a
compromise in which both parties had decided to split the difference.[9]
Second, although it is difficult to be certain about the fairness of the
outcome, the advocacy skills of the parties played a major role.
Nemesia, who had recently attended a human rights training session
run by a local NGO, was far more articulate than Laura. The main
theme of her speech was loyalty to her husband and to the community. Perhaps this was a coded way of saying that the other woman had
not been loyal to her estranged husband and had betrayed the community during the war against terrorism. Third, neither the parties
nor the members of the panel made any reference to customary law,
even though they were all members of a Quechua-speaking community. The events on which the parties based their claims were all relatively recent, and some of the interpretations they placed on these
events were based on equitable principles that could have been equally
effective had they been invoked before a state court. Fourth, the room
in which the proceedings took place was made to look like a formal
tribunal. The panel sat on a table directly facing the parties. The table,
covered with an elegant green tablecloth, had as its decoration a small
Peruvian flag. There was also a bookshelf in the room containing two
or three legal codes. Members of the public sat a few feet behind the
parties and were not allowed to intervene in the proceedings. Fifth,

although the proceedings were conducted in Quechua, one of the members of the NURAJ carefully recorded, in Spanish, the panel's decision. Record keeping is important, serving as a guarantee that the decision would be recognized and enforced by the center and the community and, eventually, by state authorities. In this respect it is important to bear in mind that two members of the NURAJ Panel were state-appointed officers. Sixth, the participation of state-appointed officials—especially a JP who, in theory, could have resolved the matter—suggests that the NURAJ has been successful in working toward reviving civil society and enhancing democratic governance (Laynes, 2004, p. 20).

Lessons

Overcoming Legal Culture

The response of Latin American lawyers and judges to community justice institutions is largely shaped by their conceptions about the rule of law and the legal system. The rule of law, as conceived by various strands of legal positivism, is conceived as a set of hierarchically related rules that derive their validity from each other and are authoritatively interpreted by officially appointed authorities. At the apex of this network of norms stands the "basic norm," which is the ultimate source of validity within the legal system. Under this conception there is no room for community justice institutions of the type discussed in this chapter. Indeed, it is precisely for these reasons that the legal profession and the judiciary in Peru, as well as in many other Latin American countries, have difficulties accepting that community justice organizations have any role to play within the legal system. Although the recent recognition of legal pluralism is helping to change attitudes, there is still a long way to go before legal experts in the region accept the legitimacy of these community organizations. In rural Peru, for example, while lawyers and judges are prepared to accept Rondas Campesinas as useful *cuida vacas* (cattle minders), they are united in regarding their members as usurpers of power and subjecting them to the criminal process.

The popularity enjoyed by community justice institutions such as the Rondas and NURAJs suggests that people in rural Peru do not understand or accept the main tenets of the prevailing legal culture. After all, these institutions are not part of the legal system, do not apply written rules, and their decisions are often arbitrary and inconsistent with the provisions of the constitution. The dissonance between the official legal culture and popular attitudes to law suggests that the soft policy approach to judicialization—the approach that seeks to incorporate community justice institutions within the official court system—deserves consideration. This approach would benefit the official court system, as it would enhance its popular legitimacy. Indeed, recent surveys indicate that, despite more than a decade of judicial reform in the region, public opinion in most countries in the region remains unimpressed with the performance of the courts. The surveys also show that citizens distrust courts as much as they distrust politicians and continue to regard judges as tools of economic and political elites (Galindo, 2003; PNUD, 2004). The main obstacle to a soft approach to judicialization is that it presupposes that these community institutions are exclusively judicial institutions and that they are all willing to become part of the official court system. Given the diverse governance functions performed by the Rondas, it is unlikely that they could be easily integrated into the official court system. NURAJs, on the other hand, because of their composition and better relations with public authorities in the region might be more willing to accept such a policy.

In any event, there is much that the official court system can learn from the success and popularity of the Rondas and NURAJs. Current efforts at judicial reform have largely addressed macro-management problems of the judiciary. The experience of community justice institutions suggests that, in rural areas, more resources should be allocated to testing and developing policies that will further good relations between local communities and the official court system. This is obviously a complex process, but there are many initiatives worth considering. For example, one of the reasons why the NURAJs emerged was simply that courts in Ayacucho are not accessible to people who live in remote communities because roads are poor and public transport is unavailable. Thus, initiatives that involve bringing courts closer to local communities can do much to further good relations between the official system and local communities. In this respect, initiatives such as the Casas de Justicia in Colombia and Guatemala (Hendrix, 2000; USAID, 2000), as well as the Módulos Básicos de Justicia in Peru (Hernández-Breña, 2003) provide interesting lessons.

The physical distance of courts from local communities may well be easier to resolve than the cultural gap. In rural Peru, language is an important barrier that remains unresolved (Bermúdez, 2002). The parties in the NURAJ case of *Laura v. Nemesia* would have not been able to argue their case before an official court since they do not speak Spanish, and the use of Quechua is not allowed in the courts in Ayacucho. Apart from measures to overcome linguistic barriers, the selection and appointment of judicial personnel in rural areas should ensure that local people are adequately represented and that training is given to lawyers and other professionals who may want to pursue a career in the judiciary.

Defying Centralism

In most countries in Latin America, the monolithic conception of the legal system is coupled with strong political centralism expressed in a chronic inability on the part of the authorities at the center to delegate power to locally elected authorities. The representatives of the executive in the provinces often have more power than representatives of local communities and through their control over the police, the military, and the budget, can undermine democratic practices at the local level. Although central governments are able to disrupt local initiatives, they are often unable, effectively, to reach remote areas of their territory. These circumstances provide the opportunity for the emergence of community justice organizations that attend to the basic governance and justice needs of their communities.

The Rondas and the NURAJs, in different ways, pose an interesting challenge to the tradition of centralism. The Rondas came into being precisely because local state authorities—the mayor, the police, and judges—did nothing to help the local community combat criminal activities that were affecting their livelihood. The Rondas responded by taking direct action to protect members of the community from cattle theft. As Rondas proved successful in performing this task, their brief expanded and they became involved in other activities, including adjudicating family disputes and taking responsibility for the general welfare of the community. From this perspective, Rondas can be regarded as an effective and creative community response to the shortcomings of the centralized model of the state. Given that today most development agencies regard decentralization as a panacea, the Rondas offers valuable lessons on what works and what doesn't in this area of state reform. The experience of the NURAJs is also interesting as it is an imaginative response by the community to the problem of establishing viable and democratic forms of public authority at the local level. This is a crucially important task in areas, such as Ayacucho, where civil strife devastated civil society.

Regulation

The examples discussed in this chapter show that, although community justice institutions may be located in remote areas of the country, they are in permanent interaction with the official institutions of the legal system. Sometimes, as in the case of the Rondas Campesinas, their objective is to resist practices and institutions of the official legal system. On other occasions, as in the case of the NURAJs, their objective is less defiant but no less effective as they seek to transform the practices of state officials through joint action at the grassroots level.

The state, for its part, rarely ignores the existence of community justice institutions. The experience of the Peruvian state in its attempt to regulate the Rondas provides interesting lessons. Despite the determined efforts by various governments to manipulate, repress, co-opt, and regulate them, the Rondas have not only managed to survive, but have achieved considerable legitimacy. Indeed, although the Rondas and their supporters failed to persuade the congress to acknowledge that they administer justice, the text of the new legislation is ambiguous enough so that, in practice, most Rondas continue to resolve disputes in their locality in defiance of the letter of the law.

It must be noted, however, that the interest in regulation does not come solely from the organs of the state. Both the Rondas and the NURAJs are interested in engaging with state institutions and achieving legal recognition, albeit under their own terms. The Rondas and their supporters vigorously lobbied the congress to make their views known and to achieve legal recognition. Likewise, the promoters of the NURAJs in Ayacucho have enlisted the services of a lawyer and have prepared a draft bill granting legal personality to the NURAJs and acknowledging their role in the resolution of local disputes. The issue of regulation is thus not one sided. Although community justice institutions constitute a rejection of the practices of state authorities in the locality, they are not lawless or subversive organizations. They are interested in good governance, but once established they cannot be easily co-opted by the state.

Human Rights

Some practices of community justice institutions discussed in this chapter give rise to serious concerns. These practices involve cruel and inhumane punishment, such as flogging and sometimes banishment, or decisions that perpetuate the subordination of women or the exploitation of children. In gauging the most appropriate policy response to these practices, it is necessary to bear in mind two factors: first, that community institutions generally come into being in response to the abuses committed by the official legal system, and, hence, invoking principles of the official legal system to judge their practices is likely to be perceived as a cynical exercise of double standards; and second, that it is often unwise, impossible and even counterproductive to attempt to remedy at once all the human rights shortcomings.

It must be borne in mind, however, that the evidence suggests that the behavior of the Rondas and the NURAJs, though illegal, is not generally inconsistent with basic principles of human rights. Although some Rondas do occasionally apply inhumane and cruel forms of punishment—as evidenced by the two cases mentioned in this chapter— today, community service seems to be the preferred form of punishment (Aranda, 2003; Ardito, 2004b). More encouraging, however, is the fact that observers report that in some localities Ronda members actively seek training in human rights (Aranda, 2003; Laynes, 2004). Their demand for human rights training should not be construed as an attempt to please the official operators of the legal system. It stems more likely from their awareness that the training provides them with a powerful tool to defend their interests and vindicate their rights.

Human rights training can undoubtedly bring about significant improvements in the practices of community justice institutions. Yet, it should be carried out with tact and caution. Resorting to human rights teaching in the way management training schemes instruct middle management on new office procedures can be offensive and even counterproductive. In order adequately to deal with the human rights issues raised by community justice institutions, it is necessary to understand that cultural perceptions may sometimes differ and thus what all sides in the cultural spectrum require is patient dialogue (Benhabib, 2002). It is important also to bear in mind that human rights violations sometimes occur because communities are driven to outrageous forms of behavior out of desperation, not because they are primitive, violent, or evil. The solution to these problems is often found by tackling structural injustices in the wider community rather than by preaching human rights standards to those whose basic rights are consistently denied by the economic and political systems.

Conclusions

As already noted, community justice institutions are far from perfect. It would be foolish, however, to reject them simply because they do not conform to the ideal vision of the rule of law or because their activities are, occasionally, inconsistent with principles of human rights. Community justice institutions play important political and legal roles in their localities and, often, in society at large. As institutions they are flexible and their members are capable of responding and adapting to external demands. Contrary to what some lawyers and judges believe, they are not subversive organizations. They are generally conservative institutions established by the community to survive in hostile environments. Their experience shows that people in rural areas are not averse either to authority or to rules, provided they are confident that obedience to authority and compliance with rules will enable them to live and work in peace.

Notes

This chapter draws from the text of a report I prepared for the DFID (U.K.) on non-state justice systems in Latin America—www.grc-exchange.org/docs/DS39.pdf

1. ILO Convention No. 169 *Concerning Indigenous and Tribal Peoples in Independent Countries*, adopted in 1989, has played a major role in this process.
2. The constitutional court of Colombia has decided some interesting cases that suggest that in that country at least, senior judges are beginning to understand the implications of legal pluralism. See Cepeda's chapter in this collection and Sanchez, 1998.
3. On violence and politics in Peru, see generally Bourque and Warren, 1989.
4. On the issue of language and ethnicity see, Ardito, 2004a; Bermúdez, 2002; Lozano, 2000.
5. Justices of the Peace are lay magistrates who, until recently were appointed by the supreme court. Nowadays the community elects them. At present there are some 4,000 JPs, mostly in rural areas and in district capitals. There are also JPs in shantytowns in most cities except Lima. Given the demography of the country—30% rural and 20% in small towns—the network of JPs provides justice services to nearly half the population. They are not salaried, but, in some areas, charge the parties for their services, based on the notion of reciprocity.
6. On popular justice see Yngvesson, 1989; Joh, 2000–2001.
7. Article 149 of the constitution provides as follows: "The authorities of campesino and native communities with the support of the Rondas Campesinas, can exercise jurisdictional functions within their territorial area in conformity with customary law as long as this does not violate the fundamental rights of the person. The law will establish the forms of coordination between this special jurisdiction and the justices of the peace, and other institutions of the judiciary."
8. On the new law see Ruiz, 2003 and Yrigoyen, 2003.
9. On the ambiguity of the notion of "harmony," see Nader, 1997 and Nader, 1990.

References

Aranda, Mirva Victoria (2003) *Las Rondas Campesinas en las provincias altas del Cusco* (Lima: Consorcio Justicia Viva, Informe Externo) www.justiciaviva.org.pe

Ardito, Wilfredo (2004a) "Cómo vencer las barreras lingüísticas en la administración de justicia?" *Justicia Viva* (Instituto de Defensa Legal), no. 12 (2004), pp. 8–9.

——— (2004b) *Los peligros de buscar la justicia* www.derechos.org/lecturas/archivos/000228.html

ASER (Asociación de Servicios Educativos Rurales) (2001) *Proceso de desarrollo social de las Rondas Campesinas y organizaciones de autodefensa rural* (Lima, ASER, Mimeo).

Benhabib, Seyla (2002) *The Claims of Culture Equality and Diversity in the Global Era* (Princeton: Princeton University Press).

Bermúdez, Manuel (2002) *Los derechos lingüísticos* (Lima: Ediciones Legales).

Bourque, Susan C. and Kay B. Warren, "Democracy Without Peace: The Cultural Politics of Terror in Peru," *Latin American Research Review*, vol. 24, no. 1 (1989), pp. 7–34.

CEAS (Comisión Episcopal de Acción Social) (n.d) *Proyecto: Rondas Campesinas en Cajamarca* (Lima, Mimeo).

Chunga, Fermín G. (1986) *La Justicia de Paz en el Perú* (Lima: Fundación Friedrich Naumann).

Comisión Andina de Juristas (1999) *Gente que hace justicia: La Justicia de Paz* (Lima: Comisión Andina de Juristas).

Comisión de la Verdad y Reconciliación (2003) *Final Report* http://www.cverdad.org.pe/ingles/ifinal/index.php

CONAPA (Comisión Nacional de Pueblos Andinos, Amazónicos y Afroperuanos) (n.d) www.conapa.gob.pe

CUPROC (2001) *Reglamento interno de la Central Unificada Provincial de Rondas Campesinas de la Provincia de Hualgayoc* (Bambamarca, Peru: Mimeo).

Degregori, Iván, José Coronel, Ponciano del Pino, and Orin Starn (1996) *Las Rondas Campesinas y la derrota de Sendero Luminoso* (Lima: Instituto de Estudios Peruanos).

Drzewieniecki, Joanna (1995) "Indigenous People, Law and Politics in Peru" (paper delivered at the meeting of the Latin American Studies Association, Washington, D.C., Mimeo).

Gálvez, Norma (ed.) (2000) *Justicia de Paz en la Región Andina* (Bogotá: Corporación Excelencia en la Justicia).

Galindo, Pedro, "Los jueces y la información: Indicadores subjetivos," *Sistemas Judiciales*, vol. 3, no. 6 (2003), pp. 4–35.

Gitlitz, John S. (2000) *Justicia Rondera y Derechos Humanos, Cajamarca: Understanding Conflict Resolution in the Rondas of Northern Perú* (Ponencia 13, Conferencia RELAJU (*Red Latinoamericana de Antropología Jurídica*) www.geocites.com/relaju/

Gitlitz, John S. and Telmo Rojas, "Peasants Vigilante Committees in Northern Perú," *Journal of Latin American Studies*, vol. 15, no. 1 (1983), pp. 163–97.

Hernández-Breña, Wilson, "Indicadores judiciales: ¿Sirvió invertir en Módulos Básicos de Justicia para reducir la carga procesal?" *Instituto de Defensa Legal, IDL (Consorcio Justicia Viva)*, no. 33 (June 16, 2003).

Hendrix, Steven E., "Guatemalan 'Justice Centres': The Centrepiece for Advancing Transparency, Due Process and Access to Justice," *American University International Law Review*, vol. 15 (2000), pp. 814–67.

IPAZ (2000) *Administración de justicia en zonas rurales de Ayacucho: El caso de las provincias de Huanta y Vilcashuamán* (Ayacucho, Peru: IPAZ).

Jiménez, Yadira (1999) *La situación de las poblaciónes indígenas* (Lima: Ministerio de Salud, Mimeo).

Joh, Elizabeth E., "Custom, Tribal Court Practice, and Popular Justice," *American Indian Review*, vol. 2000–2001, pp. 117–32.

La Rosa, Javier, "La Justicia de Paz y la Administración de Justicia," *Justicia Viva* (Instituto de Defensa Legal), no. 10 (2003), pp. 8–9.

Laynes, Emilio (2004) *Estabilización post conflicto y rehabilitación psicosocial en las comunidades Alto Andinas del Perú* (Ayacucho: IPAZ).

Lovatón, David (2000) "La Justicia de Paz en el Perú: Aspectos positivos y límites," in Galvez (ed.), *Justicia de Paz en la Región Andina* (Bogotá: Corporación Excelencia en la Justicia), pp. 19–46.

Lozano, Ruth (2000) *Análisis de la problemática de la educación bilingue en la Amazonía peruana* (Cusco, Defensoría del Pueblo: Documento de Trabajo no. 4).

Mallon, Florencia E. (1983) *The Defence of Community in Peru's Central Highlands: Peasant Struggles and Capitalist Transitions, 1860–1940* (Princeton: Princeton University Press).

———, "Indian Communities, Political Cultures, and the State in Latin America 1780–1990," *Journal of Latin American Studies*, vol. 24 (1992) (Special Issue), pp. 35–53.

Nader, Laura (1990) *Harmony Ideology: Justice and Control in a Mountain Zapotec Village* (Stanford: Stanford University Press).

———, "Controlling Processes: Tracing the Dynamic Component of Power," *Current Anthropology*, vol. 38, no. 5 (1997), pp. 711–37.

O'Donnell, Guillermo, "On the State, Democratization and Some Conceptual Problems: A Latin American View with Glances at Some Post-communist Countries," *World Development*, vol. 21, no. 8 (1993), pp. 1355–69.

Odonga-Mwaka, Beatrice (2000) "Linking the State to the Community: Uganda's Local Government Councils," in Julio Faundez, Mary Footer, and Joseph Norton (eds.), *Governance, Development and Globalization* (London: Blackstone Press Ltd.), pp. 245–54.

Paponnet-Cantat, Christiane (1994) "Gamonalismo After the Challenge of Agrarian Reform: The Case of Capamarca, Chumbivilcas (Cusco)," in Deborah Poole (ed.), *Unruly Order: Violence, Power and Cultural Identity in the High Provinces of Southern Peru* (Boulder, CO: Westview Press), pp. 199–222.

Peña, Antonio (1998) *Justicia comunal en los Andes del Perú* (Lima: Fondo Editorial, Pontificia Universidad Católica del Perú).

Peña, Antonio, Vicente Cabedo, and Francisco López (2002) *Constituciones, derecho y justicia en los pueblos indígenas de América Latina* (Lima: Pontificia Universidad Católica del Perú).

Plant, Roger and Soren Hvalkof (2001) *Land Titling and Indigenous Peoples* (Washington, DC: Inter-American Development Bank).

PNUD (2004) *El desarrollo de la democracia en América Latina* (New York: United Nations).

Poole, Deborah (ed.) (1994) *Unruly Order: Violence, Power and Cultural Identity in the High Provinces of Southern Peru* (Boulder, CO: Westview Press).

Radcliffe, Sarah A., "Marking the Boundaries Between the Community, the State and History in the Andes," *Journal of Latin American Studies*, vol. 22, no. 3 (1990), pp. 575–94.

Ruiz, Juan Carlos, "Hacia una nueva agenda sobre la justicia comunal," *Justicia Viva* (Instituto de Defensa Legal), no. 9 (2003), pp. 4–5.

Sánchez, Esther (1998) *Justicia y pueblos indígenas en Colombia* (Bogotá: Universidad Nacional).

Sieder, Rachel (ed.) (2002) *Multiculturalism in Latin America: Indigenous Rights, Diversity and Democracy* (London: Palgrave Macmillan).

Starn, Orin (1999) *The Politics of Protest in the Andes* (Durham: Duke University Press).

USAID, "Casas de Justicia," *Boletín Trimestral* (Bogotá), no. 1 (2000).

Van Cott, Donna Lee (ed.) (1994) *Indigenous People and Democracy in Latin America* (New York: St. Martin's Press).

——— (2002) "Constitutional Reform in the Andes: Redefining Indigenous-State Relations," in Rachel Sieder (ed.), *Multiculturalism in Latin America* (London: Palgrave Macmillan), pp. 45–73.

Vega, Ricardo (1998) *Pobreza, comunidades campesinas y desarrollo rural: Puno* www.condesan.org/infoandina/Foros/Gobiernos_locales/goblocl_7.htm

Yngvesson, Barbara, "Inventing Law in Local Settings: Rethinking Popular Legal Culture," *Yale Law Journal*, vol. 98 (1989), pp. 1689–1709.

Yrigoyen, Raquel (2001a) Rondas Campesinas y desafíos del pluralismo legal en el Perú, http://geocites.com/alertanet2/yrigoyen-rc.htm

——— (2001b) *Comentarios sobre el Proyecto de Ley de Rondas Campesinas presentado por el congresista Henry Pease* http://www.geocities.com/alertanet2/f2b-ryf-comentarios.htm

——— (2002) "Peru: Pluralist Constitution, Monist Judiciary—A Post Reform Assessment," in Rachel Sieder (ed.), *Multiculturalism in Latin America* (London: Palgrave Macmillan), pp. 157–83.

——— (2003) *Comentarios la Ley de Rondas Campesinas 27,908* (Toronto: Mimeo).

Chapter 9

Private Conflicts, Public Powers: Domestic Violence in the Courts in Latin America

Fiona Macaulay

Introduction

Em briga entre marido e mulher, não se mete a colher

(In a row between husband and wife, don't stick your spoon in)

This Brazilian saying signals the supposedly private character of the marital relationship, even when it is an abusive one. This chapter examines how the courts in Latin America, and specifically in Brazil, have increasingly "stuck their spoon" into the issue of spousal abuse. Other contributors to this volume have noted the judicialization of gender relations in Latin America in recent years through the production of jurisprudence upholding collective gender rights by newly empowered supreme courts and constitutional courts. This has often been the result of the successful mobilization of women's movements during earlier constitutional moments around issues of principle, such as sexual freedom, reproductive choice, and affirmative action. However, my focus here will be on a different aspect of the judicialization of social relations; that is, the way in which thousands of ordinary women have increasingly resorted to the lower-level courts for protection of their individual right to life and physical integrity in situations of domestic violence.

This chapter explores the confluence of two concurrent trends in Latin America. The first is the noticeable diversion of domestic violence cases within the justice system. The laws passed in the region in the mid-1990s tended to redirect domestic violence cases in several ways; their resolution passed from the police stations and the community to the courts, from criminal courts to family or civil courts, from criminal prosecution to conciliation or mediation, and from criminal procedures to civil court procedures. The accompanying publicity, outreach work by women's groups, and the establishment of myriad forms of support services and legal aid have encouraged an exponential rise in demand for specifically judicial mediation in intimate relationships. After the Chilean law on intra-family violence was passed in 1994, the number of cases presented in the courts increased from 1,419 in 1994 to 73,559 in 1999 (ECOSOC, 2003, paragraph 1323).[1]

The second trend has been toward informal, transactional justice through the establishment of new judicial arenas, ranging from community-based mediation or arbitration projects to new specialized or fast-track courts, all aimed at increasing access to justice, especially for the low-income population. Although these forums for alternative dispute resolution were intended to deal with other types of social violence or conflict, such as petty theft, minor criminal damage, or bar room brawls, they too have ended up being overwhelmed by domestic violence cases. After the Venezuelan Justice of the Peace system was set up in 1994 to resolve disputes between neighbors, some 95 percent of referred cases reputedly involved domestic violence,[2] while Smulovitz' chapter in this volume illustrates a similar trend in Argentina. We can therefore identify two separate dynamics in relation to the judicialization of domestic violence, one deliberate, the other inadvertent. The case of the Brazilian Special Criminal Courts (*Juizados Especiais Criminais*, known as JECrims), examined in detail later in this chapter, is a good example of the latter. In contrast to the constitutional debates mentioned above, these processes have generally been led not by the feminist movement, but by other political and judicial actors, and have produced unintended, even perverse, outcomes with which women's groups have belatedly had to engage.

This chapter focuses specifically on women victims of domestic violence for a number of reasons. The first is that myriad studies show that it is the structurally unequal nature of gender power relations that make women the overwhelming majority of victims of systematic coercive control, suffering restrictions on their sexual, physical, and mental autonomy and integrity at the hands of male partners (Stark, 2004). Equally, it is almost exclusively women who seek assistance and redress through social services and the justice system. I focus on adult female victims in order to explore issues of agency and autonomy in relation to the justice system. (A different situation would apply to legal minors.) As a form of social violence, domestic violence has unique characteristics. The nature of the abuse is cyclical, repeated, often consisting of hundreds of small acts of physical or psychological violence and control, and produces a cumulative effect. The relationship between victim and perpetrator may encompass an emotional range from affection, dependency, and inequality, to terror. Finally, the abuse has the potential to escalate suddenly from "low level" aggression to homicide or very serious assault, especially when the victim begins to seek exit strategies.[3] It also differs in terms of the victim's needs and preferences, which vary at different stages. In the immediate aftermath of an assault, women require protection for themselves and their children, both in the short and long term. Initially, most want the abuser's behavior to change so that the relationship can continue, for reasons of economic or emotional dependence. This results in many complaints being withdrawn at the police station. Finally, many victims want some public recognition of the abuse, and some form of punishment or sanction that empowers them in relation to the abuser, protects them from future assaults and prevents re-offending by the abuser.

This chapter is concerned with the gendered *quality* of justice that results from the judicialization of intimate social relations, and therefore addresses a number of interlinked questions. Can the current judicial treatment of domestic violence comprehend and respond to its specifically gendered characteristics described above? How does the way victims of domestic violence are directed within the justice system affect their degree of choice and control over the outcome of their case? How does judicialized resolution of domestic conflict differ from that provided by other actors? What legal good is the justice system protecting? I first consider the transnational influences on the development of state responses to domestic violence in Latin America, before critically examining the case of the Brazilian Special Criminal Courts.

Transnational Frames and Influences

The impetus in Latin America for the judicialization of domestic violence has been articulated through a dual transnational influence. One is a feminist discourse, developed by international development and rights institutions. The other is the promotion of justice sector reforms and systems of consensual or mediated justice by intergovernmental and international nongovernmental finance and development organizations (Domingo and Sieder, 2001). While the former shaped the strategies of local women's movements and the responses of national government, the latter primarily influenced initiatives spearheaded by legal system professionals. Curiously, these tendencies developed in a parallel manner, with very little dialogue, with the result that the ensuing justice sector reforms were often ill suited to dealing with gender violence.

Women's rights have been defined and refined in the United Nations (UN) system through world conferences and international declarations and conventions. However, domestic violence received little attention until the 1993 UN World Conference on Human Rights, whose final declaration shifted women's rights from the domain of development, where policy recommendations are not binding, to the field of international standards on human rights, where monitoring mechanisms carry more clout with governments. The text explicitly extended state accountability to the private sphere of the family and community.[4] The UN then appointed a Special Rapporteur on Violence against Women after it adopted its most comprehensive statement on the issue: the Declaration on the Elimination of Violence Against Women.[5] The latter highlighted the problem of state *negligence*, as opposed to direct responsibility, exhorting states to exercise "due diligence" in preventing and punishing all acts of violence against women. The notion of a sin of omission, rather than of commission, allowed for a critique of the inaction or masculine bias of the justice system. "Due diligence" was not defined, however, and no criteria were offered to measure the sufficiency or quality of state policies. Neither were any stipulations made as to the optimal design of legal procedures or judicial forums. Thus individual countries have had to devise their own responses.

In the mid-1990s, Latin America became the first region in the world to have its own dedicated rapporteur on gender issues, to pass laws on domestic violence on a region-wide basis and to produce its own version of the UN Declaration (ECOSOC, 2003). The 1994 Organization of American States' Convention on the Prevention, Punishment and Eradication of Violence against Women, known as the Belém do Pará Convention,[6] defined the site of domestic violence more widely to encompass any domestic unit or interpersonal relationship in which the aggressor may have cohabited with the victim. It also amplified the notion of due diligence, stressing legal reform and the importance of women's access to simple, rapid recourse through the courts. In addition, it urged states to set up fair and efficient legal procedures that would offer women effective protection and a prompt hearing. It provided an individual right of petition to the Inter-American Commission of Human Rights in cases where the state could be shown to have failed in its obligations. This provision was applied for the first time in 2001 when the commission ruled that the Brazilian authorities had been guilty of judicial tolerance of domestic violence in the case of Maria da Penha.[7]

The Platform for Action that resulted from the Fourth World Conference on Women in Beijing urged a "holistic and multi-disciplinary approach" and noted that violence against women was an "obstacle to equality, development and peace," bringing "high social, health, and economic costs to the individual and society." This echoed a growing body of research in the international development community (Biehl and Morrison, 1999) that has emphasized improved access to justice as a crucial component of social cohesion, economic growth, and governability. International agencies such as the IDB and World Bank have promoted alternative dispute resolution, a switch from written to oral proceedings, installation of justices of the peace, a strengthening of the lowest branches of the judiciary, and improved protection of women's and children's rights (Biebesheimer, 2001). Justice is deemed to be a key tool in addressing two interrelated forms of violence: "social," where the victims and perpetrators are predominantly young men, and "domestic," where the victims are overwhelmingly women of all ages, and the perpetrators are men. The use of conciliation and consensual justice for minor social conflicts is intended to decriminalize in order to unburden the mainstream courts (which are overloaded, slow, and inefficient), and to decarcerate; that is, reduce the use of custodial sentences in order to avoid overcrowded and dehumanizing prison systems. This abolitionist school of thought (Bianchi and Van Swaaningen, 1986), advocating minimum use of penal law, emerged in tandem with the movement for informal justice. Both are in part a response to the human rights violations produced by an over-stretched criminal justice system, and in part the initiative of legal system operators, such as judges, who wish to present themselves as more efficient and responsive to society. In quantitative terms, these initiatives have been victims of their own success; their introduction has been followed by a significant increase in the numbers of plaintiffs pursuing judicial (or quasi-judicial) forms of redress. Qualitative assessment is another matter, and here I argue that there is a strongly gendered, and as yet relatively unexplored, dimension to user satisfaction with these forums, depending on the nature of the conflict and the sex of perpetrator and complainant.

Domestic Violence Laws in Latin America

Latin American courts have historically judicialized relations within the home. After independence, secularizing states took it upon themselves to regulate relations between men and women, through laws on kinship, sexuality, reproduction, and property. Men's power over women's bodies was enhanced, and domestic violence has long been both legally and culturally tolerated. This is vividly illustrated in the "honor" defense invoked until recently in Brazilian courts by men who murdered their female partners whom they suspected of adultery (Americas Watch, 1991).

In the last decade, the evolution of international and regional norms has prompted the alteration of national legal texts, such as constitutions, penal and other codes and procedures, reconfiguring the state's duties in relation to the family.[8] The region's domestic violence laws have been quite progressive and wide-ranging in specifying the character of the abuse (physical and psychological, some including rape in marriage), as well as in their definition of kinship, household composition, and marital union (formal and de facto). However, they differ in the way they direct cases through the criminal justice system, frame domestic violence as a social problem (affecting human rights, health, economic development, or family cohesion), and define the legal good to be protected (Larraín, 1999).

Domestic violence is handled in Latin American justice systems in three distinct ways: exclusively within the criminal courts, exclusively within the family or civil courts, or in a hybrid combination of the two. Only a few countries (the Dominican Republic, Honduras, Nicaragua, Panama, Puerto Rico, Uruguay and Brazil) have included in their penal codes a definition of domestic violence as a discrete criminal act with particular characteristics. This reflects the feminist view that defines domestic violence within a human rights frame as an assault on the individual integrity of women, and prescribes that women should be empowered— with the assistance of the state—to seek restitution and justice through a criminal prosecution of the perpetrator.

Elsewhere, spousal abuse is still prosecuted under the terms of existing generic offences, such as assault, threatening behavior, or homicide. However, in most countries the legislation has been more concerned with designating judicial arenas and procedures,[9] with virtually all providing for domestic violence to be processed in the first instance through conciliation. This applies even in systems that use criminal rather than civil or family courts. Conciliation is obligatory in some cases, and is closely related to the degree of political influence of the Catholic Church in countries such as Chile, Argentina, and Peru. Here family unity becomes the legal good to be protected, over and above women's right to integrity. In other countries, conciliation is strongly urged by legal operators who do not want domestic violence cases to proceed beyond the stage of conciliation to the criminal courts.

In many countries a two-tier system has emerged. "Minor" incidents are dealt with in family courts, small claims courts or before judges of the peace using a conciliation procedure, while more "serious" offenses are handled in the mainstream criminal courts. In some cases it is not clear which court has jurisdiction, and the plaintiff is able to choose between judicial arenas that operate with quite different procedures, logic, and outcomes. More often, however, police, prosecutors or judges act as "filters" and decide in which forum the woman's complaint is to be considered, depending on their perception of the severity of the abuse.

This dual system, combining the concern of the feminist movement to highlight the criminal character of domestic assault with the attempts of justice reformers to decriminalize certain categories of offenses, creates a fundamental tension. The strengthening of human rights discourses and the assertion of new categories of rights (gender, sexual orientation, ethnicity) has led subaltern groups to link their rights claims and attacks on impunity to hyper-penalization of discriminatory behavior. For example, a 1999 bill was tabled in Costa Rica that aimed to raise the penalty for "femicide" (domestic murders of women) to 20–35 years, although the sentence for all other homicides would remain in the range of 12–18 years. However, the institutional capacity of Latin American states is distinctly patchy, and judicial culture is notoriously resistant to change. For example, since the 1980s both racism and torture in Brazil have been heavily penalized, defined in the constitution as non-bailable and non-pardonable crimes, yet very few successful prosecutions have been brought. The same is true of rape, which was included in Brazil's most draconian law, the 1990 Heinous Crimes bill. The result is weak rule of law, and a lack of redress for victims.

Moreover, in the retributive model of criminal justice, the state is the privileged protagonist as both the offended party and prosecutor, while the victim remains voiceless through the penal process (Zehr, 1990). This usurpation of the conflict can be more disempowering than the initial injury or loss suffered by the victim (Christie, 1977). It is argued that consensual approaches to resolving interpersonal conflict are more victim-centric, allowing the complainants more autonomy and capacity to represent themselves, without legal intermediaries. This corresponds better to the procedures of the civil courts, which are more transactional, relational, and aimed at achieving conciliation and reparation, and where the state is a mere mediator between private parties. How, then, should domestic violence be tackled within the various structures and logics of the justice system?

Gender Violence and Justice in Brazil

In 1985 Brazil pioneered the specialized women's police stations, of which there are now over 300 (Santos, 2004; Silva, 2001). The model has subsequently been replicated around the continent. The country also hosted the Belém do Pará conference in 1994, and in 2001, Brazilian feminists won the first ruling on a domestic violence case from the Inter-American human rights system. It is therefore paradoxical that Brazil should be one of the few countries in the region that by 2005 still lacked specific legislation on violence in the home. The likelihood of governments acting decisively against domestic violence seems to be a function not so much of the absolute or relative strength of the women's movement locally, but rather of its influence on the state (Weldon, 2002). In Brazil, this influence was weak by the mid-1990s, a situation that was exacerbated by the women's movement's lack of consensus on legal strategies, its focus on social service provision to victims (Macaulay, 2000a, 2000b, p. 361) and the appearance of a new judicial forum designed without public consultation.

Over the last decade, Brazil has introduced a number of measures to improve access to justice, largely without the influence of international actors.[10] Provision to set up small claims courts to deal with minor civil cases was passed into law during the transition to democracy in 1984, when the general part of the Penal Code was also altered to allow criminal courts to impose non-custodial sentences (Azevedo, 2000, p. 119). This principle was then enshrined in the 1988 constitution and regulated in 1995 by Law 9.099, which created a criminal division to handle minor offenses that would otherwise be punishable by up to one year in prison (now extended to two years). By 1999 there were over hundreds Special Criminal Courts, all guided by the principles of speed, informality, self-representation, oral argumentation, and direct plaintiff/defendant interaction with the judge or lay mediator. Judgments cannot be taken to appeal. However, rather than cases being diverted from the mainstream courts to the new special courts, the overall volume of cases rose dramatically. Studies conducted in Rio de Janeiro and Rio Grande do Sul also revealed that women comprised between 60–80 percent of complainants in the JECrims, and mainly came with complaints of bodily harm and threats, the typical "minor" offences of domestic violence (Azevedo, 2000, p. 165; Burgos, 2001; Vianna et al., 1999, pp. 208 and 213).

Before this new judicial arena was available, Brazilian women employed a repertoire of strategies for seeking outside intervention in abusive relationships, depending on their social networks and the authority wielded by the mediating figure. Some resorted to local parallel powers, such as the drug barons in the favelas, others to conversion in Pentecostal churches (Burdick, 1993; Chesnut, 1997), which allow lower-class women to deploy a ready-made moral community to police the bounds of masculinity and exercise "reintegrative shaming" (Braithwaite, 1989). However, as ethnographies of the women's police stations testify (Hautzinger, 1997, 2003; Muniz, 1996; Nelson, 1996; Santos, 2001), women often invoked the police monopoly of force and asked the station chief to teach the husband "a lesson" (often implying subjecting him to a beating), just as they now appropriate the authority of the judge in the JECrims (Soares et al., 1996). Most complaints ended in some kind of informal accord brokered by the police. Such negotiation between police, victim, and offender is a very widespread phenomenon in domestic violence cases (Hoyle, 2000).[11] Originally designated for "minor" crimes, the JECrims were allowed to investigate homicides in 1996. Where JECrims have been installed, the police stations have lost their conciliation function, but continue to act as important gatekeepers to the justice system, determining whether the woman's complaint merits referral to the mainstream or special criminal courts. Some 30 percent of cases still proceed no further than the police station (Burgos, 2001).

In order to understand the JECrims, we must distinguish between different modalities of consensual justice (Davis, 1998). In arbitration and adjudication the third party can give a decision, either at the behest of the parties, or without their consent, producing a zero-sum outcome. Mediation is more appropriate for those seeking to restore balance in complex relationships by easing the dialogue between two parties, and allowing them to reach an agreement on their own. In the family courts this is most often used for divorce. The conciliation process has elements of restorative justice, which brings victim and perpetrator into dialogue in a supervised encounter. The aim is to achieve reparation, apology, and emotional closure for the victim, and a sharp cognitive jolt for the offender. However, there are strong disagreements about whether restorative justice is appropriate where there is an emotional connection between both parties, or whether it does not rather serve to deepen the victim's trauma (Hudson, 1998). Domestic violence legislation in Latin America involves justices of the peace, family, civil or criminal court judges, and sometimes lay mediators, and procedures include mediation/conciliation in the first instance, proceeding to arbitration when the two parties do not agree.

The Special Criminal Courts in Action

In Brazil, the first port of call for a battered woman is the police station, where an incident report (*termo circunstanciado*) is filled out. This is not the same as a crime report (*boletim de ocorrência*), which generally constitutes the first stage in a process leading to police investigation and the bringing of criminal charges. At this point the woman is required to state whether she wishes to press forward with the complaint and has six months in which to do so. If she wants to proceed, the police refer her to the local JECrim, and she must take with her the incident report and forensic medical evidence. During the first hearing the judge calls together the victim, the presumed perpetrator and the public prosecutor to find out if there is a possibility of conciliation. This essentially means an agreement on reparation or damages (*composição civil*) and an acceptance of responsibility by the perpetrator. If the victim refuses, the public prosecutor offers the aggressor a second chance to accept a non-custodial sanction by accepting a *transação penal*; that is, a limited form of plea bargaining.[12] Around 90 percent of cases end in conciliation or plea bargain. If this is not accepted, or if the accused is absent, the prosecutor may bring charges, and a date is set for indictment and trial. This phase also begins with an attempt at conciliation and plea bargaining. If this fails, the judge first hears the defendant to see whether or not to proceed. Only then are the victim and witnesses heard. Once charges have been brought, the prosecutor and judge also possess the power to suspend proceedings for a period of two to four years, as a form of probation, as long as the accused does not re-offend. However, the judge may impose conditions for suspension, such as reparation, restraining orders, home curfew, monthly reporting to the judge, or participation in some therapeutic activity such as Alcoholics Anonymous.

Flaws in the Conciliation Model

The JECrims have by now attracted a range of criticisms from those working in the justice system concerned with women's rights (Campos, 2001, 2003; Koerner, 2002). The conciliation paradigm implicitly attributes some measure of blame to the women victims, and restricts their ability to escape the abuse. It naturalizes the violence by insisting that a couple can, or should, be "reconciled" even when one systematically abuses the other. The dual system of handling "minor" offenses through consensual justice forums, and "serious" offenses through the normal criminal courts, which Burgos (2001) characterizes as two "micro-systems," also introduces an economy of violence by normalizing a certain level as acceptable in a relationship. In so doing, it constructs two artificial poles, with no gradations in between. This leads to anomalous situations, such as that in Peru, where rape is not defined as a potential component of domestic violence. There, women must either prove psychological harm in a domestic violence case, or else resort to the conventional criminal courts and pay for the medical examination themselves.

The hybrid character of the JECrims (criminal courts using a civil-type procedure) combines the worst of both systems by effectively decriminalizing the offense and forcing women into a conciliation procedure that does not meet their needs. In pretending to be gender-neutral, the courts have been unable to grasp the specificity of domestic violence. Indeed, most of the Latin American laws refer to "intra-family" violence, thus ignoring its roots in structural power imbalances and women's socially constructed gender roles.

The incident-specific approach of the criminal justice system decontextualizes the offense, viewing each event and outcome as discrete, not cumulative. It therefore uses a positivist calculation of the severity of the harm, defined in Brazil—as in other Latin American countries—in relation to the number of days of medical treatment the victim requires and is prevented from working. Thus, before the case even reaches the courts, other legal system operators have imposed their own interpretations of harm. The police are the first filters in the chain, and often record death threats as simple "threats," and attempted homicide as "assault." In so doing, they minimize the intensity of the violence and ignore the real possibility of it escalating, in order to direct the case into the JECrims. The forensic medical staff play a similar role by understating the extent of the injuries in their records. Although the JECrims have, inadvertently, made domestic violence more visible by moving the conciliation procedures out of the back-rooms of police stations and into a public forum, they have also reduced it to a second-class misdemeanor equivalent to a traffic fine. Even when it is admitted that the violence occurred and guilt is accepted, these are not recorded as criminal acts at the point of conciliation. The problem therefore lies more in the process than in the letter of the law, given that Article 61 of the Penal Code already regards the domestic context as an aggravating factor in assault cases.

The conciliation process also presumes an equality of agency between husband and wife, which is clearly nonsense in domestic violence cases. Women victims become profoundly disempowered after prolonged abuse and are in no fit state to negotiate the terms of a settlement. The JECrim conciliatory procedure has effectively re-privatized domestic violence by removing the obligation on the police and prosecution service to investigate and prosecute it as a matter of public interest.[13] Women complainants have to take the initiative at several stages and actively decide whether to proceed with charges and prosecution.

In this process, the voice of the victim is actually weaker than in a criminal court, where the representation by an advocate can compensate for structural power imbalances between aggressor and victim. The JECrims require a lawyer to be present with the victim, but this is not enforced and they are rarely heard, given the judge's and prosecutor's emphasis on the initial conciliation stage. Indeed, Themis, a feminist legal advocacy NGO based in Porto Alegre, informs women in advance that they will accompany them to court only as long as they persist in their desire to press criminal charges (Campos, 2003).

In practice, the de-penalizing intention of the JECrims biases the transactional procedure in favor of the male perpetrator, who has veto power at most stages of the process—conciliation, acceptance of an immediate sanction, conditional suspension of the case, even agreement over damages. If the accused accepts conciliation, immediate punishment or conditional discharge, he leaves without a criminal record as well as little obligation to change his behavior. He loses only the right to another plea bargain within a five-year period, while violations of agreements often go unpunished. Elsewhere in the region, the consequences for breaking the terms of a conciliation agreement vary, with some courts merely reprimanding offenders, while in others this carries the threat of full prosecution and a prison sentence. The sanctions for domestic violence range across Latin America from a fine or community service to imprisonment. Fines, in cash or kind (in the form of donations of food parcels to local charities) are the most common sanction, yet this merely domesticates and commodifies the violence. It is also likely to be paid out of the household budget, if the couple continues to cohabit.

Even though this is supposedly a victim-centered process, legal system operators—police, judges, and prosecutors—steer it at all stages, often for their own professional interest, which is to "resolve" as many cases as quickly as possible. Conciliation also requires a neutral arbiter, yet these operators do not receive any statutory training in gender issues or domestic violence. They therefore tend to impose their own prejudices and values, which are then presented as "common sense." Studies of the treatment of gender violence in the criminal justice system show the tendency to ignore, minimize or justify the offense (Americas Watch, 1991; Hermann and Barsted, 1995; Izumino, 1997; Vargas, 2000). The officers who staff the women's police stations have generally been seconded by their superiors to a job that they feel is of lower status and an obstacle to career advancement (Conselho Nacional dos Direitos da Mulher, 2000). This, combined with lack of adequate training, leads them to perform their jobs in a perfunctory manner, often exhibiting hostility and frustration toward complainants (ECOSOC, 1997; Rocha, 1999; Santos, 2001; Silva, 2001). Equally, many access to justice projects are initiated from the top down by the state, and end up compelling legal operators to function in new, unfamiliar environments where their status as privileged agents of the law may collide with the democratizing intention of these new schemes. Koerner (2002) notes that promising innovations have been "sterilized by old practices," as the JECrims retain the individualist and adversarial logic of the conventional criminal courts. In São Paulo state, where his case study was carried out, the JECrims have no separate existence with exclusively dedicated space and staff; the same judges preside over conventional criminal proceedings in the morning hearings, and then switch to the consensual justice proceedings in the afternoon sessions. The feminist movement has found it hard to influence the institutional culture and practices of the criminal justice system, both in the police precincts and the courts (Macaulay, 2002). On the other hand, self-selecting staff and volunteers in NGO-run mediation projects, such as the female paralegals trained by Themis, are much more likely to prioritize the victim and support a broad human rights discourse.

The lack of protection measures available to judges is perhaps the most serious criticism of Law 9.099. While the JECrims are fast when compared to the mainstream court system, where cases take two years to come to trial, they are still agonizingly slow for a woman at risk of violence. It often takes up to three months from the time of reporting the assault to the first court hearing. Police-based conflict resolution, for all its informality, was at least faster. Obligatory conciliation drags out these cases, exposing women to violence between hearings. Every time the victim retracts her complaints, conciliation proceedings are reinitiated, which tends to reproduce the cyclical character of domestic violence itself (Campos, 2001).

Alternatives

Some professionals working with domestic violence have tried to accommodate themselves to the JECrim. They see an advantage in the informality and flexibility of the procedure and the fact that the judge serves a function of arbitrator rather than mediator, with discretionary powers to impose conditions, manipulate the legal procedure, pass sentence, force agreements and refer to other courts (Soares, 2001).[14] For example, in the JECrim in Niterói, part of the Rio de Janeiro conurbation, one judge has used Law 9.099 creatively. At the point where the process may be suspended, he orders the offender to spend six months in a men's therapy group, run by an NGO in the city.

The victim is also able, but not obliged, to attend therapy. According to the court's data, the level of re-offending is very low.[15]

The legislative responses to the inadequacies of the JECrims have, however, been varied. Bills currently pending in congress propose a range of strategies, mainly based on penalizing and hyper-penalizing offenses. One proposal has been to raise the penalty for the crime of bodily harm when committed by a spouse, tying the definition and punishment of spousal abuse into the Torture Law and introducing the concept of domestic abuse into the Penal Code article on bodily harm. The bill also suggests giving the public prosecution service mandatory powers to prosecute, and altering the law on the special courts so that they are excluded from handling cases of crimes committed against women, children, or the elderly. None focuses on women's protection, which has now become the object of a renewed wave of women's movement activism (CFEMEA, 2002).

Most feminists now argue that the courts need to address domestic violence in a different way. Increased specialization of the court system is currently in vogue around the world, for example in the United States of America, which has managed to reverse stubbornly low levels of prosecution in rape and domestic violence cases through the introduction of specialized prosecutors and courts (Tsai, 2000). A similar proposal has been circulating since 1996, when the National Women's Rights Council suggested it for the Federal District. In 2003 women's groups finally won the support for such courts in the state of São Paulo, and a national feminist coalition proposed the same on a national level as part of a new blueprint for tackling domestic violence (Consórcio sobre Violência Doméstica, 2003). This differed from previous statements (CFEMEA, 1999) in focusing less on public policy and more on the judicial branch itself, aiming at improving outcomes for battered women through provision of gender-awareness training to legal professionals and the range of services offered. These include social assistance and obligatory legal representation for the victim, prioritization of the victim's safety and health before other legal requirements, the imposition of educational and therapeutic penalties rather than monetary ones, the creation of a monitoring council (with the participation of local women's groups), and proper evaluation of the courts' impact.

Conclusions

The current judicialization of domestic violence in Latin America is a good example of the transfer of negotiated conflict resolution from informal, non-judicial arenas into the courts. While this judicial mobilization has been intensely individual, these rights claims are political as well as social in so far as they touch on the effectiveness, or "due diligence" of the state in relation to the human rights of one sector of the population. Although the international gender regime put domestic violence on the policy agenda and highlighted the general importance of the courts, women's movements have tended to focus on provision of social services to victims or on introducing criminalizing laws, not on the design of the institutional architecture of the court system. In the justice reforms in the region, it has generally been the service providers, technocrats, and jurists, who have been consulted on the nature of reforms, not plaintiffs, defendants, or other users of the justice system. Equally, the voices of some institutionally strong actors, such as the Catholic Church, have been heard over those of the women's movement. Feminist groups have been successful at inserting the issue into the public domain, but have tended to lose control of the process once laws pass into congress for debate. The justice system follows its own institutional logic and culture and women's groups have found themselves frozen out of the judicial reform processes.

The shift in court procedures away from a criminal justice paradigm to one more influenced both by civil procedures and by common law practices has not necessarily increased women's ability to seek redress and protection in the case of domestic violence, precisely because these procedures are not gender neutral. The elision of domestic conflict with family law has resulted, perversely, in a decriminalization and re-privatization of spousal abuse, despite the increased acceptance of international discourses that have attempted to do exactly the opposite. The conciliation model as it is currently implemented in the Brazilian Special Courts and similar access to justice initiatives in Latin America fails to take into account the specific nature of domestic conflict as a form of violence in social relations and, as a result, is failing to protect women from future violence.

It therefore seems a paradox that women seek legal process in large numbers, given the poor qualitative outcomes in terms of their needs. Despite the discrediting of the judiciary in many countries, judges still retain social status and gravitas, backed by the force of the law, in a way that the police do not. This may explain why women perceive the moral authority they appropriate in court to be greater. Judges also have more legitimacy and legal powers to enforce agreements or hand down sentences. Presenting the conflict to a judicial arena also provides neutral ground, something that community resolution efforts may not, when all the protagonists may be linked by personal histories. Although the conciliation logic of the JECrims obliges women to continue in an abusive relationship, clearly the *process* is providing the women who use the courts with some form of legitimation of their grievances. It has vividly demonstrated the gendered demand for judicial services and opened up further debate as to what kinds of legal procedures and arenas can best combine protection of the victim, rehabilitation of the offender, and the expression of social disapproval of the crime of domestic violence.

Notes

1. Lack of victimization studies makes it hard to estimate exactly what proportion of total potential demand this represents.
2. *Revista Venezolana de Estudios de la Mujer* website: http://cem.tripod.com.ve/jornadasdelcem/id14.html
3. Cross-national studies show that women victims of domestic violence are most likely to be murdered by their partners in the year following the end of the relationship.
4. For a full account of the evolution of initiatives on gender violence within the United Nations system, see ECOSOC, 1994.
5. Between 1994 and 2004, the Special Rapporteur visited six Latin American countries at their invitation: Brazil, Cuba, Colombia, El Salvador, Guatemala, and Mexico, examining domestic violence, murders of women, and gender violence in the context and aftermath of armed conflict.
6. It is the most widely ratified of the Inter-American human rights instruments, with 27 States Parties adhering between 1994 and 1998.
7. Her husband's assaults had left her severely disabled, but 19 years after the near fatal attack, after two trials in the mainstream criminal courts in which the aggressor was given prison sentences, delay of a final court verdict left him at liberty.
8. The passage of the laws occurred in a relatively compressed time period: Puerto Rico, 1989; Peru, 1993; Argentina and Chile, 1994; Bolivia, Ecuador, El Salvador, and Uruguay, 1995; Colombia, Costa Rica, Mexico, and Nicaragua, 1996.
9. For a comparative overview of the region's laws, see Larraín, 1999.
10. There is a history of conciliation-based justice in Brazil. The justices of the peace were instituted in 1824 with conciliation a precondition for any case to proceed. The Civil Code then introduced obligatory conciliation in property and family law, and in the twentieth century, conciliation became mandatory in the labor courts as a corporatist strategy for keeping the social peace.
11. One study reported that 42.7% of female police station chiefs saw it as their obligation to provide conciliation and mediation (Silva, 2001).
12. However, the aggressor is not eligible if he has already served a prison sentence or has received a non-custodial sentence in the past five years. The judge and prosecutor may also exercise discretion.

13. It should be noted, however, that opinion is divided as to whether it is helpful to make an arrest or make prosecution mandatory in domestic violence cases, as in some states in the United States of America.
14. See also Barbara Musumeci Soares, "Avançando contra a violência," *O Globo*, April 24, 2001.
15. Interview with judge Marcelo Anátocles, June 26, 2001.

References

Americas Watch (1991) *Criminal Injustice: Violence against Women in Brazil* (New York: Human Rights Watch).

Azevedo, Rodrigo Ghiringhelli de (2000) *Informalização da justiça e controle social: Estudo sociológico da implantação dos Juizados Especiais Criminais em Porto Alegre* (São Paulo: IBCCRIM Monograph no. 13).

Bianchi, Herman and René Van Swaaningen (eds.) (1986) *Abolitionism: Towards a Non-repressive Approach to Crime* (Amsterdam: Free University Press).

Biebesheimer, Christina (2001) "Justice Reform in Latin America and the Caribbean: The IDB Perspective," in P. Domingo and R. Sieder (eds.), *Rule of Law in Latin America: The International Promotion of Judicial Reform* (London: Institute of Latin American Studies), pp. 99–141.

Biehl, María Loreto and Andrew R. Morrison (eds.) (1999) *Too Close to Home: Domestic Violence in the Americas* (Washington and Baltimore: Johns Hopkins University Press and the Inter-American Development Bank).

Braithwaite, John (1989) *Crime, Shame and Reintegration* (Cambridge: Cambridge University Press).

Burdick, John (1993) *Looking for God In Brazil: The Progressive Catholic Church in Urban Brazil's Religious Arena* (Berkeley, CA: University of California Press).

Burgos, Marcelo Baumann, "Conflito e sociabilidade: A administração da violência pelos Juizados Especiais Criminais," *Cidadania e Justiça*, vol. 5, no. 10 (2001), pp. 222–35.

Campos, Carmen Hein de (2001) "A violência doméstica no espaço da lei," in Cristina Bruschini and Céli Regina Pinto (eds.), *Tempos e lugares de gênero* (São Paulo: Editora 34 and Fundação Carlos Chagas), pp. 301–22.

———, "Juizados Especiais Criminais e seu déficit teórico," *Revista de Estudos Feministas*, vol. 11, no. 1 (2003), pp. 155–70.

CFEMEA (1999) "Propostas para o estado brasileiro, níveis federal, estadual e municipal: Medidas concretas para o enfrentamento da violência contra a mulher no âmbito doméstico familiar." Internal document.

CFEMEA (2002) "Situação dos projetos de lei sobre violência familiar em tramitação no Congresso Nacional, acompanhados pelo CFEMEA." Internal document.

Chesnut, Andrew (1997) *Born Again in Brazil: The Pentecostal Boom and the Pathologies of Poverty* (Piscataway, NJ: Rutgers University Press).

Christie, Nils, "Conflicts as Property," *British Journal of Criminology*, vol. 17, no. 1 (1977), pp. 1–14.

Conselho Nacional dos Direitos da Mulher (2000) *Relatório final da pesquisa nacional sobre as condições de funcionamento das delegacias especializadas no atendimento às mulheres* (Brasilia: CNDM).

Consórcio sobre Violência Doméstica (2003) "Minuta de anteprojeto de lei sobre violência doméstica e familiar contra a mulher." Internal document.

Davis, Corinne M. (1998), "Favela Justice: A Study of Dispute Resolution in a Rio Slum" (Paper presented at the conference of the Latin American Studies Association, Chicago, September 24–26).

Domingo, Pilar and Rachel Sieder (eds.) (2001) *Rule of Law in Latin America: The International Promotion of Judicial Reform* (London: Institute of Latin American Studies).

ECOSOC (1994) *Preliminary Report Submitted by the Special Rapporteur on Violence against Women* (E/CN.4/1995/42, November 22, 1994, United Nations Economic and Social Council).

——— (1997) *Report of the Special Rapporteur on Violence against Women: Mission to Brazil* (E/CN.4/1997/47/Add.2. United Nations Economic and Social Council).

——— (2003) *Integration of the Human Rights of Women and the Gender Perspective: Violence against Women (Addendum 1) International, Regional and National Developments in the Area of Violence against Women* (Document reference E/CN.4/2003/75/Add.1. United Nations Economic and Social Council).

Hautzinger, Sarah, "Calling a State a State: Feminist Politics and the Policing of Violence against Women in Brazil," *Feminist Issues*, no. 1 and 2 (1997), pp. 3–30.

———, "Criminalizing Male Violence in Brazil's Women's Police Stations: From Flawed Essentialism to Imagined Communities," *Journal of Gender Studies*, vol. 11, no. 3 (2003), pp. 243–51.

Hermann, Jacqueline and Leila Linhares Barsted (1995) *O judiciário e a Viovência vontra a mulher: A ordem legal e a (des)ordem familiar* (Cadernos CEPIA, Year 1, no. 2).

Hoyle, Carolyn (2000) *Negotiating Domestic Violence: Police, Criminal Justice and Victims* (Oxford: Oxford University Press).

Hudson, Barbara, "Restorative Justice: The Challenge of Sexual and Racial Violence," *Journal of Law and Society*, vol. 25, no. 2 (1998), pp. 237–56.

Izumino, Wânia Pasinato, "Justiça criminal e violência contra a mulher: O papel da justiça na solução dos conflitos de gênero," *Revista Brasileira de Ciências Criminais*, vol. 5, no. 18 (1997), pp. 147–70.

Koerner, Andrei (2002) "Justiça consensual e conflitos de familia: Algumas reflexes," in Marcelo Labaki Agostinho (ed.), *Família: Conflitos, reflexões e intervenções* (São Paulo: Casa do Psicólogo), pp. 39–63.

Larraín, Soledad (1999) "Curbing Domestic Violence: Two Decades of Action," in María Loreto Biehl and Andrew R. Morrison (eds.), *Too Close to Home: Domestic Violence in the Americas* (Washington and

Baltimore: Johns Hopkins University Press and the Inter-American Development Bank), pp. 105–30.

Macaulay, Fiona (2000a) "Tackling Violence Against Women in Brazil: Converting International Principles into Effective Local Policy," in Susie Jacobs, Ruth Jacobson, and Jennifer Marchbank (eds.), *States of Conflict: Gender, Violence and Resistance* (London: Zed Press), pp. 144–62.

—— (2000b) "Getting Gender on the Policy Agenda: A Study of a Brazilian Feminist Lobby Group," in Elizabeth Dore and Maxine Molyneux (eds.), *The Hidden Histories of Gender and the State in Latin America* (Chapel Hill, NC: Duke University Press), pp. 346–67.

—— (2002) "Taking the Law into Their Own Hands: Women, Legal Reform and Legal Literacy in Brazil," in Nikki Craske and Maxine Molyneux (eds.), *Gender and the Politics of Rights and Democracy in Latin America* (Basingstoke: Palgrave), pp. 79–101.

Muniz, Jacqueline (1996) "Os direitos dos outros e outros direitos: Um estudo sobre a negociação de conflitos nas DEAMs/RJ," in Luiz Eduardo Soares (ed.), *Violência e política no Rio de Janeiro* (Rio de Janeiro: ISER/Relumé), pp. 125–64.

Nelson, Sara, "Constructing and Negotiating Gender in Women's Police Stations in Brazil," *Latin American Perspectives*, vol. 23, no. 1 (1996), pp. 131–48.

Rocha, Martha Mesquita (1999) "Dealing with Crimes against Women: Brazil," in Biehl and Morrison, *Too Close to Home*, pp. 149–52.

Santos, Cecília MacDowell dos (2001) "Delegacias da Mulher em São Paulo: Percursos e percalços," Website Rede Social de Justiça e Direitos Humanos: http://www.social.org.br.

——, "En-gendering the Police: Women's Police Stations and Feminism in São Paulo," *Latin American Research Review*, vol. 39, no. 3 (2004), pp. 29–55.

Silva, Kelly Cristiane da (2001) "As DEAMs, as corporações policiais e a violência contra as mulheres: Representações, dilemas e desafios." Internal report (Brasilia: Conselho Nacional dos Direitos da Mulher).

Soares, Barbara Musumeci (2001) "Os juizados especiais criminais e a violên-cia doméstica" (Rio de Janeiro: Centro de Estudos de Segurança e Cidadiania, Universidade Cândido Mendes).

Soares, Luiz Eduardo et al. (1996) "Violência contra a mulher: As DEAMs e os pactos domésticos," in Luiz Eduardo Soares (ed.), *Violência e política no Rio de Janeiro* (Rio de Janeiro: ISER/Relumé), pp. 65–105.

Stark, Evan (2004) *Coercive Control: The Entrapment of Women in Personal Life* (Oxford: Oxford University Press).

Tsai, Betsy, "The Trend Towards Specialized Domestic Violence Courts: Improvements on an Effective Innovation," *Fordham Law Review*, vol. 68, no. 4 (2000), pp. 1285–328.

Vargas, Joana Domingues (2000) *Crimes sexuais e sistema de justiça* (São Paulo: IBCCRIM).

Vianna, Luiz Werneck et al. (1999) *A judicialização da política e das relações sociais no Brasil* (Rio de Janeiro: Editora Revan).

Weldon, Laurel S. (2002) *Protest, Policy and the Problem of Violence against Women: A Cross-national Comparison* (Pittsburgh: University of Pittsburgh Press).

Zehr, Howard (1990) *Changing Lenses: A New focus for Crime and Justice* (Scottsdale, PA: Herald Press).

Chapter 10

Constitutionalism, the expansion of Justice and the Judicialization of Politics in Brazil

Rogério B. Arantes

Introduction

In the comparative analysis of contemporary democracies, Brazil seems to possess many of the elements analysts highlight as the probable causes of the "judicialisation of politics." First, political democracy was established in the 1980s followed by the approval of a new constitution in 1988 that set out an extensive charter of rights. Second, an increasingly greater number of interest groups within society are demanding judicial solutions to collective conflicts. Third, the political system is characterized by fragile and even minority coalitions supporting the government of the day, while the opposition uses the judiciary to fight government policies. Lastly, the constitutional model delegates to the judiciary and to the *Ministério Público* (Public Ministry) the task of protecting both individual rights and interests, as well as collective and social rights.

The judicialization of politics also depends on the willingness of actors within the justice system to assume responsibility for the implementation of rights, and for the resolution of social conflicts, something referred to in the literature as legal activism. Though it is difficult to characterize the political ideology that permeates the Brazilian legal milieu, recent research shows the presence of political values of social transformation, equality, and citizenship among judges and, especially, among members of the *Ministério Público* (MP). Although it is a state body, not subject to political or electoral control, the MP considers itself a legitimate representative of society and has become known for its "political voluntarism" (Arantes, 2002), leading the defense of diffuse and collective rights, and fighting political corruption.

Starting with the 1988 constitution, the Brazilian justice system experienced a significant and two-fold expansion, both in relation to the political system and in relation to society. For the first time, the judiciary became an important political institution, thanks to an extremely decentralized system of judicial review, widely accessible to individuals and to political and social actors. The judiciary thereby became a significant actor in the political decision-making process, accentuating even further the consensual model of Brazilian democracy (Lijphart, 1999). In addition, as an ever greater range of social rights became legal norms, the provision of ordinary justice was profoundly transformed: access to justice for collective causes was broadened, which in turn led the judicial system to adopt an increasingly protective role vis-à-vis civil society. At the heart of this "dual judicialisation" of both politics and society in Brazil, is one of the world's longest constitutions, with 1,855 original provisions and just as many additions, mostly containing definitions of social and economic rights and policies. (Couto and Arantes, 2003). This constitutional profile constrains the governmental agenda and forces rulers to form broad parliamentary alliances in order to change "constitutionalised policies," and paves the way for the judicial resolution of social conflicts—either by way of judicial review, or by individual and collective actors' access to the ordinary justice system.

The Two-Fold Expansion of the Justice System in Brazil

Two aspects of the evolution of constitutionalism in the nineteenth and twentieth centuries should be mentioned. The first is that the political and social democratization of liberal states led to a substantial change in the profile of contemporary constitutional texts, which effectively became three-dimensional. Besides ensuring the individual rights of "negative freedom"—the protection from arbitrary action by the government (Berlin, 1981)—, twentieth century constitutions also contained political rights of participation, or "positive freedom," as well as the constitutionalization of material rights of social well-being. The constitutionalization of welfare rights aimed at ensuring the welfare and equality of all citizens and imposed new policy obligations on the government. The second important aspect relates to the efforts of contemporary democratic theory to establish the possible links between democracy and constitutionalism. According to Elster (1979, 1999), the constitution acts as a self-restraining mechanism. In order to ensure the survival of democracy in the long term, it may be necessary to limit the power of political majorities: the function of the courts is to safeguard certain rights and principles and prevent them from being altered at the whim of new electoral outcomes. However, as Elster also notes (1999, pp. 33–48), the mutually rein-forcing relationships between democracy and constitutionalism can only be empirically assessed when a third dimension is taken into account; namely the kinds of decision-making processes which occur as a result of the combination between the majority will expressed at the ballot box and the constraints imposed on the exercise of that will. Cláudio G. Couto and I are currently developing a comparative methodology for analyzing constitutions. According to our hypothe-sis, extensively programmatic constitutions, such as the Brazilian Constitution of 1988, exacerbate difficulties in the democratic deci-sion-making process. Large government majorities are required in order to pass constitutional amendments in order to alter simple, yet constitutionalized, public policies. A pilot study of 34 constitutional amendments to the Brazilian Constitution enacted during the 1995–2002 period shows that, of the 482 provisions that altered or added new constitutional elements, no less than 68.8 percent (332) concerned policies and only 31.2 percent (150) related to general principles of the organization of government.[1]

Our secondary hypothesis, for a future research project, suggests that besides affecting the legislative decision-making process, the con-stitutionalization of public policies is one of the main driving forces behind the judicialization of politics in Brazil. This can be explained by the fact that the judiciary—and especially the Federal Supreme Court (Supremo Tribunal Federal, STF)—is called upon more often because of the length of the constitution and the profusion of new amendments. In fact, the data indicates that there has been an extraor-dinary growth in the level of activity by the Federal Supreme Court after 1988. Partly as a result of the constitutionalization of material rights and public policies, and partly because of changes in the nature and institutional roles of the judiciary and the MP, Brazil has experienced a significant process of judicialization of both politics and society since the 1980s.

The Political Dimension of Judicial Review

Studies of the constitutional control of laws have shown how the principle of judicial review was increasingly adopted by a number of countries[2] with the enactment of new constitutional texts during the twentieth century, texts that were much more substantive and rigid than those of the nineteenth century. Some countries copied the U.S. model, while others sought even more innovative alternatives for constitutional control, capable of addressing some of the shortcomings of the U.S. system. Since the U.S. Supreme Court was given the final word on a range of issues of immense importance for U.S. society, the possibilities and limits of the Court have often been at the centre of controversy, precisely because of the delicate interface such a system establishes between law and politics.[3] The U.S. Supreme Court experience in the 1920s and 1930s and its systematic opposition to the policies of the first Roosevelt administration (1933–1936)[4] produced harsh criticism; it was claimed that the court's actions had led to the distortion of the principles of separation of powers and degenerated into a "government of judges" (Lambert, 1921).

A few countries in Europe had introduced the mechanism of judicial review at the start of the twentieth century. The French attempt to institutionalize a democratic regime without judicial review was erratic, but Britain's experience proved that it was possible to sustain a democratic regime without that kind of control. The prevailing thesis during Britain's shift from absolutism to liberal government had been that of the "supremacy of parliament," as well as the principle that legislative decisions could not be reviewed by other bodies in the light of some superior law. In fact, no such superior law existed in England where, to this day, there is no written document that may be called a constitution. This situation changed significantly after World War II, when the resumption of democratic regimes in several countries led to adoption of the liberal principle of controlling the constitutionality of laws. In fact, the first step had taken place in 1920, when a new constitution in Austria introduced judicial review under the influence of the eminent jurist Hans Kelsen. The Austrian judicial review model was quite different from that of the United States.[5] In the latter, all the judges who comprise the judiciary have the authority to declare the unconstitutionality of laws and normative acts when presented with a concrete lawsuit. In the U.S. model, classified as *diffuse*, conflicts between the law and the constitution are not taken directly to the Supreme Court, but enter it through the lower levels of the judiciary. The Supreme Court can be understood as the guardian of the constitution only because its jurisprudence is binding and its decisions are final in practical terms. However, it is important to stress that the Supreme Court does not hold a monopoly on constitutional interpretation of laws and shares such authority with the other instances of the judiciary, in a system also termed decentralized.[6] The novelty introduced by the Austrian model is that judicial review is exclusive to the constitutional court. In addition, this court also has the authority to judge the law itself, by means of a direct action, since there is no possibility that other bodies will carry out judicial review in a decentralized manner. The Austrian system of judicial review, also called *concentrated*, was the model for those European countries which, after World War II, decided to adopt judicial review, such as Italy and Germany. In these countries, Nazism and Fascism led the designers of the 1947 and 1949 constitutions, respectively, to introduce mechanisms for controlling political power, among which was a special court to rule over the constitutionality of laws.[7]

The constitutional court model of concentrated judicial review attempted to avoid the ills of the U.S. system, where the decentralization of judicial review and the high level of insulation of the magistrates sometimes threatened to lead to a "government of judges." The concentrated system sought a better balance between the liberal function of judicial review and the preservation of the will of the political majority by increasing the politicization of the composition of the constitutional courts, and by restricting the number of actors authorized to bring suits before the court. Thus, besides the monopoly to declare unconstitutionality, the composition of the courts and the restrictions on who can access the court reduce the chances of legal activism on behalf of magistrates, thereby limiting the function of judicial review. Constitutional courts are separate bodies from the regular judiciary and do not coincide with its higher courts. Entry into the court is more political and the terms served by the magistrates, though often long, are based on the idea that their performance should be periodically subjected to evaluation by the political body. Lastly, judicial review may be further concentrated by restricting the number of those who may call upon the court, usually limited to two or three relevant political actors.

Between the two extremes—the diffuse and the concentrated formulas—some countries have sought to establish a mixed system[8] or, as in the unique case of Brazil, *a hybrid system*. In Brazil, thanks to the 1988 constitution, the system of judicial review is not simply diffuse. Because of the Direct Unconstitutionality Action mechanism (*Ação Direta de Inconstitucionalidade*, ADIN), by which the Federal Supreme Court may directly annul or ratify a law, the STF may be considered a quasi constitutional court. On the other hand, neither is the system purely centralized, since the STF does not hold a monopoly on declaring (un)constitutionality, sharing such authority with lower courts and judges throughout the country. When the STF receives appeals from the lower courts regarding constitutional issues, it will rule only in its role as the judiciary's highest body, and its rulings are only valid for the particular cases in question. Such dissociation between the diffuse and the concentrated aspects of the Brazilian system have led to attempts to secure reforms that would make the

STF's decisions binding on the lower levels of the judiciary. There have also been attempts to introduce mechanisms that would enable constitutional conflicts to be sent directly to the STF for a definitive evaluation that would be valid in the whole country.[9]

Some numbers will provide an idea of the dimensions of the Brazilian judiciary and its diffuse judicial review system. Brazil is a federal country, made up of 26 states and a Federal District. According to data from 1999, there were 7,231 judges in the lower level state courts. There is an appeals court in every federal unit—the Tribunal de Justiça—which, in total, had 1,167 "*desembargadores*" (judges) in 1999.[10] Alongside the ordinary state justice system, specific branches of justice were created during the twentieth century that, throughout the country, are represented by judges of the first instance as well as appeals courts. These include military courts, electoral courts, labor courts, and federal courts. Of these four, the highest number of judges is found in the labor courts, where over 2,000 judges are charged with deciding conflicts between employers and employees. This is one of the largest contingents of labor judges in the world.[11] The branch of justice with the second highest number of judges, and one that plays an extremely important role in the judicialization of politics in Brazil, is the Federal Justice, where cases involving the central government are processed. The federal government is the authority responsible for most of the administrative acts affecting the population and whose constitutionality is commonly questioned, especially in the areas of taxation and social and economic policy. According to data from 2003, around 990 judges work in the federal justice courts of the first instance and approximately 130 are spread across the five Federal Regional Courts (Tribunais Regionais Federais), which act as appeals courts.[12]

Though it is not possible to calculate accurately the number of current proceedings involving constitutional issues, two graphs give an indication of the judicialization of politics in Brazil. figure 10.1 shows the evolution of proceedings in the federal justice courts of the first instance, where individual citizens may bring a suit against the federal government (or be sued by it), and where the constitution is often used to evade laws and administrative acts that are claimed to be unconstitutional.

Though it is not possible to distinguish between cases in which the federal government is the plaintiff and those in which it appears as defendant, estimates show that around 46 percent of the cases being processed during the year 2000 concerned debts to the state (taxes, fees, and others).[13] If we consider that the remainder of the cases are actions by individuals against the government, and that this ratio has

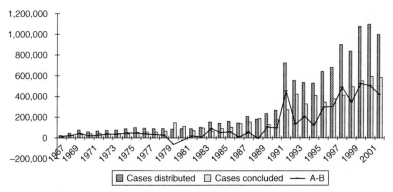

Figure 10.1   Cases distributed and concluded within the lower instance of the federal justice, 1967–2001

Source: Judiciary National Database and Supreme Federal Courts Reports (www.stf.gov.br).

been constant, we can estimate that no less than half a million cases have been brought every year against the federal government in the past few years. Though more careful investigation is required, one can suggest that such extreme litigiousness between the government and society in Brazil arises from successive government interventions in the fields of economic and fiscal policy, as well as taxation. These interventions have almost always taken the form of Provisional Measures by the federal executive branch,[14] which have altered the legal order and left both individuals and private companies discontented. In addition, as the 1988 constitution is extremely detailed (there are 1,855 provisions in total), acts by the government almost always clash with constitutional provisions and are subsequently questioned in the justice system. As becomes clear from figure 10.1, the stunning increase in the number of cases began precisely in 1990–1991, in the wake of one of the most interventionist economic plans in Brazilian history: the Collor Plan. Since then, the diffuse side of the Brazilian judicial review system has been used by thousands of people who are unhappy with acts of government. It is therefore one of the most significant examples of the judicialization of politics in Brazil, despite the fact that several magistrates have issued warnings concerning the risk of a collapse of the legal system. There are currently over five million cases awaiting decisions in the federal justice system, which corresponds to an average of over five thousand cases per judge.

The second table, which shows the increasing number of current proceedings on the diffuse side of the judicial review system, concerns

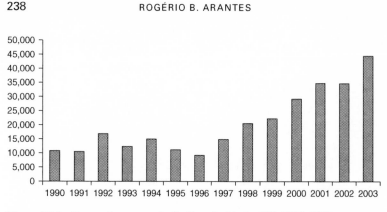

Figure 10.2   Extraordinary appeals distributed with the STF, 1990–2003

Source: Judiciary National Database. Supremo Tribunal Federal (www.stf.gov.br).

Extraordinary Appeals (Recursos Extraordinários, RE). Extraordinary Appeals allow the parties in a case involving constitutional issues to take their claims to the Federal Supreme Court. Figure 10.2 shows the number of REs that quadrupled between 1990 and 2003. Although REs concern proceedings initiated years ago in the first instance and that only much later reached the STF, their extraordinary increase has had two significant consequences. One is the overload of the STF. The STF has no case selection mechanism equivalent to that of the U.S. Supreme Court, and—in addition—finds itself obliged to rule repeatedly in similar cases, since its decisions are not binding on the lower instances. The second impact is economic: many *Recursos Extraordinários* concern financial losses by social sectors and professional groups as a result of monetary stabilization plans implemented by previous administrations, which then falls upon present and future administrations to settle. (There have been situations where the government found itself forced to spend billions of dollars to settle past accounts).

In addition to the decentralization that characterizes judicial review in Brazil, the system has also become very widely accessible, given that the 1988 constitution increased the number of agents authorized to make use of the ADIN before the Federal Supreme Court. Previously limited to the attorney general of the republic (*Procurador Geral da República*), the list of potential agents became extremely long, even surpassing countries with a system of concentrated judicial review. Article 103 of the constitution authorizes nine different categories—and at least 75 agents—to bring an ADIN before the STF, not counting nationwide trade union confederations, whose number is unknown (see table 10.1).

Table 10.1   Agents authorized to call upon constitutional courts in Brazil, Austria, and Germany

Brazil	n	Austria	n	Germany	n
1. President of the republic	1	1. Federal government	1	1. Federal government	1
2. Board of the federal senate	1	2. State government (Landers)	9	2. State government (Landers)	16
3. Board of the chamber of deputies	1	3. 1/3 of the Parliament	–	3. 1/3 of the Parliament Parliament	–
4. Board of a state legislative political parties assembly	27	(There are four political parties in the federal legislature)		(There are six in the federal legislature)	
5. State governor	27				
6. Attorney general of the republic	1				
7. Federal council of the Brazilian Bar Association	1				
8. Political parties represented in the national congress	16				
9. Confederation of labour unions or a professional association of a nationwide nature	–				
Subtotal	75	Subtotal	10	Subtotal	17

The effect of such an expansion in direct access to the court is predictable: during the 15 years in which the constitution has been in force, no less than 3,014 Direct Actions of Unconstitutionality have been brought against federal and state laws and administrative acts. Disregarding the few months of 1988, this averages about 200 actions a year. As can be seen in table 10.2, the most frequent plaintiffs are the state governors and the nationwide trade union confederations (26.4 percent and 25.5 percent, respectively), followed by the attorney general of justice and the political parties (around 20 percent). This result is in line with the trend revealed by Vianna et al. (1999). In a study which analyzed ADINs up to 1998, it was found that the STF represented an important oppositional forum both for the trade union confederations and for political parties dissatisfied with the laws promulgated by the government. In addition, the STF acts as a state-level tribunal, due to the significant amount of actions brought by state governors, almost always against laws produced by the legislative assemblies in their own states.[15]

Table 10.2 Direct actions of unconstitutionality, 1988–2003

Plaintiffs	1988	1989	1990	1991	1992	1993	1994	1995	1996	1997	1998	1999	2000	2001	2002	2003	Total
State governor	2	55	100	57	47	39	32	61	25	60	28	48	68	58	49	66	795
Confederations	4	53	51	58	21	48	64	48	59	47	69	46	62	51	35	52	768
Attorney general of the republic	0	22	63	65	63	49	68	47	12	38	27	18	22	11	6	117	628
Political parties	2	14	30	39	25	15	29	47	47	45	42	59	75	79	27	44	619
Brazilian Bar Association	1	5	9	3	4	7	3	2	8	12	9	12	20	6	14	9	124
State legislative assemblies	0	1	1	7	4	1	1	3	2	2	1	3	4	3	3	1	37
Other (*)	2	9	1	3	2	3	1	3	5	2	5	3	2	1	1	0	43
Total	11	159	255	232	166	162	198	211	158	206	181	189	253	209	135	289	3014

Note: (*) Plaintiffs who, even though not qualified according to the definitions set forth in Article 103 of the constitution, insist in initiating ADINs. In these cases, the STF declares the action inadmissible.

Source: Judiciary National Database. Supremo Tribunal Federal (www.stf.gov.br).

Although they are authorized to bring ADINs, the president of the republic and the presidents of the boards of the Federal Senate and Chamber of Deputies have never made use of such a mechanism for judicial review. This is a clear indication that the laws enacted during the period in question, as an expression of the will of the political majority, met the interests of both legislative chambers and of the executive branch. In contrast, the STF was directly called upon over 3,000 times by those dissatisfied with federal and state laws, and in addition thousands of cases involving constitutional issues arrived at the court via the diffuse path, which undoubtedly made it a major political power and guardian of the constitution. The significant political function of the STF has increasingly aroused researchers' interest in the court's performance, its level of independence, and the behavior of its judges.[16]

The Brazilian political system differs from Lijphart's majority model (1999) and adopts the liberal principle of restraining the political majority by means of an ultra-decentralized system of judicial review. This decentralized system of judicial review enables political minorities to exercise their veto power by invoking the constitution against laws and administrative acts issued by the legislative and executive branches of power. If we consider that the political decision-making process in Brazil contemplates the participation of a wide variety of institutional actors in a wide range of arenas (separation of powers between executive and legislative, two legislative bodies with equal powers within congress, exaggerated multipartisanism and a reasonably decentralized federalism), we should add the judicial review system as one of the main resources available to the political minorities against majority political decisions, reinforcing even further the consensual nature of the Brazilian political system.[17]

In the past few years analysts have argued that the Brazilian political system has operated in the form of a "coalition presidentialism," characterized by a fragmented party system, whose dispersion is compensated for by the power of the federal executive. The executive controls the legislative agenda and distributes posts and ministries as a means to unite parties and sustain the governing coalition in parliament.[18] Despite the validity of this argument, the use of judicial review by opposition parties has been one of the main ways of politically challenging the governing coalition, leading to the judicialization of politics in Brazil.

Table 10.3 shows the direct actions of unconstitutionality sponsored by the seven largest parties in the past few years (Partido do Movimento Democrático Brasileiro (PMDB), Partido da Frente Liberal (PFL), Partido da Social-Democracia Brasileira (PSDB), Partido

Table 10.3 Direct actions of unconstitutionality by political parties (1990–2003)

Parties	Collor 1990–1991	Itamar 1992–1994	FHC I 1995–1998	FHC II 1999–2002	Lula 2003	Total	%
Governing party coalition (*)	PRN PFL-PDS	PMDB-PFL-PSDB-PTB	PSDB-PFL-PMDB-PTB	PSDB-PFL-PMDB-PTB	PT-p.p.e-PTB		
Left							
Workers' Party (PT)	26	12	69	43	0	150	24.9
Democratic Labour Party (PDT)	21	10	21	16	5	73	12.1
Small left-wing parties (PCdoB/PSB/PCB/ PPS/PSTU/PV)	21	9	17	27	2	76	12.6
Left-wing parties co-authoring (PT, PDT, PCdoB, PSB, PV)	0	1	35	18	0	54	9.0
Center							
Brazilian Social Democratic Party (PSDB)	5	1	0	1	9	16	2.7
Brazilian Democratic Movement Party (PMDB)	6	3	7	9	1	26	4.3
Right-wing							
Brazilian Labour Party (PTB)	1	0	0	9	1	11	1.8
Liberal Front Party (PFL)	0	1	5	1	8	15	2.5
Progressist Party (PDS/ PPB/PP)	0	0	7	2	4	13	2.2
Social Liberal Party (PSL)	0	0	0	65	7	72	11.9
Solidarity Humanist Party (PHS)	0	0	0	25	0	25	4.1
Other (small non-ideological parties)	14	7	20	24	7	72	11.9
Total	94	44	181	240	44	603	100.0
% of actions brought by government-allied parties	0	11	6.6	8.3	6.8	4.3	

Notes: (*) Classification of party coalitions, adapted from Meneguello (1998)
PT   Partido dos Trabalhadores
PDT   Partido Democrático Trabalhista
PCdoB   Partido Comunista do Brasil
PSB   Partido Socialista Brasileiro
PCB   Partido Comunista Brasileiro
PPS   Partido Popular Socialista
PSTU   Partido Socialista dos Trabalhadores Unificado
PV   Partido Verde
PSDB   Partido da Social-Democracia Brasileira
PMDB   Partido do Movimento Democrático Brasileiro
PTB   Partido Trabalhista Brasileiro
PFL   Partido da Frente Liberal
PDS   Partido Democrático Social
PPB   Partido Progressista Brasileiro
PP   Partido Progressista
PSL   Partido Social Liberal
PHS   Partido Humanista da Solidariedade

Source: Judiciary National Database. Supremo Tribunal Federal (www.stf.gov.br).

dos Trabalhadores (PT), Partido Democrático Trabalhista (PDT), Partido Trabalhista Brasileiro (PTB), Partido Progressista Brasileiro (PPB)), listed along a left–center–right spectrum. The small left-wing parties have been grouped together, as have other small parties whose ideological profile is less well-defined. Two numerically insignificant parties (PSL and PHS) were listed separately because of the high number of ADINs they brought in the 1999–1902 period. Lastly, it is worth noting that 54 actions were coauthored by two or more parties.

The main opposition party during the 1990s—the PT (Workers' Party)—was responsible for a quarter of the total number of ADINs during the administrations of Collor de Mello, Itamar Franco, and Fernando Henrique Cardoso. Having presented 150 ADINs during that period, the PT has not called upon the STF since Lula took office in 2003. The PSDB, which resorted to the STF only once during the Fernando Henrique Cardoso administration has resorted to the STF nine times since it became part of the opposition in 2003. In this case the judicialization of politics is clearly an initiative by the opposition parties, which, defeated in the political and parliamentary arenas, resort to the STF in an attempt to defeat the government in the judicial arena. In general, governing parties brought less than five percent of actions between 1990 and 2003, and, of these, a majority concerned state and not federal laws.

Another important aspect of the judicialization of politics, expressed in the form of ADINs presented by political parties, is the fact that some 25 percent of these actions were sponsored by parties with less than five percent of the parliamentary representation in the national congress. Though insignificant from a numerical point of view, the existence of a single deputy affiliated with the party in question is sufficient to enable it to make use of ADINs to try to overturn the majority will expressed in the promulgation of a given law. The most significant case in this respect is that of the Social Liberal Party, which, in the elections of 1998 and 2002, had only one representative elected (0.19 percent of the chamber of deputies) but, during these five years has brought no less than 72 ADINs, or 25 percent of the total actions taken to the STF by parties between 1999 and 2003. Besides the number of cases brought by the PSL, their contents also stand out: the party attacked provisions in state laws that introduced external control of police activity by the *Ministério Público* and gave prosecutors the authority to carry out criminal investigations. The PSL was also responsible for actions against changes in the public safety system in some states and against some restrictions on the trade of firearms in others. The miniscule party opposed Provisional Measure 2152, which aimed to unite the whole country in combating the electricity crisis in 2001, and was responsible for an ADIN against the Acre state constitution because it did not invoke God's protection in its preamble.

One hypothesis to be explored is that a significant share of the total of 3,014 ADINS presented to the STF concern constitutional provisions relating to public policies rather than fundamental principles of Brazil's political and social organisation. As the country's charter has become noteworthy for constitutionalizing policies, it is likely that government measures may easily be confronted by the opposition via the judicial review system, transforming the STF into a sort of revising chamber of government policies and hugely increasing the level of judicialization of politics.

Broadening Access to Common Justice and the Expansion of the Judiciary

If judiciaries generally tended to expand with the installation of liberal-democratic regimes in the twentieth century, by way of protecting established freedoms, the promotion of equality by these regimes has also led to an unexpected kind of judicial expansion. This has to do with the transformation of the judiciary into a mechanism for guaranteeing social and collective rights, especially in the second half of the twentieth century. There are two main complementary aspects to such an expansion. The first is sociological and links the expansion of the judiciary and its current difficulties to the development and crisis of the welfare state during the twentieth century. The second is legal and links the expansion of the judiciary to the broadening of access to justice for collective cases, especially from the 1970s onwards. Boaventura de Sousa Santos argues that the development of the welfare state after World War II led to significant changes in the world of law and justice. Characterized by the principles of economic interventionism and the promotion of social welfare, this new state form led to the promulgation of constitutional and ordinary laws which were much more substantive than those issued under the classical liberal model. These laws detailed such social and economic rights as education, health, labor, social security, and others.[19] According to Santos, these changes led the judiciary to assume a new role: previously restricted to the role of applying the law in private conflicts, it was now called upon to make effective new social legislation, much more substantive from the standpoint of citizenship rights. Though this is not a linear process, Santos highlights that "[t]he juridification of social welfare has made room for new litigation in the fields of labor, civil, administrative and social security law, which—in some countries more than in others—has translated into an exponential increase in legal activity, a consequent boom in litigiousness."[20] According to this sociological perspective, the crisis suffered by the welfare state in the late 1970s also affected the judiciary. The core problem to be confronted was that of the state having lost much of its ability to promote social welfare as a result of reform processes guided by neoliberal ideology. Unlike the state, which saw its size shrink as a result of the crisis, the judiciary found its activities expanded even further in an attempt to conserve expanded legislated rights in the face of scarce public resources. If it was already difficult enough to ensure the effectiveness of such rights, the crisis of the state made the setting even more dramatic, setting an increase in legal demand against the judiciary's limited ability to respond.

The second analytical perspective, which describes the expansion of the judiciary in the second half of the twentieth century, emphasizes the juridical changes entailed in the development of new types of rights and new forms of access to justice. According to this line of thought, the judiciary has undergone significant expansion throughout the twentieth century because such an evolution placed justice within the formal reach of collective social actors. A study by Cappelletti and Garth (1978) discusses the changes to individualist liberal law and the opening of the legal order to the so-called diffuse and collective rights.[21] In their opinion, the recognition by law of the diffuse and collective dimensions of certain interests has led several countries to promote new procedures of access to justice, transcending the individualism of the liberal model and making room for collective action. In the context of the 1970s, the authors highlighted the vulnerability of individuals due to the growing complexity of social life and the collective dimension of various kinds of conflicts, at the same time as they pointed to the inability of state institutions to offer general protection to supra-individual rights such as the environment, consumer-related rights, public property and cultural and historical heritage, among others. In this context, the authors emphasized the importance of opening the justice system to civil associations, legally formed for the judicial defense of diffuse and collective rights, thereby challenging the judiciary to take on a completely new role.

A second aspect emphasized by the authors with respect to broadening access to justice concerns innovations in the judicial structure from the 1970s onward, such as the establishment of "small claims courts" aimed at faster and more effective solution of less complex cases (or cases involving lesser sums and/or lesser offences). This kind of judicial reform signaled an attempt by the judiciary to get closer to the poorer population, and face up to the so-called constrained litigiousness, or demands which did not even reach the courts because of difficulties in access. Overall, the expansion of the judiciary in Brazil can be linked both to the sociological and the juridical-procedural reasons indicated above.[22]

Though Brazil has not developed a welfare state similar to that of many European countries, the economic model implemented from 1930 onward—under the leadership of Getulio Vargas—led the state to assume a central role in running the economy, in combination with a high level of intervention in social relations. The Vargas model, much more corporatist than the European welfare system, also led to the development of new social legislation, especially relating to labor. It was at that time that the Brazilian judiciary underwent its first phase of expansion, when important areas of conflict were channeled into special branches of the justice system with the creation, in the 1930s, of the electoral and labor courts. Because elections in the Old Republic (1889–1930) had been marked by fraud and other political ills, the creation of electoral courts was one of the practical consequences of the 1930 Revolution. In addition, the need to expand social rights and at the same time keep the working classes under control led the Vargas administration to develop an extraordinary body of laws and institutions, including labor courts. However, the judicial solution of electoral and labor issues was not the only, nor indeed the most common, form of accommodating and resolving these conflicts (Sadek, 1995a; Santos, 1979).

Figures 10.3 and 10.4 show the volume of electoral and labor court actions in recent years. In the first case, despite the consolidation of the rules of political competition and improvements in the electoral process (ranging from voter registration to the use of electronic ballot boxes throughout the country), the volume of cases in the regional electoral courts remained in the range of 35,000 throughout the 1990s, reaching the figure of 52,808 in 2002. If we consider that there were 1,654 executive and legislative posts (federal and state) up for election, and that 18,880 candidates stood for office in the 2002 elections, this means that there were, on average, almost 32 legal actions per post and almost three per candidate in the electoral justice system, something that indicates a high level of judicialization of elections in Brazil. In addition to these quantitative measures, it is worth highlighting at least two recent decisions by the electoral justice system that have had a significant impact on the rules of the political game. In 2002, the Supreme Electoral Tribunal implemented the most important change in electoral rules since 1988, drastically limiting the freedom to form party alliances in a decision which became known as "verticalisation" of party coalitions. In 2004, the

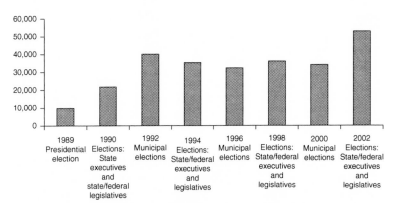

Figure 10.3 Cases distributed within regional electoral courts (selected years)

Source: Judiciary National Database. Supremo Tribunal Federal (www.stf.gov.br).

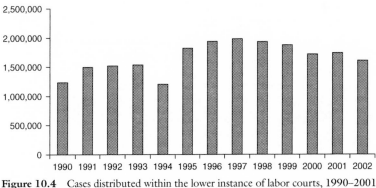

Figure 10.4 Cases distributed within the lower instance of labor courts, 1990–2001

Source: Judiciary National Database. Supremo Tribunal Federal (www.stf.gov.br).

same court abolished around 8,500 elected municipal posts in a total of approximately 2,400 municipalities.

The volume of cases in the labor courts is impressive. Although a decrease in the number of lawsuits occurred in 1994 (probably related to the inflation measures imposed by the Real Plan), subsequent years saw a return of the extraordinary growth in the number of lawsuits. In 1997, there were approximately two million cases in the first instance of the labor courts. According to studies carried out by Pastore, Brazilian labor courts are world champions in volume of lawsuits. This is possibly due to an inclination toward litigation in this area, but can also be explained by the rigidity of the legislation that regulates labor

relations and the high level of normative power entrusted to the labor
courts and their authority to intervene in conflicts between employers
and employees that concern employment rights.[23] According to
figure 10.4, there has been a gradual decrease in the number of lawsuits since 1997, though the year 2000 saw the impressive figure of
one lawsuit for every 98 inhabitants and one lawsuit for every
46 members of the economically active population.

A new wave of judicialization of conflicts took place from the
1980s onward. As I have discussed elsewhere,[24] at that time Brazil
began to legally acknowledge diffuse and collective rights, and opened
up the legal process to the representation of such rights. The main
milestone in this process was the creation of the Public Civil Action
(*Ação Civil Pública*) in 1985, whereby consumer, environmental, and
cultural heritage rights could be defended collectively in court. The
debate about the creation of Public Civil Actions engaged jurists,
judges, and members of the MP. The latter, at the time, claimed for
itself the function of defending society, though it is a state institution.
In fact, the MP has managed—through lobbying the National
Congress for the approval of the Public Civil Action Law in 1985—to
secure for itself the attribution of defending the new diffuse and
collective rights.

The 1988 constitution consolidated the expansion of justice
toward the protection of collective rights, reaffirming them as a constitutional category and enabling the legal recognition of various
other related rights. It also confirmed the MP's guardianship role,
ascribing to it an unprecedented level of institutional independence
from the other powers of state.[25] Since 1988 we have been witnessing
the development of a veritable juridical subsystem, whereby new laws
are guided by the idea of collective protection of rights and by the
reinforcement of the guardianship role of the MP.[26] The overall result
of such legislative evolution is that the Brazilian justice system has
been turned into an important arena for collective conflicts, and the
protagonism of the MP has drawn the attention of analysts concerned
with assessing the potentials and limits of this institutional model. The
MP, one of the main agents in the judicialization of politics, has made
use of its high level of independence by frequently suing politicians
and governments in cases that range from administrative impropriety
to attempts to force administrators to carry out public policies in the
areas of health, education, and so forth. Such aggressiveness has raised
considerable controversy regarding the limits of judicialization of
politics through actions by the MP.[27]

Thinking in broader terms, is it possible to speak of a *rights revolution*
in Brazil? Analyzing the examples from the United States, Canada,

Britain, and India, Epp concludes that "rights are not gifts: they are won through concerted collective action from both a vibrant civil society and public subsidy. Rights revolutions originate in pressure from below in civil society, not leadership from above" (Epp, 1998, p. 197). It is important to highlight that the expansion of access to justice in Brazil did not happen as a response to pressure from civil society associations, but rather as a result of endogenous motivations from within the judicial institutions themselves. In the case of the MP, it maintains its role as a representative of civil society, though it has no link of authority or accountability with it. Though more timidly than the MP, it was also by the judiciary's own initiative that the justice system became more accessible to the population, especially with the creation of the small claims courts—established by law in 1984 and then constitutionalised by the 1988 charter. Regulated again by law in 1995, the small claims courts represented an important step toward broadening access to ordinary justice for civil cases involving amounts up to 40 times the minimum wage and for criminal cases in which the maximum sentence did not exceed one year's imprisonment. The greater simplicity of the procedure in these courts enabled much swifter judgments, attracting to the legal arena conflicts which previously probably would have been resolved informally (see chapter by Fiona Macaulay in this volume).[28] The federal justice branch introduced its courts in 2002, and after little more than two years in existence, the 242 courts experienced one of the most spectacular avalanches of cases in history when 1,265,251 lawsuits were initiated.[29] These were mostly actions brought by citizens against the federal government, and concerned welfare and social security issues (approximately 2,500 lawsuits a day). Parallel to the special courts, and guided by the same principle of offering swifter and more accessible legal services, several other initiatives were taken by the state and federal justice system in the 1990s when informal conciliation courts, traveling courts (which operate from coaches that travel around the city) and special courts housed at law schools were introduced. In many states, governments have sought to bring together the various public services related to the justice system and to citizenship rights, and to offer these services to the population in an integrated manner under the same roof.[30]

In short, the double expansion of the Brazilian justice system, both in political-constitutional terms and in the area of ordinary justice, was facilitated by important institutional transformations, and by changes in the legal order in general. However, as pointed out by Tate and Vallinder (1995), the judicialization of politics and of society is only complete when judges and other members of judicial institutions are willing to act assertively and to make use of all the legal opportunities available to them. With respect to the members of the MP, qualitative research indicates that their ideology can be classified as one of "political voluntarism," which embodies a belief in the institution's protective role in a society that is incapable of defending itself and in the context of a representative political power that is corrupt or incapable of fulfilling its duties.[31] Among judges, surveys conducted by IDESP since the beginning of the 1990s demonstrate a strong political and social sensitivity on the part of magistrates, and in the last survey carried out by the Institute (2000), 73.1 percent of judges went as far as stating that "the judge has a social role to fulfill," and that "the pursuit of social justice justifies *decisions that breach contracts.*" Only 19.7 percent of judges stated that "contracts must be complied with regardless of their social repercussions."[32]

Regardless of the difficulties and contradictions that still mark the process of expansion of Brazilian justice, it seems unquestionable that the judiciary and the MP have taken on tasks of major significance, fitting with the Brazilian statist tradition whereby the central state exercises institutional guardianship over society. However, and in spite of this trend, at times the central function of these institutions contrasts with their ability in practice to deliver the expected responses.

Crisis and Prospects for Judicial Reform in Brazil

The expansion of the justice system in Brazil is explained by the combination of institutional factors and the activism of judges and prosecutors. However, alongside expansion, much public debate has also focused on the poor performance of the judiciary. This debate has concentrated on a number of features: first, the excessive slowness of procedures, which means that it can take many years to reach a final judgment. The extraordinary backlog of proceedings at all instances, and in all branches, of the justice system is exacerbated by the great variety of appeals allowed by procedural legislation (many merely dilatory in nature) and the antiquated administrative organization of courts and ancillary bodies of justice. A second factor refers to the judiciary and the MP's high level of insulation from society, and their reticence to institutional and organizational change, which generates suspicion and a low level of legitimacy. Third, whenever corruption scandals in government or common crimes shocking to public opinion occur, the justice system is harshly criticized for its inability to respond promptly to tackle impunity. Sometimes these scandals and crimes can drag on for years before the courts, without reaching a final verdict on the guilt or innocence of those involved. When these scandals involve judges, the picture is even grimmer and leads to fierce attacks, reviving attempts to reform the judiciary.

In more analytical terms, the crisis of the judiciary occurs both within the political-constitutional sphere (this is essentially a political crisis) and in the realm of ordinary justice—which has more to do with efficiency. A judicial reform project that addresses these issues has lingered in congress for over ten years, but the various actors involved (government, political parties, the highest bodies of the judiciary, judges' associations, and the Brazilian Bar Association) have ended up creating a situation of crossed vetoes, whereby two or more of them ally to support one proposition, but find themselves in internal disagreement with respect to many others. In terms of the political dimensions of the crisis, the major conflict has revolved around proposals to concentrate the authority for judicial review in the STF, decreasing participation on the diffuse side of the system. During the 1990s, presidents of the republic and governing parties (the political majority) tried to approve constitutional changes that would have achieved this concentration, but the opposition—though a minority—managed to stop them. The opposition in this case was under the principal leadership of the Workers' Party, and had the support of the lower instances of the judiciary, judges' associations and the MP and the Brazilian Bar Association.

The hybrid system of judicial review, in addition to being highly decentralized, has an added peculiarity. Even if the STF is the last instance in the Brazilian judiciary, its decisions have no binding effect on the lower courts, which may continue to rule contrary to the STF's decisions. Such an institutional peculiarity becomes even more serious in the cases of appeals arising from the lower courts: sometimes these appeals concern thousands of similar cases, but the court's decision is only valid for the specific case under review and may not be extended to all others. The perverse effect is that those who might benefit from court decisions need to enter the legal *via crucis* and go through all instances to arrive at a decision that has already been applied to previous similar cases. On the other hand, in cases where the lower court judges decide to apply the same interpretation as the supreme court, those harmed by the decision manage to drag the case to the STF, thereby postponing for as long as they can the negative result of the claim. To have an idea of the impact of such systemic irrationality on the volume of cases, figures presented by one of the court's justices, Nelson Jobim, showed that, in 2002, the court had "ruled" on 171,980 cases. (An average of 17.1 thousand per justice, which means up to 85 cases per working day). Jobim stated that it would be impossible to judge them individually and revealed that the judges had developed the practice of selecting a batch of similar cases and ruling on all of them in a few minutes. Such practices aggravate distortions in the court's decisions, hamper judicial efficiency, and create an unflattering situation for the country's highest court.[33] In 1998, another STF judge had already revealed that 80 percent of the appeals appraised by the court were repeated.[34]

In order to remedy this state of affairs, some proposals have been formulated to concentrate constitutional control in the STF. Among these is the *súmula de efeito vinculante* (SEV) (binding effect summary), an instrument by means of which the court could—once decisions were reiterated—establish jurisprudence in certain cases and make it binding on the lower instances of the judiciary. Notwithstanding its aim to reduce the excess of cases in the highest court, the SEV proposition was harshly opposed for its alleged centralizing character and soon became the focus of a fierce dispute between government and opposition in the 1990s. Resistance to adopting the SEV comes precisely from the sectors which make use of the judiciary as a space for political struggle against the government by taking advantage of the decentralized and hybrid character of the judicial review system. Defeated in the political-representative sphere, opposition parties find in the judicialization of politics the possibility of reversing—or at least postponing—the implementation of measures adopted by the government. During the 1990s, and early in the year 2000, the Workers' Party was one of the parties that most often resorted to this strategy, and one of the most radical opponents to the adoption of the SEV. In the same manner, sectors of society displeased by political decisions also have easy access to the judiciary, and have used this to circumvent political majority decisions, or at least to postpone their immediate impact. For this reason, despite the flagrant incongruities of the judicial review model, opponents of the SEV strive to defend the system of diffuse judicial review, not only for the possibility of being able to take the government to court throughout the country, but also because the hybrid nature of the Brazilian system prevents STF interpretations from being binding on the lower instances of the judiciary. The belief held by opposition sectors that the supreme court is susceptible to pressures by the ruling political majority, due to the fact that justices are appointed by the president of the republic with the approval of the Federal Senate, only reinforces such stances. The Brazilian Bar Association has also engaged in a noteworthy campaign against the adoption of the binding effect. Despite its ideological arguments, the Bar Association's main motivation seems to be the defense of the lawyers' labor market, given that they have much to gain from the unjustifiable multiplication of cases and the slow speed of the proceedings.[35]

With the ascent of the Workers' Party to the presidency in 2003, the opposition became the government and a major shift occurred. The party's parliamentary representation in congress now changed to support the adoption of the binding effect mechanism and proceeded to vote for it when the project for judicial reform was taken up again by the senate in mid 2004.[36] This was a surprising change since the Workers' Party had opposed the proposition for almost ten years and Lula, during his presidential campaign in 2002, stated several times that he would work to prevent all attempts to adopt the SEV.

Proposals to broaden and differentiate the structure of the judiciary to address the issues of efficiency and poor performance are less controversial. Many of them managed to garner the support of the magistrates, the Brazilian Bar Association and opposition parties. This is in sharp contrast to the practically indifferent stance of the government. The creation of new appellate courts in the federal justice sphere, the creation of new small claims courts, functional and administrative autonomy for the Public Defense Services, transferring human rights trials to the sphere of federal justice, reviewing the procedural codes and decreasing the types of appeals are some of the propositions which have been met with a reasonable level of consensus. Propositions that have intended to review the extension of diffuse and collective rights, and the increasingly important role of the MP as an independent body in the defense of such rights, have been more problematic. After being at the forefront of the political scene in the 1990s, the MP has faced attempts to reduce its power in important areas. By the end of 2002 a new law had transferred the trials of high political authorities from the lower to the higher courts. This transfer removed the possibility of using administrative impropriety suits against mayors, governors, and other authorities from an army of almost 9,000 prosecutors. The more than 4,000 cases currently before the courts may suffer a fatal setback, since—according to the new law—they now have to be sent to the higher courts for appraisal and await trial on a long waiting list. On a nationwide level, the MP has pledged to fight the change and is exerting pressure on the Federal Supreme Court to declare the law unconstitutional. [37]

Another important point concerns the practice of criminal investigations by the MP in lieu of the police. Since the 1988 constitution, prosecutors have assumed the role of investigators, especially in cases of political corruption and organized crime. In view of the crisis and ineffectiveness of the Brazilian police apparatus, the MP aimed to replace the police in these areas, which it considered strategic. In reaction to this encroachment by the MP, the police corporation has defended its monopoly on criminal investigations, and the issue is currently pending a constitutional ruling at the STF. Such setbacks regarding the operation of the MP have taken place in a context of increasing criticism of the institution's excessive autonomy and of abuses perpetrated by certain individual prosecutors, to the extent of raising questions about the constitutional model which gave the MP its independence.

To the two reform fronts—the political and the functional—we should add a third: the attempt to set up bodies to exert external control over the judiciary and the MP. It should be remembered that one of the dimensions of the redemocratization process in Brazil was and has been the republicanization of the state. The emphasis given to the theme of political corruption is an example of the importance of the "republican wave," which removed a president of the republic (Collor's impeachment in 1992) and has led to the removal from office of several representatives of executive and legislative bodies in various regions of the country. It should come as no surprise that this tendency would reach the magistrates and the MP, special bodies of officials who, safeguarded by so many guarantees and privileges, constitute what de Tocqueville (1977) considered modern society's new aristocracy. As prophesized by the French thinker, the democratic trend could place the guarantees of this group at risk when—overwhelmed by a desire for equality and by the ideal of the res publica—people and political representatives seek to increase their control over the whole state administration, including judges. At such critical moments judges face enormous difficulties in maintaining their institutional independence and privileged working conditions. The proposal to create external control mechanisms, such as the National Justice Council, has greatly vexed judges and prosecutors. Some fear political interference and the end of the judiciary's position as a political power capable of keeping the ruling majority in check. Those who simply benefit from the judiciary's guarantees and privileges fear that republican equality will level things out at the bottom. During the 1990s, the intricate political game around the main points of judicial reform kept the magistrates and the MP safe from the creation of these control bodies, thanks to the crossed vetoes involving themselves, the government, the opposition parties, and the Brazilian Bar Association. With the Workers' Party being one of the main champions of the republican wave, its ascent to power has threatened to dissolve the tacit alliance with the magistrates and the MP of times past. The president of the republic is now openly advocating the introduction of bodies for external control of these institutions.

Table 10.4 shows a graphic representation of the prevailing trends among the different players involved in the judicial reform

Table 10.4 Predominant trends in attempts at judicial reform during the FHC (1994–2002) and Lula (2003–) administrations

Propositions	Concentrating judicial review with the STF		External control of the judiciary		Broadening and differentiating the judiciary structure	
Administrations	FHC (1994–2002)	Lula (2003–)	FHC (1994–2002)	Lula (2003–)	FHC (1994–2002)	Lula (2003–)
Federal executive branch and governing parties in congress	3	3	0	3	0	3
Opposition parties in congress	−2	2	2	0	2	0
Magistrature: Higher level bodies	0.5	0.5	−0.5	−0.5	0.5	0.5
Associations of magistrates and "first instance" judges	−0.5	−0.5	−0.5	−0.5	0.5	0.5
Brazilian Bar Association	−1	−1	1	1	1	1
Total	0	4	2	3	4	5

process—before and after the change of government in 2003. As a numerical representation of the different levels of capacity to influence the results of the parliamentary political process, the number 3 was the weight attributed to the federal executive and its majority bench in congress; the number 2 to the opposition parties; and the number 1 was the weight attributed to outside players, the Brazilian Bar Association, and the magistrates. The latter, in turn, is divided and its strength in the political game varies according to the degree of unity among the higher courts, class associations, and lower court judges. A positive value was attributed when the actors' position was favorable to the proposition and a negative one when their position was contrary to the suggested change. Zero was attributed to actors indifferent to the reform proposition.

This table translates with some accuracy the result of the first rounds of voting on the judicial reform project in the Chamber of Deputies in 2000. After lengthy negotiations, which lasted for several years and involved various versions of the project, the reform was approved in the chamber of deputies. Proposals to broaden and differentiate the structure of the judiciary were easily approved; the creation of the Conselho Nacional de Justiça (National Justice Council) to control the judiciary was approved because the left-wing parties and the Brazilian Bar Association strongly supported it (Cardoso's government was less dedicated to the issue). Lastly, the question of concentrating judicial review in the STF remained deadlocked during the entire legislative process and was only approved by the Chamber of Deputies because the Cardoso administration put all its political strength behind it.

With Lula taking office in 2003, not only did the government and the opposition change sides, but the PT converted to the proposition of concentrating judicial review in the STF. If the PT had maintained the position it had held for 10 years as an opposition party it might have tilted the balance in favor of those opposed to adopting the SEV. However, the first round of voting in the Federal Senate, in 2004, dealt a harsh blow to the magistrates' associations, first instance judges, and Brazilian Bar Association. It also led to a profound disappointment by these sectors with their former left-wing ally (the Workers' Party), which surrendered to the logic of governability and supported the creation of the SEV. As the trends in table 7.8 confirm, it is possible that the judicial reform will be approved in a future vote during the Lula administration. In that case, its main consequences will be: (1) Some degree of broadening and differentiation of the judicial structure; (2) a significant reinforcement of governability with the concentration of judicial review in the STF and; (3) a greater degree of indirect control by elected representatives over the judiciary, with the introduction of external control of the magistrates and the MP, and even some weakening of their functional guarantees and career privileges.

The future of the judiciary in Brazil thus depends on achieving a balance between the political, functional, and "republican" dimensions of reform. In the meantime, the role of the judiciary and its functions in Brazilian democracy continue to be problematic. The judiciary has to balance the dual tasks of restraining the power of ruling political majorities in the name of protecting individual freedoms by means of judicial review (liberal function) and supporting egalitarian claims of social groups by means of collective access to justice (social function). And all this amid the constant challenge to maintain its independence at the heart of a democratic republic.

Notes

1. The overall result we reach is that the set of constitutional amendments enacted during the FHC administration led to the change of only 8.8% of the total original provisions and to twice as much growth in the text: the FHC administration increased the constitution enacted in 1988 by 15.3%. (Couto and Arantes, 2003)
2. See, in this sense, Cappelletti, 1984.
3. The issue of the relationship between constitutionalism and democracy, a highly significant and lasting one, dates back to the classical *Federalist*

Papers (Madison et al., 1993) and the literature about it in the United States is vast, especially with regard to the supreme court's role in the political system.

4. There is vast literature on this period in which the court confronted the president and on other stages in the history of the U.S. Supreme Court. Amongst others, see Baum, 1987.

5. In order to describe the level of judicialization of politics in Brazil, I shall repeat the description of the existing models of judicial review and of the Brazilian case in particular, already presented in previous work. (Arantes, 1997, 2000, 2001).

6. Some countries which adopt the US diffuse model: in Europe—Denmark, Ireland, Norway, Sweden; In the Middle East—Israel; in Asia and Australia—Japan, India, and New Zealand; in the Americas—Canada, Argentina, Bahamas, Bolivia, Dominican Republic, Jamaica, Mexico, and Trinidad and Tobago. Source: http://www.concourts. net (by Dr. Arne Mavčič)

7. Examples of countries which adopt the concentrated model of constitutional courts: in Europe—Hungary, Spain, and several Eastern European countries which have recently redemocratized themselves, such as Bulgaria, Czech Republic, Lithuania, Poland, Rumania, Russia, Slovenia, and Ukraine; in Asia and Australia—Armenia, Georgia, South Korea, Sri Lanka, and Thailand; in the Americas: Chile and Surinam. Source: http://www.concourts.net (by Dr. Arne Mavčič).

8. Some examples of countries where the two models were combined: Greece, Indonesia, Taiwan, El Salvador, Honduras, and Venezuela. Source: http://www.concourts.net (by Dr. Arne Mavčič).

9. I shall analyze such reform proposals, which have been in congress for over ten years, in the next section.

10. Data from the National Judiciary Database. http://www.stf.gov.br/ bndpj/movimento/

11. Information from the *Tribunal Superior do Trabalho*: http://www. tst.gov.br

12. Data from the Federal Justice Council: http://www.cjf.gov.br/ Estatisticas/Estatisticas.asp

13. Prudente, 2001.

14. The Provisional Measures introduced by the 1988 constitution are edited by the president of the republic and come into full force immediately, producing effects for a given period of time until congress ratifies them as ordinary laws or denies their validity. Widely used by all presidents since 1988, Provisional Measures are usually blamed for destabilizing legal ordering and give cause to various legal actions which question their constitutionality.

15. Vianna et al. (1999) revealed that almost 90% of the 507 ADINs proposed by state governors until 1998 aimed to obtain a declaration of unconstitutionality for laws enacted by their respective state legislative assemblies.

16. On the attempt to identify behavioral patterns of the STF judges and the issue of the court's independence, see the study by Oliveira, 2002.

17. The *consensual* model opposes the *majority* model, in which the political majorities are formed more easily and where they rule without so much resistance. According to Lijphart (1999), the following would be traits of that second model: concentration of power by the executive branch of power, a single-chamber legislative, bipartisanism, the unitary state, and the absence of judicial review. In Brazil, recent analyses have been trying to show how the Provisional Measure instrument and the relative control over the legislative agenda by the executive branch of power offset the high level of *consensual* fragmentation of the political system. What these analyses do not take into account is the cost of democratic governability of such a model, and, from the perspective of substantive results, who it benefits.

18. See, amongst others, Meneguello, 1998 and Figueiredo and Limongi, 1999.

19. A good synthesis of that argument can be found in Santos et al., 1996.

20. Santos et al., 1996, pp. 34–35.

21. A general formulation of diffuse and collective rights can be as follows: transindividual and indivisible rights by nature, of individuals (diffuse rights) or groups of persons, connected among themselves through some kind of legal relationship (collective rights). Another important trait is that these new rights can be represented legally by social and collective players, extraordinarily legitimized to go before courts to defend rights which are not particularly their own, but which belong, rather, to a set of dispersed and not always identifiable individuals. Examples of diffuse rights are those relating to the environment, of which all citizens benefit, though indivisibly. Examples of collective rights can be found in consumer relationships, when individual consumers are connected among themselves or with the opposing party by a juridical relationship which, when disrespected, affects them collectively; in the same manner, reparation may benefit all, indistinctively.

22. Below is a list of the most important works, in chronological order and according to topic. As for the magistrates' profile and opinions of judges on certain themes and values relating to Justice, see Sadek and Arantes, 1994; Sadek, 1995b; Vianna, Carvalho, Melo and Burgos, 1997. As for the two-fold expansion of the Brazilian Judiciary in the political-constitutional dimension and in the social dimension, see work by Sadek, 1999 and Vianna et al., 1999. For a balance of the new experiences in access to justice, especially with regards to the judiciary, see Sadek, 2001a. For some special topics such as the concept of judicialization of politics and an empirical assessment of the system of protection of collective rights in Rio de Janeiro, among other topics relating to justice, see Vianna, 2002. For an examination of the relationships between justice and economy, see Castelar, 2000. For the issue of judicial reform, see Sadek, 2001b; Castelar, 2003; and Macaulay, 2003.

23. The various articles by José Pastore on these issues can be found at: http://www.josepastore.com.br

24. Arantes, 2002.

25. On the uniqueness of the Brazilian MP's institutional independence model, see Kerche, 2002.

26. Examples of such are Law 7853/89, which addresses the protection of the disabled; Law 7913/89, which instituted collective protection for investors in the securities market; Law 8069/90, which created the Statute of Children and Adolescents; Law 8078/90, which created the Consumer Code, certainly the most important document in this new juridical subsystem; Law 8429/92, which addresses administrative impropriety and delegates important functions to the MP; Law 8884/94, which deals with violations against the economic order and, lastly, Law 8974/95, which establishes rules on biosafety and legitimises the MP to act in that area.

27. Vianna and Burgos, 2002, p. 445, based on broad ranging research on public civil actions in Rio de Janeiro, contest the thesis of excessive predominance of the MP in relation to society, in the proposition of collective actions and, adopting a more optimistic perspective on that relationship, conclude that "between society and the MP the relationship is not so much of asymmetry and dependence on the former *vis-à-vis* the latter, but rather of interdependence, which, as it consolidates further, the more it legitimises the new roles of the MP and removes the sense from the perspective that considers them polarities, opposing instances."

28. According to Cunha (2001), there were, in 2001, around 1702 special courts in ordinary justice. In the State of Rio Grande do Sul there were 220, 218 in Paraná and 170 in Rio de Janeiro. Such courts are already responsible for a great number of cases, sometimes greater than the lower instance of ordinary justice, as is the case of the State of Amapá, described by the author.

29. Information from the *Centro de Estudos Judiciários* (Centre for Judiciary Studies). CEJ/SPI/DIEPE-03/02/2004.

30. A balance of these various experiences can be found in Sadek, 2001a. Vianna et al. (1999) examined the work of special courts in Rio de Janeiro and demonstrated their importance to the process of judicialization of social relations, not without identifying problems and limitations of that model of access to justice.

31. Arantes, 2002.

32. The full result of the survey may be found in Castelar, 2003.

33. At the same event when Nelson Jobim presented these figures, the justice revealed the existence of a "black market" of judicial credits, encouraged by the slow speed in which cases are processed: "if a citizen who has a right, already recognised in the first and second levels, but has to wait for the special appeal or extraordinary appeal and cannot afford to do that, what does he do? He sells that right in the black market at 10 percent of the face value. And the one who can

afford to wait receives it, further on, 100 percent of the face value, plus inflation, plus compensatory interest, plus composite interest, plus penalty interest, etc." Jornal *O Estado de S.Paulo*, October 7, 2004, p. A4.

34. Velloso, 1998.
35. A judge from the STF, Nelson Jobim, endorses the hypothesis that such a system benefits mainly lawyers. See Jobim, 2003.
36. The judicial reform has been in congress since 1992, when it was presented as a Constitutional Amendment Project (PEC, in Portuguese). In Brazil, the constitutional amendment process requires two rounds of voting in the chamber of deputies and two rounds in the federal senate, all of which must achieve a 3/5 parliamentary majority. After much deliberation and several adjustments, the PEC was approved in the first round in the chamber of deputies in January 2000 and in the second round in June 2000. After that it was discussed for four years in the federal senate and only in July 2004 the basic text was approved in the first round in that legislative body, not without leaving 175 topics earmarked for specific voting and which may postpone the second round until 2005, making it almost two decades of legislative progress.
37. On December 27, 2002, the National Association of MP Members (*Associação Nacional dos Membros do Ministério Público*) brought a Direct Unconstitutionality Action before the Supremo Tribunal Federal but did not obtain a preliminary injunction against introduction of the special "instance." The case still awaits judgement of its merit. To follow up on the development of the case see the supreme federal court's website STF (www.stf.gov.br), ADI/2797.

References

Arantes, Rogério B. (1997) *Judiciário e Política no Brasil* (São Paulo: Idesp/Sumaré/Educ).

——— (2000) "The Judiciary, Democracy, and Economic Policy in Brazil," in Stuart Nagel (ed.), *Handbook of Global Legal Policy* (New York: Marcel Dekker), pp. 335–49.

——— (2001) "Jurisdição Política Constitucional," in Maria Tereza Sadek (ed.), *Reforma do Judiciário* (São Paulo: Fundação Konrad Adenauer), pp. 23–89.

——— (2002) *Ministério Público e política no Brasil* (São Paulo: Sumaré/ Educ).

Baum, Lawrence (1987) *The Supreme Court* (Port.trans.) (Rio de Janeiro: Forense Universitária).

Berlin, Isayah (1981) *Four Essays on Liberty* (Port.trans.) (Brasília: Ed. UnB).

Cappelletti, Mauro (1984) *Il controllo giudiziario di constituzionalità delle leggi nel diritto comparato* (Port.trans) (Porto Allegre: Fabris).

Cappelletti, Mauro and Bryant Garth (1978) *Access to Justice: The Worldwide Movement to Make Rights Effective. A General Report* (Milan: Dott. A.Giuffrè).

Castelar, Armando (ed.) (2000) *Judiciário e economia no Brasil* (São Paulo: Sumaré).

—— (2003) *Reforma do Judiciário: Problemas, desafios e perspectivas* (São Paulo: Idesp; Rio de Janeiro: Book Link).

Couto, Cláudio G. and Rogério B. Arantes (2003) "Constitución o políticas públicas? Una evaluación de los años FHC," in Vicente Palermo (ed.), *Política brasileña contemporánea: De Collor a Lula en años de transformación* (Buenos Aires: Siglo XXI, Instituto Di Tella), pp. 95–154.

Cunha, Luciana G. S (2001) "Juizado Especial: Ampliação do acesso à Justiça?" in Maria T. Sadek (ed.), *Acesso à Justiça* (São Paulo: Fundação Konrad Adenauer), pp. 43–73.

Elster, Jon (1979) *Ulysses and the Sirens* (Cambridge University Press).

Elster, Jon and Rune Slagstad (eds.) (1999) *Constitucionalismo y democracia* (Buenos Aires: Fondo de Cultura Económica).

Epp, Charles R. (1998) *The Rights Revolution: Lawyers, Activists, and Supreme Courts in Comparative Perspective* (Chicago and London: The University Chicago Press).

Figueiredo, Argelina C. and Fernando Limongi (1999) *Executivo e Legislativo na nova ordem constitucional* (Rio de Janeiro: Editora FGV).

Jobim, Nelson (2003) "O processo de reforma sob a ótica do Judiciário," in Armando Castelar (ed.), *Reforma do Judiciário: Problemas, desafios e perspectivas* (São Paulo: Idesp; Rio de Janeiro: Book Link.), pp. 13–40.

Kerche, Fábio (2002) "O Ministério Público no Brasil: Autonomia, organização e atribuições" (Ph.D. dissertation, Department of Political Science, University of São Paulo).

Lambert, Edouard (1921) *Le gouvernement des juges et la lutte contre la législation sociale aux États-Unis: L'expérience américaine du contrôle judiciaire de la constitutionnalité des lois* (Paris: M. Giard & Cie).

Lijphart, Arend (1999) *Patterns of Democracy: Government Forms and Performance in Thirty-six Countries* (New Haven: Yale University Press).

Macaulay, Fiona (2003) "Democratisation and the Judiciary: Competing Reform Agendas," in Maria D'Alva Kinzo and James Dunkerley (eds.), *Brazil since 1985: Economy, Polity and Society* (London: Institute of Latin American Studies, University of London), pp. 84–104.

Madison, James, Alexander Hamilton and John Jay (1993) *The Federalist Papers, 1787–1788* (Port.trans.) (Rio de Janeiro: Nova Fronteira).

Meneguello, Raquel (1998) *Partidos e governos no Brasil contemporáneo* (São Paulo, Paz e Terra).

Oliveira, Fabiana L., "Ministros do STF: Profissionais versus politicos," *Teoria e Pesquisa* (Revista do Programa de Pós-Graduação em Ciências Sociais e do Departamento de Ciências Sociais da UFSCar), no. 40/41 (Jan/July, 2002), pp. 183–205.

Pastore, José (1995) *Flexibilização dos mercados de trabalho e contratação coletiva* (LTR editora).

Prudente, Antonio de Souza, "Cobrança administrativa do crédito da Fazenda Pública," *Revista CEJ*, Conselho da Justiça Federal, Centro de Estudos Judiciários, no. 13 (2001), pp. 66–72.

Sadek, Maria Tereza (ed.) (2001a) *Acesso à Justiça* (São Paulo: Fundação Konrad Adenauer).

———— (ed.) (2001b) *Reforma do Judiciário* (São Paulo: Fundação Konrad Adenauer).

———— (1999) "O poder judiciário na reforma do estado," in Luiz Carlos Bresser Pereira, Jorge Wilheim and Lourdes Sola (eds.), *Sociedade e estado em transformação* (São Paulo: Editora Unesp; Brasília: Enap), (chap. 12), pp. 293–324.

———— (1995a) *A Justiça Eleitoral e a consolidação da democracia no Brasil* (São Paulo: Fund. Konrad-Adenauer).

———— (ed.) (1995b) *O Judiciário em debate* (São Paulo: Sumaré).

Sadek, Maria Tereza and Rogério B. Arantes, "A crise do Judiciário e a visão dos juízes," in *Revista da USP*, no. 21, (March–May 1994), pp. 34–45.

Santos, Boaventura de Sousa et al., "Os tribunais nas sociedades contemporâneas," *Revista Brasileira de Ciências Sociais*, no. 30 (February 1996), pp. 29–62.

Santos, Wanderley G (1979) *Cidadania e Justiça* (Rio de Janeiro: Ed. Campus).

Tate, C. Neal and Torbjorn Vallinder (eds.) (1995) *The Global Expansion of Judicial Power* (New York: New York University Press).

Tocqueville, Alexis de (1977) *Democracy in America* (Port.trans.) (São Paulo: Edusp).

Velloso, Carlos M.S., "Do Poder Judiciário: Como torná-lo mais ágil e dinâmico: Efeito vinculante e outros temas," *Revista de Informação Legislativa* (Brasília: Senado Federal), a. 35, no. 138 (April/June 1998), pp. 75–87.

Vianna, Luiz Werneck (ed.) (2002) *A democracia e os três poderes no Brasil* (Belo Horizonte: Editora UFMG; Rio de Janeiro: Iuperj/Faperj).

Vianna, Luiz Werneck and Marcelo B. Burgos (2002) "Revolução processual do direito e democracia progressive," in Luiz Werneck Vianna (ed.) *A democracia e os três poderes no Brasil* (Belo Horizonte: Editora UFMG; Rio de Janeiro: Iuperj/Faperj), pp. 337–491.

Vianna, Luiz Werneck, Maria Alice R. Carvalho, Manoel P. C. Melo, Marcelo B. Burgos (1997) *Corpo e alma da magistratura brasileira* (Rio de Janeiro: Revan).

———— (1999) *Judicialização da política e das relações sociais no Brasil* (Rio de Janeiro: Revan).

Chapter 11

The Transnational Dimension of the Judicialization of Politics in Latin America

Kathryn Sikkink

Current trends toward the judicialization of politics in Latin America are deeply embedded in a context of regional and international legalization. In this chapter I argue that one cannot fully understand the domestic judicialization of politics in most Latin American countries without taking this regional and international context into account. For example, to understand outcomes in the area of the judicialization of human rights politics in many countries in Latin America, we also need to be attentive to developments in international and regional human rights law, as well as the role of transnational advocacy groups. Borrowing a concept from social movement theory, I believe that to understand the current level of judicialization of human rights policy in Latin America, it is necessary to situate it within its relevant international and domestic *political and legal opportunity structure*.

The specific case I examine is the judicialization of the politics of accountability for past human rights violations. I am explicitly interested in what Epp has called "rights-enhancing judicialisation" (1998). As the editors to this volume point out in the introduction, however, the human rights cases considered here are not about the creation of new rights, but about claims for the enforcement of existing rights where those rights have not been effectively upheld in practice. We are talking about the right to be free from summary execution, torture, kidnapping, and arbitrary imprisonment without trial, all rights long protected in the constitutions of most Latin American countries. But amnesty laws blocked judicial accountability for the violations of these rights, and thus the rights were not upheld in practice. I explore how the dynamic interaction of domestic and international opportunity structures helps explain outcomes with regard to justice for these past human rights violations. Although the bulk of the case material will focus on Argentina, for purposes of comparison I will also discuss the situation in Chile and Uruguay.

The puzzle at hand is that Argentina, Chile, and Uruguay, all of which experienced repressive authoritarian regimes at roughly the same time, adopted such different approaches to transitional justice. Argentina opted for a truth commission, far-reaching human rights trials, and eventual amnesty; Chile had an amnesty law and a truth commission but no far-reaching human rights trials, and Uruguay, after a political struggle, adopted an amnesty law with neither a full truth commission nor human rights trials. Yet by 2004, amnesty laws had been overturned in Argentina, skirted in Chile, and questioned again in Uruguay. In order to understand these changes, we need to see how new openness in international institutions provided opportunities for domestic and transnational human rights activists to bring pressure for change in their domestic systems. The model I propose would help us understand the initial differences in the three countries, and in understanding why and how these original choices began to break down.

Regime change to democracy in many countries in Latin America in the 1980s and 1990s opened the possibility for accountability for past human rights violations. But domestic political pressures in most countries in the region led to amnesty for perpetrators of past human rights abuses. In the past in Latin America, the story always stopped there, and no further efforts at accountability were possible.[1] But the international and regional political and legal opportunity structure had changed in the 1970s and 1980s, giving human rights activists new options. They sought out international allies (transnational advocacy networks) and brought their cases before regional and foreign courts. The degree to which foreign courts were open to their cases depended in turn on the characteristics of their domestic legal system: different domestic laws, bases for jurisdiction, and the possibility of trials in absentia, for example, made such trials possible in some countries and not in others (Lutz and Sikkink, 2001). These foreign judicial processes led to the issuing of hundreds of extradition requests and international arrest warrants for military officers in Latin America (and very occasional arrests and convictions). This created pressures or incentives in some countries where the human rights violations occurred to open new or reopen old domestic human rights cases. Judicial decisions in these domestic cases in turn drew on both domestic and international law, especially in countries in Latin America with monist approaches to international law. Understanding this process requires attention to the interactive effects of opportunity structures at the domestic, regional, and international level.

Much of the debate in this area has been framed in either/or terms: is it *either* domestic *or* international factors that are responsible for changes. This is a particularly unhelpful and sterile way of framing the question. In my opinion, one cannot understand the nature of the judicialization of human rights politics in Latin America without taking into account the *interaction* of domestic *and* international factors. This is evident from looking at the judicialization trends, not only in Latin America and elsewhere in the world. Before 1985, when the trials of the juntas for past human rights abuses began in Argentina, there had been no such previous trials anywhere in the region. Since 1985, hundreds of such trials are underway, in virtually every country in the region that experienced severe human rights violations. Dozens of foreign human rights judicial proceedings are also underway in the United States and European courts for human rights violations in Latin America. This is what Ellen Lutz and I have called the "justice cascade" (2001). It is a regional and global phenomenon. When similar phenomena occur in different countries simultaneously, it makes sense to ask how the regional and international context contributes to these outcomes. However, the international context doesn't simply cause certain national outcomes. Rather it interacts with different political and legal situations to create unique domestic outcomes.

The doctrine of complementarity built into the statute of the International Criminal Court (ICC) can be seen as a metaphor for this much broader form of interaction of the international and domestic legal and political spheres. Developments at the international level depend upon processes at the domestic level, and vice versa. But we lack a theoretical apparatus to allow us to understand and explain these kinds of interactive developments. To offer a theoretical explanation, I build on two literatures that I believe offer possibilities: the comparative politics literature on social movements and the international relations literature on the interaction between domestic politics and the international system.

One way to begin to think about these characteristic patterns of interactions is to use a concept developed by social movement theorists, that of political opportunity structures. Political opportunity structures can be defined as consistent dimensions of the political environment that provide incentives and constraints for people to undertake collective action by affecting their expectations of success or failure (Gamson and Meyer, 1996; Tarrow, 1994). It should be emphasized that political opportunities structures include both incentives *and* constraints for collective action. So an opportunity structure is not only about opportunities; it is about opportunities and *threats*. Social movement theorists increasingly also emphasize the fact that opportunities and threats are not objective structural factors, but will only invite or constrain mobilization if they are perceived by activists (McAdam, Tarrow, and Tilly, 2001). Social movement literature has also argued that social movements not only face existing opportunity structures, but can also help create them. Social movements also engage in "venue shopping," as activists search out the most receptive venue for their demands.

While a promising concept, there is not yet a systematic theory of how domestic and international opportunity structures interact. McAdam, Tarrow, and Tilly (2001) have discussed the phenomena of "scale shift" to describe this move of contention from the national to the transnational level, and identify the mechanisms and paths through which it occurs. But more work still needs to be done to identify, not just the scale shift from the national to the transnational, but the ongoing dynamic interaction between the national and the transnational level. Second, social movement theorists rarely take legal factors into account when thinking about opportunity structures. Nevertheless, I believe that the concept can be modified to allow us to focus on those consistent dimensions of the *political and legal* environment at the domestic and international level that provide incentives and constraints for activists by affecting their expectations of success or failure. The idea of a domestic legal opportunity structure is related to Epp's concept of a "support structure for legal mobilization" (1998). Epp, however, looks only at the domestic factors that facilitate legal mobilization, while I am interested in both domestic and international opportunity structures that both facilitate and constrain legal mobilization. In order to understand how such domestic and international legal opportunity structures interact, however, it may be useful to turn to an older debate in international relations theory about the relationship between domestic politics and the international system.

Most international relations literature grants primacy to the international level, while most comparative politics literature grants primacy to the domestic level, and then both hold the other constant for the purposes of their research. There are relatively few genuinely interactive theories (Gourevitch, 2002, p. 310). For many research puzzles, it is entirely appropriate to focus on either a domestic or international problem and hold the other constant. But I argue that for some international issues, including the study of transnational legal processes, an interactive approach is necessary to understand the potential for change and innovation in the international system.

One sophisticated version of domestic/international interaction is the two-level game model (Putnam, 1988), which has the virtue of being truly interactive and dynamic. For some issues, however, the two-level game's concentration on the chief negotiator or head of government as the lynchpin mediating between the international and the domestic simply misses what is most important theoretically and empirically.

In *Activists Beyond Borders*, Margaret Keck and I developed one type of alternative to the two-level game that we called the "boomerang effect," where non-state actors, faced with repression and obstructions at home, sought out state and non-state allies in the international arena, and in some cases were able to bring pressure to bear from above on their government to carry out domestic political change (Keck and Sikkink, 1998). Thomas Risse and I later expanded the boomerang effect into what we called the spiral model (Risse and Sikkink, 1999). The spiral model integrated the boomerang into a more dynamic five-phase conceptualization of the effects that domestic-transnational linkages have on domestic political change.

But the boomerang and spiral models did not adequately conceptualize domestic political and legal opportunity structures, in part because they focused mainly on human rights change in authoritarian regimes. A more nuanced version is needed that can conceptualize the ongoing interaction of domestic and international opportunity structures in democratic or transitional societies. Earlier work by Risse, focused on the importance of "domestic structures" for understanding international outcomes, is a useful starting place for thinking about the interaction of domestic and international legal and political processes. However, the notion of "domestic structures" would have to be modified to reflect political and *legal* opportunity structures at both the domestic and international level (Risse-Kappen, 1995; Risse, 2000). Risse argues that the impact of transnational actors on outcomes "depends on the domestic structures of the policy to be affected and the extent to which transnational actors operate in an environment regulated by international institutions" (Risse, 2002, p. 258). Risse now recognizes that this argument to some extent resembles the social movement argument that political opportunity structures are an important factor for explaining the success of movements (Risse, 2002).

Interaction of Domestic and International Opportunity Structures

To explore these characteristic patterns of interactions, I focus on an essential aspect of political and legal opportunity structure at both the

Table 11.1   Dynamic multilevel governance

International Opportunity Structures

Domestic Opportunity Structure	Closed	Open
Closed	A. Diminished chances of activism	B. Boomerang pattern and spiral model
Open	D. Democratic deficit/defensive transnationalisation[a]	C. Insider/outsider coalition model

Note: [a]There are essentially no modern human rights cases here, but many anti-globalization actions, however fit in this box, where farmers, labor or environmental activists fear that international institutions like the World Trade Organisation (WTO) or the International Monetary Fund (IMF) will work to undermine national standards they have won in past struggles, and will undermine national influence over domestic economic policy.

domestic and the international level; namely, that of access to institutions. Or—in other words—how open or closed domestic and international institutions, including but not limited to courts, are to network or social movement pressures and participation. In this particular case, the focus is on how open or closed domestic and international institutions are to networks of activists using international human rights law, but the framework also permits us to look at a wider range of issues. Using the basic idea of closed and open structures at the domestic and international level as an analytical starting point, one can think of at least four different characteristic patterns of activism (see table 11.1).

Here, international legal and political opportunity structure refers mainly to the degree of openness of international institutions to the participation of transnational NGOs, networks, and coalitions. International opportunity structure takes into account that there is not a single international structure, but one that varies over time and across intergovernmental institutions. It also varies according to issues and across regions. For example, international institutions were considerably more open in the 1990s than in the 1960s; international institutions that deal with human rights are more open to transnational activists than those that deal with trade; and regional institutions in Europe are more open than those in Asia. We can operationalize this understanding of international opportunity structure by looking at the formal and informal mechanisms or procedures for inclusions and participation in different international institutions. For example, the institutions connected to the UN's Economic and Social Council (ECOSOC) not only have provisions for NGOs to seek and be granted consultative status, but many have also developed practices that permit some NGOs to speak at meetings and present written materials for inclusion in the record. On the other hand the WTO, or the IMF, has no such provisions for NGO participation. Thus, international opportunity structures can provide *either* incentives or constraints for collective action. As such, international influences and actors are clearly not all pushing in the same direction on the issue of human rights. When the Bush administration, for example, success-fully pressured the Belgian government to limit the application of universal jurisdiction in its law, it closed down a previously open inter-national opportunity structure for accountability for past human rights abuses.

Domestic opportunity structure here refers primarily to how open or closed domestic legal and political institutions are to domestic social movement or NGO influence. It varies primarily across countries, but it also varies over time and according to issues within countries. As in the case of international opportunity structures, we can operationalize it by looking at the formal and informal mechanisms or procedures for participation on different issues. Here, three important factors are: (1) regime type; (2) type of transition to democratic regimes; and (3) types of laws and legal systems. Just as in the international realm, opportunity structures offer incentives or constraints for collective action.

With respect to regime type, clearly authoritarian regimes are a more closed domestic political opportunity structure for social movements.[2] But knowing if a country is democratic or authoritarian is only a start-ing point for understanding how open domestic institutions may be to social movements. For human rights activists, whether or not a coun-try has ratified major human rights treaties, and whether or not it is a monist system that incorporates those treaties directly into domestic law, openness of the domestic legal system for activists making arguments using international human rights law. So, for example, in the case of Argentina, the fact that the 1994 constitution gives inter-national human rights treaties constitutional status offers more legal opportunities on the human rights issue than the Chilean Constitution of 1980, which does not clarify the relation between international law and internal Chilean law (Detzner, 1988). Specific laws or institutions determine the degree of openness or closure on particular issues. For example, amnesty laws close off the opportunity for legal accountabil-ity for past human rights abuses. Democratic countries with amnesty laws may therefore still be "closed" legal opportunity structures when it comes to issues of legal accountability. Likewise, political and legal opportunities and threats are not objective structural factors, but are perceived by activists. Activists need to perceive and attribute opportunities and threats at both the international and the domestic level.

In the short term, it is possible to analyze the dynamics of social movement activity as groups operating rationally within international and domestic contexts of opportunities and constraints. As Stone Sweet has argued, the judicialization of politics "shapes the strategic behaviour of political actors engaged in interactions with one another" (1999, p. 164). For example, for perpetrators of past human rights abuses, if the choice is trials or no trials, they will prefer "no trials" and will work strategically for that outcome. But if changes at the international level mean that the choice may increasingly be "international trials" or "domestic trials" then strategic behavior may change, if those accused of human rights crimes prefer domestic trials to international trials.

Social movements not only operate within existing domestic opportunity structures. They can also make or expand existing opportunity structures (Gamson and Meyer, 1996; Tarrow, 1996). The same is the case at the international level. Over a longer term, the goal of many transnational activists is to transform or recreate the very opportunity structures within which they work. Obviously, human rights activists are not the only actors working to affect international opportunity structures. At the same time as human rights activists are working to expand existing opportunity structures, other actors are working to limit access of social movements. So, for example, various states are now making an effort to constrain the granting of consultative status of many NGOs to ECOSOC. Consultative status has been an important vehicle for opening the UN to the influence of social movements. States recognize this, and some states are now working to reduce this avenue for access.

Domestic Political and Legal Opportunity Structures

The literature suggests that we should pay attention to three key aspects of domestic political and legal structures: (1) regime type; (2) type of transition to democratic rule; (3) types of laws and type of legal system. There has been considerable debate over how exactly regime type influences the willingness of countries to accept binding human rights norms, but there is general agreement that regime (democratic, newly democratic, or authoritarian) is a relevant factor to explain the adoption of human rights norms (Hathaway, 2003; Moravcsik, 2000). Not surprisingly, virtually all moves toward accountability for past human rights violations have happened after transitions to democratic or semi-democratic regimes. Transition to democratic rule would therefore appear to be a necessary condition for establishing accountability for past human rights abuses, although it is not a sufficient condition. Because the countries in Latin America under review have all experienced transitions to democratic regimes, this factor cannot help us explain the differences among the countries in the region. Some authors have also observed that there is a significant difference between common law and civil law systems, both in terms of their propensity for treaty ratification, and in terms of their compliance with international law. We still lack a theoretical understanding of why this is the case. My work on Latin American human rights regimes suggests that the types of legal systems do adopted play an important role in the acceptance of binding human rights obligations. By 1998 all the civil law countries in the region had ratified the American Convention on Human Rights and accepted the compulsory jurisdiction of the Inter-American Court, while all the remaining countries that had not ratified the convention and not accepted the jurisdiction of the court were common law countries, including the United States and Canada.

We do not yet understand the reasons why the type of legal system adopted affects treaty ratification or compliance with international law. But, it is possible that it is not common law or civil law per se, but the association between common law and dualism and civil law and monism that is the relevant factor. In monist systems, constitutions provide that international law is automatically enforceable as domestic law. Dualist systems, on the other hand, require the incorporation of international law obligations through the adoption of national legislation. But the contrast between monist and dualist systems is deeper than such definitions suggest, and embody entire belief systems about the appropriate relation between international and domestic law. Judges and lawyers in dualist system can be "rather contemptuous of everything to do with international law, which they doggedly regard as 'unreal' " (Higgins, 1994, p. 206), while judges and lawyers in monist systems are by definition required to see law as a single system, with international law as an element alongside domestic law.

For much of Latin America, the prospects for greater influence of international law are heightened by the fact that most countries are civil law systems with substantially monist approaches to law. In general, we can say that democratic countries, with civil and monist legal systems and majority ratification rules, will offer a more propitious environment for the influence of international law. In a study comparing Latin America to other regions or other countries, these factors would be important for explaining differences. But for the countries in this study, two of the four factors of comparison identified above as potentially relevant aspects of domestic political and legal opportunity structure become irrelevant (regime type, and type of legal system). However, there are still important and interesting differences among Latin American countries with regard to issues of accountability for past human rights violations. The remaining factors that may be relevant for helping explain these differences are: (1) type of transition to democratic rule; (2) specific laws or institutional characteristics of the judicial system that may close off the legal and political system to social movement activity for accountability for human rights violations; (3) the strength and dynamism of human rights social movements.

The transitions literature has called our attention to the differences between the so-called negotiated or "pacted" transitions, where the military negotiates the transition and ensures significant protections and guarantees from prosecution for human rights violations, and the "society-led" transitions, where the military is forced to give up power without negotiating specific protections (Stepan, 1986). Of the cases considered here, Argentina is an example of a society led-transition, after the failure in the Malvinas war, and Chile and Uruguay are "pacted" transitions. These differences in transitions help explain why it was more possible for Argentina to hold trials of the Junta immediately following the transition, and why it was more difficult to hold such trials in either Chile or Uruguay. By 1988, however, Argentina had passed two laws (*Ley de Obediencia Debida* and *Ley de Punto Final*) that were essentially amnesty laws and put Argentina on the same footing with Chile and Uruguay in terms of closing off domestic opportunity for accountability for past trials.[3] By the mid-1990s, the Chilean, Argentine, and Uruguayan governments believed they had put the issue of trials for human rights violations behind them. At this point, the existence of international and regional opportunity structures again became important.

International and Regional Opportunity Structures

International opportunity structures also vary over time, according to issue, and across regions. Over the last few decades, there has been an increased judicialization or legalization of world politics (Goldstein et al, 2001; Stone Sweet, 1999). Depending on how we count, there are now between seventeen and forty international courts and tribunals. The expansion of the international judiciary has been described by one analyst as "the single most important development of the post-Cold War age" (Romano, 1999, p. 709). This expansion of international legalization, however, is uneven. Trade issues have high levels of international legalization in treaty law, while regional security regimes display less legalization. In terms of region, Europe is by far the most legalized, but Latin America is also relatively highly legalized in comparative terms. Latin America has a more propitious regional opportunity structure for human rights activism than Asia, for example, because of the existence and density of the Inter-American human rights norms and institutions. Asia has no such regional human rights regime.[4]

The mere existence of these domestic and international opportunity structures, however, does not matter unless there are actors poised to take advantage of them. Here domestic and international movements become important. Domestic human rights organizations and transnational human rights networks both operate in existing opportunity structures and either take advantage of them or not. They can also help create new opportunity structures. During the years of repression, Argentina and Chile had many human rights NGOs, while Uruguay had none or few. These more numerous human rights groups in Argentina and Chile worked to keep human rights issues on the political agenda. But after the transition to democracy in Chile, the most important human rights organization, the Vicaria de Solidaridad, closed its doors. This weakened the NGO pressure for ongoing accountability in Chile. In the 1990s, Argentina continued not only to have more active human rights organizations than either Uruguay or Chile, but also to have groups committed to innovative legal strategies for accountability for past human rights violations. The Grandmothers of the Plaza de Mayo and the Centre for Legal and Social Studies (Centro de Estudios Legales y Sociales, CELS) had particularly active and innovative legal teams that worked to find a way to press ahead on human rights trials, even after the amnesty laws were passed.

When amnesty laws blocked domestic prosecution for past human rights violations in most countries, regional and international opportunity structures gave activists an avenue to try to bring pressures on their legal systems and their political systems from outside. The first regional legal opportunity structure that activists turned to was that offered by the Inter-American human rights system (made up of the Inter-American Commission on Human Rights (IACHR) and the Inter-American Court of Human Rights (Inter-American Court). In 1992, the IACHR concluded that the Argentine laws of *Punto Final* and *Obediencia Debida*, and the pardon issued by President Menem for crimes committed during the dictatorship, were incompatible with the American Convention.[5] This created a regional legal opportunity structure that human rights activists could take advantage of by bringing the case of the amnesty laws again to the Inter-American system, should they be completely stymied in the domestic legal arena. In 2001, this possibility was heightened when the Inter-American Court of Human Rights declared in the Barrios Altos case that two Peruvian amnesty laws were invalid and incompatible with the American Convention on Human Rights.[6] The recommendations of the IACHR and the sentences of the Inter-American Court also provided jurisprudential resources for more activist judges in domestic cases against the amnesty laws. When human rights lawyers brought cases against the amnesty laws before domestic courts, some judges began to declare such laws contrary to domestic and international law.[7]

An additional regional opportunity structure was provided by the Inter-American Convention on the Forced Disappearance of Persons, which entered into force in 1994 and was ratified by Argentina in 1995 and Uruguay in 1996. The Inter-American Convention defines disappearances as a permanent or ongoing crime as long as the whereabouts or fate of the victim has not been determined. If disappearances are a permanent ongoing offence, this gives grounds to argue that they are not subject to amnesty laws—which provide amnesty for crimes committed only during a certain delimited period. Likewise, the convention obliges states to punish those who "commit" disappearances, alongwith their accomplices and accessories, and states that such criminal prosecution shall not be subject to statutes of limitations. After the convention entered into force, lawyers and judges throughout the region began to make use of these provisions and arguments to skirt amnesty laws. Even though Chile has not ratified the convention, the Chilean Supreme Court eventually used the argument that disappearances were a permanent and ongoing crime to permit disappearances cases to be reopened when Pinochet was detained in London. It is an even more effective argument in countries that have ratified the convention, and where the convention has entered into domestic law.

In addition to regional opportunity structures, there were also international opportunity structures in the realm of accountability for past human rights violations. Argentine and Chilean human rights activists, blocked by amnesty laws in their own judicial system, took cases abroad, mainly to Spain, but also to Italy, France, Germany, Sweden, and Belgium. In each of these countries they found somewhat different bases for jurisdiction, but in all cases they were able to open cases that had been closed in their own judicial systems. They succeeded in securing convictions in a handful of cases (since France and Italy allow trial in absentia), or in securing indictments, and generated international arrest warrants for hundreds of military officers and their collaborators. Initially, most of these indicted individuals did not face judicial processes in their home countries. But they began to discover that they could not travel beyond their borders for fear of arrest. The Pinochet case is the best known. It has received extensive attention from legal scholars, so there is no need to repeat any of the political or legal details of the case. The political and legal impact of Pinochet's arrest and trial in London on politics and human rights trials in Chile and elsewhere was significant (Angell, 2003; Bravo Lopez, 2003), but the Pinochet case is simply the high profile version of dynamics at work in many other parts of the world with less prominent and well-known individuals. The broader point is that a very complex interactive game is occurring, where moves at a national, regional, and international level affect developments at the other level. To understand the evolving situation, it is necessary to look at the interactions of these different levels.

Box A: Diminished Opportunities for Activism

In Box A, where activists perceive that they face closed opportunity structures both nationally and internationally, we would expect to see the least activism, and thus fewer chances of success. This would apply to most cases of accountability for past human rights violations before the mid-1980s. It was the situation in which human rights activists in Chile, Uruguay, and Argentina found themselves after the coups in 1973 and 1976. Repression at home made it impossible for them to pursue accountability domestically. But international and regional institutions were still relatively closed. Their countries had not ratified the Inter-American Convention on Human Rights nor accepted the compulsory jurisdiction of the Inter-American Court. Most had not ratified the Covenant on Civil and Political Rights (CCPR), or the optional protocol.

Yet the figure does not describe a set of static structural conditions. Much of the most interesting bi-level social movement activity aims to move from one box to another. The early period of human rights activity in Chile, Uruguay, and later in Argentina, can be seen as a moment when human rights activists, closed off from domestic institutions by authoritarianism and repression, tried to create new international opportunities within existing international and regional human rights organizations. So, for example, Chileans managed to open new international space in the UN Commission on Human Rights and in the General Assembly to work explicitly on human rights in Chile. The Chilean case was the first time the UN responded to a human rights situation that was not seen as a threat to international peace and security. Uruguayan human rights activists took advantage of the fact that Uruguay had ratified the Covenant on Civil and Political Rights, and its first Optional Protocol, giving Uruguayan citizens the right to bring complaints against their government before the UN Human Rights Committee, which had been set up when the covenant entered into force in 1976. In its early years, the Human Rights Committee decided more cases against the Uruguayan government than any other government in the world. Argentine human rights activists were especially active in the IACHR. The IACHR did its first major country report based on an on-site visit to Argentina.

In the case of Uruguay, the decision of the (democratic) Uruguayan government to ratify the Optional Protocol to the CCPR before the coup created an international opportunity structure that was not open to the other countries, Chile and Argentina, whose governments had not ratified the Optional Protocol. Chilean human rights activists, on the other hand, taking advantage of the situation in the UN where they had the support of both the USSR and the United States (after Carter took office in 1977), were able to help create international political opportunities within the UN Human Rights Commission and the General Assembly that were not open to other countries without this broad support. Essentially, these groups took a situation where both domestic and international institutions were closed to them (Box A) and converted it into a situation where at least some international political opportunities were more open to their demands.

Box B: Boomerangs and Spirals

Once international institutions are more open, and when domestic structures are perceived as closed and international as open, activists may seek international allies and attempt to bring pressure to bear from above on their governments to implement changes. The case of justice for human rights violations in Chile, and the arrest of Pinochet in London, can be explained using a boomerang or spiral model. Even after democratization in Chile, the amnesty law effectively blocked human rights activists from seeking justice for past human rights violations in domestic courts. In turn, they sought out allies and alternative institutions abroad to pursue their justice claims, most importantly the Spanish National Audience Court, which was empowered to hear cases involving international crimes. Note that in this case the "open international opportunity structure" was not an international or regional organization. Rather, activists were "borrowing" domestic courts in other countries that are empowered by universal jurisdiction to hear human rights cases from abroad. Chilean activists emulated a tactic used initially by Argentine human rights activists in Spain, and introduced a case against Pinochet and other Chilean military officers before the Spanish National Audience Court. In doing so, they also formed new coalitions with groups in Spain, including members of the Progressive Prosecutors Association and the United Left Political Party (Lutz and Sikkink, 2001; Roht-Arriaza, 2004).

The cases in Spain led to the arrest of Pinochet in Britain in 1998. The British Law Lords eventually determined that Pinochet could be extradited to Spain to stand trial because international institutions (in this case the Torture Convention that had been ratified by Chile, Spain, and the UK) provided for universal jurisdiction in the case of torture. The "open political opportunity structure" was therefore provided here by an international institution (a treaty), as this was interpreted and implemented in domestic courts. This emphasizes the important point that while international opportunity structures are often found in international organizations and spaces like the United Nations, they can also be found in domestic spaces where the opportunities or constraints are created by international institutions like treaties.

Although Pinochet was eventually released and allowed to return to Chile for health and political reasons, his detention led to important changes in the political opportunity structure in Chile, most specifically the opening of a previously blocked space in the Chilean judicial system for victims of human rights violations to pursue their claims (Davis, 2003; Loveman and Lira, 2002; Lutz and Sikkink, 2001). Despite allowing various human rights trials to move ahead in Chilean courts, in 2002, the supreme court found that Pinochet was too frail and mentally ill to stand trial for his involvement in the Caravan of Death case. In mid-2004, however, the Santiago Appeals Court denied immunity to Pinochet and opened the way for the general to face prosecution in the Operation Condor case, involving the cooperation of security forces of Southern Cone countries in repression.

The international-domestic dynamics here fit the boomerang pattern well, and illustrate that while the boomerang has been used primarily to describe political change under authoritarian regimes, even formally democratic regimes may have the kinds of domestic political blockages that lead domestic actors to seek international help to press for domestic change. As the spiral model points out, however, one of the goals of boomerang activism is to open domestic space for political activism. Primarily through a process of re-democratization, previously closed domestic political institutions are opened for domestic human rights activism. Part of what makes this model of multilevel governance dynamic is that the goal of social movement activity is very often to change or transform the structures.

Box C: Activists Within and Beyond Borders:
Insider–Outsider Coalitions

When both international and domestic opportunity structures are relatively open, domestic activists will, I believe, privilege domestic political change, but will keep international activism as a complementary and compensatory option. Domestic political change is closer to home and more directly addresses the problems activists' face, so they will concentrate their attention there. However, activists who have learned how to use international institutions in an earlier boomerang phase will keep this avenue open in case of need. I call this the insider–outsider coalition category. This is the current situation of Argentine human rights organizations on the topic of transitional justice in Argentina. The insider–outsider model is of particular importance because it is not limited to cases like Argentina, but may be a key element in explaining how many protest movements located in democratic countries relate to the international.

The Argentine Case: Insider–Outsider Coalitions
in the Demand for Justice and Accountability

Argentine human rights groups displayed virtuosity in playing the boomerang game when their domestic opportunity structures were blocked during the dictatorship of the period 1976–1983. With the return to democracy, these groups returned to focus their attention on the now much more open domestic polity, pressing for and securing a path-breaking Truth Commission, trials of the nine top leaders of the military juntas, reparations for victims of human rights violations, and other significant domestic changes. The domestic space for securing justice for past human rights violations narrowed when the Argentine government passed the two amnesty laws and when President Carlos Menem issued pardons for already convicted and imprisoned military commanders. Human rights organizations, recognizing that there was still some important openness in the relevant domestic institutions (especially the judicial system), implemented a two-track strategy. They launched a series of innovative legal challenges to try to circumvent the amnesty laws, and they cooperated with and initiated some international and regional tactics as well.

The innovative domestic legal challenges included efforts by the legal team of the Grandmothers of the Plaza de Mayo to hold military officers responsible for the kidnapping and identity change of the children of the disappeared, who in many cases had been given up for adoption to allies of the military regime. The Grandmothers' lawyers argued that because the crime of kidnapping had not been covered in the amnesty laws, they were not blocked from pursuing justice for these crimes. Their legal strategy began to succeed by the mid-1990s, but initially most of those found guilty were lower-level military and the adoptive families.[8] However, on June 9, 1998, Federal Judge Roberto Marquevich ordered preventative prison for ex-president General Rafael Videla for the crimes of kidnapping babies and falsifying public documents. It is often overlooked that, when Pinochet was detained in London three months later, Argentine courts had already done the equivalent by ordering the preventative detention of an ex-president for human rights violations. And they had done it using domestic political institutions. But, even in this case, the international dimension was also involved. Videla had been tried for human rights violations during the trials of the Juntas in 1985, had been convicted and sentenced to life in prison, but was released in 1990 under President Menem's pardon. Why, all of a sudden, was Videla back under arrest?

At the end of May of 1998, President Menem came back from a diplomatic trip to the Scandinavian countries. Instead of the economic contacts he had been seeking, both the Finnish and the Swedish governments asked for an investigation into two cases of disappearances: that of the Swede Dagmar Hagelin and Finnish Hanna Hietala. European human rights activists and family members of the disappeared had made these cases causes célèbres in their respective countries and had recruited allies at the highest levels of the relevant European governments. The European press focused its coverage of the Menem visit on these two cases. They were, in turn, connected to two other cases of disappearances, that of two French nuns, Alice Domon and Leonie Duquet. All four women had been kidnapped by a navy group in which the notorious Captain Alfredo Astiz had participated. Menem realized that in his upcoming visit to Paris a week later he would also face demands for the extradition of Astiz to France, where he had been condemned in absentia for the kidnapping of the nuns. Menem was scheduled to meet with French President Jacques Chirac, who had publicly stated that he wanted Astiz to be extradited to France. Just a few hours before the Chirac-Menem meeting, Judge Marquevich decided to detain Videla. In his meeting with the French press, instead of facing criticism, Menem was greeted as a human rights hero. Menem told reporters that "this is one more sign that we have one of the best justice systems in the world."[9]

This is an excellent example of the kinds of insider–outsider coalitions discussed here. Domestic human rights organizations, by using innovative legal strategies, had done all the preliminary legal and political work to secure Videla's arrest. They still needed some help from their international allies, however, for the final push to put a top-level military leader in jail. The judge that ordered Videla's arrest was not known for his commitment to human rights, but for his intense loyalty to President Menem, who had appointed him. There is strong reason to believe that Judge Marquevich was responding to Menem's political agenda on his trip to France when he ordered the detention.[10]

Four months later, after Pinochet had been detained in London, and the Spanish court had issued arrest warrants for a wide range of Argentine military officers, another Menem loyalist on the bench ordered the preventive detention of Admiral Emilio Massera, former head of the Navy and Junta member, and—after Videla—the second most powerful leader in Argentina during the most intense period of repression. The context and timing of Massera's arrest suggests that the decision by another Argentine judge to imprison Massera was a preemptive measure in response to Spanish international arrest warrants for Argentine military officers.[11] On November 2, 1998, Judge Garzon in Spain issued indictments for 98 members of the Argentine military for genocide and terrorism. Three weeks later, the Argentine judge ordered the preventative imprisonment of Massera for kidnapping babies.

Why would international arrest warrants lead local judges to order arrests in Argentina? International arrest warrants for Argentine military officers created international and domestic pressure to extradite the officers to Spain to stand trial. The Argentine military was adamantly opposed to extradition, and nationalist sentiment in Argentine political parties resisted the idea of extradition. But the relevant international legal precept was that a state must either extradite or try the accused domestically. To fend off political pressures to extradite many officers, the Argentine government apparently decided to place under preventative prison a few high-profile, but now politically marginalized, officers, like Videla and Massera. Argentine human rights activists actively cooperated with the foreign trials. Many Argentine family members of the disappeared traveled to Spain to present testimony and to add their cases. Argentine human rights organizations cooperated actively with requests from the Spanish, French, and German courts and from human rights organizations based in Europe to provide documentation and case material for foreign human rights trials.

One of the most surprising developments is that, in 2001, the Mexican government agreed to extradite an Argentine national living in Mexico, Ricardo Miguel Cavallo, to the Audiencia Nacional of Spain, to stand trial for human rights violations he was accused of committing in Argentina during the dictatorship. This is the first case where a third country extradites a national of another country to stand trial in yet another different country, for human rights abuses committed in his country of origin. The Argentine government did not oppose Cavallo's extradition to Spain, nor did it submit its own extradition request. In other words, Cavallo is the minor official now following the path that Pinochet could have followed, were it not for all the political capital expended by the Chilean government to secure his return to Chile. Meanwhile, France continues to request the extradition of Alfredo Astiz, and Germany has issued extradition requests for Argentines accused of human rights violations during the dictatorship.

Perhaps the most challenging of the legal battles was the case led by CELS to have the amnesty laws declared null, or unconstitutional. Once again, using the case of a kidnapped child of the disappeared, CELS argued that the amnesty laws allowed for the Argentine judicial system to find people criminally responsible for kidnapping a child and falsely changing her identity (more minor crimes), but not for the more serious original crime of murder and disappearance of the parents that later gave rise to the crime of kidnapping. Additionally, they argued that the amnesty laws were a violation of international and regional human rights treaties to which Argentina was party, and which were directly incorporated into Argentine law. A judge of the first instance found the arguments compelling and wrote a judgment that was a 185-page treatise on the significance of international human rights law in Argentine criminal law.[12] The appeals court supported the decision, and the case came before the Argentine Supreme Court. The supreme court, embroiled in a crisis as its members faced impeachment, lacked the consensus to decide on the case, and sent the case to the Court of Cassation. The case remains in a situation of "legal paralysis" where neither the supreme court nor the Court of Cassation is willing to take a decision. In the meantime, however, the actions of the executive have rendered some of the legal issues in the Poblete case moot.

In 2003, the new President of Argentina, Nestor Kirchner, announced that he was revoking the decree of the De La Rua government that denied all extradition requests, and was devolving the decision and control of extradition to the judiciary.[13] Although no individual has yet been extradited from Argentina to stand trial abroad, Kirchner's announcement signaled a return to a more activist human rights policy on behalf of the executive. In August 2003, the Argentine Congress, with the support of the Kirchner administration passed a law that declared the amnesty laws (*Obediencia Debida* and *Punto Final*) null and void. The effect of this new law was to permit the reopening of the human rights cases that had been closed for the past fifteen years. According to all observers, this was an unexpected political and legal development.[14] It took place in the context of the international legal opportunity structure discussed earlier. Just days before the law was passed, Judge Canicoba Corral, following the government's new policy on extraditions, had provided for the extradition of 45 members of the military and one civilian, to Spain, requested by Garzón. The day before the congressional debate regarding the repeal of the amnesty laws, the Kirchner government signed a decree implementing the "Convention on the Non-Applicability of Statutory Limitations to War Crimes and Crimes Against Humanity." In addition to declaring that no statutory limitation shall apply to war crimes and crimes against humanity, the convention obliges governments to punish these crimes and to adopt all necessary measures to make extradition possible, irrespective of the date the crimes were committed. The convention essentially prohibits amnesties.[15] The convention entered into force in 1970. The Argentine Congress ratified the convention in 1995, but the executive had never deposited the ratification instrument. By its decree, the Kirchner government assured that the treaty would enter into effect in Argentina, and at the same time, it sent to congress a law that would give the norm constitutional status. Through this move, the government provided additional incentives for congress to annul the amnesty laws. At the same time, it also opened up new international opportunities for activists, in the event that congress would have decided not to annul the amnesty laws, by providing additional reasons why the amnesty laws should be seen as contrary to international law and to the Argentine constitution. In this we have the case of the government explicitly creating international opportunity structures to support its domestic political moves.

Likewise, the Grandmothers of the Plaza de Mayo pursued an insider–outsider coalition strategy. During the international process of drafting the Convention on the Rights of the Child, the Grandmothers lobbied the Argentine government to include specific provisions in the convention that they believed would enhance the success of their domestic trials. Specifically, they realized that domestic law did not provide a legal basis for arguing that the kidnapped children had a standing in court. So the Grandmothers convinced the Argentine foreign ministry to press for provisions on the "right to identity" in the Convention on the Rights of the Child. They are included in the Convention as Articles 7 and 8, and are informally called the "Argentine articles." Because the Argentine constitution incorporates international law directly into domestic law, once Argentina had ratified the convention, these articles provided the Grandmothers with the legal bases to argue that children had a right to identity. Subsequently, judges were permitted to order blood tests, even though they were opposed by the adoptive parents, to establish whether the children in question were the sons and daughters of the disappeared.[16] In this case, the Grandmothers of the Plaza de Mayo, a domestic Argentine human rights movement, helped to change international opportunity structure by changing the wording of a treaty, which in turn changed their domestic opportunity structure and made it easier to obtain convictions.

CELS solicited international groups to write amicus briefs for their cases, and succeeded in establishing for the first time in the Argentine judicial system the practice of using foreign amicus briefs. Local groups stayed in close contact with the Inter-American Commission on Human Rights, and at one point when progress on the truth trials stalled, they brought a case before the Inter-American Commission. The commission, in negotiations with the Argentine government, was able to secure a commitment from the government to allow the trials to continue.[17] The human rights groups are also poised, should the supreme court uphold the validity of the amnesty laws, to reopen a case before the Inter-American Commission, which has already found such laws to be a violation of the Inter-American Convention on Human Rights. In other words, domestic groups are concentrating primarily on their very active domestic judicial agenda, but moving with relative ease and fluidity in foreign, international, and regional institutions as a complement and/or backup to their domestic work. This is neither the boomerang nor an example of defensive transnationalization, but an example of a mixed coalition of insiders and outsiders, or Box C. International and regional activism remains one of the tactics in the repertoires of these groups. At times it is more latent that others, but always there. But it is not a privileged sphere, largely because there has been so much domestic space in which to participate.

Uruguay: A Case of "Immobilised" Opposition

In Uruguay, the character of repression was different that in either Argentina or Chile. Repression in Uruguay was not characterized by large-scale massacres or thousands of disappeared people. Instead, the military implemented a program of far-reaching arrests, routine torture of prisoners, and complete surveillance of the population. In 1976, Amnesty International estimated that 60,000 people had been arrested and detained in Uruguay; one out of 50 Uruguayans had been through some period of imprisonment since the coup. Seventy-eight prisoners died in prison, many as a result of torture. But the

Uruguayan case also illustrates the interconnected nature of the repression, especially in the Southern Cone. Of the 173 disappeared Uruguayans, 32 were forcibly disappeared in Uruguay, 135 in Argentina, 4 in Chile, and 2 in Paraguay, as a result of cooperation of security forces in the region (SERPAJ, Uruguay, 1989).

The transition to democracy in Uruguay came through a negotiated agreement in 1984—the "Naval Club Agreement"—in which the military received explicit and implicit assurances that they would not be prosecuted for human rights violations during the military regime. So, both the nature of the repression, in which there were fewer disappeared victims, and the nature of the transition influenced the type of transitional justice in Uruguay. The congress created an investigative commission to look into the situation of the disappeared during the 1971–1981 period (La Comisión Investigadora sobre la Situación de Personas Desaparecidas y Hechos que la Motivaron).[18] In scope and scale it was inferior to the Argentine and Chilean commissions and did not issue a published report. As such, I do not classify it as a truth commission in the same sense as the Argentine, Chilean, Guatemalan, or Salvadorean cases.

In December 1986, the Uruguayan Parliament passed the amnesty law (Ley de Caducidad de la prevención punitiva del Estado). In 1988, the supreme court sustained the constitutionality of the law by a three to two vote. Uruguayans opposed to the amnesty organized a huge petition campaign to put the topic of the amnesty to a popular vote. In a plebiscite in 1989, 57 percent of the public voted in favor of sustaining the law in a situation where many still feared that trials could lead to a military coup. In the words of one human rights advocate, the results of the plebiscite "immobilised the popular movement, and especially the human rights movement, which lacked initiative for a long time" (Peralta, 2002). Their respect for the voice of the people expressed through the plebiscite made it difficult for the human rights movement to respond to the legitimate political and legal demands against impunity. In addition, the post-transition democratic government held up the results of the plebiscite as evidence of the popular support for their policies of not investigating the past (Peralta, 2002). As a result, the situation of impunity was stable for over ten years and there were few domestic legal initiatives to try to undermine the amnesty law. With reference to table 11.1, objectively the amnesty law put Uruguay in Box B, with closed domestic institutions to the demands for accountability for past human rights violations. But as a result of the plebiscite, the Uruguayan human rights movement acted as if they were in Box A, where domestic, regional, and international institutions were closed to their demands.

Various regional and international initiatives helped to prod the movement for change in Uruguay. The IACHR, in its 1992 report, and the UN Human Rights Committee in its report in 1998, expressed deep concern because the amnesty law blocked access to justice for the victims. The detention of Pinochet in London in 1998 also made an impact on the human rights movement by providing new legal and political arguments against impunity. But it was the international campaign of Argentine poet Juan Gelman that made the greatest impact on the Uruguayan government. Gelman denounced the Uruguayan government for its failure to assist him in locating his disappeared granddaughter who was living with an adoptive family in Uruguay. Eventually, the new Kirchner administration in Argentina took up Gelman's case and put direct pressure on the Uruguayan government to exhume the body of Gelman's daughter-in-law. Contrary to Argentina, prior to 2002, Uruguay had never undertaken exhumation of graves with the help of a forensic anthropology team to provide forensic evidence for human rights trials.

In 2000, under international and increasing domestic pressure, President Jorge Batlle set up a "Peace Commission" to investigate the topic of the disappearances. The work of the commission was to locate information about the fate of the disappeared in Uruguay and to make that information available to family members. It lacked, however, the necessary mandate, resources, and the cooperation of the military to fully complete its task. The commission did not have the authority to identify those responsible for the disappearances. One of the purposes of the commission was to put to rest once and for all the inquiries into the fate of the disappeared. However, this purpose has not been fulfilled, because while the commission was functioning, activists for the first time initiated judicial proceedings for human rights violations committed during the dictatorship.

In 2001, the human rights secretariat of the national labor union, the PIT-CNT (Plenario Intersindical de Trabajadores—Convención Nacional de Trabajadores), presented an accusation against the ex-foreign minister during the dictatorship, Juan Carlos Blanco, for being an accessory to the kidnapping of Elena Quinteros in 1976. Quinteros was kidnapped after she had already entered the grounds of the Venezuelan embassy where she sought asylum. The amnesty law protects the military and police from prosecution, but does not explicitly protect civilians, so human rights groups eventually realized that one way to evade the amnesty law was to bring lawsuits against the civilian members of the military regime and, in particular, ex-President Bordaberry and Foreign Minister Juan Carlos Blanco. Blanco spent six months in preventative prison before being released to await the conclusion of the trial. The Uruguayan government has worked to block the trial and support Blanco. For example, the government appointed Blanco to serve as one of ten arbitrators for the Mercosur Tribunal for the Solution of Controversies. The executive branch claims that the amnesty law covers Blanco and that the judicial branch must dismiss the case, but the judges do not agree. The court of appeals in Uruguay refused to dismiss the case and used the argument of the Inter-American Convention Against the Forced Disappearances of Persons that the crime of kidnapping was a permanent one. Blanco's lawyers then requested that the Peace Commission provide information that Quinteros was dead, and later the charge was changed from kidnapping to murder, apparently because a murder charge is subject to a statute of limitations, while a disappearance—seen as an ongoing crime—is not. The judge in charge of the case has ordered the exhumation of the area where Quinteros is thought to be buried, and has cited military officers to testify about the case in court.[19]

In 2002, the Uruguayan Association of the Relatives of the Disappeared filed a lawsuit against ex-President Juan Maria Bordaberry for having violated the constitution in 1973 by carrying out a coup against the democratic government. Bordaberry was the elected civilian president of Uruguay, but he cooperated with the military when they dissolved congress and created an authoritarian regime. The lawsuit was initially referred to the supreme court because it involved alleged crimes that Bordaberry committed while president, and was thus seen as a political case. The supreme court, however, decided in March 2004 that a criminal judge could try the case, since Bordaberry is no longer president.[20] Since that time, two judges have recused themselves from the case. There is also another case filed against Bordaberry for the murder of eight communists in April 1972.

Argentine courts also continue to be actively involved in Uruguayan human rights cases, since more Uruguayans disappeared in Argentina than in Uruguay. They continue to search out evidence of collaboration in repression between Argentine and Uruguayan security forces, under the guise of Operation Condor. In this case, an Argentine judge has requested extradition of Uruguayan military officers to Argentina, but the request was turned down by the conservative Uruguayan government of Jorge Battle.[21] In early 2004, Argentine lawyers filed a case in Argentine courts on behalf of the families of Senator Michelini and Representative Gutierrez Ruiz, exiled and murdered in Argentina in 1976.

What is most striking about the Uruguayan case is how long it took for human rights groups or lawyers of the victims to make concerted judicial efforts to hold people accountable for past human rights violations. The amnesty law, upheld both by the supreme court and by a democratic vote, was seen as an impenetrable barrier to prosecutions. But the existence of regional and international opportunity structures was finally perceived by legal activists in Uruguay, especially after the arrest of Pinochet, and subsequently used to open their own front against the amnesty laws. The main explanation for this difference, I believe, is the nature of repression in Uruguay, and the smaller size and dynamism of the Uruguayan human rights sector. Much now depends on what policy the new leftist Broad Front government will adopt on the issue of accountability for past human rights abuses.

Conclusions

This chapter has attempted to outline a framework for the dynamic interaction of domestic and international politics to help explain the emergence and success of efforts to hold individuals legally accountable for past human rights violations. Human rights activists, aware of the possibilities created by this dynamic interaction, may choose strategies attuned to opportunities at both the international and domestic levels. Specifically, the puzzle the article addresses is why three countries in similar situations—Argentina, Chile, and Uruguay— initially adopted different strategies to address past human rights violations.

In the past, after episodes of authoritarianism in the region, there were never any trials for human rights violations. The fact that there were strong demands and expectations for obtaining some accountability for past abuses in the 1980s and 1990s was the result of a different domestic and international context. The major human rights treaties had entered into force, the Inter-American Court of Human Rights was up and running, and domestic and transnational human rights movement demanded some form of accountability. But the *form* these efforts initially took was influenced by the scope of repression in each country and the nature of transition. In countries that recorded higher rates of disappearances and deaths, there was more pressure for legal accountability, because more family members sought justice.[22] Thus, we would expect more demands for accountability in Argentina—where there were a documented 10,000 disappeared—than in Chile—with 3,000 disappeared, and less demands in Uruguay—with 170 disappeared. But the level of repression is not the only factor influencing demands for justice. If this were the main factor, we would expect to see the greatest legal accountability in the region in Guatemala, which had by far the largest number of disappeared and dead, and yet this has not been the case. The nature of transition was also important. Legal accountability was more possible in a country like Argentina that had experienced a ruptured transition than in countries like Chile, Uruguay, or Guatemala that had experienced a negotiated or pacted transition. By the early 1990s, however, all countries were in a similar situation, with amnesty laws effectively blocking almost all forms of legal accountability for past human rights violations. Despite the similarity in domestic situation, Argentine human rights movements sought out domestic, regional, and international opportunities to overturn or undermine the amnesty laws, coming up with a wide range of innovative legal tactics that put the amnesty laws under constant challenge. These trials put dozens of members of the Argentine military and their associates in jail. In Chile and Uruguay, however, the amnesty laws held firm until the very late 1990s. But finally, in 1999 in Chile, and after 2001 in Uruguay, substantial legal challenges to full impunity under the amnesty law were mounted. How can we account for these changes?

Changes in Argentina, Chile, and Uruguay in the 1990s cannot be understood without taking into account the interaction of domestic and international opportunity structures. In Argentina, human rights groups used international law in domestic courts and gained access to foreign courts to bring pressure on the amnesty law. In Chile, the detention of Pinochet in London gave impetus to legal developments already underway in the Chilean judicial system to reopen space for domestic human rights trials. In Uruguay, the domestic impact of developments in Argentina and Chile, and the detention of Pinochet, energized and motivated a popular movement immobilized over ten years earlier by the plebiscite vote in favor of the amnesty law. In each case, there is a combination of domestic and international factors that helps explain the outcomes. But the Chilean and Uruguayan cases correspond more closely to Box B in table 11.1, where the amnesty law created a more essentially closed domestic opportunity structure for human rights trials. The Argentine case, however, is an example of Box C, where the prior trials and the ongoing efforts of domestic human rights groups never permitted a situation of full closure of domestic opportunity structures for human rights trials.

Some of the differences correspond to objective differences in the cases—especially the greater scope of repression in Argentina. Some differences correspond to the nature of the transition, especially the ruptured transition in Argentina, which weakened the legitimacy and influence of the military, and made it difficult for them to impose conditions on the transition. Yet in the end, the greater number and greater dynamism of the human rights movement in Argentina helps explain why they were more able to create new political opportunities at the domestic and international level through innovative legal and political tactics. The Argentine case also illustrates a point frequently made by social movement theorists that political opportunities are not only perceived and taken advantage of, but they are also created by social actors. Uruguayan groups chose an electoral strategy against the amnesty law, and when they lost the vote, they, until recently, almost gave up looking for innovative judicial strategies to limit impunity. Argentine activists felt no such compulsion to respect majoritarian sentiment on human rights issues, and pursued legal strategies in the face of political opposition. These social movement and legal strategies are so extensive that I consider Argentine social movement activists, and at times, even members of the Argentine government to be among the most innovative protagonists in the area of domestic human rights activism. They are not emulating tactics they discovered elsewhere, but are developing new ones. On a number of occasions, they have then exported or diffused their institutional and tactical innovations abroad. Argentina, which never was a passive recipient of international human rights action, but was a classic case of the boomerang effect, has gone well "beyond the boomerang," to become an important international protagonist in the human rights realm, involved in actively modifying the international structure of political opportunities for human rights activism. For example, Argentina was one of the four or five most active countries in the development of the International Criminal Court, and an Argentine activist was named the prosecutor for the ICC, perhaps the most important position in the court. This dynamism of the Argentine human rights sector is even more interesting and important in the context of active U.S. opposition to the expansion of international human rights law, because it suggests that the advancement of human rights institutions may proceed even in the face of opposition from the hegemonic power in the system, exactly because new actors have emerged who are committed to building, or at least maintaining, existing regional and international opportunity structures in the area of human rights.

Notes

1. For the most complete study of amnesties historically, see Loveman and Lira, 1999, 2000.
2. For social movement theorists, political opportunity structure is more than access and repression, but these elements appear in many typologies of the concept. Although repression is often seen as a separate aspect of political opportunity structure, I see it as an aspect of access, since repression can be an extreme form of closing domestic institutions to political participation. See McAdam, 1996.
3. Couso (this volume) and Hilbink (2003) have also pointed to other institutional aspects of the judicial system that complicated the possibility for accountability, including the career trajectories of the judges.
4. On the low level of legalization in Asia, see Kahler, 2001.

5. IACHR reports are generally not seen as binding on member governments. But the opinion of the IACHR may reveal a position that the court might later adopt or embrace, should the case be brought before it (Filippini, 2004).
6. Inter-American Court of Human Rights, Sentence of March 14, 2001, Barrios Altos case (Chumbipuma Aguirre y otros vs. Peru), paragraph 41.
7. Decision by judge Gabriel Cavallo, Juzgado Federal No. 4, March 6, 2001, in the Poblete-Hlaczik case.
8. Interview with Alcira Rios, Buenos Aires, December 2002.
9. "Cuatro historias escandalosas en el legajo del juez Marquevich," *Clarin*, December 22, 2002.
10. Interview with Luis Moreno Ocampo, December 21, 2002, Buenos Aires, Argentina.
11. Interview with Martin Abregu, July 1999, Buenos Aires.
12. Decision by judge Gabriel Cavallo, Juzgado Federal No. 4, March 6, 2001, Poblete-Hlaczik case.
13. *La Nación*, June 20, 2003.
14. See, for example, the essays in Natanson, 2004.
15. G.A. Res 2391 (XXIII) annex, 23 UN GAOR Supp (No. 18) at 40, UN Doc. A/7218 (1968).
16. Abuelas de la Plaza de Mayo, 2001 and interview with Alcira Rios, December 2, 2002, Buenos Aires.
17. Interview with Victor Abramovitz, November 13, 2002, Buenos Aires.
18. Created November 1985. See *Diario de Sesiones de la Cámara de Representantes*, vol. 620, no. 1856, pp. 511–17.
19. "El Jues Recarey citará como testigos a los coroneles 'Pajarito' Silveira y Cordero en el caso de Elena Quinteros," *La República*, December 2, 2003, p. 21.
20. Uruguay FBIS Report, *Highlights: Uruguay Press*, March 23, 2004.
21. Dante Montero, "Uruguay-Argentina: Stalking Operation Condor, 28 Years On," IPS-Inter Press Service/Global Information Network, May 20, 2004.
22. O'Donnell and Schmitter (1986, p.29) also argued that the sheer magnitude and quality of physical repression affected the nature of transition.

References

Abuelas de la Plaza de Mayo (2001) *Juventud e Identidad*, vol. 2 (Buenos Aires, Argentina: Espacio Editorial.
Angell, Alan (2003) "The Pinochet Factor in Chilean Politics," in Madeleine Davis (ed.), *The Pinochet Case: Origins, Progress and Implications* (London: Institute of Latin American Studies), pp. 63–84.
Bravo Lopez, Francisco (2003) "The Pinochet Case in the Chilean Courts," in Madeleine Davis (ed.), *The Pinochet Case: Origins, Progress and Implications* (London: Institute of Latin American Studies), pp. 107–22.
Davis, Madeleine (ed.) (2003) *The Pinochet Case: Origins, Progress and Implications* (London: Institute of Latin American Studies).

Detzner, John A. (1988) *Tribunales Chilenos y Derecho Internacional de Derechos Humanos* (Santiago, Chile: Editorial Tiempo Nuevo).

Epp, Charles (1998) *The Rights Revolution: Lawyers, Activists and Supreme Courts in Comparative Perspective* (Chicago: University of Chicago Press).

Filippini, Leonardo (2004) "La Corte Suprema Argentina y la Convención Americana sobre Derechos Humanos: Análisis Jurisprudencial" (LLM thesis, Palermo University).

Gamson, William and David S. Meyer (1996) "Framing Political Opportunity," in Doug McAdam, John McCarthy and Mayer Zald (eds.), *Comparative Perspectives on Social Movements: Political Opportunities, Mobilizing Structures, and Cultural Framings* (New York: Cambridge University Press).

Goldstein, Judith, Miles Kahler, Robert O. Keohane, and Anne-Marie Slaughter (eds.) (2001) *Legalization and World Politics* (Cambridge: MIT Press).

Gourevitch, Peter (2002) "Domestic Politics and International Relations," in Walter Carlsnaes, Thomas Risse, and Beth Simmons (eds.), *The Handbook of International Relations* (New York: Sage Publications).

Hathaway, Oona, "The Cost of Commitment," *Stanford Law Review*, vol. 55, no. 5 (2003), pp. 1821–62.

Higgins, Rosalyn (1994) *Problems and Process: International Law and How we Use It* (New York: Oxford University Press).

Hilbink, Lisa (2003) "An Exception to Chilean Exceptionalism? The Historical Role of Chile's Judiciary," in Susan Eckstein and Timothy Wickham-Crowley (eds.), *What Justice? Whose Justice? Fighting for Fairness in Latin America* (Berkeley: University of California Press), pp. 64–97.

Kahler, Miles (2001) "Legalization as Strategy: The Asia-Pacific Case," in Judith Goldstein, Miles Kahler, Rober O. Keohane, and Anne-Marie Slaughter (eds.), *Legalization and World Politics* (Cambridge: MIT Press).

Keck, Margaret and Kathryn Sikkink (1998) *Activists Beyond Borders: Advocacy Networks in International Politics* (Ithaca: Cornell University Press).

Loveman, Brian and Elizabeth Lira (1999) *Las suaves cenizas del olvido: Vía chilena de reconciliación política 1814–1932* (Santiago, Chile: LOM Ediciones).

——— (2000) *Las ardientes cenizas del olvido: Vía chilena de reconciliación política 1932–1994* (Santiago, Chile: LOM Ediciones).

Loveman, Brian and Elizabeth Lira (2002) *El espejismo de la reconciliacion: Chile 1990–2002* (Santiago, Chile: LOM Ediciones).

Lutz, Ellen and Kathryn Sikkink, "The Justice Cascade: The Evolution and Impact of Foreign Human Rights Trials," *Chicago Journal of International Law*, vol. 2, no. 1 (2001), pp. 1–33.

McAdam, Doug (1996) "Conceptual Origins, Current Problems, Future Direction," in Doug McAdam, John McCarthy and Mayer Zald (eds.), *Comparative Perspectives on Social Movements: Political Opportunities, Mobilizing Structures, and Cultural Framings* (New York: Cambridge University Press), pp. 23–40.

McAdam, Douglas, Sidney Tarrow and Charles Tilly (2001) *Dynamics of Contention* (New York: Cambridge University Press).

Moravcsik, Andrew, "The Origins of Human Rights Regimes: Democratic Delegation in Postwar Europe," *International Organization*, vol. 54, no. 2 (2000), pp. 217–52.

Natanson, José (ed.) (2004) *El Presidente inesperado: El gobierno de Kirchner según los intelectuales argentinos* (Buenos Aires: Homo Sapiens).

O'Donnell, Guillermo and Phillippe C. Schmitter (1986) *Transitions from Authoritarian Rule: Tentative Conclusions about Uncertain Democracies* (Baltimore, MD: The Johns Hopkins University Press).

Putnam, Robert, 1988. "Diplomacy and Domestic Politics: The Logic of Two-Level Games," *International Organization*, vol. 42, no. 3, pp. 427–60.

Risse, Thomas (2002) "Transnational Actors and World Politics," in Walter Carlsnaes, Thomas Risse, and Beth Simmons (eds.), *Handbook of International Relations* (New York: Sage Publications).

Risse, Thomas and Kathryn Sikkink (1999) "The Socialization of International Human Rights Norms into Domestic Practices," in Thomas Risse, Stephen C. Ropp, and Kathryn Sikkink (eds.), *The Power of Human Rights: International Norms and Domestic Politics* (Cambridge: Cambridge University Press), pp. 1–38.

Risse-Kappen, Thomas (1995) "Bringing Transnational Relations Back In: An Introduction," in Thomas Risse-Kappen (ed.), *Bringing Transnational Relations Back In: Non-State Actors, Domestic Structures, and International Institutions* (Cambridge: Cambridge University Press).

Roht-Arriaza, Naomi (2004) *The Pinochet Effect: Transnational Justice in the Age of Human Rights* (Philadelphia, Pennsylvania: University of Pennsylvania Press).

Romano, Cesare, "The Proliferation of International Judicial Bodies: The Pieces of the Puzzle," *New York University Journal of International Law and Politics*, vol. 31, no. 4 (1999), pp. 709–51.

Peralta Ariela (2002), Servicio Paz y Justicia Uruguay, unpublished manuscript.

Servicio Paz y Justicia (SERPAJ) Uruguay (1989) *Uruguay Nunca Más: Informe sobre la violación a los derechos humanos (1972–1985)* (Montevideo: Altamira), pp. 417–30.

Stepan, Alfred (1986) "Paths toward Redemocratization: Theoretical and Comparative Considerations," in Guillermo O'Donnell, Phillippe C. Schmitter, and Laurence Whitehead (eds.), *Transitions from Authoritarian Rule: Comparative Perspectives* (Baltimore, MD: The Johns Hopkins University Press), pp. 64–84.

Stone Sweet, Alec, "Judicialization and the Construction of Governance," *Comparative Political Studies*, vol. 32, no. 2 (1999), pp. 147–84.

Tarrow, Sidney (1994) *Power in Movement: Social Movements, Collective Action, and Politics* (2nd edition) (Cambridge University Press).

Tarrow, Sidney (1996) "States and Opportunities: The Political Structuring of Social Movements," in Doug McAdam, John McCarthy, and Mayer N. Zald. (eds.), *Comparative Perspectives on Social Movements: Political Opportunities, Mobilizing Structures, and Cultural Framings* (New York: Cambridge University Press).

Afterword

Guillermo O'Donnell

I was delighted to be invited as a discussant at the conference that gave rise to the present volume. I was also worried because, even though I have done some writing on the rule of law,[1] I am not a specialist on the judiciary. My pleasure was confirmed by learning a lot from a lively and challenging conference, a spirit that is well echoed by the present volume. And my concern was confirmed when the organizers of the conference and this volume invited me to write down for publication the rather assorted and unsystematic comments I offered at the end of the sessions. Such comments follow.

The judicialization of politics should be seen, in part, as part of the broader phenomenon of the judicialization of social relations as a whole. To a significant extent, the *judicialization* of social relations (whereby social claims are pursued through the courts or court-like structures) is probably an expression of the increasing *juridification* of social relations: the mounting degree to which social relations, formerly left to autonomous and/or informal regulation, are being textured by formal legal rules. This mounting juridification is a worldwide phenomenon that has been extensively noted and discussed. Juridification, of course, is not identical to judicialization. But we may surmise that, as more social relations are legalized and regulated, more incentives and opportunities for claiming them in courts would arise. So one would expect a positive correlation, albeit of magnitude impossible to determine a priori, between juridification and judicialization.

In respect of *judicialization*, the very concept alludes to some kind of excess or surplus of judicial action with relation to an underlying comparative standard. This standard may be diachronic, referred to judicial action at some period in the past of a given case; or it may be synchronic, related to some average or degree of judicial action in other cases (countries or regions) deemed relevant for such comparative purposes. Obviously, the choice of the standard of comparison will depend on the questions asked by the researcher, and usually the conclusions will be deeply influenced by that choice.

In light of the above, for each case examined one would want to draw maps that show across time varying degrees of what I would call the penetration and densification of the overall legal system, comprising various rules and institutions, across society. This, however, is a Herculean task, which does not seem feasible in the foreseeable future of Latin America. As an approximation to future drafts of that map, however, it might be useful to consider that the processes of judicialization (and, I add, juridification) that the chapters in this volume detect and discuss have been simultaneously accompanied by some important processes of both de facto and de jure *de-judicialization.* I refer in particular to the following.

First, the sharp increase of arbitration and other kinds of "alternative dispute resolution" (ADR) in (broadly defined) commercial matters, both within each country and, arguably more dramatic and consequential, transnationally. Also, as far as I can tell there has been a no less sharp increase in numerous business matters as well as in agreements with international financial institutions, in the abdication of domestic jurisdiction in favor of courts located in the great financial centers of the world.[2] This means that when governments establish or accept domestic or transnational arbitration mechanisms and/or when ceding jurisdiction to foreign courts, they are *de-judicializing* decisions that sometimes involve momentous interests and consequences for their countries. Second, there is a worrisome tendency in a significant number of countries to de-judicialize several aspects of criminal law and procedure. All too often demands for "order" and "security" lead to systematic judicial tolerance—including indeed sheer inaction—of unlawful actions perpetrated by the police and various vigilante groups. This amounts to a de facto withdrawal of judicial jurisdiction. Third, even further away from formal legal relationships, we should take into account the existence and, in some countries, the recent expansion of what I have called "brown areas,"[3] those where state legality has at best a tenuous hold. In these areas (both in the geographical peripheries of the countries and in parts of their large cities) what actually rule are various versions of mafia law enacted by assorted drug dealers, smugglers, vigilante groups, and violent political bosses. Fourth, in a different, and in this case beneficial direction is the recognition that some countries, many of them following recent constitutional changes, have made of the legal systems and adjudication patterns of indigenous peoples.[4] These are just some examples of changes that run contrary to the processes of judicialization of politics and other social relations that form the focus of this volume. As a consequence, we seem to be left with a complex map of simultaneous expansions and contractions of the judicialization and, to a large extent, also of the juridification of social relations, all of which have important political implications.

Of course, none of this is to deny the great importance of the judicialization that this volume discusses in a fruitful and timely manner. It is simply meant to induce further efforts at mapping the complex contractions and expansions that seem to animate our present legal systems. The expansions registered in this volume evince, in general, a growth of the activity of the state by means of one of its constituent set of institutions, the judiciary. In contrast, most of the contractions I have mentioned signal a withdrawal of the state from some of its most traditional, and arguably central, tasks. The abdication of the state to adjudicate in commercial matters that may be of great importance for the country, its sheer impossibility (or unwillingness) to impose the law in the brown areas, and the sidestepping of basic legal procedures in important aspects of criminal law, all point out to an abdication of basic state responsibilities. On the other hand, the formal recognition of indigenous peoples and their legal systems in Latin America, however reluctantly and poorly implemented, should be seen as a constructive devolution of long-usurped rights.

This volume provides ample evidence of the vigorous juridification and judicialization that has occurred in Latin America during roughly the past three decades. This is undeniable, although I wonder to what extent the changes have, on one hand, echoed the world-wide processes of juridification I mention above and, on the other, may be due to a rather specific conjuncture in the region. In this respect I refer to the transitions to democratic regimes that occurred in most countries in Latin America during the 1980s and 1990s. Often these transitions were accompanied by changes in the respective constitutions. Perhaps more importantly, during these transitions broad and vigorous demands for legal change emerged. As a consequence, numerous updating and revisions of various aspects of legislation which had been pending during authoritarian rule occurred. This affected family law, gender, some minorities, habeas corpus, *habeas data*, association, expression, judicial procedures and the like, not to say anything of rules dealing with the electoral process and its concomitants. This process of updating and correcting statutory changes not only expanded the juridification of social relations; it also provided paths through which the legal mobilization documented by several chapters in this book could be channeled, including the judicialization of many of those claims. It remains to be seen whether the rate of increase of judicialization will diminish, or even become negative, once many of the new legal opportunities that resulted from transitions become, so to speak, normalized by repeated practice and the establishment of relevant precedents.

Drawing on valuable suggestions from several chapters in this volume, it would also be relevant to create a typology of areas, or arenas, where judicialization (and as far as possible, juridification) is taking place. This exercise would be valuable in and of itself. It would also be a step toward typologically complementing the thoughtful listing of pros and cons of judicialization that the editors present in their Introduction. With no claim to comprehensiveness, I believe that the following arenas might be usefully considered in future typologies.

Processes in which Judicial Activity Is in Principle a Good Thing, At Least Insofar as It Is a Result of Deficiencies in the Action of Other Responsible State Agencies and/or of Gaps in the Laws or Their Implementation

The juridification and eventually the judicialization of the protection of the integrity of democratic electoral process, at the national and subnational levels.

- The installation of institutions, of a judicial and/or nonjudicial character, of what in previous works I have called "horizontal accountability"; that is, actions aimed at preventing and eventually punishing presumably illegal actions and omissions of state officers (O'Donnell, 2003).
- The installation of institutions, of a judicial and/or nonjudicial character in relation to actions or undue omissions by state agencies in matters of civil and human rights.
- The installation of institutions, of a judicial and/or nonjudicial character in relation to the protection of the environment.

The four arenas listed above refer mostly, albeit not exclusively, to interactions within the state. There is another kind of relationship, mostly among actors in society, about which expanding juridification and the concomitant judicialization also seem positive. I refer here to the statutory establishment and, when needed, the legal prosecution of gender rights, private violence prevention, consumer rights, labor legislation, prevention of work-related accidents, and the like. As already noted, the expansion of juridification in these matters is a worldwide phenomenon, which, with some significant lags (especially in the implementation of the respective rules), Latin America seems to be following.

Processes in which the consequences of judicial activity seem at best ambivalent

The consequences of legislation or judicial activism making social and economic rights actionable seem to me in most cases questionable. Courts may irresponsibly ignore fiscal constraints, provoke the creation of powerful antagonistic coalitions and, in general, erode their authority by forcefully and legitimately adjudicating in matters such as those listed. Furthermore, the awarding of social and economic rights by courts has an intrinsically paternalistic component; historically these rights have been acquired and, more importantly, secured as a consequence of political struggles.

There is also the issue of who and in what circumstances promotes judicialization. Obviously, this is not only a result of judicial activism. I will not elaborate here because the editor's Introduction as well as several chapters in this volume fruitfully deals with this matter.

In synthesis, it has been a pleasure and a challenge to comment upon this volume, for which we should be grateful to the organizers of the conference that preceded it and, in the same persons, to the editors of this volume. It has the marks of truly pioneering work on an important and complex theme: it surveys a multifaceted field, offers a series of interesting findings and hypotheses, and poses a number of intriguing questions that future research will endeavor to answer.

Notes

1. See, for example, O'Donnell, 1999.
2. For interesting critical commentary on these matters, see Jayasuriya, 2002.
3. See O'Donnell, 1993.
4. See the chapter of Julio Faundez in this volume and Sieder, 2002.

References

Jayasuriya, Kanishka, "Globalization, Sovereignty, and the Rule of Law: From Political to Economic Constitutionalism?" *Constellations*, vol. 8, no. 4 (2002), pp. 442–60.

———(1999) "Polyarchies and the (Un)Rule of Law in Latin America: A Partial Conclusion," in Juan E. Méndez, Guillermo O'Donnell and Paulo Sérgio Pinheiro (eds.), *The (Un)Rule of Law and the Underprivileged in Latin America* (Notre Dame, Indiana: University of Notre Dame Press), pp. 303–37.

Jayasuriya, Kanishka (2003) "Horizontal Accountability: The Legal Institutionalisation of Mistrust," in Scott Mainwaring and Christopher Welna (eds.), *Democratic Accountabiilty in Latin America* (Oxford: Oxford University Press), pp. 34–54.

O'Donnell, Guillermo "On the State, Democratization and Some Conceptual Problems: A Latin American View with Glances at Some Post-communist Countries," *World Development*, vol. 21, no. 8 (1993), pp. 1355–69.

Sieder, Rachel (ed.) (2002) *Multiculturalism in Latin America: Indigenous Rights, Diversity and Democracy* (London: Institute of Latin American Studies).

Index

Printed in the United States
108500LV00001B